HIS MASTER'S VOICE

SIR JOSEPH LOCKWOOD AND ME

WILLIAM CAVENDISH

HIS MASTER'S VOICE

SIR JOSEPH LOCKWOOD AND ME

www.emigrouparchivetrust.org

Published in 2017 by Unicorn
an imprint of Unicorn Publishing Group LLP
101 Wardour Street
London
W1F 0UG
www.unicornpublishing.org

ISBN 978-1-910787-700

Designed by TJ INK, Padstow (www.tjink.co.uk)

Printed and bound in Great Britain by TJ International, Padstow

To my parents because they never asked.

Acknowledgements

Without my partner Charles Selby's computer skills this book would never have existed.

My grateful thanks to Ruth Robinson for allowing me to quote from letters Joe sent her father, John Caudwell, and her grandfather, Charles Caudwell.

I have quoted from:
Lindsay Anderson "The Diaries", Methuen 2004; "Peter Hall's Diaries", Hamish Hamilton 1983; Arnold Haskell "Balletomane at Large", Heinemann 1972; Nick Mason "Inside Out: A Personal History of Pink Floyd", Phoenix Paperback 2004; David Sherwin "Going Mad in Hollywood", Andre Deutsch 1996.

I have reproduced:
"King's Reach and the National Theatre" from a watercolour by © David Gentleman, by kind permission of the Rayne family. Drawing by © John Lennon from the Christmas edition of "John Lennon in his own write".

Also, the works of many photographers have been included, I am able to name:
Michael Wallis
Anne ffrench
Eddie Ryle-Hodges John Dove (EMI)
Peter Vernon (EMI)
Donald Southern (Royal Opera House)
Reg Wilson (Royal Opera House)

And apologies for those I have overlooked.

The majority of the photographs are my personal property.

I have received invaluable assistance from:
Rupert and Carolyn Ryle-Hodges
Jackie Bishop and Joanna Hughes (EMI Archives)
Richard Waltham (EMI Electronics)
Hannah Vaughan & Magda Pieta (TJ International – TJ INK)
And, above all from
Ian Strathcarron (Unicorn Publishing Group)

"The Cavendish Collection" forms part of, and is controlled by, the EMI Group Archive Trust. It consists of items relating to Sir Joseph Lockwood's relationship with the Beatles, personal correspondence, gifts and other memorabilia.

The Cavendish Collection also holds documents and items relating to EMI's history (mentioned in the text) such as The Gramophone Company's "Golden Book" of signatures from famous recording artists and celebrities visiting Hayes.

Contents

PART 1

"Joe"

1904 – 1964

Joseph Lockwood,
Mayor of Doncaster, a direct ancestor

CHAPTER 1

Nottinghamshire Mill Boy

When I met Sir Joseph Lockwood, I was twenty-three and had no future plans. At a similar age, Joe (as I will call him) had successfully run two large flour mills in South America. How did his long business career come about? This was 1964, and for the last ten years he had been Chairman of Electric & Musical Industries Ltd (EMI). He was in his sixtieth year.

The Dictionary of Business Biography lists him as an "Industrialist". So helpful. *The Times Lives Remembered 1991* carried his obituary in March of that year, which ended with the traditional three words: "He never married". That's about as dry as one can get.

Some of Sir Joe's ancestors showed ability, of which he had little knowledge and less interest. He knew he was a distant cousin of Sir Frank Lockwood, Solicitor General in the Lord Rosebery Liberal Government. It was Sir Frank who successfully convicted Oscar Wilde for sodomy, and in doing so, saved the Prime Minister's reputation. Joe owned a copy of *Sir Frank Lockwood, a Biographical Sketch* by Augustine Birrell. Sir Frank progressed from barrister to judge, a career Joe might have pursued, had he come from a privileged background. Another cousin was Henry Francis Lockwood, Victorian architect of church and industrial buildings, such as Sir Titus Salt's Saltire textile factory. And then there was the beautiful film star Margaret Lockwood.

All these cousins were descended from Joseph Lockwood (1759 – 1837), Joe's great, great, great, great grandfather, who, yes, was a successful Industrialist. Apart from that, he was Mayor of Doncaster, twice, when Doncaster's grand Mansion House was on a par with London's. He was Steward of Doncaster Racecourse, which Joe would cap as Director of Epsom and Sandown, two other great racecourses.

Augustine Birrell recorded that Joseph Lockwood came to Doncaster from "over the hills far away" in another part of Yorkshire. He was "what is called a self-made man. Of his nobility his son spoke frequently." His birthplace was probably Huddersfield, a modest town before the Industrial Revolution, depending on sheep and gritstone quarries. His parents, about whom he never spoke, were not married, but later produced legitimate offspring. He decided to make his fortune elsewhere, and did not return.

This Dick Whittington figure found the streets of Doncaster were not paved with gold. Self-confident and undeterred, he did not "turn again". Rather, he married the sixteen-year-old daughter of a local builder. He was aged nineteen.

Described by Robert Southey, Doncaster was "one of the most comfortable towns in England, for it is clean, spacious and has no manufacturers". Famous for horse fairs, markets and annual race meetings attended by the Prince Regent, such evident signs of prosperity would stimulate the ambition of a young man like Joseph Lockwood. By 1814, he had the means to lease a limestone quarry called Levitt Hagg on the River Don, from the owners of the local stately home, Cusworth Hall. The quarry lease enabled him to extract limestone from the cliff face without incurring mineral royalty rights, provided the price remained fixed: maximum extraction meant maximum profit. Registered as Lockwood, Blagden and Crawshaw Ltd, the company was still operating as a 100% subsidiary of Pilkington Brothers Ltd, the glass manufacturers, in 1971, and was described as "Limestone Quarry" in the Report & Accounts. Ownership remained with Lockwoods for three generations. But none of this benefited Joe's branch of the family.

On a narrow strip of land between quarry face and river bank, the miners' families lived in damp, airless conditions alongside baking hot and toxic beehive-shaped kilns. There was no escape from the noise of rock being extracted and shaped into paving stone and brick. With the arrival of the railways, Doncaster became a main hub of the system. It was no longer a market town. The quarry no longer depended on the River Don to bring coal for the kilns, or transport stone and quicklime to the big cities. Joseph Lockwood's grandson was sent to Manchester to open a depot. There he settled and sent Frank to Manchester Grammar School, leading to Cambridge University, Lincoln's Inn and the House of Commons.

William Lockwood, Joseph's younger son, was sent to run the company builders' yard in York. A respected citizen of the city, and owner of the Black Swan Inn, his descendants rapidly descended the social scale. Joe's great-grandfather was a vet, and his grandfather, William Horner Lockwood, farmed 240 Yorkshire acres, assisted by one labourer. William Horner and Elizabeth Ellen Lockwood lived at Thornton-Le-Clay Cottage where, between 1865 and 1882, they produced ten children, six daughters and four sons. Joseph Agnew, the seventh child, Joe's father, was born in 1876.

First to break away was Elizabeth, the eldest daughter, who married a prosperous York flour merchant and mill owner. Joe's own future was coming into focus when his father was invited by Elizabeth's husband to learn milling. Joseph Agnew, barely fifteen, was no longer on the 1891 census for Thornton-Le-Clay. By the turn of the century, fully qualified and ambitious, he applied for a post as engineer to a small flour mill at Southwell in Nottinghamshire. Travelling to his destination through Lincolnshire, Joseph Agnew realised he was the first Lockwood to leave Yorkshire since Viking days.

Caudwell's Mill – or Burgage Mill as it was called when Joe's great-grandfather, Charles Thomas Caudwell, bought it in 1851 – was fed by the Greet, "one of the best trout streams in England". By the time of Joseph Agnew's arrival, water was replaced by coal and a steam engine. The Caudwells adopted modern methods. Joe's grandfather, Edward, prospered to become the richest man in Southwell and the first to own a motor car. His parents were from Manchester, where his father sold coal, and mother's family were flour dealers. He remembered coming to Southwell aged four, where the mill boasted three pairs of water-driven stones producing provender and flour of average quality and quantity. Under his management, "Greet Lily" flour, from E. Caudwell Flour Mills, became acknowledged as one of the finest, purest flours, making "large loaves, which when cut show an even texture of bread, with an exquisite creamy shade — not a starved, bleached-looking white". Between 1876 and 1900 the mill rose to six storeys, including a separate power plant and new boiler, with an output of six sacks (of 280 lbs each) per hour. Further improvements coincided with Joseph Agnew's arrival. Thirteen double rollers were supplied by Henry Simon Ltd of Manchester. Output rose to eight sacks, and then twelve sacks an hour. The installation of an H. Simon elevator in 1905 made possible delivery of a hundred sacks of wheat an hour from railway trucks and farm wagons. There is little doubt that this ever-greater-efficiency-seeking grandfather was a major influence in Joe's life. Edward's motto was, "A pennyworth of coal makes a sack of flour."

Edward had ten children: eight girls and two boys. One son died, leaving twenty-four-year-old Charles still living at Burgage House with his parents. Also at home was nineteen-year-old Mabel, Joe's mother. Charles Caudwell would inevitably inherit the family mill,

Joe's father, flour mill manager, the year he died

but Edward saw the need to engage an experienced engineer.

A photograph depicts Joseph Agnew as slight in stature but up-right and confident in manner. At his command, the thirty mill work-ers would return to their eight-hour shifts when summoned from the New Castle Arms. He lodged next door at Flour Mill House in Station Street. He was soon re-ceiving visits from Mabel when he was not at the mill. She was a big, plain girl with a large mole on her face, and a will of her own. The mutual attraction must have been immediate. Their wedding took place on 14th May 1901 at the Parish Church of Southwell, in the presence of the bride's brother and sister. No photograph was taken to show the couple, he slim and serious, she more robust than at their introduction. Departure to Africa was hasty. Edward explained to inquisitive townsfolk that Joseph Agnew had been offered a mill to manage on the Gold Coast. The couple had gone to investigate. They got as far as Madeira and were back in Southampton to register the birth of their first son, Frank, on 14th November 1901. Mabel claimed Africa "was full of foreigners".

Life returned to normal. The family moved into an end-of-terrace Victorian two-up two-down red-brick house, Albion Villas, situated across the street from the mill in Station Road. A younger brother, Fred, joined Frank at the end of 1902, and Joe arrived, after an extended gap, on 14th November 1904.

There was little doubt who was now running things at Caudwell's. The 1906 edition of *Milling* magazine reported: "Mr Lockwood manages the mill well, including provender milling." Greet Lily won the Bakers Cup in 1907, 1908 and 1909. Joseph Agnew was ambitious to enlarge the company. He was impressed by the massive mills built by Joseph Rank across the Humber at Hull. These were constructed by Henry Simon Ltd of Manchester. Old Joe Rank dominated the Industry. Foreign wheat came direct to his mills by sea, whereas Caudwell's was fed by canal and road from the Trent.

Joseph Agnew envisaged rebuilding at Newark-on-Trent, with the assistance of Henry Simon Ltd This meant a business trip to Manchester to discuss contracts. He planned to be back for Joe's fifth birthday in November 1909, and the imminent arrival of his fourth child. A noticeable rapport had developed between the two Josephs. They were quite inseparable, whereas the older brothers were closer to their mother. Both father and grandfather recognised something special about the little boy.

On 9th November, Joseph Agnew was at the offices of Henry Simon Ltd when he was struck down with acute appendicitis. Rushed to the Royal Infirmary, he was operated on by Harry Platt, a twenty-three-year-old, recently qualified surgeon from London. He died of untreatable peritonitis on the operating table. There was no hope. He was only thirty-three. The hospital was part of Manchester's Victoria University, where medical techniques were the most advanced in the country. Platt was the outstanding graduate of his year, gaining honours and the Gold Medal. Ironically, he lived to be a hundred, retiring as a Baronet, and President of the Royal College of Surgeons.

It was impossible to foresee the impact the news would have on young Joe. The shock was too much. Whooping cough was diagnosed; but virus alone could not account for the fever and dangerously high temperature, pointing to acute pneumonia. Mabel Lockwood claimed that Joe had "brain fever". The doctor told her to prepare for one of two outcomes. He would either make a complete recovery and be "very clever", or become permanently mentally defective and "be an imbecile". He was obviously suffering from some sort of psychosomatic reaction. Medical practice in the provinces was still primitive. Glass cups were applied to his back and chest, heated to draw out the poison in his system.

No effort was spared to ensure Mr Edward Caudwell's grandson's recovery. Oxygen was ordered from Nottingham by Dr Willoughby, who carried the heavy cylinder on his back from the station. He remarked on his little patient's exceptionally large lungs, and attributed them to his recovery. They were the "envy of any professional boxer".

For some time, Joe was unable to speak. This did not mean his mind was not in turmoil. A new emotion arose to engulf the black despair that threatened to strangle him. This was ANGER, unspoken now, but the same anger that would punctuate every episode of his life: strong enough to broach the many challenges that were to come his way. Kept under self-control and rarely used, it would erupt without warning. The shock created had maximum – and intended – effect. It was a controlled anger that disappeared as quickly as it arose. Schoolmasters, doctors, academics, interior designers and executives would all witness it, and not forget it.

Joe's fatherless younger brother, Charles, was born on 18th January 1910. A weak little fellow, his diaphragmatic hernia was described by Mabel as: "His heart was over here, his lungs were down there, his stomach was up here." Upside-down stomach could be operated on. Like his brother, he determined to use such an early setback as a means to survive and succeed.

Mother and four little boys were now destitute. The mill would only remind them of their sad predicament, and it was decided they should move.

Southwell is divided in half by Burgage Green, which is raised on a promontory and surrounded with grand houses such as Burgage Manor, Lord Byron's childhood home. Down one side are the railway station, the mill, the coal yard, the lace works and the house of correction. Down the other side exists a different world, centred on the medieval Minster and

Joe, with his mother, Frank, baby Charles, and "Donkey man" Fred

the Saracen's Head, a coaching inn. There are the ruins of the Archbishop of York's palace, the modern Bishop's Residence, and the elegant prebendal town houses, all very desirable and individual residences. These were to be Mabel's new surroundings.

Number 11, Westgate is a church property on the corner of Bishops Drive, leading to the Residence and the Minster precincts. It is another two-up two-down end of terrace brick house with a large coal cellar. The front door opened on the main thoroughfare. Here Mabel would live for sixty years, her strong personality firmly established among the townsfolk. The name Mrs Lockwood became practically synonymous with Southwell itself. Her husband was buried beside the North Door of the Minster, where she would one day join him.

Southwell Minster

From his earliest moments, Joe knew that Charles needed his mother's full attention. His older brothers could not be relied upon. She said: "Joe, I can feed you, I can clothe you, but I cannot educate you." Although there were good schools in Southwell, he had to leave home. Aged six, he was sent to Lincoln for four years. He claimed to have been a choral scholar at Lincoln Cathedral. But, as the Cathedral had no choir school until 1921, he was probably educated at a prep school, paid for by his grandfather. Boy choristers were selected from these schools by the organist, and some were accommodated in the Choir House.

Put on the Nottingham-Lincoln train, with a label tied to his neck, he left behind his childhood memories of Southwell. He recalled sitting on his grandfather's knee. Edward lectured him to avoid the church and hide when they came calling. He recalled seeing King Edward VII "drive out to Southwell in his motor car" when His Majesty was staying nearby at Welbeck Abbey for the shooting.

The City of Lincoln rose dramatically from the plain, and it was quite a climb from the station. Surely someone would have met Joe with his heavy trunk to escort him up "Steep Hill" to school. Despite its magnificent cathedral, Lincoln was a bleak city, with its ruined castle, notorious Victorian prison, asylum and court house, not to mention the remains of the Roman garrison. School holidays did not mean Southwell. Instead, Joe was put on a train to York with a label attached. There he was taken by Lockwood uncles and aunts to farms they owned or rented. These were mellow red-brick homesteads, with stackyards behind and a single sturdy copper beech tree in front. They resembled Joe's father's and grandfather's birthplace cottage, at Thornton-Le-Clay. Aunt Anny and Uncle Charlie were his favourite aunt and uncle. Charlie ran his farmland near Malton from horseback, "like one's idea of the perfect gentleman farmer", as Joe's brother Charles remembered him.

Frederick, the eldest uncle, was a JP and loved hunting. He bred "Pat the Giant", a famous bull weighing 1½ tons, which toured agricultural shows around the country. Another uncle recalled leading "Pat" to and from the railway station.

Joe was learning at an early age about arable farming, that would feed the mills he was to run and build. He heard about harvests, hay-making, crop yields, advantages of winter and spring wheat, strength and moisture content. Cereals were required for provender (cattle food): oats, barley, maize and rye. Descended from farmers and millers (Mabel boasted "a miller's thumb"), Joe's veins flowed with the finest flour.

Sometimes he was sent to Manchester. Here he witnessed the wealth of Lancashire and Cheshire, created by the Industrial Revolution. His youngest Caudwell aunt was married to a "Cotton King". They lived at Pott Shrigley Hall in the Peak District, which is now a Golf and Country Club.

At eight or nine, Joe lived at home. He became a day pupil at the Magnus Grammar School in Newark. Founded by Archdeacon Magnus in 1529, the school moved to a red-brick Victorian building in the suburbs in 1890. Joe was excused morning prayers. The long journey to and from school depended on branch and mainline train times, lifts on mill lorries, and the weather. A much-repeated story involved Mabel taking a job as secretary to the large maltster's company chairman in Newark:

"You are late this morning, Mrs Lockwood," said her employer.

"Yes, Mr Cherry Downs, so would you be if you had walked from Southwell!"

It was time for the older brothers to leave home. Frank went to boarding school in Bedford, but did not fit in. Mabel saw his interest in farming, and arranged a fee-paying apprenticeship with a local lady landowner. It was a success. He achieved his ambition to become a dairy farmer, to build up his herd, and to establish a milk round for his son and grandson to inherit.

In the words of Alexander Pope:

Happy the man whose wish and care
A few paternal acres bound
Content to breathe his native air
In his own ground.

Joe worshipped brother number two. When Fred was accepted as a Naval Cadet, the family burst with pride. The uniform was unbelievably smart: gold-braided peaked cap, bum freezer jacket, round collar, waistcoat and trousers. Joe recalled the excitement the day Fred departed, followed by the shock of his return. It was rumoured that Mabel had to buy him out of the Navy. It led to a picaresque life, causing distress to his mother and the disapproval of his brothers. For Joe, Fred no longer existed, and Charles vowed never to speak to him again. Like the proverbial bad penny, he was to crop up again, with a new name and a new calling.

Other than the circumstances of his leaving, nothing is known of Joe's time at the Magnus. Here was his first massive anger attack, fully recorded as a confrontation with the Headmaster, the Reverend H. Gorse, who had presented him with a copy of *The Romance of Modern Photography*. This was a prize for Mathematics and Science, and Gorse had plans for Joe to study Latin. But Joe had other ideas. Prizegiving was on 29th July 1920, just four months short of his sixteenth birthday. He intended to leave school at sixteen just like his father.

Gorse would have nothing of the sort. He was a firm disciplinarian, resembling Dr Arnold's "tall figure in cap and gown", a formidable figure not to be disobeyed. But he had met his match. If he planned for Joe to learn Latin and go to university, he could forget it. There was an angry scene. Joe was not prepared to have conditions imposed by authority. He wrote to the chairman of the governors of the School to complain about his treatment by the Headmaster. The School reluctantly allowed Joe to go.

Caudwell's Mill

To further emulate his father, Joe was drawn to the mill. But here lay a problem that would thwart his ambition. There was nothing to stop him working in the mill alongside Edward and John, Charles Caudwell's sons, but they would own it one day.

They were public school boys and, as Mabel reminded him, they were rich. To get on, he would have to leave Southwell, especially if he was to be a miller. But in the meantime, he could learn everything a miller needed to know.

Another reason for leaving Southwell would be to get away from the poor relation syndrome, something that affected his mother. As a girl, she was sent down in the dark evenings from Burgage House to read to her grandfather, who had failing sight. Charles Thomas

Caudwell lived at Normanton House, the largest and grandest prebendal house. She told Joe that she had been scared. As a result, Joe passed the house cautiously, barely daring to look over the garden wall, even when he grew up. And Easthorpe Lodge, where her brother brought up Edward and John, could be seen from Westgate across the meadows behind the Minster. She and Joe would have a sense of trepidation that they were trespassing, even by looking in that direction.

Joe blended in with the town. On the way to the mill in King Street, he noted that the butcher's boy was sixteen and already earning money to support his mother. He did not envy the job, but worried about how he himself was to be a breadwinner. Further up the street were the photographer's premises. The photographer's son was Harold Cottam, the heroic young Marconi operator on the SS Carpathia who picked up the distress signals from the Titanic. Cottam was the youthful celebrity who everyone, including Joe, worshipped. Here was someone who had left Southwell to achieve his ambitions. And there were other local celebrities he could emulate. Sir Edwyn Hoskyns, the Bishop of Southwell, was a keen angler. Together he and Joe would fish for trout in the Greet. And in the Minster, the organist was not averse to Joe covering for him "when he went for a cup of tea". The local MP the Marquis of Titchfield was guest of honour at a "Smoker" hosted by uncle Charles, a JP, County Councillor and Chairman of the Church Lads Brigade.

Joe and Mabel joined the mill workers' families on annual works "junketings" to Skeggies (Skegness) and Mablethorpe. They saw seaside concert parties, Pierrot shows and "coons". Joe befriended ex-champion boxer Bombardier "Beautiful" Billy Wells, on holiday with his young wife in Mablethorpe. He got on well with the heavyweight celebrity, who had a large female following and banged the gong for J. Arthur Rank films. Joe was not shy to swim with him to compare his burgeoning manliness, tall for his age at 6', with the boxer's magnificent 6'3" physique.

Back at the mill, Joe found other attractions. From earliest times "mill boys" were employed to sweep floors and do odd jobs. Spaces were provided for them to sleep in cubicles, as the mill ran continuously for twenty-four hours in eight-hour shifts.

Anthony Trollope has a character remark:

"I remember hearing of people who lived in a mill, and couldn't sleep when the mill stopped!"

And as a mill boy with other mill boys, accompanied to the sound of Caudwell's mill, Joe had his first sexual experiences.

Charles Caudwell noted his sixteen-year-old nephew's growing confidence. It was clear he was ambitious to get on. And there was a way this might be achieved. At his uncle's expense, Joe was sent to study milling at the Analytical and Technical Laboratories, Grange-over-Sands, Lancashire.

Forget the Magnus School! This was the education Joe craved, as can be seen from the letter he wrote home on 13th July 1921:

Dear Uncle,

…The Remington process is very simple but could be of use to us. They have a very nice baker up here. He is rather young but has got about fifty medals for baking. He and others have been teaching me how to do the undermentioned tests, and I can manage them quite well:

Test to see if Saloss is in the flour, test for yeast, two tests to find water absorbing power of flour and of gluten, etc …

With his horizons beginning to expand, it would take another three frustrating years to get the break he yearned. In February 1923, he wrote to cousin John from the Victoria Hotel, Strabane, near Londonderry:

Strabane is the slowest place I have ever been in, there are about three street lights. In fact it is like living in Southwell. The Irishmen at the mill are very amusing. Mr Smyth, is a very keen sportsman, and I am going horse riding with him tomorrow … I have not yet heard date of sailing, although I have had a letter from the Santa Rosa Co.

An offer had come to assist the manager of a mill in Chile. He could not wait. He shared Lord Byron's view, writing from Cambridge aged nineteen: "To forget or be forgotten by the people of Southwell is all I aspire to!"

A job awaited him, but the mill owners, Balfour Williamson, had no vessel sailing to Chile carrying supplies for a further year. Time on his hands found Joe reluctantly acting as secretary to his uncle's Church Lads Brigade branch.

Southwell Church Lads Brigade, (off to camp)

With growing anticipation, he ordered a dinner jacket and several linen suits suitable for overseas posting. He had already mastered the latest milling techniques. He had his appendix removed in memory of his father. It was benign. He told Mabel he would be away for five years. She did not object. There was a berth for him on a boat sailing from Liverpool. He was nineteen, the same age as Byron.

CHAPTER 2
Chile Flour Mill Manager

Joe left home a boy, and arrived in South America a man. Edward and John received a much-awaited letter in 29th April 1924, from the RMS Oropesa:

> We are just about to arrive in Rio. I shall go ashore as I particularly want to get some Brazilian tobacco and cigars which are about 1 1/2d each!

(Joe took to pipe smoking when an aunt told him it was unmanly not to do so. She would also impress his younger brother: Charles claimed he practically fainted at her sophistication and femininity.) Joe continued to boast:

Mr Webster, 4th Officer, S.S. Oropesa

All the officers are very good fellows and they spend most of their time with us. One of them, Webster, keeps us in roars of laughter. He says he wishes he had known me a bit sooner so he could have given me a good time the night before the boat sailed. I am beginning to look like a nigger. I have had dozens of photographs taken. I think there are eight meals. We start with early morning tea. There are sandwiches after dinner and again just before bed. The orchestra is now playing. We have got quite a decent second class deck. In fact, we have two decks. Every night we have a dance. Well, I'm hot, so goodbye, your loving cousin Joe.

He was at sea for five weeks.

News got to him that Edward Caudwell Ltd was formed into a Limited Liability company, with Charles, Edward and John as directors in his absence. He was not needed. But they should see what he was now running. Letters home described the Santa Rosa Milling Company Ltd, in Concepción, as one of the largest companies in Chile.

All the three mills are electrically driven and we run them day and night until Sunday morning. I have control over all the men in the firm except for Mr Vasey and the other miller. After they have gone home, I am responsible for the whole place. I live in part of Mr Vasey's house and have a youth to clean my rooms and wait on me generally. I am about almost from 6.30am to 6pm. This is a terrible place for accidents. During the last six months we have had two men killed, one got round a shaft, the other was electrocuted!

That irresponsible anger, never far from the surface, from which no one was safe, made itself felt back in Southwell. To cousin John he wrote:

The first thing I am going to do is blow you up for the two letters had insufficient postage. There is very little to pay, only the annoying part is the letters are kept at the post office and they won't deliver to a servant and I have to go and sign for them, and they send a sort of income tax demand. I have to pay income tax here and it is a bit too bad!

He was too poor to buy a newspaper and relied on the British Club in Concepción to keep copies. He was receptive to news from home.

> I am glad you are catching a few trout. With a little patience and practice you'll be able to empty the Greet …

> Well, I'm having a fine time here, not manual, there is no need to do a stroke. These men here think I look rather strong and are very obedient. Since I have been here I have sacked some 30 men and lads and kicked several drunkards into the gutter. They'll probably be waiting for me at night with a revolver when I go to dinner but it doesn't bother me. When any man comes to speak to you, you make him stand at attention and take his hat off. You can imagine how important it makes you feel walking around the mill and sort of thinking "All this is mine", but I'm not getting swollen headed!

To his uncle he wrote in October 1925:

> I am sorry to hear things are still bad in England but there seems to be a tremendous lot of communists there nowadays.

> Yes, I have settled down quite well here and like it very much and have no great hope to live in England any more, although I would like to visit the family often.

> I hope to stay here about 4 years, and then if possible I would like to get on Simon's staff either at home or abroad and retire here in years to come.

In December he learnt that his younger brother Charles, at sixteen, like himself, "is coming to the mill this month. Keep him at it anyway, and find him plenty of work!"

In 1926, the senior partner of Balfour Williamson visited Chile:

Joe, in the Plaza Concepción, 1924

Me, in the Plaza Concepción, 1993

Lord Forres laid the law down when he was out here as the whole place had to be painted inside and out at a cost of £1000. But he is a very different Lord to those I have ever seen here and is exceptionally clever. He even knows the strength of wheat and everything an engineer miller would understand. You can't fool him. He is worth about £10 million I am told.

Another fellow and myself are going to have Mr Vasey's house and keep a cook, and servant, and a youth. But following Lord F's instructions we have to get an old cook of course. He says it wouldn't do to get in a young!

I am sorry to hear that the Bishop has died. No doubt you will have a new one by now.

Lord Forres was impressed enough to consider that Joe was capable of running a flour mill single-handed, because that is what was to happen. The next two years have to be considered the best period of his whole life.

In April 1927 he wrote:

Joe, aged 23 in Santiago

Compania Molinera San Cristobal Santiago — you will see I have changed my address to the Capital. I have been lent to this milling company while the manager visits England. S. seems to be the best place and miles ahead of London. I AM FEELING QUITE A BIG PERSONAGE NOW. The S. racecourse is the finest in the world. As I have always been accustomed to getting up at 7 am, I can't now get in the habit of staying in bed, so have to spend two miserable hours as prestige won't allow me to walk to my office with Managing Director on the door until 9 am. I have brought several white suits with me but prestige won't allow me to use them and I have to use me Sunday best with a hard collar. I have a house near the mill which is in the residential part and it has sixteen rooms and I have it all to myself!

Joe would have found his surroundings intoxicating. The mill in Concepción looked out on the railway yards. But here his mill was at the base of the San Cristobal sugar loaf mountain, facing the Andes, beckoning exploration on horseback across the river and into foothills.

With the international port of Valparaiso situated so close to the capital, many nationalities made up the cosmopolitan population of Santiago. Joe remarked on how Germans, Swiss and Norwegians celebrated their National Days. He was attracted to a young Norwegian visitor to the mill and invited him to his residence. All would have been well in normal circumstances, where advantage could have been taken of privacy. Unfortunately, another member of staff was staying at the time in a spare adjoining bedroom. This person's silent prurient disapproval spoilt everything. It may have been that person's jealousy, something Joe considered outrageous. Joe was frustrated, but more than that, he was plain angry that anyone should interfere with his pleasure.

Apart from this setback to his self-esteem, everything was going well for Joe, and he decided it was time to share his success with his uncle:

> It seems a long time since I wrote to you, so here goes. The time of my contract with Santa Rosa is up and I have signed on for another two years as I think it is the best thing to stay here for a while longer. I have been lent to this firm for 3 or 4 months.

> Santiago is the nicest city I have ever lived in. We have 45 horses at the mill and 4 saddle horses, so that I can get plenty of riding when I want, but there seems plenty to do without that.

> I should very much like to come to Southwell but I am afraid I should want to remodel your mill as the whole time I have been in Chile I have spent more time remodelling than milling!

And, in even higher spirits, he wrote to John:

> Our brothers and cousins seem in a great hurry to get married. I haven't begun to think about it yet, "tampoco", I can't afford it. I am going to buy a car first, then a wife afterwards.

In August, back in Concepción, he wrote:

> I saw the Charleston in Santiago, but the Black Bottom is quite the new thing and caused quite a stir here. Needless to say we have all been every night!

Nevertheless, the return to Concepción from the capital must have been an anti-climax. Doubts arose as to whether he might be at a dead end, staying in South America. In a letter dated 2nd March 1928, he criticises its unstable economy, where previously, everything he described had been so wonderful. On English Club Concepción notepaper, he wrote:

> I am trying to save some money now, ready for when I come home, but it is very difficult. To enter the club here means at least 20 pesos, as one has to throw the dice for cocktails etc. every time you look at anyone. The peso has a nominal value of 6d but the spending power of 1d. It costs 4 1/2d to send a letter and 3/- to get a haircut and it used to be so cheap in 1924/1925!

The British Community, Concepción

CHAPTER 3

Paris/Brussels Flour Mills Technical Manager

Joe was back in England on holiday at the end of 1928. He decided not to return to South America to complete his contract with Balfour Williamson. Instead, he offered his services, "with expert knowledge on long extraction milling", to Henry Simon Ltd. To arrive at the head office of that company in Manchester, and to be welcomed, would fulfil his ambition. It would complete the Odyssey his father failed to accomplish in 1910.

As luck would have it, there was a job waiting, and it was just the sort of thing he was after. It did not mean a move to Manchester. That would have to wait another four years. He was off to the Continent to solve a problem.

The Hungaria Mill in Louvain, remodelled by H. Simon's office in Brussels, had failed to meet the guarantee under its contract. It was under-producing, and it was suggested flour was being sacked off secretly. Simon's staff could find no other explanation. The owner was incensed at being accused of cheating and complained volubly to the chairman, Ernest Simon, back in England. Joe began by listening to the stories that were going round. Joe then found his way round the mill, tapped a few walls, sat down in his office, and lit his pipe. He compared how much the owner would make under the guarantee with the hypothetical income from secret sacks, and concluded there was no advantage in cheating. The mill must be made to work.

He sent everyone back to Brussels except a bright young mill starter he had picked out. Dick Adderley's family owned a flour mill in Yorkshire. Together they replaced useless scrapers with wads of sacking. In a remarkably short time, rollers were grinding as they should be. The guaranteed output was achieved. It was all a matter of instinct.

Joe and Dick Adderley relaxing in Belgium

Joe and Dick became close friends and were to work together on many future projects. Dick, small and built like a jockey, was a keen equestrian. In fact, he was to meet his future bride, Joseph Rank's granddaughter, hunting in Ireland. Bright, witty, irreverent, and three years younger than Joe, he was attractive, and Joe made no secret he was attracted. They went swimming together. "He offered me his body, but I declined," Joe claimed later.

Dick introduced him to Gus and Fred Wolff, heirs to the London Metal Exchange merchants, Rudolf Wolff & Sons. Fred was a wonderful-looking athlete aged nineteen, who became a Gold Medallist in the 1936 Berlin Olympics. Joe fitted in effortlessly with this group of self-confident, wealthy, fun-loving young men. They replaced his provincial Southwell cousins, who were somewhat forgotten.

On the occasion of his knighthood in 1960, among the letters of congratulation, came one from Gus Wolff:

Fred and myself are very fond of you and there is no doubt you duly benefit from your Belgian training. "Ponky Pete" alias Dick Adderley will have to get a move on if wishes to emulate his former Henry Simon and Young Farmer associate!

Dick may have kept his nickname for thirty years; Joe was quite unlikely to have had one. For "Young Farmer", the current reference should have been made to the "Young Millers", a social group who invited Joe to address their meetings, when he became famous.

It is not certain whether it was by intention or by coincidence that Joe found himself travelling on the same train between Brussels and Paris as Ernest Simon. He introduced himself to the formidable Governing Director of Henry Simon, who instructed him to "Make me a note", before dismissing him.

Joe recommended that the company should close down the Brussels branch and put the work through the Paris office. His success at Louvain added strength to his proposal. And so that is what happened, and Joe found himself appointed Technical Manager of Etablissements, Henry Simon S.A., a post he held from 1928 to 1932.

That meeting on the train could not have been more opportune. Much as Dick may, possibly, have "emulated" Joe, this was nothing compared to Joe's emulation of Ernest Simon, whose father had chosen "Darwin" as his second Christian name. Henry Simon came to Manchester from Germany in 1860, and built up a company based on two major industrial processes: by-product coke ovens and roller milling. He instilled in Ernest a determination "to acquire a sound technical education, to avoid the well-trodden arts and professions for a career, to keep in close contact with scientific development, and to search for engineering specialities and patents which could improve the efficiency of large scale industrial enterprise". To run a business successfully he should endeavour to increase the company's capital base, and to be in a position to summon, rather than be summoned by, his bankers.

Ernest was still studying and playing cricket at Cambridge when his father died suddenly from overwork in 1899, aged sixty-four. Overnight he was put in charge of the business. He was twenty. He may not have completed an engineering degree; instead, he built on his father's experience. He inherited a gift to infect others, including Joe, with the determination to succeed in industry.

Henry Simon's office in Paris was at 1 Rue de Mondetour, between

Les Halles and the Gare du Nord. Joe lodged at the Hotel Corona, 8 Cité Bergère, "Situé à proximité de l'Opéra et des Grands Boulevards, entree 6 Rue du Faubourg Montmartre". It is still there, but the office went with the redevelopment of Les Halles.

Paris was the most exciting city in the world. It was home to "good Americans, elegant Argentinians and refined English expatriates". Joe conveyed something of its flavour to his cousins in 1931:

> I got back from Brussels on Thursday accompanied by our commercial head. I saw the Duke and Duchess of York arrive while I was seeing him off at the Gare du Nord yesterday. Last night I went to the Folies Bergère. There is a good show there!

He entertained business associates and their wives at jazz clubs, dancing "the foxtrot" and listening to "Le chanson". Chanteuses such as Edith Piaf and Lucienne Boyer ('Parlez-moi d' Amour'), and chanteurs Charles Trenet and Jean Sablon, filled music halls with La Revue. Colette observed the scene in an early novel, *Mitsou*:

> First showgirl: "I must go back to my guests. They are two millers I have left in my box. They own a flour mill".
>
> Second showgirl: "Pff! A couple of flour-sifters!"

"Next time you come to Paris I shall have a lot to show you. Every day I discover something new," Joe boasted to John and Edward. Business associates expected him to take them to brothels and the lowest dives. Other nights were less thrill-seeking: "Owing to the bad weather I was forced to go to the cinema this evening with Stamford who is on the milling staff here!"

The French film industry was going through a golden patch, with famous directors René Clair, Jean Renoir, Carl Dreyer and Marcel Carné. A cinema at the Madeleine re-ran *Ben-Hur* continuously. Joe was very taken by Ramon Novarro. Sometimes he would go to the cinema alone. On one occasion, he sat next to a young Argentinian and responded to his overtures. It was not just a casual pick-up. The boy was very respectable and wanted Joe to meet his parents. Years later he was to have a similar experience with another Argentinian boy on an overnight train journey in South America. Again, he was assured of a gracious welcome from the parents.

Joe's area of responsibility stretched from Alsace in the north to Algeria in the south. A typical tour inspecting mills took him to the Port of Algiers, Malta, Monte Carlo, and finally Choisy, where he addressed a group of young French millers.

In 1931, he was "having a devil of a job to get permission from the French authorities to work in France and Mr Simon has taken the matter up in Parliament with the Secretary of the Board of Trade who has asked the Foreign Office to instruct the British Embassy to work on my behalf. I feel very important after having to deal with common or garden Consulates."

In June 1932, he wrote home:

To tell the latest news about my promotion. From the end of September I am going to come back to England permanently and make my headquarters at Manchester. There I am to supervise all technical H.S. work in the Continent of Europe from Russia, Scandinavia, Germany, France etc. In addition I have been appointed assistant to Mr Fowler for all the technical work in Great Britain and the rest of the World. He is going on half time. It is Sir Ernest who has decided this. Needless there will be a good deal of opposition from certain quarters. 5 days in 7 I am in Paris. I have clients to entertain, and the number of late nights means I have to sleep 12 hours to make up for the previous 4 or 5 nights. Mussolini has made some new decrees which have made it difficult for milling engineers in Italy. I am still touring thousands of miles. On Monday I am going to Strasbourg and Germany. On Saturday next I leave for Africa, either direct to Algiers or through Spain to Spanish Morocco. I must be in London on July 18th to meet Mr Levy who controls the largest group of flour mills in the World.

CHAPTER 4

Manchester Flour Mills Expert

Joe's rise within Henry Simon was rapid. Within a year of returning to England he became a director of the company. The summer of 1933 found him at Turnberry Hotel Millers' Convention, co-presenting a technical paper on Water Cooling of Rolls with Sir Ernest Simon.

Milling magazine noted, "Mr Lockwood's experience is international in scope; he is unquestionably one of the most capable and progressive of the younger school of millers. He deals with the diagrams, flow sheets, and all the milling matters in their technical sense."

Each year, the National Association of British and Irish Millers arranged a get-together. It was a social occasion and the wives, sons and daughters were included. Joe was a good mixer. He was tall, personable, successful, aged twenty-eight, and unmarried. Late one night at the Turnberry Hotel, a miller's daughter slipped into his bedroom uninvited. The young millers thought it a huge joke. They had put the girl up to it for a bet.

With mother Mabel in Skegness, 1934

Highley Sugden, another mill owner's son who, like Dick Adderley, chose to work for Joe permanently, described Joe's success with Sir Ernest: "Sir Ernest was a great believer in giving responsibility to people when they were young; he worked on the principle that a young man would make mistakes, but unless he was a fool he would not make the same mistake twice. If he did he would be sacked immediately. He had a very quick brain, he would pester you with questions requiring immediate, concise and constructive answers, or he would make you prepare half-page reports, and if they contained any padding he would chuck these back at you and make you do them again, often over the weekend!

"Joe told me that, when he first got the top job and was summoned to Simon's office, he would nip off to the nearest pub for a large gin; 'to make me sparkle'.

"But Joe had a remarkably quick and clear brain too, and he soon learnt how to stand up to him and handle him. He used to say Simon's instinct was brilliant, but if he tried to reason things out he could sometimes reach the very wrong conclusions.

"Simon liked to hear about successes, and Joe was delighted to have success stories to tell him."

"Good. I do like success!" were Simon's very words, addressed to astronomer Sir Bernard Lovell, by his benefactor, at Jodrell Bank in 1949.

Joe said Simon was not inclined to digress: "Different subject. Keep for separate meeting." Wives were not included in dinner invitations unless they had something to contribute.

In 1934, Fowler left, and Joe was now "milling expert at headquarters". As in Paris, he chose to live in a hotel near his work. This was all to change as a result of a lucky meeting on a routine train journey from Manchester to Euston. Sharing his third-class carriage was a fair-haired young man, who politely asked him to remove his feet from the seat opposite. A deep friendship resulted from this unpromising start. Harold Rodier was training as a solicitor in London. He introduced Joe to his friend Tommy Russell, a tall Cambridge rowing blue. Harold and Tommy drew him away from his Stockport hotel and office, with long walks in the Derbyshire countryside. He shared their love for the peaks and dales of the Pennines on Manchester's doorstep. Unresisting, he was adopted into the Rodier and Russell families, and in due course Harold's and Tommy's sons became his first godchildren.

Letters to Southwell illustrate these developments. Beforehand he wrote:

> Busy, dictating 36 letters at office. Planning to go to Paris, Brittany, Marseilles, Strasbourg, Brussels. The result is my nerves are all on edge and I cannot settle down. I find the easiest way to work it off is to go on writing, or go to the cinema.

Then came the change:

> I had a grand weekend – Rodier and I walked 18 miles yesterday on Derbyshire moors and then got back to tea and remained for supper also. They are a charming family.

Tommy's family owned a major construction company with its roots in Scotland, like McAlpines. He and his older brother shared a large house in Whaley Bridge, and they invited Joe to join their bachelor existence. One night they were thrown out of a hotel in Buxton for rowdy behaviour. Joe found his name in the local newspaper the next day.

Work and pleasure formed an enviable partnership, as Joe recounted, writing in a spare moment from the Great Eastern Hotel at Liverpool Street Station on 27th May 1936:

> Tommy and I have had a grand weekend fishing in the West of Ireland. We arrived back at Liverpool, and here I am leaving for Brussels tonight, but hope to get back on Friday so that we will make four days at sea in the seven days on Tommy's yacht. I got a big order from Hovis Manchester last week which has pleased me a lot. Tomorrow I hope to get the reconstruction of the Grands Moulins de Brussels, a 100-sack plant. I am not feeling too well today. Very late to bed last night on the boat. Adderley got left on the boat as it sailed from Dublin without

warning. I had to persuade the Captain to turn round and take A. back to Dublin which he did. We have a big pull with the steamship company owing to the amount of freight we give them.

In 1933, Joe paid the first of many visits to North America. He was critical of the milling methods in the United States and Canada, which he considered out of date. Spoilt by sheer volume of output, complacency led to reluctance to adopt new technology. Joe made an intensive tour of mills in Buffalo, Chicago, Minneapolis and Ontario.

He sailed on the *SS Normandie* three months after her maiden voyage, when she won the Blue Riband for the fastest crossing of the Atlantic. Travelling with him were the Belgian directors of the two largest flour milling companies in Europe. Paul Baumann's family owned the above-mentioned Grands Moulins de Brussels, and G. A. Stein was a director of the funny-sounding Bunge and Born, the company with mills in Brazil and Argentina of particular interest to Henry Simon. But also aboard was someone who reminded Joe of his days in Paris. Josephine Baker was on her way to appear in the Ziegfield Follies in New York. She signed her photograph with Joe, "A Monsieur Lockwood with best wishes from Josephine Baker, 1935". Once notorious for nudity, it was rare to see her fully-clothed, fashionable and demure.

Aboard the Normandie with Josephine Baker and Belgian millers

In December 1937, Joe was back in America, travelling 25,000 miles through the United States, Mexico and South America. Writing of his experiences in *Milling* magazine, he gave a glimpse of that anger punctuating his long career:

In spite of two visits to the Mexican Consul in Liverpool I had some trouble crossing the Mexican frontier, and although I produced proof that I only intended to stay in Mexico five days, I was compelled to deposit 500 Mexican pesos (about £25) as a bond that I would leave the country again, even this was not as simple as it sounds, for I had nothing but Sterling and the frontier authorities had no notion of the rate of exchange. This regulation apparently does not apply to citizens of the USA, and my few American fellow passengers had no difficulty. In Mexico City I at once started trying to recover my deposit, and, after considerable difficulty I got it back. But I was disgusted to find that it had shrunk a good deal owing to losses in exchange and the Mexican tax on converting pesos into Sterling. As though to make it perfectly plain I was unwelcome, Mexico City produced a series of earthquakes during my visit!

This incident would always put him in a bad mood when he landed in Mexico.

Joe had sent his brother Charles and Dick Adderley to run a newly-installed Henry Simon mill in Sao Paulo, at the urgent request of Bunge and Born. When in Brazil he checked on their progress, and Charles was able to complain to his brother he had to get up at 5 a.m. every morning to start the mill. Charles's career in milling had followed a similar pattern, and he had gained experience in Kenya. He would stress he never worked for Henry Simon, nor was he employed by his older brother. Nevertheless, the Sao Paulo project led to his running all the Bunge and Born companies in South America.

Personal contact with his major customers was a high priority for Joe. By travelling with them, there was no better opportunity. G. A. Stein had autographed a photograph: "Delighted to have had this nice opportunity to be with Mr Lockwood on the Normandie. Here is to the friend."

Spillers, Ranks and the Co-op were Henry Simon's largest customers, accounting for two-thirds of the UK's output of flour. Spillers was owned by the Vernon family. Returning to England from the South American tour aboard the *Alacantara*, Joe:

was pleased to find that Mrs J. Jackson and Mr and Mrs Wilfred Vernon would be travelling with me.

Nobody who know Mrs Jackson will be surprised to hear that she was one of the most popular people on the ship; she was as full of energy as ever, and she and I had daily Tango lessons. Mrs Vernon (Nancy, her daughter) either won or got into the finals of nearly all the sports events.

The Vernon and Jackson families had intermarried, two daughters marrying two sons. Wilfred and Nancy Vernon became Joe's best friends, on a par with the Rodiers and the Russells. They monopolised him at Millers' Conventions, playing tennis, dining and dancing in full evening dress, elegant in white tie and tails, doing the Eightsome Reel with "Ma" Jackson. Wilfred and Nancy invited him to attend their sons' passing out parades at the Royal Naval College, Dartmouth.

Joseph Rank reminded Joe of Edward Caudwell; both spent their earliest childhoods in their father's flour mills. "My grandfather was very irate when he first discovered some flour from Rank being delivered to our district which included Nottinghamshire. My family were competitive millers of Joseph Rank."

It amused Joe that Mr Rank, reputed to be the richest man in England, "travelled third class on the railways until the end and always took sandwiches to prevent having to pay for lunch." Business meetings were held at station hotels. A strict Methodist, he banned his mills from running on the Sabbath. When the great Clarence Mill in Hull was bombed, his first concern was for the horses. And that was in 1941. Despite a fifty-year age gap, the two Joes got on well, something that Mr Rank's sons appreciated. Shortly before he died, aged ninety, he was staying with J. Arthur Rank (later Lord Rank), and Joe visited them. The photograph taken by Joe that day was the last picture the family were to have of the grand old man.

Provender Milling by J. F. Lockwood was published in January 1939. It was hailed as "The First Complete Book on Feed Milling Technology" and consisting of 370 pages of text and diagrams – where had Joe found the time to produce this volume? A second edition soon appeared, and remained the first and only authority on the subject. Brother Charles said the book absolutely amazed him. Cereals, leguminous seeds, oil cakes and minerals are used to produce animal feed stuffs. It is a technical subject and does not make light reading. Even popcorn is deprived of any connection with confectionery: it is one of 300 varieties of maize, and "has a large proportion of endosperm which owing to its horny nature pops when subject to heat".

The unexpected success of the book coincided with the outbreak of war. The country would depend on home production of livestock and poultry, feeding on locally milled pellets and mixtures. There were to be food shortages. Prisoners of war in German concentration camps looked forward to returning to a country where work on the land would be essential. Copies of *Provender Milling* topped the list of books requested from home.

War interfered with Joe's next masterpiece, *Flour Milling*, but it did not prevent his ordering a copy of Fowler's *The King's English*.

CHAPTER 5

War

Joe claimed he had the most interesting war of anyone. His services were required on the home front and overseas. On both, he had "a very good war". He was in charge of fire prevention in the North-West Area, including Liverpool and Manchester. He was brought in to plan the feeding of the populations of Europe where the mills had been destroyed.

"FIRE! FIRE!"

January 1940 found Joe moving to a home of his own for the very first time. At the same time, he was in Belgium inspecting mills destroyed in the First World War and about to receive a similar fate. An American milling magazine reported:

> Up almost to the very last moment of Belgium's invasion, English milling
> engineers were carrying on with the coolness under fire, or the threat of
> war, that has helped make British commerce hold fast around the world.

All the mills in both wars were destroyed, bringing an enormous amount of work Henry Simon's way. Rumour had it that the only mill left standing in Belgium was an ancient windmill. Spared on Hitler's orders, its reprieve was attributed to the fact the Führer's grandfather was an obscure miller.

Returning to Manchester, having avoided floating mines in the Channel, Joe commissioned an £80 armoured car for the protection of his factory.

Tommy Russell was getting married and his brother was overseas. So Joe moved to a cottage he had found in the Peak District National

Park. Yew Tree Cottage was actually two cottages joined together, formerly the home and forge of the Combs village blacksmith. Set in beautiful scenery and isolated, Joe could walk out of his back door into the countryside. Yet further up the pass from Combs was the main road to Manchester. With a devoted housekeeper, Mrs Drage, who made excellent fish pies, and a spaniel, Rufus, who took him for long walks, Joe settled into a familiar bachelor routine. Punctually off to work each morning, the cottage windows would be flung open after his departure at 8 a.m. to let out the pipe smoke.

Yew Tree Cottage, Combs

In October 1940, the Provost Marshal of the Royal Air Force issued his "Certificate of Employment in Essential Services in War with the Ministry of Aircraft Production, as a Member of the local reconstruction panel for the Repair of War Damage to factories North Western Area."

The following March, he was appointed "Joint Fire Prevention Executive Officer" for the region, Coventry having suffered massive destruction in the neighbouring area the previous November. The word soon got around Lord Beaverbrook's Ministry in London that an overnight billeting at Combs was an enjoyable experience: "You proved yourself to be a perfect host by providing stimulation for the mind by day and great comfort for the body as well as interesting talk when the day's work is over." The "interesting talk" led this official to indiscreetly reveal the newest bombers, by some oversight, included the place of manufacture; but "it was too late to change as the handbooks had already been issued".

Joe liked Captain Spencer Freeman, who was famous for running the Irish National Sweepstake which raised £3 million for Irish hospitals. This provided a means of bidding for runners in the Epsom Derby, despite gambling being illegal in England. For his book *Self Analysis for Success*, he asked Joe to contribute to the question: "If something made you change your mind completely would you be prepared to admit it openly?"

Stephen King-Hall and chauffeur at Combs

Commander Stephen King-Hall and Colonel Guy Symonds were further Beaverbrook-inspired appointees. King-Hall, the author whose monthly newsletter was widely distributed, came up to open the War Weapons Week in Buxton. He arrived in full Naval uniform, accompanied by Miss Bond, his driver. He inscribed "Fire! Fire!" in the 1000-page copy of *Our Own Times 1913–1939* he left for Joe. Symonds, who invented the stirrup pump as an antidote to incendiary bombs, presented him with a fifty-page report on a visit to Moscow made the month after Hitler declared war on Russia, where "the fire brigade appears to be a very efficient force".

Colonel Moore-Brabazon's term as Beaverbrook's successor came to a sudden end during a visit to Manchester. A private conversation was overheard where "Brab" rejoiced that Germany and Russia would be at each other's throats now Hitler had changed sides. It was not the way to treat our new ally. Despite Churchill's support, he had to go. Joe sympathised with his minister's predicament, but was secretly amused at his indiscretion.

In 1942 the country was divided into six regions, each with their own Commissioner given full control in the event of enemy invasion. Hartley Shawcross, QC was appointed Commissioner for the North-West Region and Joe was his second-in-command. They reported to the Home Secretary and Minister for Home Security, Herbert Morrison, through his Joint Parliamentary Secretary Ellen Wilkinson MP.

Joe had no previous experience of reporting to a woman, but was immediately impressed by this feisty MP for Jarrow, who had been on the Miners' March to London. She was a small, tough, ex-communist socialist firebrand orator. On 5th October 1942, he accompanied her on her visit to Liverpool and Bootle dockyards.

Ellen Wilkinson MP, in Bootle

She was representing the Home Secretary in an area more heavily bombed than London, where secret factories were employing 30,000 workers to produce vital munitions. Addressing a large audience about the urgency for women to become fire watchers, she was interrupted by Bessie Braddock, the extremely large and voluble Labour Councillor: "Why doesn't Herbert Morrison come in person? Women in London are being exempted, so why not us in Bootle Docks?"

E. W. passed Joe a note: "Your face suddenly registered horror, anything wrong?"

He need not to have worried: "Her voice and mine are about equal when it comes to shouting!"

He visited London occasionally, "to have lunch with my boss". He was staying at the Cumberland Hotel near Marble Arch in June 1943, when National Registration Identity Cards were issued to a population of 40 million. His registration number was 140.

Joe received another note at a meeting supporting Miss Wilkinson. This time it was from the Regional Commissioner himself, Hartley Shawcross: "Tell the Mayor's daughter I thought she was supposed to look after me. She seems to have been looking after you all the afternoon."

As senior honorary Fire Prevention Officer, Joe umpired exercises, praised women on fire guard duties, received a commendation for dealing with a massive gas explosion, and was introduced to the King and Queen at National Fire Service Headquarters.

In anticipation of the war ending, Henry Simon's were developing pre-fabricated ports and portable mills for feeding 50,000 people a day in liberated countries. Joe was constantly receiving messages of support from millers in Chile, Argentina, Ireland and Kenya, where work continued unimpeded. Bread was not rationed, and great efforts went into making what was nicknamed "The Woolton Loaf" more palatable. Joe's advice was sought to achieve 80% extraction from wartime flour: "Good colour must NOT be achieved at the expense of nutritional quality."

To obtain an acceptable balance there must be maximum Vitamin B and minimum fibre. Army bread was superior. Best of all was

American bread for those who could afford it. The Woolton Loaf was generally condemned.

"WE HAVE BEEN WAITING FOR YOU!"

Towards the end of the war, Joe found himself in demand by both our American and our Russian allies. He had been of equal service to these countries in peacetime. Russia was once the largest grain exporter in the world. Delegations responsible for building silos would visit Manchester and find their national flag flying above H. Simon's factory. "Once you sign a contract with Russians they stick to it," said Joe.

Shortly after D-Day, he was summoned to Lancaster House in London to be greeted by familiar faces. It was the Soviet Delegation: "Where have you been? We have been waiting FOR YOU!" Plans were drawn up for the restoration of food supplies to Europe. But the end of the war was delayed by the German counter-offensive in the Ardennes, and Joe was put on standby.

On 8th April 1945, he was "ordered" by the Supreme Commander of the Allied Expeditionary Forces to travel to Brussels as a civilian and join the US 21st Army Group, using military vehicles and aircraft "to examine ways of developing flour production". With no mills to produce flour, bread was almost non-existent during the occupation of Belgium, and what there was was terrible.

With the American Army in Holland

Joe told *Milling* magazine he:

> left England in early April without any money or any idea where he was going, but with the assurance the Army would feed him, billet and transport him. He reported to an address in London and was taken to an American aerodrome in Hertfordshire; two hours later he landed in Belgium, having flown over Lille and the heavily bombed coast of Northern France to avoid Dunkirk, which was still in German hands. He was given an office at 21 Army Group Headquarters and then reported to SHAEF main HQ for further directions.

> After five days he was "ordered" to Paris by command of General Bradley. Colonel Wooll, a British Army Officer provided him with transport. Escorted by two Americans, Major Hiatt and Major Lishman, and two drivers, but still in civilian clothes, he arrived at the Hotel Majestic, as guest of the 1st French Army.

Between April and June he travelled 6,000 miles, visiting HQs of all Army Groups right up to the Russian lines in Germany. Holland capitulated whilst he was there. The starving population bartered for food. A single cigarette was worth 7/6d. A Dutch boy offered himself to Joe for this sum. This was the only period his American escorts had to subsist on Army rations. On 8th May he was in Brussels with the Americans to celebrate VE Day. The menu at the Palace Transit Hotel included Trifle aux Liqueurs Victoire. On 23rd May, he reported to the British Camp at Luneburg Heath. He heard a scuffle in the next room where an anonymous prisoner was being held. Heinrich Himmler managed to swallow a cyanide pill and died instantly.

Germany lost 70% of its milling capacity. Harbours and bridges were destroyed, rivers and waterways blocked. An American General told Joe: "You want a bridge? You shall have a pontoon!"

It would take Germany about fifty years to start thinking about building another armaments industry. That was Joe's assessment: "The war should certainly have taught them a lesson. The Allies are treating them very sternly, and I never saw a British or American soldier fraternising with a German or even thanking him for any service or information he had demanded."

AFTERMATH

On 4th July, the Soviets handed over a sector of Berlin to the British Control Commission for Germany. Percy Mills (later Lord Mills), the Commissioner, occupied offices in Fehrbelliner-Platz where he was protected by a dragon of a secretary. According to Joe, she fiercely guarded access to his London HQ. Later that month Churchill arrived, and was escorted to Hitler's bunker by the Red Army. Unlike Joe, who had the opportunity, he declined the offer to go inside.

"Entering Germany" warning sign

Joe was back in Germany in September, on a two-week Allied Expeditionary Forces permit. He noted that Nazi-owned mills had taken a greater bashing than those in enemy occupied countries. They were unlikely to be fully operational until 1950, and the population would be eating wholemeal bread for years.

Wearing uniform with the equivalent rank of Colonel, Joe:

was accompanied throughout my journey by Captain Willis, who was with Spillers Ltd before the war and is milling advisor to B.A.O.R. Headquarters. We spent a few days in the North Rhineland province, where I was intrigued to see some modern Simon roller mills being installed in a mill in Cologne. They had been requisitioned from our associated Belgian company by the Nazis, and when I said they had simply been stolen, I was at once told that the man who stole them was dead.

Joe came upon a derelict Simon roller mill abandoned by Nazis, about twenty-five miles from Berlin. He photographed the terrible devastation in the city at considerable risk to himself, as the Russians clamped down on such activity. Not a single house had avoided damage, and tanks, armoured cars and smashed automobiles lay everywhere. Wreckage strewed the pavements for miles. He was able to move freely between the four zones. He saw into the Bunker, which, despite looting all around, he found the contents largely untouched. He saw the button-board on the Führer's desk with numbers for each of his staff. Nothing prevented his taking it. The unreality of the situation was brought home, when a Russian soldier asked him for his watch. Joe explained he preferred to keep it himself.

Russian soldier in Berlin

For his final visit to Germany, under the auspices of Allied Control Commission, Colonel Lockwood took Major Highley Sugden, who wrote:

> We were accompanied by Dr Tom Moran, Scientific Adviser to the Ministry of Food and head of the Millers' Research Establishment in St Albans. It turned out to be a hilarious visit from the moment Dr Moran arrived at the air terminal. He had clearly had some difficulty getting into his battledress and had to summon help from his little local tailor, who arrived hot-foot saying: "I'll do anything for a soldier, Sir". I remember how mystified Dr Moran was to see the Germans going about their business so briskly, which in his view was impossible on the limited number of calories they were supposed to be getting in their rations.

Joe photographed the black market carried on in the Tiergarten near the Chancellery, and the sad-looking "people's cars" which he realised were the first VWs. By now, the Russians had put the Bunker out-of-bounds. Menus at the 10th Infantry Brigade Officers' Club were in English, and at the Allied Control Administered Berlin Law Courts they were in Russian. Two nights at the Savoy Visitors Hotel cost six marks. Joe had signed a letter confirming he travelled to North-West Europe entirely at his own risk, bluntly refusing inoculation for typhus, typhoid, tetanus, paratyphoid and vaccination against smallpox. No such safeguards had been offered on the two previous visits as time had not permitted.

Joe's war ended in January 1946. It had taken a mere eight months for enough wheat to be ground in the British zone alone to feed 22 million starving Germans. No one was more surprised.

CHAPTER 6

Flour Milling Spreads the Word Abroad

Back at the "biggest flour milling engineering firm in the world" staff numbers rose to 3000, to keep abreast of orders to replace damaged equipment. It was necessary to strengthen the management, and Joe's reputation attracted recruits from the Army. He had the choice of its two youngest full colonels, Val Duncan and Harold Wooll. The latter had impressed him at SHAEF and was appointed joint manager with Highley, who returned with the rank of Lt Colonel. Val Duncan had also attracted the attention of the City. He became a banker, created the Rio Tinto Zinc Corporation, "the biggest mining firm in the world", and gained a knighthood.

News travelled fast when Joe was in Berlin and many were after him for a job. The story went round that a Jew pushed himself forward and invited Joe to lunch. On the way to a Wannsee restaurant, his host discovered he had left his wallet behind. "So have I!" said Joe quick as a flash, and ordered the car back to base.

Highley bought a house near Joe in the Peak District, plus a housekeeper and a dog. They met at weekends to go for long dog walks. The area is famous for ten-foot-deep snowdrifts in winter. Yet they claimed never to have missed a day's work. They would struggle to the top of the pass, where they would be collected by a car from the office.

The success of *Provender Milling*, which went into a second edition, was eclipsed in June 1945 by the publication of *Flour Milling* by J. F. Lockwood, with a Foreword by Sir Ernest Simon.

This 520-page book made Joe famous internationally. It was adopted
as a standard textbook for the Industry, and was translated into French,
German, Serbo-Croat and Spanish
(by his brother). It ran into four
editions, the last being published in
1960, this time with a Foreword by
Lord Simon of Withenshawe, and
the author Sir Joseph Lockwood.
Lord Simon wrote of, "the encouraging signs that the author and the

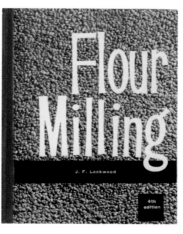

"Flour Milling",
4th Edition, 1960

milling engineering business with which he is connected are rendering
a really valuable scientific service to the world-wide industry that
gives us our daily bread."

Switzerland remained unaffected by the war. Zurich wine
merchants and flower shops were well stocked. Davos winter sports
and ski jumping competitions carried on as normal. It was here the
plan was made to rebuild Europe's flour mills.

Joe was staying with René Bühler, head of the family-owned
Gebruder Bühler, manufacturers and designers of mills, and rivals to
Henry Simon. Joe and René belonged an informal dining club, or
"Société Anonyme", with the initials SACO. As the principal members,
they agreed to divide Europe in half, Simons taking the north, and
Bühler the southern region. Together they stood firm against MIAG,
the German firms who were breaking up the market with aggressive
price-cutting tactics. This trust and mutual respect between the two
strongest manufacturers was considered good for the Industry. No
mention was made of anti-trust, collusion or cartels. Dinners were
convivial affairs, held annually, and a SACO anthem ran:

> Now we will sing the SACO song
> The Words are very clear
> And Every Member has a verse
> You'll see just what we mean...

> Now Mr Lockwood was there
> And he was quite ecstatic:
> "My latest book explains how we
> Do everything pneumatic".

Despite their wealth, the Bühlers lived modestly in a small village in a remote Canton. Their young son excused himself from having lunch with Joe. He explained he got a much better meal with the village butcher's family. René was fond of Joe, and presented him with a treasured Swiss cowbell sporting a green and white ribbon, the Canton's colours.

There was a warm welcome for the author of *Flour Milling* in Denmark, Sweden and Norway. The book had large sales and he was famous. Joe found these countries largely unaffected by the war. It was now possible to travel to North and South America again. Aboard the *Queen Elizabeth* on the outward, and the *Queen Mary* for the return crossing, life in First Class was luxurious. Sharing the comforts were Sir Patrick and Lady Hamilton. Joe and Hamilton, who was Sir Ernest Simon's nephew, were co-directors of the company, Hamilton in charge of engineering and Joe, the non-engineer, running research and sales. Joe was to tell the shop stewards at Simons that the large orders, which he had finalised in Canada, made up for the "harrowing life he had to endure aboard the *Queen Mary*". This included (unmentioned to his staff) sharing a Turkish bath with Robert Taylor, the Hollywood film star of *Ivanhoe*, whose handsome face adorned schoolgirls' bedroom walls.

This was 1947. Joe set off with his brother Charles, whom he had not seen for ten years, on a month-long tour of flour mills in twenty-four cities in America and Canada. Charles was now Technical Manager for Molinos Rio de la Plata in Buenos Aires, responsible for Bunge and Born's sixty flour mills. Life had been good for him in Brazil. He had a girlfriend. He told the story of how he was dancing with her one night, unaware there was only one other couple on the floor, which had been cleared for the President and his wife. He had no intention of moving to Argentina when his contract expired. This was not acceptable to Alberto Hirsch, the autocratic, German, Jewish President of Bunge and Born, who told Joe he must instruct his brother to accept.

Charles would come to admire Hirsch, who had arrived as a wheat buyer from Belgium in 1890 and built an empire of mills largely designed by Simons. He was little short of obsessive in his methods, restricting stakes in companies acquired to 30%, and retaining a small research laboratory for his own personal use.

Charles had no need to resent his brother's intrusion. He married an English girl, Mabel Roberts, whose father's insurance and banking company prospered when Argentina was one of the wealthiest countries in the world. Charles and Mabel built a house in an exclusive part of BA, close to the Hurlingham Club, popular with ex-patriates. They produced four fair-haired daughters who were educated in England.

Joe's only dampener on this ideal situation was to voice disapproval of Mabel's brothers, who stayed at the Ritz and kept a Rolls Royce permanently available for their visits to London and the Continent.

During that tour of America, Charles was never allowed to forget he was only the younger brother. Wherever they went, Joe was treated as a celebrity, the author of *Flour Milling*, the world expert. Yet this was the area in which Charles's status was greater, and he resented being relegated to a minor role. Worse still was being instructed by his brother to take his feet off the seat opposite in the train. That was something he never forgot. Nor did it help to hear Joe boasting to anyone who would listen that British milling methods were thirty years ahead of America.

Henry Simon Ltd, Manchester, 1946

CHAPTER 7

"They always referred to each other as Mr Lockwood and Mr Sugden"

Ernest Simon was spending less time on company matters. He held prominent positions in Manchester as Mayor and at the University. But as an MP, and then a Lord, he would be in London more often than not. Lord Simon of Wythenshawe was appointed Chairman of the Governors of the BBC, a role he devoted more time to than was considered necessary by some. For example, already branded "the Millionaire Socialist", he gained notoriety by banning a television play against the wishes of the Director General. Intended as a comedy, it concerned a fictitious Cabinet Minister revealing atom bomb secrets in order to win an election. This meant he was only available on weekends, hence making it a seven-day week for Joe, who was at the office from 8 a.m. to 10 p.m.

Joe's office was in the building in Cheadle Heath where he installed an "Experimental Mill" in 1946. There he patented a method for improving cereal purification and a machine for conditioning wheat with heat stabilisation. Royalties for both patents and book sales were paid to the company. To get to his air-conditioned room, where his secretary was working with the first IBM electric typewriter imported from America, he would pass ranks of draughtsmen standing at their drawing boards: "Good morning Mr Lockwood," they greeted him individually. The activity to keep up with orders, 80% of which were from abroad, impressed a reporter from the *Daily Express* in 1950: "It was Mr J. F. Lockwood, the Managing Director, keen, quick smiling and massive enough to suggest he used to be a Rugby footballer, who really got me excited."

In 1951, Joe and Highley decided they needed to be closer to their workplace. They jointly bought a property in Mobberley. Hill House was Grade II, black and white timbered, dating from 1590, at one time home of the Reverend Symonds Attlee, the Prime Minister's uncle. They lived there for four years. There were house rules, which Highley described:

Hill House, Mobberley

1) Joe would be responsible for the house, housekeeper and catering.
2) I would be responsible for the wine store, gardener and large gardens.
3) We would have meals together and then retire to our own quarters.
4) Neither of us would invite relatives whilst the other was in residence.

Sir Vincent de Ferranti, a neighbour, described the situation: "They always referred to each other as Mr Lockwood and Mr Sugden." Sir Vincent was the dynamic buccaneering chairman of the Manchester electrical engineering company that bore his name. His son Sebastian said he thought very highly of Joe.

Highley, living in such close proximity, was able to access Joe's character: "Though he had no training in legal or financial matters, such things seemed so simple to him. I have watched him reading through a complicated legal patent incredibly quickly; his finger would travel rapidly over the page and suddenly stop. 'This is the key point,' he would say, and then almost as quickly; 'And I'll tell you how we can turn it around'. Moreover Joe himself often made the first draft for a patent or legal agreement, leaving the lawyers to check the details. He was fascinated by new developments and was prepared to take considerable risks, provided conventional equipment was still available if needed.

Highley Sugden

"He mentioned he could have been a playboy; indeed he showed signs of it when given such rapid promotion. But then his burning ambition overcame such weakness. He was shrewd, had remarkable common sense and could be ruthless with staff that did not measure up. He did not believe people really needed holidays and rarely took any. For example if he needed someone who was on holiday he had no compunction in instructing the man to return forthwith. But at the same time, when in the right mood, he would be the life and soul of the party, brilliantly witty and delightfully indiscreet, and often the outstanding personality at any "top brass" meeting.

"Bill Bloor, manager of the Co-op mills, loved to come to lunch at Simon's (and a few whiskeys) and monopolised a high-back armchair with large side wings, suitable for an after-lunch snooze. He was delighted when Joe gave it to him when he retired. He always told the same tale in broadest Rochdale accent: 'Ah've been in t'Kremlin tha' knows. Ah told Stalin that t'ole wealth o'Mankind comes from t'brawn and muscle o'Man.'

"Joe could always get on with people like this and encouraged them to come – it was good for business too.

"Regrettably his ambition caused him to drop former friends, especially the Vernon family who had been exceptionally kind and helpful to him in his younger day."

Congratulating Young Millers

CHAPTER 8

Boffins and Bankers

In 1951, Joe was appointed a Member of the National Research Development Corporation, his first non-war unpaid Government role. The letter appointing him for a three-year term was signed by Sir Hartley Shawcross, now a Labour MP and President of the Board of Trade. Created by Harold Wilson when President of the BOT, the NRDC was made up of an equal number of scientists and businessmen (financiers/industrialists). It was established to promote technology and to prevent a recurrence of the loss of royalty rights for British inventions to America. This happened in the case of penicillin.

Joe's sponsor was Lord (Patrick) Blackett, Pro-Chancellor of the University of Manchester, nuclear physicist, and later President of the Royal Society and OM. Blackett wrote:

> I am sure you are going to be a most valuable Member. There is at present very little representation of Industry who have recently had and still have intimate contact with rapidly developing technology. If I may say so strictly in confidence two of our Industrial Members have rather too much accounting interest for my liking – I won't tell who they are!

He was referring to Sir Edward de Stein, a businessman and banker, but neither an industrialist nor (obviously) a scientist. Blackett marvelled at Joe's ease with scientists despite his lack of formal training. He threatened to resign unless Joe joined.

The scientist to be appointed at the same time as Joe was Sir Henry Tizard. In 1935 it was Tizard's Air Defence Committee, which included Blackett, who sponsored the development of radar. These two boffins deserve the credit for the saving Britain and winning the war. Churchill foisted his Chief Scientific Adviser, Professor

Lindemann (later Lord Cherwell) on to the committee. As Lindemann did not share Tizard's view on radar, this was taken as a snub, and caused Blackett and Archibald Hill, a University of Manchester physicist, to resign. With Labour now in government, Blackett and Tizard were again in favour. Joe was an early admirer of radar, in so much that, on the night Coventry was firebombed in November 1940, he flippantly and indiscreetly boasted Manchester had been the intended target, but his boffins had "bent the beam onto Coventry".

Sir Percy Mills, his wartime boss, was Chairman of NRDC, and another industrialist he greatly admired was Sir Rowland Smith, Chairman of the Ford Motor Company. Joe was prepared to forgive Churchill's poor judgement, and attended his great funeral service at St Paul's Cathedral with Percy Mills in 1965.

Managing Director of NRDC was Tony Halsbury (the Earl of Halsbury). It was with good intentions that Halsbury invited the new member to be his guest at the dining club where he was President. Quite seriously the club was called "The Sette of Odd Volumes", and Joe was at a disadvantage to discover the evening's proceedings were in Latin.

NRDC had a tight budget, with £2 million limited to any one project. Joe came up against Christopher Cockerell, the inventor of the hovercraft. He was openly angry at how that man pestered the Government for funds. Under pressure, lasting nine years, NRDC did sponsor a prototype which carried its logo, but the invention failed to live up to its potential.

Joe was better disposed towards Sebastian and Basil de Ferranti in 1959. The brothers learnt that NRDC was allocating £5 million to the computer industry, and Joe was prepared to be lobbied and to offer them lunch. He knew them as teenagers, and they were still only thirty-two and twenty-nine. Naturally, they were after preferential treatment for Ferranti.

Joe's re-appointment for a further three-year term came when the Conservatives were in office. Looking back on his twenty-four periods of unpaid Government Service, appointments made equally by the two Governments, for example Frank Cousins at Technology and

Margaret Thatcher at Education, he decided all politicians were much the same. By appeasing them he had a better chance of gaining Government contracts for his own company. Sometimes this had an unexpected outcome: "When Lord Thorneycroft returned to the Government as Minister of Defence in 1960 he asked me to take on the Royal Ballet School. I could not refuse – he was my Minister!

"Another Minister of Defence, Harold Watkinson, did not like me, because I showed him up in front of his Civil Servants."

CHAPTER 9

Rockets, Radio, Radar and Records

One day, after a NRDC meeting, Joe turned his back on flour milling. On 30th July 1954, the *Financial Times* reported:

> Mr J. F. Lockwood, Chairman of Henry Simon Ltd has been offered the post of Deputy Chairman of Electric & Musical Industries. In view of the National importance of the post, Henry Simon Ltd, with grateful recognition of his outstanding services, felt it their duty to advise him to accept it and released him from full time executive duties. Lord Simon of Wythenshaw has agreed to resume his former position as Chairman of Henry Simon.

There had been an almighty row. This time Joe's anger attack, as usual totally unexpected, exceeded all those that had gone before. Patrick Hamilton, Simon's nephew, told him one day: "You know, there's only room for one of us in this company." Joe replied: "Right! I'm gone." And with that he ended a lifetime's career.

Sir Edward de Stein had been nagging Joe at NRDC to put one of his companies right. He had been a Director of EMI, created by the merger of the Gramophone Company and the Columbia Graphophone Company, since 1931. For three years, Joe had fobbed him off. But now he said "What the hell!" and decided to give it a go. He was very, very angry and looked around to find a calming influence. Luckily his uncle Frederick Lockwood's son lived nearby. Richard came home one afternoon with his wife to find Joe playing football in the garden with their young son.

Harold Wooll saw what had happened as inevitable:

The running conflict between Lockwood and Hamilton had intensified as trading became more difficult after the post-war boom. Lord Simon, now 75, was not the decisive arbiter and peace-keeper of earlier years. The Simon family regarded Lockwood as "only a miller" and untrained for top management. He had no engineering knowledge and a somewhat abrasive personality. His success as the boss of a much larger and more complicated business in EMI, showed how poor the Simon's family judgement was in this case."

When Simon Engineering Ltd became a publicly listed company in 1960, Lord Simon insisted the family make over some of their shares to Joe, who said that apart from his grandfather's £100, this was the only capital he had ever been given.

Often asked why he had been invited to become Chairman of EMI, Joe would reply: "Because they were bust! If they had been doing well they would have gone for an Earl or a Lord."

The net loss in 1954 was £377,000. As one of the thirty companies to make up the original FT 30 Index, EMMIES stood at 35/- at their height, making the company worth £150 million. They were now 17/-. At the end of Joe's first year they rose to 25/-, making Edward de Stein a happy man. Joe quickly found where the problem lay. There was only one executive on the board, and he was conveying incorrect information to the non-executive directors. When he found Joe talking directly to executives, he made them make a written note of what they had told him. Once Joe found out, he realised there had been a conspiracy, which went on for some time, until the company secretary confessed. It was a brave man who kept secrets from Joe. If that wasn't bad enough, the managing director was having sex with his secretary in the office after hours. Everyone knew about it and it was setting a bad example to staff. "There's a right bastard running our company now," a stranger on a train told Joe, who found out his informant was an EMI employee, and had him in the next day.

The company needed a full-time Executive Chairman, and Joe inevitably assumed that role. He was officially boss of the greatest number of employees in London. Ford Motor Company employed more, but it was outside the city's conurbation, whereas EMI's head office in Hayes, Middlesex, qualified. Joe learnt he also employed the largest number of card-carrying communist and Union members.

Most of EMI's businesses were enclosed in one vast 150-acre site squeezed between the Great Western Railway and the Grand Union Canal. As the original headquarters of the Gramophone Company, it was best known for its record factory. But the basic manufacture of records, radio and television shared space with the more sophisticated electronics of radar, rocket fuses and computers. At the heart of all this, feeding new technology to all manufacturing departments, was the five-storey Central Research Laboratories building, which was first to catch Joe's attention and admiration. By chance he had recently read an article in the *Manchester Guardian* about Isaac Shoenberg, the Director of CRL, receiving the Faraday Medal. This was "in tardy recognition" for developing electronic high definition television with cathode ray tubes in 1934 and its vital adaptation to radar during the war. Shoenberg and his team, "My Boys", including Alan Blumlein, had chosen the 405-line TV display system. EMI, not Baird, was the true inventor of television. One of Joe's first actions was to put seventy-five-year-old Shoenberg on the EMI Board and lobby for his knighthood.

EMI had no cash or reserves. For the first time in his life, Joe had to ask to see his bankers. He was given a hard time. The company held founder shares in Associated Broadcasting Development Company, which, as ATV, in 1956 became the first commercial television station. With no funds to take up EMI's entitlement, Joe allowed the offer to lapse. Worse still, he found the shares were held in the name of the chairman he replaced, who kept the proceeds at their disposal. Or that is what Joe claimed happened. There was another investment available. $3 million was required, and Joe was determined not to lose it this time. He approached EMI's official bankers which were Barclays, Samuel Montagu, and Edward de Stein. None was forthcoming. De Stein had some excuse. He was selling his bank to Lord Cowdray's Lazards, part of the S. Pearson Group. To replace himself on the EMI Board, de Stein, who was gay, offered Joe "two of my boys", who were both now with Lazards. These were Mark Norman, nephew of Montagu Norman, Governor of the Bank of England, and Lt Colonel Christopher (Kit) Dawnay, also of a banking family. Joe chose Dawnay, who had been on Montgomery's staff in North Africa, and whose hobby was needlework, a pastime he had learnt from Sir Edward.

Joe was not prepared to take rejection lightly. He turned to Warburgs, a new arrival in the City, considered an upstart by the establishment. They were delighted to take on a new client. When the news got out, Lord Catto of Morgan Grenfell put a stop to this interference. He offered £3 million in the form of 5.5% Cumulative Second Preference Loan Stock, such a good rate that Joe kept the loan, which he recouped in two years, on the balance sheet indefinitely.

CHAPTER 10

Capitol Records, Hollywood, USA

Joe now had £3 million. He would dismiss those unhelpful merchant banks and their grand city offices as "convenient places for directors' wives to drop off the day's shopping from Harrods". The loan was for the purchase of Capitol Records Inc., a Californian company founded in 1942.

Capitol Tower, Hollywood

For fifty years, all the best popular music was American. EMI had automatic access to Columbia and RCA recordings. Reciprocal arrangements with both companies were about to lapse. It was essential to find another source, and to fail to capture an American company such as Capitol would be as bad as losing ATV, Britain's first commercial television company. Music was the principal activity of the company. Based on Berliner's invention of the gramophone in America and the establishment of the Gramophone Company in 1897 in London, EMI issued the recordings of the two major American companies on its Columbia and HMV labels in the UK and overseas where it had subsidiary companies.

American Columbia had already gone. By the time Joe came on the scene there was little he could do to save RCA. General David Sarnoff, President of RCA had recently turned up at Hayes. There was no one to greet him. He noted broken windows, peeling corridor walls, depressingly dated offices. There was no question of his renewing the contract. Elvis Presley's first recording for RCA appeared on the HMV label in England. None followed. 'All Shook Up', on HMV Pops, was issued in July 1957 and held the top spot in the charts for seven weeks.

The Singles Chart, listing top-selling 7" records, had frequently included Capitol label artists since its inception. Frank Sinatra, Dean Martin and Tennessee Ernie Ford were household names. Al Martino's 'Here in My Heart' was the first chart-topper to sell a million copies in the UK.

The founders of Capitol, including the chairman, Glenn Wallichs, sold all their shares in the company, in the mistaken belief radio would kill the record industry. Wallichs and his brother had a large radio store in Hollywood. However, he stayed on as chairman. He became a Director of EMI and Joe joined the Capitol Board as a non-executive.

The *Daily Express* compared Wallichs's £54,000 salary and profit-sharing contract with the £10,000 paid to the British Prime Minister, Anthony Eden. Joe responded that Wallichs was "worth every penny he gets". Compared to the larger American companies, his pay was modest. But with EMI's accounts showing combined fees of the other non-execs as £6,000, and Joe's salary at £5,000, it did stick out a bit.

To avoid strict US Anti-Trust laws, Wallichs was given total control of Capitol. Rather than the time difference between Los Angeles and London being a problem, it worked to the two Chairmen's advantage. They phoned each other late, or early in the day at home, away from the office. The US Justice Department sensed the possibility of a famous American company being influenced by its British owner and opened enquiries. Joe put Hartley Shawcross on to the job. The famous QC's comment, "It would need the Queen Mary to convey all the documents the Americans are demanding!" was enough to silence Washington.

This understanding between the Chairmen lasted fifteen years and worked well. It was good for the shares too, as EMI was already quoted on the New York Stock Exchange. Thirty per cent of the shares were held by Americans. With this new forged American connection, Wall Street brokers piled into more EMMIES.

With The King Sisters, glamorous Capitol artists

Joe and Wallichs visited each other regularly. They both enjoyed travelling. Capitol took on EMI's responsibility for Canada, Mexico and Japan, which gave Wallichs the excuse to explore the world. He and Dorothy, his wife, became addicted to shopping in Hong Kong.

Joe was no stranger to America. If Capitol executives had expected him to arrive sporting a bowler hat and neatly furled umbrella, they were to be disappointed. The first thing to confront him was the new company headquarters rising, circular floor by circular floor, on Hollywood and Vine Streets. Shaped like a stack of gramophone records, the building rose to the thirteen storeys height permitted in Los Angeles. It was the first fully air-conditioned structure in the city. The takeover of the company did not obstruct it opening for business in March 1956. At its base were brand new recording studios. Frank Sinatra was on hand to conduct the first session in the Capitol Tower, Hollywood's newest landmark.

Glenn and Dorothy Wallichs introduce Tommy Sands

CHAPTER 11

"King of Pop"

Joe made himself available to recording artists and found he was sharing their celebrity. Their success was very important to the profits of EMI. He set out to make pop music as respectable in England as it was in America — everything was more glamorous over there. They had colour television, which we lacked until 1967. Also, California basked in sunshine and produced Technicolor movies to promote stars of sound and screen. One of the most famous, for her films and records, was Doris Day. She had sold 50 million records on the Philips label, and was available to move to another company. Somehow her name and Joe's became linked, and there were rumours of "a signing". Nothing came of it. But Joe found the experience invaluable. He learnt that it was essential to make oneself pleasant to the artiste's manager, something at which he was adept. In Doris Day's case it was her husband, Marty Melcher.

A quiet word with the manager of the punk rock band, the Sex Pistols, might so easily have saved the group making EMI the laughing stock of the record industry, twenty years later.

1955 was a wonderful year for Joe to start in "pop". Columbia artiste Ruby Murray had five discs simultaneously in the "Top 20", which was to be an unbroken record for years. With her soft lilting Irish brogue she had no need to appeal to TV viewers.

Alma Cogan, on HMV, used black and white cameras to best effect. Her exaggerated ball gowns, hairstyle and bubbly personality helped 'Dreamboat', her biggest hit, to the top of the charts. Victor Silvester and his Ballroom Orchestra demonstrated dance steps to viewers. But it was as much his radio show as his TV show that brought Victor Silvester sales exceeding £30 million. He was a worthy recipient of a gold disc, the first to be presented by the new Chairman

With Alma Cogan and Laurie London

of EMI. Joe was on hand to carry out similar ceremonies for another twenty years. By the time the Beatles beat Ruby Murray's record, with their five singles topping the US charts in April 1964, Joe had earned the title "The King of Pop".

It was not an easy job to convince the Directors of EMI how important pop music was for the company's profitability. Classical music was something they professed to appreciate. "How are the sales of the new *Magic Flute?*" was the sort of question asked at board meetings. Joe would brush this aside: "We are having a fantastic hit with The Three Black Crows." It did not matter if he had got the group's name wrong. It was just to make an effect. He had nothing against the more prestigious, but less profitable, classical music, and knew perfectly well how the *Magic Flute* was doing. He would spend hours chatting with Sir Thomas Beecham after a concert at the Royal Festival Hall. They both bemoaned the 60% luxury purchase tax on classical records, whereas books were considered educational and went tax-free. Beecham had been recording for RCA in America, and doing his best to avoid our Inland Revenue. His father, Sir Joseph, was responsible for building up the pharmaceutical company in Lancashire. Joe responded to Beecham's North Country wit and ability to share anecdotes at his own expense: he had been touring the United States in grand style by train. When his private carriage halted at one station he was gratified to be met by crowds of excitable girls. Only later did he learn Frank Sinatra was travelling on the same train.

It was important for Joe to know he had the support of the directors at all times, even when they found it difficult to understand the music industry. Luckily, seventy-year-old Lord Brabazon, the longest-serving board member, told Joe he could always count on his vote. No one was more free of prejudice, or more full of humour, than "Brab". He was the first Englishman to fly, hence his car number plate "FLY 1", and to prove "pigs can fly" he took one up with him aloft.

Joe soon had to shield the board from criticism in the newspapers. *The People*'s headline in June 1956 screamed: "DIRTY DISCS – SCANDAL", with a front-page story:

> A new menace to the morals of young people is on open sale in shops all over the country. It takes the form of gramophone records that are sold purely on the appeal of their smutty lyrics!

The paper had latched on to a comedy album made for Capitol by Stan Freberg, the popular writer and entertainer. One track entitled 'John and Martha' had the two performers sharing an orgasm, or that is how it sounded from the way they emoted each other's names. There was no conversation. The BBC refused to play the record. Joe decided to ignore the scandal, and EMI's reputation remained intact.

Brab was a man of many interests, issues which he was prepared to raise in the House of Lords. Joe put him to use when the "Copyright Bill" came before the House in 1956, and threatened the record industry's future. As a member of the Church of England Moral Welfare Council, Brab tackled wide-ranging subjects. In 1942, he introduced the Insemination Bill to increase cattle production in wartime. In 1954, he spoke in the pre-Wolfenden Report Sexual Offences Debate, and his speech is worth recording:

> Not all people are produced perfectly, there are hunch-backs, the dumb ... but of all the dreadful abnormalities surely abnormal sexual instincts must become of the worst ... It must colour the whole of a man's life, and it is more a subject for our pity than our rage ... This extreme penal legislation can go too far, and it becomes quite illogical ... You might as well condemn an hermaphrodite to penal servitude for life.

No sooner had Joe joined EMI than C. B. Dawson Pane, Manager of the Copyright Department, came to him in a great state. The bill the Lords were debating put record companies in danger of losing their long-established copyright in sound recordings. Known as Mechanical Rights and extending over 50 years, these were Intellectual Property Rights, as important to composers, music publishers, songwriters and artists as they were to record companies.

Joe took a copy of the white paper home, "put a damp towel over my head", and studied the incredibly complicated subject, determined to become an expert in copyright. Realising two Lords were required to put the Industry's brief, he went straight to Brab, who in turn conscripted Lord Mancroft.

When the Copyright Act of 1956 was published, it came out that Brab had used the same debate, as Chairman of the Greyhound Racing Association, to establish that racetracks owned the copyright of their live commentaries. Betting shops would eventually pay the tracks for permission to relay the broadcasts.

Brab retired, and Joe replaced him on the board with his wartime boss, Sir Percy Mills, giving him the title of Chairman of EMI Electronics Ltd. This subsidiary company was expanding commercial and industrial activities not involving military contracts where the only customer was the Ministry of Defence.

Mills had overseen the Government's massive house-building scheme after the war. Harold Macmillan appointed him Minister of Power in charge of Atomic Energy, with a peerage as it was a Cabinet post. This meant resignation from EMI. He returned as a viscount. Joe did not meet the Prime Minister, but surmised his own knighthood in 1960 may have come as a favour from Macmillan to Mills.

Another appointment to the board was Lt General Sir Ian Jacob, on his retirement as Director General of the BBC. Ernest Simon had been his chairman. Joe and Jacob shared many anecdotes about Lord Simon's proclivities.

Sir Ian was as much a disciplinarian as Simon. On Churchill's wartime Cabinet staff, and on duty during the Blitz, he would sleep on the hard, wooden bed provided in the bunker deep under Whitehall, earning the nickname "Iron Pants". At the BBC, he vetoed a programme on homosexuality scheduled to be aired on the Home Service: "I presume we are not putting anything out on this subject."

CHAPTER 12

Disposals

Manufacture of HMV and Marconiphone gramophones, radiograms, radios and TV sets accounted for much of the Hayes workforce. Beautifully designed as living-room furniture, they were built in the magnificent cabinet factory, visible from the Great Western Railway line, and labour costs were high.

Joe was aware of a rival factory in Enfield putting out a similar product range and making good profits. This was Jules Thorn's Thorn Electrical Industries Ltd.

Thorn, a diminutive hyperactive Austrian Jew, had "arrived in this country selling light bulbs". A publicly listed company since 1936, Thorn Electrical had become the country's leader in lighting and TV rental.

Over lunch at Hayes in 1957, Joe and Jules agreed to merge their radio and TV activities. The decision was as dramatic as it was sudden, as it meant EMI would no longer be manufacturing receivers. These would now be produced under license by Thorn, using the famous HMV and Marconiphone trademarks. As the Royal Warrant holder for His Master's Voice, EMI remained responsible for the quality and performance of products bearing the HMV logo. This applied to the first colour TV sets, which were manufactured in the 1960s, and were of course manufactured by Thorn.

Everyone, from the Royal Household down, wanted to be the first to own a colour TV set. EMI's Mr Gibson was delegated to look after Royal Residences, and was much in demand at Buckingham Palace. It was not unusual for new models to develop faults. When Very Important People found fault with their status-symbol HMV set, they were mollified to learn Mr Gibson also looked after the Queen's TV. Those who used Joe's influence to get a set also expected to use Mr

Gibson, and were not prepared to deal with Thorn as they should. They even bribed him to get preferential treatment. It was impossible to please everyone. Ernest Marples, former Conservative Postmaster General and Shadow Minister of Technology, thought Gibson "was not up to the job".

EMI continued to manufacture television cameras and studio equipment for the BBC. The first colour cameras, in 1967, bore the "EMI Colour" emblem before being replaced by "BBC". This caused confusion, as it had become accepted that colour was Thorn's preserve.

Joe had to sack 2,500 EMI employees from the workforce. He decided to make the announcement in person. He walked across from head office to the shop floor, only to discover the microphone had been deliberately cut off. With voluntary redundancies, retirement and relocation of labour, Joe would claim no one was left jobless.

Joe and Jules became close friends, but it was not all plain sailing. The merger was successful and beneficial to both companies, but Jules was not the sort of person to stick to the rules. To avoid exceeding agreed quotas, thus incurring additional royalty payments, he was caught selling sets without the HMV and Marconiphone trademark.

Joe joked you could have a row with Jules and issue a writ on him in the morning, and still have lunch with him the same day. Some years later, Jules discovered that the managing directors of Thorn and EMI were concocting a merger behind his back. "Who is planning to be chairman of the combined company?" he enquired. "I am!" said the EMI MD.

Joe and Jules laughed together. They thought such wishful thinking was hilarious, as neither intended any such thing should happen.

CHAPTER 13

Country Squire, Tycoon and Darling of the City

When Joe came to London, he rented a service flat in Grosvenor House, intending to keep Mobberley for weekends. Learning that the Inland Revenue did not accept the flat as an allowable expense, Joe's anger was beyond outrage. He erupted: "In that case sell Mobberley!" he instructed. This was not the first time Highley had the rug removed from under his feet. On a previous occasion, Joe had sacked the gardener at Hill House without consulting him. It had always been agreed that the garden and gardener were Highley's responsibility.

In 1957, Joe moved back to the country. East Burnham Well, near Farnham Royal, was a good-sized house on the corner of a quiet lane. It had a large garden stocked with rose bushes and a two-acre hayfield. It was chosen as it was in easy reach of EMI.

East Burnham Well

Mrs Crosby was the new housekeeper and "Prince" was the new dog: Joe chose an Alsatian. The neighbourhood attracted burglaries, and he felt it wise to have a guard dog. The place suited him perfectly, and he found he could relax at weekends, when it was known he did not like interruptions. He should only be contacted in emergencies.

Weekend scything at East Burnham Well

It was with trepidation that L. G. Wood, Manager of EMI Records, approached him with an urgent request to present a gold record on Sunday 22nd December. It was Joe's first Christmas in his new home. Yet he accepted, to LG's immense gratitude, knowing that no one would have come to him unless it was important to the company.

So, Joe found himself on the stage of the Regal Cinema, Edmonton with sixteen-year-old Paul Anka. He claimed he received more screams from the girl fans than the diminutive pop star. 'Diana', on the Columbia label, written and sung by Anka, had sold 1,240,000 copies, making it the second-highest seller after Bill Haley's 'Rock Around the Clock' in the 1950s.

There was another reason for justifying Joe's presence at the ceremony. He had discovered the pop star. It had been pure luck, but that was no reason not to boast. The American Broadcast Corporation started a record label, ABC Records, and Joe's friend Sam Clark, the vice-president, discussed using EMI as their UK outlet. He sent over a disc, which being American had a large hole in the middle for playing on jukeboxes. So, Joe was not equipped to play it, and sent it over to EMI Records to assess. The Columbia people thought they had better release 'Diana', because "it had come from the Chairman's office".

Paul Anka Gold Disc presentation 1957

On 30th August 1957 Joe appeared on *Press Conference*, a BBC TV programme, where he told viewers that EMI and not Baird had invented television. He was grilled by a panel of four media personalities for twenty-five minutes. Francis Williams was a former Editor of the *Daily Herald* and press officer for Clement Attlee; Wolf Mankowitz was a journalist and playwright, whose "pop" stage musical was turned into a film in 1959 starring Cliff Richard, the year 'Living Doll', Cliff's first hit, sold 770,000 copies; Cecil Pollard was Editor of *The Gramophone* magazine; L. Marsland Gander was radio critic for the *Daily Telegraph*. Joe was introduced to the strains of 'Royal Progress', which also concluded the programme. A large contemporary ashtray "for speaker's table" was provided for his pipe.

The programme resulted in his being labelled a "tycoon". As a salaried employee of a company he did not own, he considered it inappropriate. His 4,000 EMI 10/- ordinary shares were the statutory minimum director's holding. He was against having shares in companies where he was a director.

TV appearances would make "Joe" a favourite with the press, "no longer the more formal Mr Lockwood". In 1961, the *News Chronicle* composed a poem:

Son of a miller, left school at 16;
To take up milling (fishing in between);
Bachelor (dear 'EMMIE' is his love);
Still finds time for fishing (see above);
Pet hate? The Purchase Tax (Ah well!);
Favourite records? Those that sell (and sell).

EMI's shares rose from 25/- in 1954 to 80/- in 1959, as a result of Joe's strict financial discipline. For the first three years, he refused to pay a dividend. He appeased shareholders by issuing scrip and rights issues. These would normally lower a share price but had the opposite effect. The issue of £3.2 million unclassified shares to strengthen the capital base worried shareholders temporarily. The stock market was experiencing the upset caused by a new phenomenon, the acrimonious hostile "Take-Over Battle". Warburgs, the upstart bankers, met with disapproval for the way they acquired British Aluminium. However, any concern that Joe might be using his new shares to mount a take-over, and depress their value, was groundless.

Forbes magazine boosted the share price further, claiming EMI could justifiably boast to be "THE GREATEST RECORDING COMPANY IN THE WORLD", ahead of RCA Victor and CBS.

Joe was prepared to use unpopular methods to achieve this success. Costs were cut ruthlessly. His hatred of extravagance, his tight-fistedness, bordered on stinginess.

Fundraising for charity and "whip-rounds" for retiring staff were banned on office premises. Having once had no money of his own, Joe disapproved of people who could not afford to donate being pressured to contribute. He confiscated the liqueurs in the Chairman's Dining Room, used for entertaining visitors. Unable to sell them, be bought them himself. He limited the number of free records requested by non-executive directors. Most unpopular of all, he cancelled the annual Christmas party at Abbey Road studios. All these restrictions, however small, were accompanied by a very public attack of anger. He blew his top when he was unable to leave the Christmas party. The commissionaires had abandoned their post. Hugh O'Brien, the TV Wyatt Earp cowboy, also wanted to get away early. They were both locked in. The press loved it, with headlines the next day: "Chairman had to shoot his way out!"

As the party had been a traditional and boozy way of entertaining artists, managers, session musicians and engineers, Joe was considered by some to be killing the goose that lays the golden egg. He was stopping people enjoying themselves.

Joe had a better way to demonstrate his support for his artists. From 1957, the previously featureless EMI Annual Report and Accounts would display photographs of all the artists, leading off with a roster of seventy well known and popular portrayals. He would visit the studios and look in on sessions. He told his mother he was there in 1959 when Russ Conway was recording 'Side Saddle', which topped the charts. "We never see the chairman, please come more often!" the popular pianist called over to him.

Joe had no alternative to acting as an autocrat in those first years at EMI, where so much needed putting right. As soon as he had staff he could rely on, he would be happy to delegate. He claimed to be lazy and interfered as little as possible. Surely there must be someone in the 17,500 workforce worthy of promotion? They couldn't all be duds if properly led. The two executives he decided to take a chance on justified the confidence he showed in them.

Percy Allaway, a former engineering apprentice, became Managing Director of EMI Electronics, and Leonard Wood (LG), a record salesman, became Managing Director of EMI Records. Both spent their whole careers with EMI, and both went on to be awarded CBEs. Allaway was President of the Institute of Electrical and Radio Engineering, and Wood was President of the British Photographic Industry. The latter implored Joe not to promote him; he felt inadequate to take on responsibility, but Joe recognised his ability.

In 1959, with the board's encouragement, Joe appointed an outsider as Group Managing Director. John Wall came from the Ministry of Food and from Unilever, where he had been in charge of "Organisation". Steady, compliant and non-aggressive, he complimented Joe's maverick, abrasive, even aggressive qualities. The titles "Chairman" and "Managing Director" sat comfortably on their shoulders. The title "Executive" did not apply, as it was clear inside and outside the company that Joe was the Chief Executive.

Wall never addressed Joe as Joseph or Mr Lockwood, it was always as "Chairman". Somewhat bureaucratic, his innovations did not always work out. Unlike Joe, he was keen to introduce share options for directors and senior management, to take advantage of the company's ever-increasing share price. The initial issue was made, as so often the case, when the shares were standing at their highest point. The price failed to move over the next four years, and the scheme was quietly discontinued.

Wall was the MD who had secret ambitions to become chairman of a combined Thorn EMI company, much to the amusement of Jules and Joe. He subsequently had a successful career as Chairman of International Computers (ICL) and of the Post Office, was knighted and became a life peer, but depression and money worries led to his committing suicide, drowning in the Thames.

CHAPTER 14

Digital Clocks and Watches

Nowadays it is common to hear of company chairmen "collecting directorships". Joe was reluctant to accept non-executive directorships. EMI deserved his full attention. Companies generally fixed monthly board meeting dates a year ahead. His diary would require spending half a day a month at another company's head office, apart from his own.

Rio Flour (Holdings) Ltd, was a company in decline. The largest mill operator in South America was for years controlled by City bankers, who had no idea of the business. The chairman was John Hansard, a Director of Samuel Montagu & Co., and now in 1957, at Joe's invitation, a Director of EMI. Joe clearly knew more about flour milling and South America than Hansard, who persuaded him to join the board. Rio de Janeiro Flour Mills and Granaries Ltd went inevitably into liquidation, and was sold to American Deltec Corporation for $2 million in 1967. Joe provided the company secretary with temporary accommodation at EMI, and was constantly interrupted with requests for signatures "as no one else was available". It had been a thankless task.

Ralph Gordon-Smith, Chairman of S. Smith & Son (later Smiths Industries) manufacturer of clocks and watches, known to his staff as "Mr Ralph", owed his position on the EMI Board to his late father. Sir Allen Gordon-Smith was an original non-executive director and, in patrician fashion, presented a silver Challenge Cup to the EMI Sports and Social Club in his name.

By 1959, Joe could no longer delay Ralph's invitation to join his board. This involved travelling to Smith's Cricklewood headquarters monthly for the next twenty years. Fortunately, he was fascinated by the company's electrical products. Clocks and watches were now powered by miniature cells, as were precision instruments for the motor industry and aircraft. Car radios, introduced as an innovation, became a standard feature. Ralph was third-generation, but as he and his wife Beryl failed to produce an heir, Joe would play a leading role among the non-executive directors when it came to appointing the next chairman. Ralph was less assertive than his father and would rely on Joe's support. The other non-executive directors reflected Smiths Industries' dependence on the Ministry of Defence for orders.

Air Chief Marshal Sir Harry Broadhurst, the Battle of Britain air ace, had a wealth of amusing stories. He was to share a love of ballet with Joe.

Earl Jellicoe, son of the Battle of Jutland Admiral, had a complicated private life. Embroiled in an unfortunate sex scandal, he was obliged to resign all his directorships, including Smiths. After a respectable period had elapsed, Ralph wrote to the board members about re-appointing him. Joe replied:

> As far as the Non-executive directors are concerned I would be entirely in favour of inviting Lord Jellicoe to return to the Board. If all males who have anything to do with call-girls are to be banned from being Non-executive directors I fear that industry would come to a stop. I am quite sure he will be very pleased to be invited to join the Board again.

CHAPTER 15

The Chairman's Overseas Visits

EMI's business was international. Whatever the time of day or night, somewhere a recording was being made in one of thirty-five languages, in one of thirty countries. Joe visited them all in a space of three years. Trips lasted up to a month. He set off for a warmer climate in January, usually California. He visited Los Angeles and New York at least once a year. In the business quarter of LA, he was considered smart for buying Capitol. Lunches were put on in his honour. Evenings were spent at parties in Hollywood with artists. Deep-voiced Tennessee Ernie Ford, whose 'Sixteen Tons' topped the UK charts, teased Joe on his English accent. Heartthrob ('Teen-age Crush') Tommy Sands charmed him.

"Well, he put himself out and came over specially from San Francisco to attend a reception, which was given for me in Hollywood, and I talked to him for quite a long time and he really is a very, very nice charming modest person, and I believe he is going to be a tremendous success in the future."

Tommy Sands went on to marry Nancy Sinatra, Frank Sinatra's daughter. Sinatra did not come to meet Joe. He walked out of Capitol Records after five years, "the years of his greatest recordings". Between 1953 and 1959 he made eighteen albums, having been picked up by Capitol recording manager Dave Dexter, when his career was at a low ebb. By matching his voice with Nelson Riddle's orchestra and arrangements, his popularity was restored to unassailable heights. He erupted (Dave Dexter said handling him "was like defusing a ticking bomb") when he learnt that a pop duo, Louis Prima and Keely Smith, were on a higher royalty rate. Jealousy also played a part: Louis

Prima's Las Vegas nightspot was more popular than his. Determined to damage Capitol, he started the Reprise record label with Warner Brothers, and smashed a stack of thirteen albums representing the Capitol Tower. Joe was forever angry at such disloyalty. Whenever the name came up, he asserted: "That man can't sing!" Glenn Wallichs was relieved to let him go, but Joe claimed he would have been able to persuade him to stay.

In South Africa, Joe was struck by the enormous range of repertoire the company catered for. He could not help remarking on the black artists arriving to entertain him at the offices in Johannesburg, let down from the backs of lorries: "They look like convicts on day release!"

He was introduced to Kwala music, and in particular an infectious number played on a flute: 'Tom Hark'. It simply must be released in the UK. It was, and it entered the charts in the Top Ten. When Joe returned to Farnham Royal, he heard boys whistling 'Tom Hark' in the streets.

In Pakistan, he was entertained by Field-Marshal Sir Claude Auchinleck, chairman of the local company. Auchinleck would call on him when in England. Noshir Soparivala, a millionaire mill-owner friend, invited Joe to inspect his Sind Roller Flour Mills in Karachi. Joe had a massive anger attack when accompanying Mr and Mrs Soparivala on a shopping trip in London. They reached Asprey's in Bond Street at lunch time on the Saturday morning, just as the store closed and refused to re-open. Joe remonstrated with the commissionaire, who was told these wealthy customers could buy up the whole store. The Soparivalas were uncomplimentary about the type of their fellow countrymen we were allowing into the UK.

Joe's visit to India was greeted with great anticipation. The Gramophone Company of India, established for fifty years on the Continent, was welcoming a chairman from the parent company in Blyth Road, Hayes, Middlesex, England, for the first time. He had the status of a viceroy from the Mother Country representing Queen Victoria. He was garlanded in Bombay at the Britannia Talking Machine Company, and in Calcutta at The Oriental Watch and

Gramophone Dealers of Northern India: Silk scroll of welcome

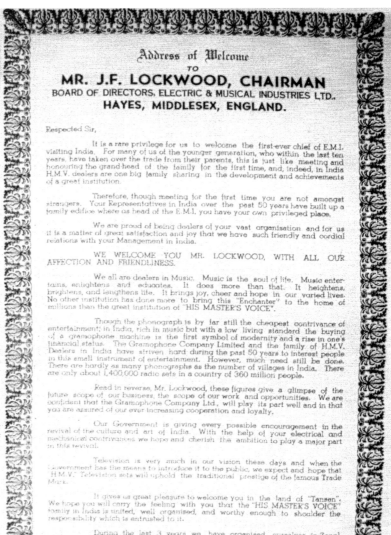

Address of Welcome
TO
MR. J.F. LOCKWOOD, CHAIRMAN
BOARD OF DIRECTORS, ELECTRIC & MUSICAL INDUSTRIES LTD.
HAYES, MIDDLESEX, ENGLAND.

Respected Sir,

It is a rare privilege for us to welcome the first-ever chief of E.M.I. visiting India. For many of us of the younger generation, who within the last ten years, have taken over the trade from their parents, this is just like meeting and honouring the grand-head of the family for the first time, and, indeed, in India H.M.V. dealers are one big family sharing in the development and achievements of a great institution.

Therefore, though meeting for the first time you are not amongst strangers. Your Representatives in India over the past 50 years have built up a family edifice where as head of the E.M.I. you have your own privileged place.

We are proud of being dealers of your vast organisation and for us it is a matter of great satisfaction and joy that we have such friendly and cordial relations with your Management in India.

WE WELCOME YOU MR. LOCKWOOD, WITH ALL OUR AFFECTION AND FRIENDLINESS.

We all are dealers in Music. Music is the soul of life. Music entertains, enlightens and educates. It does more than that. It heightens, brightens, and lengthens life. It brings joy, cheer and hope in our varied lives. No other institution has done more to bring this "Enchanter" to the home of millions than the great institution of "HIS MASTER'S VOICE".

Though the phonograph is by far still the cheapest contrivance of entertainment; in India, rich in music but with a low living standard the buying of a gramophone machine is the first symbol of modernity and a rise in one's financial status. The Gramophone Company Limited and the family of H.M.V. Dealers in India have striven hard during the past 50 years to interest people in this small instrument of entertainment. However, much need still be done. There are hardly as many phonographs as the number of villages in India. There are only about 1,400,000 radio sets in a country of 360 million people.

Read in reverse, Mr. Lockwood, these figures give a glimpse of the future scope of our business, the scope of our work and opportunities. We are confident that the Gramophone Company Ltd., will play its part well and in that you are assured of our ever increasing cooperation and loyalty.

Our Government is giving every possible encouragement in the revival of the culture and art of India. With the help of your electrical and mechanical contrivances we hope and cherish the ambition to play a major part in this revival.

Television is very much in our vision these days and when the Government has the means to introduce it to the public, we expect and hope that H.M.V." Television sets will uphold the traditional prestige of the famous Trade Mark.

It gives us great pleasure to welcome you in the land of "Tansen". We hope you will carry the feeling with you that the "HIS MASTER'S VOICE" family in India is united, well organised, and worthy enough to shoulder the responsibility which is entrusted to it.

During the last 3 years we have organised ourselves in Zonal Associations and through mutual help and goodwill have achieved a fair amount of success in implementing the policy of your Management in India of Price Maintenance. The Associations are doing constructive and useful work under the guidance of the Gramophone Company Ltd. We are earning a reasonable margin of profit on our business and devoting ourselves to the work of improving our turnover, our Show Rooms and general display. We shall, however, be much happier when present foreign exchange restrictions and their strangling effect on business have been removed.

WE WELCOME YOU AGAIN SIR, WITH THE BEST OF WISHES AND RESPECT AND INVITE YOU TO COME AGAIN.

We remain Sir,
Yours truly;

DELHI
Dated 16th Jany. 1959   THE GRAMOPHONE DEALERS OF NORTHERN INDIA.

Gramophone Company. In Delhi, he was presented with a scroll of welcome printed on silk. It extolled "the future scope for business in this Country of 360 million people". Joe was not so sure. There was little hope for a country where lawns were being cut with nail scissors. Numerous receptions and sightseeings at the Taj Mahal exhausted him. The pompous managing director sent out from Hayes bored him. The record factory at Dum Dum was fondly nicknamed "The Black Hole of Calcutta". He swore never to return.

CHAPTER 16

Sir Joseph Ponders
Next Day Disc Delivery

The 1950s ended on a high for EMI and its chairman. But there was a setback in the world of classical music.

Herbert von Karajan, whose recordings with the Philharmonia Orchestra dominated the HMV catalogue, left the company. For fifteen years, all his recordings were made with Walter Legge, who picked him up at the close of atrocities in wartime Austria. He announced his intention to record the Beethoven Symphonies with the Berlin Philharmonic Orchestra for Deutsche Grammophon. This meant breaking his contract and depreciating his Beethoven repertoire on HMV. He was permitted to go.

As far as Joe was concerned, Karajan no longer existed. There was nothing special about conductors. He played a Furtwängler and a Karajan interpretation of the same piece, and challenged a member of the Classical Department to guess who was conducting. The Philharmonia's reputation remained unimpaired and strengthened under Principal Conductor Otto Klemperer and Manager Legge.

British pop artists were overtaking Americans at the top of the UK Charts. Sinatra's hit 'Three Coins in a Fountain' on Capitol was way back in 1954, and not repeated. Columbia led the way now with Michael Holliday, Cliff Richard and the Shadows, and Russ Conway. Parlophone had a brief moment at the top with Adam Faith's 'What do you Want?' and 'Poor Me'.

Youthfulness was pre-eminent, and Joe relished it. He was intoxicated. Nineteen-year-old Cliff Richard toured the record factory at Hayes in November 1959, and was met with screams. His parents joined the chairman for lunch, and Joe presented him with a gold pen and pencil for selling a million copies of 'Living Doll'.

"The bump-and-grind rock'n'roller Cliff Richard appeals more to the UK's leather jacket set than to British Industrialist Joseph Lockwood. But financially Lockwood loves his Cockney Elvis Presley," *Forbes* magazine reported. Cliff's father died not long after, and Joe assumed pastoral responsibility for the nineteen-year-old.

Managing director John Wall was keen on the privileges that went with the job. He persuaded Joe to accept the invitation from the owners of *The Times* to dine and watch the next day's edition come off the presses. They presented themselves at the back door of *The Times*'s offices in Printing House Square at 7.30 p.m. on 14th December 1959 as requested, to be met by Gavin and Hugh Astor, the joint proprietors.

Joe was deep in thought. Why were these newspapers reaching the next morning's breakfast tables, when it took record shops days to receive their orders? The station master at Ashton-Under-Lyne in the Midlands complained he had to wait a week for something he wanted. By making record distribution his priority, Joe achieved fame by getting them on to the newspaper trains, but it would take four years of persuasion.

Joe kept secret the fact that he was receiving a knighthood as a Knight Bachelor for two weeks. The first of the 500 letters and telegrams on 1st January 1960 came from Printing House Square. Air Commodore Colin Cadell, *The Times*'s efficiency expert, wrote: "All of us who had the pleasure of welcoming you to *The Times* recently would have had the impression that they were in the presence of a very great man who was very much worthy of this honour." Cadell was flattered to be the target of Joe's probing questions.

Sixty messages came from his mother, his family and his friends. Eighty came from the milling fraternity, one hundred and sixty from EMI, a hundred from fellow industrialists, eighty from the Government, the civil service, trade unions and the arts. Walter Legge and Elizabeth Schwarzkopf represented classical music, Sam Costa and Norrie Paramor, Cliff's recording manager, represented pop.

Eighty-year-old Lord Simon, who died that year, was generous in praise: "You have not indeed wasted much time."

Old enemy Sir Patrick Hamilton, whose Baronetcy was inherited, wrote graciously: "Industrial Knighthoods are very difficult to get. I understand you are easily the youngest appointment from the Industrial World."

He was right. George Nelson at English Electric waited until he was sixty-eight, and Leslie Gamage seventy-three, after fifty years with GEC. Ted Lewis of Decca was considered more deserving than Joe by the *Sunday Times* and *Sunday Express*, and was honoured the following year. Jules Thorn's came in 1964, and Wilfred Vernon in 1965.

Alfred Clark's widow wrote. Her husband was the first Chairman of EMI. Congratulations came from Alan Blumlein's widow. Blumlein was the most brilliant of Shoenberg's team of scientists. Merchant banker Lionel Fraser cabled: "Delightful! Delicious! D' Lovely! Deserved!" quoting Cole Porter.

A Gloucester Mill Engineering Company owner wrote: "I must also include a tribute from the young. Some months ago, I asked my son who is still at Cheadle Heath what he would like to do as soon as he has passed his final exams for his A.M.I Mech E. He replied: 'I would like to be Mr Lockwood's office boy for 12 months'". Joe was brought down to earth by a Mr Ashwell of East Burnham:

As a neighbour, may I be the first to congratulate you on your New Year Honour. Also, in that capacity, please may I ask a favour of you. Your dog barks daily soon after six in the morning and disturbs myself and my household with unfailing regularity. If you could prevail on your housekeeper to keep him until after say 7 am, I shall be indeed grateful.

Book-plate showing East Burnham Well

Clarenceux King of Arms, I.R.A.F.B.

Joe chose the HMV dog "Nipper", a Fox Terrier, for his coat of arms. Alongside it was a lyre, representing music, and a wheat-sheaf surrounded by millrinds. His motto, "Persevere", alluded to five years of grind at EMI, and the prospect of more needing doing.

L. Coat of Arms
R. HMV's Nipper

The day Joe was dubbed by Prince Philip at Buckingham Palace clashed with the Rio Flour board meeting. So instead of his mother accompanying him, as might be expected, he took John Hansard. They both went in top hat and tails to the private lunch at the Dorchester Hotel, arranged by the non-executive directors and their wives. Gordon-Smith

Knights Bachelor insignia

and Mills speculated in speeches at the possibility of a Lady Lockwood one day joining Sir Joseph.

EMI Director Ralph Gordon-Smith presents Sir Joseph with Danish porcelain figures at the Dorchester Hotel

A knighthood meant Joe must fend off tempting distractions to take him away from EMI. He turned down the request to sort out British Railways, and the job went to Dr Beeching. Every time he was reported as taking over a company, the rumour had to be quashed. This meant time-consuming interviews with financial journalists, which never failed to engender further publicity.

Joe was not as enthusiastic about financial journalists as they were about him. As a rule, he found them nondescript and poorly dressed: "Why are they always so scruffy?" he complained, as they cornered him at press conferences and pop receptions.

A prominent exception to the rule was flamboyant Lord Boothby, who had a column in the *Sunday Express*. And Timothy Raisin, a young Tory, was a breath of fresh air. Describing Joe in an article for the *New Scientist* he wrote: "There is something of the 19th Century entrepreneur about him". William Davis, Rabelaisian wit, Editor of *Punch* and representing the *Evening Standard*, was treated to Joe's favourite epigram: "Chairmen are the worst judges of their Company's shares". Patrick Sergeant, City Editor of the *Daily Mail*, claimed Joe as a friend after regular lunch meetings and even an invitation to East

Burnham Well with his wife. Grander than the company chairmen he courted, Sergeant famously compared the 1970s merger of Vickers and Rolls Royce Motors to "two Dukes falling upstairs out of Annabel's propping one another up".

Joe resisted the board's and the bankers' ambition to take over companies. Frederick Ellis, City Editor of the *Daily Express*, was Joe's greatest fan, admiring his strong line, sharing the view that takeovers can damage a company's share price. Joe told him and others: "I refuse to pay more than I consider fair".

In January 1960, a £11.5 million bid for Lancashire Dynamo, suggested by one of its directors, Tony Halsbury, fell through, as did £15.8 million for Henry Simon in March. Sir Edward de Stein, who was still around, had the most audacious proposal of all: this was for EMI to take over the massive GEC, worth £116 million and four times the size of EMI. As EMI's p/e (price relative to earnings) was four times higher than GEC, this was feasible, but Joe protested: why should he be left to manage such a massive mess? De Stein, who would have claimed this as his final coup, may have been thwarted, but he still had one more scheme. And that would be the one Joe was to permit against his better judgement.

Morphy Richards was a big name in domestic electrical appliances, and still is. EMI's Commercial Non-Military Electronics Division also made kitchen equipment, such as kettles, under the HMV name. There was even a Cavendish room-heater. In August, Mr Morphy and Mr Richards fell out.

Mr Morphy left, and that could damage the company's value, as happened at H. Simon when Joe left. Joe stepped in and bought Mr Morphy's 12% stake for £800,000 as a trade investment, which could be sold at a profit. He had no intention of taking over the company, despite the commercial sense of combining Morphy Richards' famous toasters and irons with EMI's products. As long as Mr Richards stayed as a major shareholder, its future was safe.

By September, the situation had changed. City Editors admired Joe's resolve, but the EMI Board and bankers were frustrated because EMI's share price had not yet been used effectively by Joe "to take over" another company. Mergers generated fees for bankers, but brought no guarantee of gain for shareholders.

At a press conference the previous November, Joe had clearly indicated that the issue of shares would not be used for takeover purposes. The market reacted favourably with the shares going up 9/-.

Frederick Ellis ran headlines in the *Daily Express*:

> NO CASH ISSUE SAYS THE BOSS … he is increasing EMI Capital so that there will be five million New Shares, for future issue. The Directors solemnly say there is no intention of making a cash issue. And Mr Lockwood added "We mean what we say". I am inclined to believe Mr Lockwood; for he is the most honestly outspoken Company boss I have met in Q and A for a long time.

He sent Joe a Greetings telegram, quoting Peggy Lee's current hit on the Capitol label:

> All Too Soon Came Music for Loving. Wife and self swooning. Congratulations Today's Press Conference. Wish More Long Playing Bosses.

Less than a year later, Joe received an unexpected visit at East Burnham Well. Wearing old gardening clothes, he greeted four men in grey suits, who looked out of place in his sunny rose garden. John Wall, Kit Dawnay, David Montagu and John Hansard (both of Samuel Montagu & Co Ltd), were on a mission.

On Thursday 8th September 1960, the *Daily Express* announced EMI was taking over Morphy Richards for £13 million.

No longer a fan, Frederick Ellis wrote:

> The glib way in which company chiefs flatly deny market reports of take-over bids, even when they know the bids to be true – EMI denied it was taking over Morphy-Richards.

CHAPTER 17

Manchester and Grosvenor Squares "On the Fringe of High Society"

EMI House, Manchester Square, 1962

Joe had been looking for a new London location for EMI's music activities. It did not seem appropriate for board meetings to be held in the manager's office above the HMV store on Oxford Street.

He set his heart on the Old Queens Hall in Langham Place, conveniently next to the BBC. But the price was too high, and the St George's Hotel now stands on the site where he would have built offices. Instead, he found a ready-made block put up by property tycoon Max Rayne to fill a bomb site, in the otherwise untouched Georgian Manchester Square north of Oxford Street. It was available for immediate occupation with a reasonable seven-year rent review.

EMI Records moved into EMI House, 20 Manchester Square, in November 1960. Joe retained the sixth-floor penthouse as the "Chairman's Office", with the same facilities as at Hayes, i.e. there was a boardroom-cum-dining room, kitchen, and an extra loo for his own personal use, separate from visitors. He divided his time between London and Hayes, which remained untouched, but London gradually took precedence over head office. LG was on the fifth floor, with immediate access to Joe, and to his own personal loo, which he kept locked. The four Artists and Repertoire (A&R) Managers were on the fourth floor. Each had assistants and secretaries. They were away at Abbey Road studios much of the time. Of the four managers, Norrie Paramor, synonymous with Columbia, was the senior, although there was no obvious hierarchy. Walter Ridley looked after HMV. Norman Newell recorded with Columbia and HMV. The junior member was George Martin at Parlophone.

A single lift served the building, described in the prospectus as follows: "electric brains of the lift sorts out demands, and arranges its journeys to serve everyone's needs in the minimum time". Joe was not "everyone". He had an override button installed which summoned the lift to the top floor where it remained, if forgotten, until the commissionaire rang to request that it be sent down. On arrival each morning, Joe found the lift awaiting him. Anyone unlucky enough to be in it as he approached across Manchester Square was requested to vacate the lift, which was being held for the chairman. This caused resentment among less obsequious staff, which only the installation of a second lift would have forestalled.

This new London base influenced Joe's decision to come and "live in town" and commute to Hayes.

He kept in touch with the friends he made in Farnham Royal. There was Don "Pathfinder" Bennett, wartime hero and airline pioneer, whose Swiss wife Ly admired Joe's legs when playing tennis. The white shorts he kept for these occasions were unprepossessing. Being well endowed, it was not only the legs that caught Ly's attention. Lord and Lady Chatfield invited Joe to their family occasions. Modest, unassuming Lady Chatfield, wife of the distinguished First Sea Lord and Chief of the Naval Staff, would wait patiently for her turn in the local shop. The wives of "no-body stockbrokers", full of self-importance, demanded attention. These were the types who infuriated Joe to unsuppressed anger: "Why can't people be more like Lady Chatfield?" he fumed, and was glad to be rid of them.

He would miss the two polite young Jeffery boys' "Good morning Mr Lockwood". The brothers never failed to greet him as they bicycled past the house on the way to prep school. Another time, two little girls peeked over the garden wall: "We are your nieces!" they explained. "Well, you can push off!" Joe replied, angry that bad penny brother Fred dared to show his face.

East Burnham Well was sold in November 1961 to the Chairman of Glaxo, who had offices in Hayes. The Managing Director of Philips agreed to take Prince. In April, EMI had provided Joe with a flat in a new block, next to the American Embassy in Grosvenor Square. The first tenants included the Niarchos Greek shipping family, Henry Lazell (Chairman of Beechams) and Sandor Gorlinsky, Maria Callas's manager. Joe's kitchen window overlooked the back of the Duchess of Argyll's house in Upper Grosvenor Street. He relished the vicarious reports in the morning papers of the depravity he had witnessed the night before.

Tax deductible hospitality could be provided again, as at Mobberley, where there had been a constant string of flour millers from Argentina, Japan and the Lebanon. Now EMI executives from America, France, Germany and Australia came to dine. Joe enjoyed dinner parties. As a titled bachelor, he received many invitations, and lived "on the fringe of High Society". But Caudwells, Lockwoods, Vernons, Rodiers, Russells and of course Highley Sugden were not neglected. There was a spare room for his mother's visit. Mabel was left to her own devices during the day. She had lunch at Fortnum & Mason, and, when asked by Joe, told him she had walked there.

His greatest pleasure came from inviting the most successful recording artists to dinner. The first to sign the visitors' book was Adam Faith, already an established star. He came with his managers, Maurice Press and Eve Taylor. Also there was Norman Newell, who had produced Adam's number one singles, 'What do you Want' and 'Poor Me' on Parlophone, and LG, who rarely mixed with artists. LG was uncomfortable with the two managers' coarse language: he considered Press very common. Invited to sign the visitors' book, the couple entered "British Museum" as their address, which was in fact true. Norman responded with "San Quentin".

At the next dinner, when Norman Newell brought John Barry, of the John Barry Seven, the composer of James Bond film theme music, LG sent a deputy. Not to be outdone, Norrie Paramor brought Cliff Richard and his mother. Also at the dinner were David Jacobs, the disc jockey, and Michael Holliday.

George Martin was not in evidence. His artists were not yet on a par with Norman and Norrie.

In June 1962, Norman surpassed himself by bringing along, on one evening, Vera Lynn, Alma Cogan, Dorothy Squires and Peggy Mount.

By now the most familiar name signing the visitors' book was Robert Stigwood, and that involves a story. In August 1961, John Leyton, a handsome young radio and TV actor, had an unexpected hit with 'Johnny Remember Me' on the failed Top Rank label which EMI rescued from oblivion.

Over lunch at Hayes, during the pop star's obligatory tour of the record factory, Joe was intrigued at such success, which came without EMI's involvement other than supplying the demand for the records. The song was recorded, reputedly, in the bathroom of independent producer Joe Meek's Holloway Road flat. It was sung by Leyton in a popular BBC TV series, *Harpers West One*, set in a department store. The actor's young Australian agent, Robert Stigwood, claimed sole credit. He was Leyton's manager, album producer, sleeve note writer, cover designer, song chooser, in fact everything. Joe was sold, and the aforementioned album *The Two Sides of John Leyton* was issued on HMV, with credit given to Joe Meek's R.G.M. Sound Recording Company. A follow-up album, *Always Yours, John Leyton* more assertively came as "A Robert Stigwood Production for R.G.M. Sound".

Joe noted how obsessed Stigwood was with his pop idol: "He gets upset if anyone stands too close to him in the Gents!"

He invited both to dinner and included Stigwood's business partner, Stephen Komlosy, whose father had put up the money to back them. They soon had a hit with another actor-singer, Mike Sarne, whose 'Come Outside', a comedy record, came out on the Parlophone label. No further number ones followed, and Stigwood concentrated on launching a fan magazine, *Pop Weekly*. Joe was invited to make a speech at the launch party. Girls bought the magazine for the glamorous pin-up photographs and stories about their idols. It was good exposure for EMI artists. Bobby Vee, the eighteen-year-old Liberty Records artist Joe had met in America, was described as a modest young singer "whose average and likeable ways and manners are refreshing ... the heartbreaking touch!"

For three years, Stigwood, Komlosy and Leyton maintained a strong relationship with Joe, meeting on thirty-four occasions, and creating jealousy in EMI. This ended suddenly in 1965.

CHAPTER 18

The Chairman Falls in Love

Sir Ian Jacob's younger son, William, had a golfing friend who needed a job. EMI had introduced a management trainee scheme, intended to strengthen the Overseas Division. Sir Ian collared Bill Stanford, the staff manager responsible for recruitment, recommending William's friend. Joe of course did not approve of people getting into the company that way. Stanford took it as an instruction to engage the twenty-two-year-old reprobate Etonian, BC (see Part II).

By chance, Joe was looking for a new personal assistant, and Stanford sent BC, who was learning the record business at Hayes, up for interview. During his time at EMI, Joe kept a male PA. The occupant would move on after a couple of years into senior management, following the tradition Joe started at Henry Simon with Dick Adderley.

BC was preceded by three PAs at EMI. The first was from Eton, despite Joe's public aversion to public schoolboys. Charles Strachey came as a favour to the boy's father. He was the failure of the three. The others were absorbed successfully into the organisation. Strachey's father was the Rt. Hon. John Strachey PC, OE, ex-Communist Labour Minister in Attlee's Cabinet. He was tipped as a future Prime Minister, but died suddenly. As Minister of Food, Strachey was responsible for the disastrous Tanganyika groundnut scheme. As Secretary of State for War, he was lambasted in the press for his "Red" sympathies. He was brilliant, but, as a politician maverick, was strongly attracted to Joe's personality. He pestered Joe with invitations to dinner. He was just like Lord Mountbatten, Captain "Bob" Maxwell and David Frost, who were all persistently after Joe for their own purposes.

Charles Strachey did not last, and was remembered for "wandering into Abbey Road Studios whenever Maria Callas was making a recording".

On 24th January 1962, BC was sent up to see the chairman "after lunch". The meeting was to change Joe's life dramatically. This round-faced, stocky, half-Danish, blond young man found instant favour. A natural humorist, with a quick wit, quips, aphorisms and repartee, was on display. There was an easy-going confidence, so seductive, so destructive. No references were required: he was already an employee on the staff. Sir Ian Jacob was a family friend, and his father was a magistrate. His Eton background disgrace was probably dismissed. The job was his.

It is interesting to speculate how things might have been different had Charles Rodier's appointment with the chairman preceded BC's. But Joe's sweet fair-haired godson's slot was for the following afternoon. Harold Rodier claimed "Joe got my son into EMI", but this was only partly true. As a boy, Charles had received gramophone records from Joe, which led to a passion for classical music. By training and qualifying as a solicitor, he joined the company to look after legal affairs in the International Classical Artists Department. He would be on hand to support Joe in resisting Boris Christoff, Yehudi Menuhin and other classical artists' demands.

With Otto Klemperer and Walter Legge

Rodier would have relished accompanying Joe to the Kingsway Hall on Saturday 3rd February at 9.45 a.m. But it was not to be. Walter Legge was recording the much-acclaimed version of *Fidelio* with Otto Kemperer and the Philharmonia Orchestra. Engineers and lab technicians found Legge reluctant to use new the Stereo Sound technique, preferring to stick with Mono. Joe was angry and came with the intention "to take over the Recording Session". Legge watched impassively as he commandeered the microphones, re-arranging them and instructing the recordists to send the sound down the line to Abbey Road Studios. By bouncing the sound back after miniscule delay, the effect of a deep, dark dungeon was created. The following April, both Joe's and Legge's versions were played at the listening session. Christa Ludwig and Jon Vickers enthusiastically agreed Joe's version added realism. His stormy intrusion proved to be justified, and no one was allowed to forget it.

EMI executives noticed a fresh vigour, and even mellowness, about their chairman, which may have caused them to speculate. Joe and his PA were indeed in a relationship. Scrutiny of the "X's" appearing in the chairman's desk appointments diary indicated when he was privately occupied. He was delighted with the good impression his new PA was making with business colleagues. Sir Isaac Wolfson, the boss of GUS, offered BC "a large discount" on a Burberry raincoat.

On 19th February, Joe and BC set off on the first of the twenty overseas trips, during which they covered twenty countries in two years. Two weeks were spent in New York and Los Angeles. They were Glenn Wallichs' guests in Palm Springs. Glenn gave Joe an album for his photographs entitled "My Palm Springs Weekend". The pictures of BC beside the swimming pool, at Glenn's hacienda in unspoilt desert surroundings, gave the impression the album was intended for honeymooning couples.

Whilst in Hollywood, BC met the President of Liberty Records. Al Bennett and Joe had a deal to release each other's records. EMI got Bobby Vee and the Chipmunks. Liberty got the artists Capitol did not want. Unknown to Joe, BC had with him some Parlophone demo discs George Martin wanted him to plug. Martin had given up trying to interest Capitol in his artists, as was the case with his new signings, the Beatles, four months later. BC made quite a conquest with Bennett, who sent him gifts in appreciation. This was a rare case of the chairman not knowing what was going on in the company.

On their return to London, Joe made an appointment to visit his and EMI's solicitors in the city. Etiquette would normally expect Herbert Smiths to send a partner to the client. But Joe was breaking a life-time habit and planning to lend £8000. BC had no money to buy the bijou little cottage in Chelsea he had set his heart on. Joe took out the deeds in his own name, to be kept at the solicitors. Parents were informed over dinner at Grosvenor Square. BC might even pay interest on the loan.

Previously reluctant to take on new responsibilities, Joe was now more available. Inevitably, having run the Royal Ballet School's endowment fund for two years to please Lord Thorneycroft, he became Governor of the School and now its chairman. The approach came on a fishing weekend with the current chairman, Viscount Soulbury. Joe found the company of this ex-Secretary of State at the Department of Education delightful. They visited the pretty fishing cottage on the River Itchen belonging to Soulbury's brother-in-law, Edward de Stein. Freshly primed about the RB School, Joe found himself staying in Bath a couple of weekends later with the director, Arnold Haskell, balletomane brother-in-law of Dame Alicia Markova.

Although Joe had not been to a ballet performance until he was in his fifties, he was hooked. His love of the Royal Ballet Company and the School was exclusive. None other existed. He was told the School's two previous chairmen were no good, but Lord Wakehurst had been responsible for gaining the School and Company a Royal Charter in 1956.

Considering Joe's dislike for charity fundraising, his next appointment as Honorary Treasurer of the British Empire Cancer Campaign (later: Cancer Research Campaign) came as a surprise. A letter of invitation from his predecessor, the Duke of Devonshire, went to the wrong address before eventually reaching him. Grand Council Meetings were held at St James's Palace. Sitting beside his

President, the Duke of Gloucester, Joe was less than impressed with the Queen's uncle, who had to read every word of his address to the Council. The executives responsible for fundraising and expenditure, Admiral Balfour and Captain Tours, had to put up with Joe's: "All that money being spent on cocktail parties!" which was a constant refrain. Joe took an instant dislike to Arthur Dickson Wright, father of Clarissa the cook, chairman of the rival Imperial Society for Cancer Research. The two funds were identical with a joint income of £50 million a year, and the only reason they did not merge until 1998 lay with the unbearable self-importance of Dickson Wright, who was surgeon to the Queen Mother and a popular after-dinner speaker. Joe was credited with raising the BECC's income by 70% and building a £1 million reserve fund.

Still wary of taking on non-executive directorships, Joe was courted vigorously for his second fee-paying post at expensive restaurants and fishing weekends. Separate approaches were made by the Chairman and Managing Director of Hawker Siddeley Group, the company formed by the amalgamation of Sir Thomas Sopwith's First World War aviation company, de Havilland, and A. V. Roe.

Strong personalities were involved, and it was essential for Joe to remain impartial should there be a clash. Dinners with the MD, Sir Arnold Hall, former Principal Scientific Officer at the Royal Aircraft Establishment, and solver of the defect causing Comet aircraft crashes, were at White's Club and the Savoy Hotel. Fellow guest one evening was Lord Beeching, who had taken the British Railways job offered Joe. Dinner with the chairman, Sir Roy Dobson, was at the Mirabelle. Dobson had merged his company A. V. Roe (Avro) with HS. A close friend of Sopwith, his hobbies included gliding and fishing. The evening ended with an invitation to an exclusive stretch of the Test, where Dobson had a rod, close to Sopwith's estate at Compton Manor, and the Houghton Fishing Club at Stockbridge.

And now, much to his surprise Joe found himself taking on another new role. The Press called him an IMPRESARIO.

EMI's show business activities were confined to issuing Original Cast albums of film and stage musicals. Capitol provided *Oklahoma*,

The King and I, *Pal Joey* and *The Music Man*. Norman Newell recorded London cast albums of shows that transferred from Broadway. Investing in shows and owning theatres were areas to be avoided. All this changed when Glenn Wallichs invited Alan Livingston back to Capitol as President. Originally producing successful children's records in the 1940s, he left to manage his wife, Betty Hutton's, affairs, when she starred in *Annie Get Your Gun*. Now divorced and married to film actress Nancy Olsen, former wife of *My Fair Lady* composer Alan Jay Lerner, he was steeped in show business. Confusingly, Alan Livingston had a brother, Jay Livingston, who was a composer. Jay Livingston and Nancy Olsen appeared in the film *Sunset Boulevard* with Gloria Swanson and William Holden.

Alan Livingston set up a meeting in London with Cy Feuer and Ernie Martin, currently producers of successful Broadway musicals. Over dinner at the Mirabelle on 17th April, a plan was hatched to make Joe a theatre owner and showman. Capitol and EMI would jointly create a million-dollar revolving fund to invest in Feuer and Martin shows, which would be put on in a London-owned theatre. Although the venture was short-lived, Joe loved *How To Succeed in Business*, the first musical to be put on in "his" theatre the following year.

Bernard Delfont, already an impresario, was given executive management of the theatrical side of the enterprise. Joe and BC met up with him in May in Monte Carlo. They were returning from visiting Turkey, Greece, Italy and Germany. The Managing Director of Electrola, EMI's German subsidiary, invited them to his holiday home at Cap Martin, where they were rather surprised at the opulence of the villa overlooking the Mediterranean.

In Monte Carlo, they found Delfont and his operetta star wife, Carole Lynne, sunbathing by the hotel pool. With his brothers Lew and Leslie (Joe knew and liked all three), Delfont operated the Grade Organisation, which ran theatres and agencies, representing several EMI artists. They owned Moss Empires, the Palladium, Pye Records and ATV.

*Robert Stigwood in
St. Tropez*

Monte Carlo was very much the favourite destination for show business people and tycoons at that time, much as Barbados is today. On a second visit, this time with Robert Stigwood, Joe met fellow impresarios Jack Hylton, Tom Arnold and Val Parnell. Between them they controlled much of London's theatre-land. Joe took a shine to Hylton, who made three hundred 78 rpm records on HMV with his orchestra in the 1920s, which defined popular music for a generation. Hylton's TWW Company would sell the Shaftesbury Theatre, at the time called The Prince's Theatre, to Delfont for £280,000, on behalf of EMI and Charles Clore's property development company. As joint owners, Joe and Clore were christened "The Two Tycoons" by the press.

Another weekend, Joe was the guest of washing machine tycoon John Bloom at his villa in St Tropez. The invitation was an excuse for Bloom to show Joe his new yacht.

In August, Joe accepted an invitation from Air France, who were inaugurating Caravelle Flights to the South of France. After lunch with the board of BOAC and BEA at Heathrow, he boarded a plane for Nice with a party of business VIPs from Plessey and Rolls Royce. They were put up at the Hotel Bel Air in Cap Ferrat, the Côte d'Azur resort made famous by Somerset Maugham. Strolling near the shore late the first night, Joe spied John Clark, the highly respectable, recently divorced Managing Director of Plessey Electronics, picking up a young man in tight white trousers.

That month, Joe and B.C visited Scandinavia. In Helsinki, business affiliates, as was the custom, invited them to a stag night of vodka, toasts, saunas and nude bathing in an ice-covered lake at a remote snow-covered pine log cabin. They were provided with birch twigs and encouraged to scourge themselves to restore circulation. Recovering in the morning, Joe found evidence on his body that he had been severely beaten. Convinced he had been attacked by his PA, he kept his suspicion to himself.

Joe enjoyed the company of the young. He socialised with two groups, joined by BC when it suited him. There were, of course, Stigwood, Komlosy and Leyton, who treated Joe as their meal-ticket, tempting him to take a break in Brighton away from the office. And there was a threesome of City types, Julian Gibbs, Tommy Frankland and Richard Broome, who introduced him to young men at dinner parties.

Being seen around with such people did him no harm. But impervious as he was to scandal, danger cannot have been far away. He was lucky not to have been drawn into the Profumo Affair, when he associated with two of Christine Keeler's boyfriends. It was a routine custom to celebrate Russia's National Day with a glass of vodka at their embassy in Kensington. Yvgeny Ivanov, the Naval attaché, Keeler's lover and self-confessed spy, was a most attentive host. But nothing resembling business was mentioned. Joe laughed at the thought or assumption that he had access to sensitive information. A journalist wrote to him in 1964: "According to Stephen (Ward) you once met Ivanov to discuss a putative deal with EMI." He ignored the letter.

Fortunately, Joe never knowingly met Stephen Ward. But he did know Keeler's other boyfriend, whom she called "the best looking man I have ever seen". At a Stigwood party, Joe was introduced to Noel Howard Jones, who invited him to "7.15 pm. Cocktails. Dinner" at his flat in Chelsea. This was 17 Vale Court, Mallard Street, SW3, the address where Ward committed suicide whilst on trial for living off prostitution. Joe was not the only person to sleep with Howard Jones, who was married to a Japanese lady. Joe asked why he had got married. "Because I was sorry for her!" was the characteristic reply of someone who stood by his friends, such as Ward, when others abandoned them. His reward was to be drawn into a major scandal with the accompanying notoriety.

At another Stigwood party, Joe met Dick Kallman, a young American actor, who was in London auditioning for the lead role in *How to Succeed in Business Without Really Trying*. This was the big Feuer and Martin musical, "Broadway's Greatest Smash Hit!", to launch EMI's Shaftesbury Theatre the following spring.

Many considered Kallman outrageously camp, but Joe found him immensely entertaining and relished his sense of humour. The couple were frequently seen dining together at the two most popular gay restaurants, The Popote on Walton Street and the Casserole on the King's Road. Kallman did not get the part, which made a name for Robert Morse in the original production and later in the film, and he returned to America. They kept in touch.

Joe did not allow show business to interfere with his devotion to the more serious aspects of EMI's manufacturing activities. On Sunday 1st July, he boarded the overnight sleeper for Newcastle-on-Tyne with EMI Electronics Managing Director Percy Allaway. On Monday morning, they attended the Queen Mother opening the computer installation in the Central Office of the Ministry of Pensions and National Insurance. The EMI DEC 2400 was capable of handling 25 million pensions a day. The Queen Mother wanted to know if she was one of the 25 million. Joe explained that indeed she and Princess Margaret were included, as only the Queen's details were not stored. The Government had ordered the equipment four years previously and there was not much money in it. Despite being a pioneer in the computer industry, completing large orders for Glaxo and Kodak, Joe decided it was time to get out. Personal "user friendly" desktop models were for a future market. Instead, EMI's technology (he avoided the word "automation") was channelled into pattern recognition. CRL concentrated on FRED (Figure Reading Electronic Devices). This pointed the way to the EMI Scanner, the World's first brain-scanner. invented by Godfrey Hounsfield at Hayes.

Brain-scanners, or CATs, were still years off, but Joe was ready with another breakthrough: "There is nothing like it anywhere!" he exclaimed. This was EMI's new Colour Television Camera. Again, this was an innovation that the public would have to wait for – five years in fact – before colour would be transmitted. In the meantime, a colour closed circuit system was installed at Hammersmith Hospital. So dramatic was the colour on monitor screens during heart surgery that a theatre nurse stood by to provide a seat and a cup of tea for anyone taken faint at the sight.

The chairman's overseas trips were covered by local press. This was something the managing director in each territory was expected to arrange, sending back press clippings to head office. On a trip to Africa in October, Joe had a major anger attack, which reverberated around the continent, and was duly reported.

After an exhausting few days in the heat of Johannesburg, Durban and Cape Town, Joe and BC flew to Bulawayo in Southern Rhodesia, en route to Salisbury, to publicise the building of a £50,000 record factory. On 12th October, the *Daily Express* ran a headline: "POMPOUS ASSES AT AIRPORT ANGER SIR JOE". Completing a lengthy immigration form in the aeroplane before disembarking, which he "did perfectly", he was called to the Immigration Office: "An officious young man started asking inane questions about my grandmother, and I'm only to be in the country four days", he said explosively. "They messed me around for nearly thirty minutes. If there had been another 'plane out of Rhodesia from Bulawayo this morning I'd have taken it!"

Although he had visited almost every country outside the Iron Curtain, he had never received treatment compared to that at Bulawayo. "It's always the tinpot little Ruritanian Countries that behave in this way. I'm shocked to find Rhodesia doing it."

A Federal Government statement claimed that Sir Joseph's

examination lasted thirty seconds, and that he was asked only two questions – neither of which was out of the ordinary. An editorial in the *Rhodesia Herald* defended Joe:

> This is the type of treatment about which African Leaders returning from abroad have repeatedly complained. It is significant that Sir Joseph described the officer who ill-treated him as being about 25 years of age. In our experience this is the type of European who daily ill-treats Africans and uses vile language to them. This habit has become such second nature that their bad manners are affecting even their own people.

As usual, Joe's anger disappeared as quickly as it rose. EMI's area manager in Kenya arranged a stay at the Safari Club near Nairobi. Joe was pictured in a relaxed and composed mood. Several photographs were taken of BC posing at Treetops and the Equator, for another album.

CHAPTER 19

Sir Joe Intoxicated with Beatlemania

In January 1963, Joe undertook a four-week tour of the Far East. His arrival in New Zealand was greeted by the press with a banner headline: "RECORD GIANT'S ADVICE – TELEVISION BRINGS CHANCE FOR POP IDOL HERE".

Joe went straight to the point:

> Now that New Zealand has television, there could be a big future for some handsome young man, about 19 or 20, with sex-appeal and a flair for singing with rhythm. When launching a new record star it is essential that he should be seen by the Public. Young people who bought pop records liked to visualise the singer.

Joe would like to have said his "pop idol" should waggle his hips like Cliff Richard. His evidence was based on a conversation with an eminent psychologist over dinner, who asserted that a male gyrating his hips only meant one thing. This was the Permissive Sixties, and "sexual intercourse began in 1963", according to Philip Larkin. Pop entrepreneur Larry Parnes had a stable of such pop idols, and Joe was determined EMI should do as well. It was under his pressure that George Martin signed the Beatles. Joe was intoxicated with Beatlemania, and he was now infecting New Zealand.

Since being put in charge of Parlophone by Joe in 1959, the twenty-nine-year-old Martin had had limited success. Measured by the charts, this was confined to The Temperance Seven, and The Vipers skiffle group. He had not recovered from the disgrace, and Joe's anger, at failing to sign Tommy Steele at the 2 i's coffee bar in 1956 and letting Decca get in first.

Joe caught flu in Hong Kong and cut short his trip. News of his early return preceded him. Rumours spread he would require a stretcher or wheelchair on arrival at Heathrow. EMI shares dropped 1/6d. The *Daily Mirror* reported on 7th February: "One sneeze cost the giant EMI electrical company £1,400,000 yesterday. The man who sneezed is Sir Joseph Lockwood, 58, the Company's Chairman." A cartoon appeared in a Swiss satirical magazine showing Joe drawing a rising graph on a blackboard. Joe sneezes and his hand is jogged, only for the line to rise again when he recovers. The Scharz-Deutsch caption explained: "Within a few minutes the value of EMI shares sank by about 17 million francs. In high-up business circles, even a nose cold can be worth much." Yehudi Menuhin, who lived in Switzerland, sent Joe a copy: "Although an unflattering portrait – I thought you would be amused."

The City hates this sort of volatility. Kit Dawnay began a secret campaign to retire Joe at sixty, which failed. This was partly based on jealousy and irritation at Joe's inflexibility when presented with takeover opportunities. Dawnay's prestige was limited to City Livery Companies and directorships, whereas Joe's success was widely reported. Under headlines: "STANLEY LUNCHES AT THE PALACE", the *Evening News* elaborated: "Stanley Matthews footballer of the year, was one of the guests when the Queen and Prince Philip gave one of their small informal lunch parties at Buckingham Palace today. Other guests included Sir Joseph Lockwood and Mr Oliver Messel." The Queen took Joe on to the balcony and confided she was experimenting with wearing glasses for her eyesight.

The newspapers praised EMI throughout 1963: "No doubt about it, this was the Beatles year in the disc business. With pop stars like Frank Ifield, Cliff Richard and the Beatles on its lists, records were the Company's biggest money spinner." But Joe had grounds for frustration in his business and in his private life.

He was very angry with George Martin for giving "The Beatles' music publishing to a little man with an office around the corner". It was Joe's idea to put EMI's own small publishing company, Ardmore and Beechwood, into the HMV store, with the object of

*Beatles Gold Disc presentation
at EMI House, 1963*

listening to demo discs transferred from tapes brought in off the streets by unknowns. Brian Epstein used this service for the Beatles, and Sid Coleman, Ardmore and Beechwood's manager, published the first two Lennon–McCartney songs. It was an act of disloyalty for George Martin, as an EMI manager, to take the Beatles' future publishing away from the company. LG wanted to sack him, but Joe decided against it. By docking his Christmas bonus as a punishment, LG created a permanent rift between the two of them. Fortunately, this failed to damage EMI, as Martin and the Beatles were firmly committed by contract to record for the company. Also, Brian Epstein was not really responsible for the situation. This was helpful, as managers were so often the first to create difficulties. One such was Kenneth Hume, Shirley Bassey's husband, who was dissolute, and someone Joe preferred to have as little to do with as possible, despite the pleasure it gave him to associate with the successful artist.

Joe's standards regarding behaviour and morality were high. He was particularly averse to open displays of drunkenness. This applied equally to Cabinet Ministers and film stars. Dining with Norman Newell, Lionel Bart and Lionel Blair one evening at an expensive restaurant, he was so outraged and angry at the film star Peter O'Toole's disgustingly atrocious drunken lack of self-control at the next table, he had to be restrained from making a scene.

BC was a social success around London, but his position in the company was less settled. Joe was keen for him to be made a director of one of EMI's subsidiaries, so that he could call himself a company director. Humphrey Tilling, the group company secretary, vetoed the idea, and the suggestion was quietly dropped. When there was a leak of sensitive company information to the press, BC was suspected as its source. He openly speculated on EMI's share price by taking out "put and call options", which was a minor form of gambling, but gambling nevertheless. Joe quashed the rumour.

Being a social success meant that BC gave parties and received phone calls at the office. The phone calls irritated Joe, who must have realised his PA was less than perfect. Never being invited to the cottage in Chelsea for the parties must have rankled Joe, who had never previously been jealous of anyone.

Julian Gibbs made sure he was not excluded. During the summer, he had Joe to stay at the coastguard's cottage he rented with Tommy and Richard on the Beaulieu Estate in Hampshire. Lord Montagu entertained them down at the beach rather than up at Palace House, and the weekends flew by. Julian also included Joe in a sightseeing visit to Tuscany, where he was not permitted to visit La Voce del Padrone SpA, EMI's Italian Company.

Undeterred by the undistinguished return from their visit to the Far East in February, Joe and BC undertook tours of South America in September and Northern Nigeria in November.

In Santiago, Chile, Joe discovered that his San Cristobal flour mill no longer existed, and had given place to one of the city's smartest residential areas. In Argentina, Joe and BC stayed with Charles and Mabel Lockwood. To keep them entertained his brother suggested an outing to the Viña del Mar seaside resort, famous for its Song Festival. When he indicated he had no intention of accompanying them, the suggestion was promptly shelved.

Nigeria became an independent country in 1960, but traditional rulers retained their influence. In the north, where EMI Electronics had the contract to install a television station at Kaduna, the population was predominantly Muslim. Joe had met the Sardauna of Sokoto, the impressive premier of Northern Nigeria, back in London. Descended from Sultans, the Sardauna was otherwise known as Sir Alhasi Ahmadu Bello K.B.E. A former

Bored in Buenos Aires

schoolmaster, he had held ministerial roles and was chancellor of a university named after him. He invited Joe to attend the opening ceremony of the TV station which he was to conduct with the Emir of Zaria. Making sure his inoculation against yellow fever was in order, Joe arrived to be greeted by his hosts, who were wearing their long, flowing white robes.

Whist in the country, Joe and BC visited the Emir of Kano's palace, and watched a football match between the staff of EMI (Nigeria) Ltd, and a local team in Jos.

Sadly, the Sardauna of Sokoto was murdered in 1966, most likely by a Christian faction, alongside other ministers. Heads of state in Africa were reputed to build personal fortunes, but the Sardauna left a mere £20,000.

BC dutifully posed for numerous photographs during their travels, but as usual, was keen to get home as soon as possible.

Doing the Twist with Mrs Val Parnell, 1963

1963 ended with a New Year's Eve party given by John and Anne Bloom at their Park Lane penthouse. The invitation card read: "8.30 p.m. until dawn". As predicted by Joe, John Bloom's washing machine empire collapsed in 1964.

Joe's first social engagement for the new year was a harpsichord recital to be given by George Malcolm. The invitation was for 9 p.m. on Tuesday 14th January. I was there.

Cliff Richard shares a joke with the Chairman

PART 2

Me
(College – City –
Cambridge – City Again)

Me, aged 12, posing for a milk advertisement

College

My parents collected me from Cothill one summer's day in Coronation year. I remember the rumble of the cattle grids as Daddy's Bristol crossed Dorney Common. A huge castle filled the distant skyline.

My future Housemaster whispered in Daddy's ear that the boy Charles Goodhart (the economist), showing us my future room, was the cleverest pupil he had ever taught. At the same time My Dame was advising Mummy where to order curtains. My mother, economical by nature, preferring to buy crockery from the local homeware shop rather than Thomas Goode, now excelled herself. A rich-red, thick-pile fitted carpet was ordered from the High Street upholsterers. With it came curtains, bedhead valance and ottoman cover to match. My Dame was impressed. Fitted carpets were a rare luxury in My Tutor's. A russet-leafed motif softened bright red curtain material. Of nine new boys, I was to become My Dame's favourite. Those curtains contributed to my downfall that first Winter Half at Eton.

I was still at prep school aged twelve. Major Pike summoned me shortly before the end of term. He warned against being "taken up by an older boy who would offer me the earth". I was advised to reject any such favours. To succumb would be a disaster. I would be dumped, left in the lurch etc. etc. I had no idea what he was talking about. Had he used the word "seduction", I would have been none the wiser. There was no one to compare notes with, as I was the only leaving boy to get this lecture. Flower sketching in Mrs Pike's rose garden may have made him consider me a likely target. What he had not noticed was the Classics master who was already "at it". Unexpectedly good marks in Common Entrance exams led to special tuition in Greek, to gain a higher remove. This subject was normally reserved for cleverer boys than myself. Another reward was to be taken out to tea by the Greek beak in the holidays.

Dear Mrs Cavendish,

As I live near you in Chelsea I wonder whether William would like to come to the cinema one afternoon?

Yours sincerely, H. A. G. Phillimore.

My mother was delighted to have me off her hands. There were two cinemas on the King's Road to choose from, Classic and Essoldo. Mr P's housekeeper served tea in his large bachelor flat in Cadogan Gardens. An extra pleasure was to be read to from Sir Walter Scott's Waverley novels; a hand stroking my bare knee, but nothing more.

I was a "goody goody", never failing to earn my "V badge" every year. This treasured little brass V-shaped brooch gained the lucky "sap" a place on the summer term school treat. The reward was a Thames River trip with strawberries, cream and iced coffee from Salter's Boatyard in Abingdon. I never missed a trip. Major Pike's records incorrectly showed a gap of one year, denying me a full-house, leaving me with an axe to grind. But I had another matter on my mind when I returned for Old Boy Day the following year.

Things were wonderful that first Half at Eton. I could do no wrong. It was a privilege to fag for Charlie Benson, the Captain of the House. He had three fags, and called us all Harold, although our names were Henry, Robin and William. There must be some reason for this tradition which I have never discovered. He was a good picker, as all three became House Captain when our turn came. His talents turned to the horse track, where he became a high-class racing correspondent and gambler. He was the mysterious "Mr B." at the Clermont Club's backgammon tables the night Lord Lucan disappeared.

On my first morning, I knocked on my neighbour's door. My Dame told me Robin would teach me how to tie my tie. It was the start of a forty-year friendship. It was pure chance our mutual attraction was formed that very first day. We set off to Early Morning School glowing with golden suntans from wonderful holidays in different parts of Cornwall.

Across the corridor from us, Henry shared a room with his older brother. Henry was Robin's senior by a year, as Robin was mine. Henry and Robin were close. For some reason, Old Cothillian Henry took against me. There was no cause for jealousy, as he was superior in every way. He was Major Pike's star pupil, blessed with brains and beauty, an Oppidan Scholar who was also a star at games. His smouldering dark good-looks were flawed, if you could call it that, by the ridiculous black beauty spot on his cheek. Boys had to leave their bedroom doors open until evening prayers. Henry observed me repeating my name aloud: "My name is Cavendish." I was rehearsing introducing myself. Relentlessly he would mock me, day in day out: "My name is Cavendish!" It became tiresome.

My first Half at Eton

Teasing can be painful and the memory endures. My father had a similar experience at Cambridge. He was entertaining in his rooms when there was a knock at the door. The stranger introduced himself: "I'm your couthin Dougleth Cooper," he pronounced with a lisp. From that day forward my father's friends greeted him with: "I'm your couthin Dougleth Cooper."

Despite this small matter, the first two Halves were very rewarding. Fellow new boy Jeremy Reiss and I found we were compatible, and messed together for the next five years. As one had tea with the same person every day, this was desirable. School reports were so good my grandmother circulated them among her friends. Sadly, they were not returned. I won the Milner Prize for Literature, on H. G. Wells's *The*

First Men in the Moon. My Tutor, a History Master, was so impressed he put me in for the Rosebery History Prize. Unfortunately, I failed that dismally. On the sporting field, I would perform the position of post in our victorious house side each Winter Half at the Field Game. "Post" in the bully is similar to hooker in rugger. I was supported by two massive props, or "sideposts", and a "BUP" (back-up post). It was invigorating. Chosen for my stockiness, I regretted not taking up rugger in the Lent Half. Winning the House sides meant I earned my House colours. One previous owner of the second-hand cherry-and-grey cap was cousin Caryll Waterpark. This was my sporting achievement.

Raef Payne was my Classics tutor. He came back to Eton, where he had been Captain of the School, after university. Aged twenty-three, it was as if he had never left. The distance from his rooms in Baldwin's Shore to the Drill Hall Schools, where he taught, indicated he was just a "junior" beak. Warm and avuncular, his arm cradled my bottom standing at his desk. He corrected my prose. Intimacy was discreetly concealed by the tails of my school dress. Smaller boys in Eton jackets, or "bum freezers", offered more temptation but were less accessible. I was drawn to Raef's nicotine-stained fingers and his hirsute chest.

Physical contact with classmates was called "fiddling". Why older boys, who had gone through puberty, are interested in the private parts of younger boys is strange. Anyway, I enjoyed being fiddled in the back row of "Div". Even in the Science Schools, darkened for the slide shows, with benches raked steeply, my suitor was able to pleasure me from the lower row. Back in his House, he boasted: "It was heaven!" Outside class, one was still vulnerable. I was "de-bagged" by two aggressors beneath a glass display cabinet in the Natural History School. And in the High Street we new boys were warned to cross the road and avoid eye contact with the lecherous President of Pop, Peter Palumbo.

Living in a House, occupied by forty-five boys aged between twelve and eighteen, all experiencing physical and emotional development, strong relationships inevitably evolve. My Tutor's wife had the crazy idea of turning the end-of-Half Christmas "sock supper" into a Fancy Dress Competition. She was little aware of what she was starting. In a general panic, with no idea what to go as, I grabbed the nearest item. This was the red curtain My Dame had so admired. What a picture I must have made! Cloaked and hooded, I became Little Red Riding Hood. The evening ended with prize-giving for Lower and Upper boys. Inevitably, I won first prize. Returning to our rooms I glimpsed the ostrich outfit of the senior prizewinner. Above thin legs in orange tights was a pillow case topped with an umbrella handle. The occupant was JC. Little did I realise that Ostrich had fallen for Red Riding Hood.

I make no apologies for what happened during my second Half. I resisted, and succumbed. It was the first morning. After breakfast, we Lower Boys, or "squits", reclined on my thick red carpet reading the *Daily Mirror*. My bed was folded against the wall, as per House instructions. JC entered and settled beside me, with his arm around me in search of what he was after. Squits snooped pruriently behind papers raised to screen their modesty. I asked Robin what to do. He said I should close the door in JC's face next time. Of course, he was right. I obeyed his stricture, which I immediately regretted. My room was out-of-bounds by rules to JC, but that did not apply to Robin. I noticed they were often in each other's company.

Pretty boys by tradition were "tarts", a ridiculous generalisation. With my kiss-curl, and provocative choice of fancy dress, I was now firmly in that category. Attention was exciting and enjoyable. During that Lent Half, I experienced many exhilarating emotions. First came remorse that I had closed the door in JC's face. Next, the ravishing moment when he gave me a nickname. I became his own private "Schnook". It was an expression picked up from *The Goon Show*, which he listened to with his friends. I have not come upon the word since. Schnuk is German for a pet, whereas Schnook is tinned fish, popular in the war. I was given a ring to wear. Our feet played footy-footy under the table at Boys' Dinner. Hands were held, with little fingers pressed into sensitive palms, which held a special significance. A holiday together in Moscow, where JC's father was based, seemed possible. Passion grew and peaked on the last night of the Half. There was joy in being the centre of desire and attention. Before evening prayers, JC steered me to his room, pressing me against the closed door to prevent intrusion. Where was Robin now? One's first kiss is never forgotten. The surprise was total. My cheeks burned from his rough mouth. The stale, pungent smell of perspiration and unpressed Eton tails and trousers regaled my senses. Somehow we reached the pupil-room in time for prayers. I took my place standing in the front row, directly facing My Tutor. Behind, and so close I could feel his breath on my neck, was JC.

A day or two into the holidays, a large, pustulous spot spread across my face. Impetigo, or doglopaedia, is as unpleasant as its ugly name implies. It was obvious from where the adolescent infection had sprung. JC's "shag spots" had gone unnoticed. Visual impairments are of no consequence when one is overcome by testosterone-inflated virility.

One look in the mirror and guilty pleasures turned to revulsion, frustration, repression, jealousy and, ultimately, rejection.

JC came to my room on the first morning of the Summer Half, and I turned him out. Robin witnessed the scene. They were both mildly surprised. When JC rejected my overtures two years later, I doubt he reflected on the irony of the situation.

Robin and JC had crushes on boys in other Houses. They were sensible. My Tutor was positively homophobic and intolerant of anything, having inherited a House rife with buggery. Drastic measures were taken to eliminate corruption. Sackings were still talked about. One story concerned a boys' maid finding the Captain of Games in bed with his fag. My prurient mind was regaled with a vivid picture of the scene: "The spunk was flowing freely". Threatened that she would be killed if she told the Housemaster, she reported the matter to the Dame instead.

Arthur Koestler described the English Public School system in *Thieves in the Night*. His advice was to restrain rash impulses, established to a degree where the suppression almost preceded the impulses themselves, and second thoughts came first. By doing the right thing myself, I should have been satisfied. But I was merely suppressing the inevitable.

My father showed how risky these rash impulses can be. His best friend was sacked "for the usual". Dandy Wallace was told to pack his bags and leave on the first train in the morning. Alan Pryce-Jones, who was gay, described the event in his memoirs *The Bonus of Laughter*. He was the innocent subject of Dandy's attentions. He bore Dandy no ill will. That they were caught out and reported was just bad luck. My father showed solidarity by getting up early to accompany Dandy to Windsor Station to see him off. Alan, Dandy and my father's shared sense of humour allowed them to reminisce over past indiscretions. After Eton, my father and Dandy set off on a tour of Europe in Dandy's "faithful" Rolls Royce with Hector the chauffeur. They made a strange pair. Freakishly tall and thin, Dandy was photographed on the Yugoslav border, standing to attention beside a ramshackle hut in the middle of nowhere. Beneath is written: "Hungarian Customs Officials disarmed."

I was unable to laugh at my own predicament. That destructive emotion of jealousy overwhelmed and consumed me. It is something girls suffer from, boys to a lesser degree, but experience shows me it can even affect grown men. Robin had moved to be close to JC, and a new boy was now in his room. My neighbour had golden hair, cornflower blue eyes and looks to kill for. Twelve-year-old baronet Sir John Bradford had the added attraction of possessing a pretty older sister. Even without the older sister, he would have been the centre of attraction.

Bradford's door was open, conforming to the rules. But who was that pinning him to the floor in a suggestive fashion? None other than my other neighbour, Henry! The spectacle caused a welling sense of jealousy, which was quite uncalled for, as I had no interest in either of the participants.

At the end of the Summer Half, Bradford was missing from the House group photograph. He had not returned from Long Leave. We were told he was driving a tractor which overturned and crushed him to death. My rival's name was not mentioned again. Like some angel, he was too good for this world.

Returning to my prep school for Old Boy Day, I was summoned to see the Headmaster. The last time I stood before Major Pike was to be warned about older boys. What he prophesied had occurred. He would certainly enquire about my progress. How would I respond? I was taken aback by the strength of his concern. But it was not about me. He adopted the tone of a commanding officer: "I have called you here because I believe you can tell me something. I gather that Henry has formed an inappropriate relationship with someone called Hoare. Can you tell me about it?" And that was all. I was dismissed. Back at Eton, I checked Hoare's name against the School List, and decided Henry could have done better.

Boys are not particularly concerned about each other's inclinations. Masters approach the subject from contrasting angles. My Tutor was interested in catching rule-breakers and heart-breakers. That put him on the offensive. Raef was easy-going and unlikely to criticise. He observed my progress over three years. His reports were masterpieces of tact, and, from what I remember, impressed my father. Written in italic script, learnt from his friend Wilfred Blunt, he reported to My Tutor: "He is the cleverest boy in the Pupil Room, and I can understand how tantalising it must be to assert his superiority. But other the boys will acknowledge it and respect it

My grandmother, seated on Eton's "Long Walk" wall

more readily if he keeps quiet about it. In general, his zeal and charming personality have made him very good company and a most rewarding pupil."

I was thirteen at the time. Two years later, he wrote: "He could safely undo a button or two." Poor Raef! Unaware of the reason for my shyness, it would only be a matter of time before his suggestion took literal effect.

One of the great joys of

Eton is to be allowed to choose a subject to specialise in, and the Modern Tutor to go with it, after finishing with Latin and Greek. I was spoilt for choice. Standard attire for Assistant Masters consisted of grey suit, usually of expensive cut, allowing a touch of sartorial elegance, plain white shirt, stiff collar and white bow tie. The ensemble contributed to the distinction of any good-looking "beak".

The first time I saw David Cornwell, riding his bicycle around the school, I was struck by his old blue rugger shorts. His fair hair and light downy knees were becoming. He was a new beak, teaching French and German, my subjects. Jeremy and I chose him as our exclusive Modern Tutor. Hearing his attractive voice again recently, reading from his John le Carré novels on the radio, reminded me of what a good choice we made. My handwritten reports revealed a perception foreign to My Tutor: "There is, unless I am mistaken, a new note of bitterness almost of resentment in his reaction to some problems we have raised ... this is ultimately, I imagine, a matter for his House Tutor rather than me however." On leaving after two short years, he wrote: "I shall follow his career with interest, even if it's only scribbled on the back of a Christmas Card! And I shall always remember him as the best kind of Etonian."

We were to bump into each other after Eton, in Upper St Martin's Lane near Cambridge Circus, in the vicinity of MI6. His mind was on other matters.

Another young Master with a beautiful speaking voice, reading to us, was Richard Bull, later Headmaster of Rugby and Oakham

With cousin Eddie, just elected to Pop

Schools. He chose short stories by Saki, and ended English Extra Studies by singing entrancingly to his guitar. I was bewitched.

But, enough of Masters. I was quite surprised to find it was not uncommon for boys of similar age to form crushes. I assumed the attraction would have been in the age difference. One day Jeremy asked me to go round to College with him to see his tennis partner. It turned out he needed a chaperone. We were aged sixteen, and it was my first visit to College. I imagined "tugs" slept in curtained off cubicles along "Long Chamber". In fact, WW had a spacious room to himself in the Victorian New Buildings overlooking Weston's Yard. Somehow the three of us became entangled in a heap on the floor, hands groping private parts, and generally out of control. The door opened and the intruder, pausing to observe the scene, theatrically withdrew with the quip: "Retires Embarrassed!" I recognised the stocky, fair-haired Colleger as my opposite number in the Field Game House sides. BC gained notoriety shortly afterwards when he was sacked for buggery, or for "acting in an importunate manner towards a younger boy" who complained. It was a very public sacking, and the unwelcome reputation would be difficult to throw off. When I met BC seven years later, it was the first thing I thought of. He had the misfortune of having Steven McWatters as his Master in College. McWatters had recently unearthed a scandal involving Jeremy Wolfenden, whose incriminating letters to a boy still at school were revealed after he had left Eton. Sebastian Faulks described Wolfenden's decadent behaviour in his *The Fatal Englishman* biography. Raef succeeded McWatters, and would have handled matters differently. Jeremy Reiss and WW had a successful tennis partnership, and won the School's Doubles Cup.

I moved to another room, taking my red carpet with me. My window faced the river. I sulked, watching Robin and JC set off for long walks along the Brocas beside the Thames. Life seemed so unfair. Outwardly, I maintained a stiff upper lip. In the 1956 House Group photograph there I am, aged fifteen, standing beside the spurned JC, aged seventeen. How is it I appear so normal? How demeaning to be sent down to Rafts by My Tutor to have my rowing ability assessed by

JC. As I struggled with the oar in the rowing machine, JC stood over me, distinctly unimpressed.

A small incident shows how ridiculous things were becoming. The Library, consisting of the most senior boys, were last to join the rest of the House for evening prayers. The boys in Debate, one level down from the Library, were privileged to delay entering Pupil Room until shortly before the Library. One evening I was fooling around with the other members of Debate. On a mad spur-of-the-moment impulse, I hid under the pile of School Dress Tails left for the cleaners outside the Library, leaving my hand exposed. It was a convincing impression of a severed limb. Debate dispersed, and the Library processed past. I felt my hand being raised to someone's lips. The lips belonged to JC.

JC shared the room above mine with his younger brother. Towards the end of his leaving Half, I discovered a fresh yearning for attention. One hot summer night, after lights out, we were leaning out of our windows. I attempted to draw his attention, only to be rewarded with a shower of earth from his window box. My intentions had been recognised. The next night, a colleague of JC had the cheek to come to my room uninvited, completely without warning. That was not quite the end of the story. One afternoon, when all was quiet, I found myself perched on JC's lap. We were in full School-dress. The door opened without warning. It was JC's brother. "Get out you oaf!" JC screamed. But it was too late. "I've come," he explained in frustration, as he dismissed me. After he left he came back to see us all. It was another warm summer evening. He joined My Tutor and the Library for a dip in the open-air swimming pool, which was a rare treat. He came to my room afterwards. He exposed himself, and I felt his penis brush my cheek briefly as I sat by the window. Then he was gone, to take sherry with My Dame. It was a meaningless gesture, reminiscent of kissing my hand before evening prayers. Similarly, when I was Captain for the House and wrote inviting him down, his terse refusal brought a surprise. He revealed he had had the same letter from Henry when he was Captain of the House, and from Robin when he was Captain of the House. Now I wanted him, and he "had enough of all that!"

Robin became a regular night-time visitor. It was a pleasure to have a satisfactory relationship without any emotional involvement. We enjoyed a physical attraction for a further thirty years. He was Captain of the School Boxing Team, and would come for solace the nights before "the big match".

Despite my Tutor imploring me to stay on for another Half, I left suffering from a deep lack of self-esteem. The gloomy expression on my leaving photograph spoke for itself. Entitled to have my name carved in Upper School's ancient oak panelling alongside my father, I did not take up the option. Headmaster Robert Birley was enthusiastic about my future when he heard I was off to Germany. He spent the post-war years rebuilding the German educational system. I planned to return in the summer speaking perfect fluent German for the A Level exams.

l. Band of Brothers: With two Members of Pop

R. My sulky leaving photograph

On the Channel crossing I avoided a fellow passenger sporting an OE tie. Nuns engaged me in conversation, as the train stopped briefly in Cologne.

Bavaria and Munich, which had so impressed my mother at a similar age in the 1930s, were up to expectations. But I was so lonely, exploring Chiemsee and Wendelstein on a borrowed moped. I stayed with my mother's adored Gräfin, on a farm below a castle her family formerly owned. The castle was now a public school for boys, who were away on holiday. A teacher came down to give me private German lessons.

In Munich, I bought postcards to send home in the Neue Pinakothek gallery, famous for its modern art collection. I sent Marc Chagall's *Daphnis and Chloe* to Raef, with an apology for not calling on him to say goodbye. The truth was I had been too shy. I indicated that the beauty of the naked Daphnis had tempted me to choose that particular card.

On receipt of the card, Raef instructed me to call on him as soon as I returned. He had been promoted from Assistant Master to Master-in-College. As I crossed School Yard, stories about him crossed my mind. They came from Martin Parsons, the most amoral boy in my House. I had dismissed them as a fantasy. In one, he claimed Raef locked him into his rooms in Baldwin's Shore with threats not to release him "until he had had his way". In another, which seemed more credible, a similar event took place in Parsons' bedroom. When my Tutor was away, Raef stood in for him. After evening prayers he made the rounds of the House, picking up requests left on the slab by boys needing his signature on reports and exeats. He left Parsons until last deliberately, so as to be in his room when the lights went out at 10 p.m.

The Master-in-College's accommodation consisted of a large sitting room and bedroom, with an oriel window overlooking School Yard. With the briefest of preliminary greetings, and "If only I had known", we were in each other's arms. This was all I needed to restore my self-esteem. Joy was mutual. At last I had caught up. Until now I had been what Christopher Isherwood referred to as "out of step".

Friends gave me free use of their house in Ascot while they were away. Raef would come over. After exams, we drove up to London in his open-top Derby Bentley. The wind blew through our hair. We were elated. That same car had taken us to swim in Slough Baths five years previously, before Eton afforded its own pool. Our affair remained secret, apart from a single hint of discovery. Later, Raef would visit me at Cambridge. An ex-Colleger was heard to remark: "Raef's come up to see his little friend." We were close to disaster on one occasion, whilst I was sitting the exam. It would have been common courtesy for an ex-House Captain to call on his House Master. In my emotional state, I never gave it a second thought. My Tutor was nicknamed "Spot", appropriately, for invariably turning up when least expected. Crossing Long Walk, and approaching the Porter's Lodge entrance to School Yard, I spotted him taking the same route. Fortunately, the venerable lime trees lining our route were of massive girth, and I was able to conceal myself behind the nearest trunk. I held my breath. It was a close thing. My gratitude went out to the former Provost who planted the trees at the time of King Charles II. They have since been cut down and replaced with hornbeam. To hide from a Master was once called "shirking" in Eton terminology.

It was a glorious Summer. Raef and I drove out to the surrounding countryside. We found seclusion on the thickly-wooded banks of the Cliveden Estate overlooking the Thames at Taplow. In London, we met at homes lent by Gavin Maxwell and other friends. Our relationship would last a lifetime.

City

I had a year to fill in before going up to Cambridge. Apart from six months in America, where Jeremy Reiss and I felt very grown-up visiting Hollywood and Las Vegas, I was based with my parents in Belgravia. Having spent my nineteenth birthday evening at the Metropolitan Opera, in New York, life in London was a come-down. I had a job in the City to go to.

My mother, who had shown little concern for my welfare previously, now exploded quite dramatically on three separate occasions during this period.

The first drama occurred in a men's outfitters. I frequently bought clothes at John Michael, the men's shop on the King's Road. This was before the Swinging Sixties when John Steven opened his famous store. Even before then, I found "Vince Man's Shop" in Foubert Place, just round the corner from Carnaby Street. My cousin Eddie and I discovered it in 1956, when we were aged seventeen and fifteen. We had seen the sophisticated West End revue, *Cranks*, staged by John Cranko, the Royal Ballet choreographer. A cast of four boys and girls wore identical, fetching, and very tight hipster jeans. Eddie decided he, or we, should have some. Vince Leisure Ware was credited in the programme. It turned out to cater exclusively for a gay clientele.

John Michael in Chelsea was expensive and classy. My mother and I were examining Italian suits in the downstairs department. Suddenly she pushed me behind a pillar: "Don't let that man see you!" she instructed. "He's a homosexual!" She was referring to harmless Peter Williams, distinguished critic and Editor of *Dance and Dancers Magazine*., who once escorted my mother and her sisters to Deb Dances, and was my grandmother's favourite escort.

Customers were looked after by Joe Besser, John Michael's top fitter. He was so camp. Once, when serving a good-looking boy, he whispered to me: "Shit! That boy isn't wearing underpants! Why does he have to have his girlfriend with him?!"

Charles, during National Service in Germany

In May 1960, my parents gave a cocktail party for Eddie's twenty-first birthday, and for completion of his National Service in Germany. Some of his officer friends came along. One tall fellow stood aloof in the corner of our small sitting room, observing the gathering. This was Charles Selby. I was to learn he invariably chose the best vantage point, be it in a restaurant or elsewhere. That was my first recollection. His, of me, followed at Eddie's "bottle party" at the Bistro d'Agran, the popular restaurant in Pavilion Row, a few nights later. He describes how we found ourselves upstairs "sitting on the floor in darkness, lit only by an open 'fridge' door". A letter arrived a couple of days later from Blackbird Hill Garage, in Hendon:

My Dear Billum,

I hope you will forgive my writing to you but I have decided not to race at Trewin Water on Saturday ... I hope I will hear from you.

Yours (I never know how to end letters to people like you so that they are honest and not conventional)

Charles.

Charles, exercising with a medicine ball in Cornwall

Charles and me beside the sea with Timmy and Sara-Jane Trusted

That led to the first of many weekends together. He made it clear our friendship was platonic. I expressed surprise and made an effort to break his code. He was sympathetic. He made no secret of his attraction to me, but there was no mistaking his reluctance to make an exception. I had to accept the situation. This was difficult, as the more I got to know him, the more I wanted him. He was attracted to "people like you". As there were plenty of people like me, there were bound to be misunderstandings.

After a weekend under canvas on the Sussex Downs, he delivered me home early on the Monday morning. As I turned the key in the lock, the door was wrenched open. I had never seen my mother quite so distraught, standing in the hallway in her nightdress. She explained why she had been up all night: "I am so worried it is physical!" My reassurance that nothing was going on brought tangible relief. I had not lied, but I had not spoken with a clear conscience. Charles was relieved too. He wrote:

Seeing Charles off, in his all-purpose van

Dearest Bin,

I was overjoyed to get your letter, as I thought she was thinking that, although it doesn't say much for my character to be thought of as such a bad influence! I am very glad we should understand each other more fully now and hope that it will be easier for us in future years. Thank you for standing up for me in so noble a way … I just love you, and that love spreads out and embraces my entire life, with all my love

Your own Charles.

Many such letters followed. It was a thrilling time. Then the blow came. It was like being back at Eton. Rejection shattered my self-esteem once again. We had known each other such a short time. It was my first visit to his North London flat. I arrived for supper, to find someone changed beyond recognition. Charles was in a state of shock: "Ian is dead!" The exclamation spoke for itself. I had no choice but to leave. Ian, his army friend, had been killed in a car crash, and Charles had only just returned from holidaying with him in Scotland. I could understand the despair. I could understand the remorse too. Ian had wanted more than Charles had been prepared to give, despite the devotion.

It was hard to have a relationship terminated in such a dramatic fashion. Yet a future together had not been discussed, and no thought had been given to the pressures we would face. There would have been some sort of inevitable break anyway, when I went up to Cambridge in September. That was to cause a separation from my mother too, and the reason for her final outburst.

All this while, I had been working as an articled clerk in the City. Chartered accountancy was considered a suitable career. At the head of the profession was Henry Benson, a senior partner of Cooper Brothers (now part of PwC / Price Waterhouse Coopers). Benson had formed an action committee of fathers, dissatisfied with Eton's failure to get their sons into Oxford and Cambridge. Through this connection (although I did get into Cambridge), my father arranged for Benson to see me at his office in the City. The firm is now a household name, but at the time its city office was undistinguished, although close to Mansion House. The street and the building were demolished later. The elevator was an old-fashioned iron cage, and the interview room was almost too small for the desk at which Benson sat. Standing behind him in what space remained was David Corsan, the young partner in charge of articled clerks. The firm agreed to take me on until I went up to Cambridge, on the understanding I return on graduation, to complete my articles. A clerk is articled to an individual partner, and it boiled down to the fact I would be "breaking" my articles whilst I was away. This was a very special concession.

Articles were achieved after three years with a degree, or five years without. Either way, the work was unbelievably dull and routine in those pounds, shilling and pence days. Clerks were mainly male. If there was a girl in the team sent out "on an audit", she was generally a comptometer operator, which is as dreary as it sounds.

I reported for work on 1st January 1960 at Abacus House, the firm's appropriately named, newly-opened headquarters in Gutter Lane. From day one, there were reminders of Eton. Did I know Martin Parsons? Not only did I know him, he was the one who put those ideas into my head about Raef. His career at Cooper Brothers had been short. He was considered as having a bad influence on another younger OE, and it was decided he should leave. That relationship continued, affecting the younger OE's work, and he had to go too. Parsons was still up to it. I was careful to remain uncontaminated by his notoriety.

One day, the manager I was allocated to asked me to deliver some papers to his flat as a favour. The door was opened by his flatmate, as he was out. It was obvious the two were in a gay relationship. Eton again!

It was like being fagged round to another boy's House, bearing a note for the recipient, which read: "What do you think of my fag? Isn't he delicious!"

Familiar faces continued to crop up. I was in Oxford, on the audit of the Rhodes Scholarship Trust books, when I bumped into Henry in Beaumont Street. We were happy to meet again. Dressed dandily, he sported a silver and ebony cane; all very ostentatious. Lacking in the ensemble was a top hat. He was evidently going through an Oscar Wilde–Max Beerbohm phase, and the cane symbolised some exclusive Oxford society.

Another encounter, less welcome, occurred in the West End of London. I had popped into the Red Lion, on Duke of York Street off St. James's, for a lunchtime lager and prawn sandwich. Coming in soon after was the squit I remembered as JC's younger brother and room-mate. He rushed up with his companion, who he introduced as JC. There was a similarity, but I knew it was not JC. He watched my reaction, knowing I was vulnerable. It was a twisted and cruel thing to do. There was a distinct remembrance. It was the middle brother, who shared JC's good looks. He was an innocent party to this deception, made in extremely poor taste.

Cambridge

My father's role in setting up the interview that helped me into the City was no less effective at getting me into Cambridge. He hoped I would go up to Trinity, where he had had such a good time. To make sure I had a good chance, he accepted invitations to college reunion dinners whenever his year came up, so that he could network with the Dons. As a result, I was invited for interview by John Morrison, the Senior Admissions Tutor. This was whilst I was still at Eton. I had little preconception of university life, which I looked upon as a sort of finishing school filling three years. If I had any warning, it came from an unexpected quarter: my mother! "I am so worried that the Dons are going to lead you astray when you get to Cambridge!" I did not get the point. The only Dons I had heard of were in the hugely successful Julian Slade and Dorothy Reynolds musical *Salad Days*, which we had all seen in 1954. A catchy song went like this:

> The things that are done by a Don,
> The mad mad things that are done by a Don.

Surely this did not imply Dons went around seducing undergraduates. Nothing could be more respectable than the way my father was setting up my future. As a natural clubman and backgammon player, he had used his contacts at the Bachelor's Club, St James's Club and White's, consecutively, to advance the careers of lots of young men. This was the Old Boy Network.

When my Tutor learnt of the date I had to be in Cambridge, he declared, by amazing coincidence, that he had to be there on the same day. He drove me up. Late in the afternoon we arrived at the Porter's Lodge of Trinity. There had been a change of plan. Dr Morrison was taking up the post of Vice-Master of Churchill College, and I was to be seen by the Dean of College instead. My Tutor delivered me to the Rev. Harry Williams's door in the corner of Great Court. Harry explained later how impressed he was that a Housemaster had taken such special trouble to bring his pupil to Cambridge. Chatting over tea and crumpets beside a coal fire, this was not the sort of interview I was expecting. If asked, I would have been able to boast one A Level in French, but German came later. When I was safely "up", and able to claim I had two A Levels, Harry countered: "I did not know you had any!"

He was unable to offer me a place immediately. He agreed to take me a year hence, when I was nineteen. In the intervening period, he would be pleased to see me again. By chance, the Institute of Chartered Accountants booked a residential course in Trinity when the college was empty during the Long Vacation in 1960. Harry was still in residence at the time of the weekend seminar, and I called on him. We walked over to the Fitzwilliam Museum. It was my first visit and I was interested to see the Nicholas Hilliard and Isaac Oliver miniatures.

My father was delighted at the way things had turned out. One day he was playing backgammon in the St James's Club with Ludovic Kennedy. The BBC correspondent volunteered that he had recently interviewed Harry. "He is tipped to be the future Archbishop of Canterbury."

University provides the ideal surroundings where one can find oneself and "come out". Girls went to finishing school in France. There were no girls at Trinity in those days, just as there were no boys at finishing school in France. Men at Trinity come up after doing National Service. Boys came straight from school. Trinity was the largest college. With so many to choose from, I did not sleep around. There matters would have rested, had not B. Griffiths had rooms on my staircase, making our acquaintance inevitable. Griffiths was just like Parsons. He was an amoral fantasist, who claimed to have slept with everyone in Trinity. He also knew all the gay Dons, those monsters my mother so feared. At the first gay party he took me to, I was introduced to a gay Don, who knew my family. Rather than eating me alive, Peter Avery, the distinguished expert on Persian poets, exuded respectability. We discussed matters of mutual interest. In particular, he described his mother attending an auction of horse-drawn carriages from our stately home in Derbyshire. My grandmother sold the contents of the stables to pay death duties.

One of my first social duties was to invite Harry, my Tutor, to tea. We were joined by a Don who Griffiths had introduced me to. Whilst I was out of the room, boiling a kettle in the pantry, both Dons turned to each other and asked in unison: "How do you know William?" I was already seeing the Music Tutor, Raymond Leppard, who had rooms above Harry in Great Court. Ray had a reputation for pinching other Dons' conquests. He decided I was his "find", and I became part of his life for a short time. We met in London during the vacation. We went to see *The Beggar's Opera* at the Aldwych. The production was by the Royal Shakespeare Company, where Ray was music adviser. He brought Andrew Gow, the eighty-four-year-old Trinity Don, who had once taught my father at Eton. Seeing him in Great Court, Daddy could not believe he was still alive. "Grannie" Gow was in love with thirty-year-old Dorothy Tutin, who was repeating her Polly Peachum role, which she performed in the screen version with Laurence Olivier. Andrew had been struck by her boyish appearance as she rode in breeches on horseback.

Finding myself at last: On the Backs at Cambridge

She was the finest actress of her generation. She should have been made a Dame. As the three of us trooped backstage into her dressing room, she embraced her "Darling Andrew!" It was obvious their love was mutual.

I found Ray warm, attractive, generous and without the affectation expected of a musical maestro. He was very open with me, and confided that he planned to marry the Duke of Devonshire's sister, Elizabeth Cavendish. This was a strange and uncharacteristic boast. Even at that time, Elizabeth was John Betjeman's devoted and long-standing companion.

Maybe Harry felt left out. Nevertheless, he was taking a risk sleeping with a pupil in his pastoral care. It was a single lapse. I considered it a Christian act of kindness, and certainly had no intention of telling anyone, or making it a habit. The bedroom was as cold as a monastery, and bare, apart from the crucifix on the wall. But Harry could not resist boasting. It got around. A mutual friend challenged me: "How could you? You can do much better!"

It must have reached Ray's ears. One evening, we were dining alone in his beautifully oak-panelled set, paid for by his friend Leo Rothschild. After the meal, I was treated to a private harpsichord recital. In the candlelight it could have been Frederic Chopin playing to the Rothschilds in Paris. Instead, it was Ray, protégé of the present-day Rothschilds, playing for me. But the spell was shattered by a wrong note. I lacked the maturity to respond to the sensuality, the romance, the seduction of wine and music. At the moment of greatest intimacy, I giggled. In so doing I insulted Ray, who told me to get out. The spell was broken. Rejected and humiliated, I slunk back across Great Court to my room. I had learnt my lesson.

Had Sir Malcolm Bullock heard of this incident, he would have treated it as a huge joke. Ray introduced this merry seventy-year-old widower, who drew me into his busy social life. Malcolm entertained at his Lutyens house in Great Shelford outside Cambridge, and at his London clubs. Invitations to dine were issued well in advance. They continued regularly until a certain day in 1966, when I received a note dictated to his butler: "Very sorry having an operation after motor smash so dinner must be off." By the time I received this, he was already dead. It was sad, but saved having to find a way out from his future hospitality.

Totally irreverent, and a great tease, Malcolm's stories were as much against himself as against his friends. Somerset Maugham was a particular target. Malcolm featured in Chips Channon's and Harold Nicolson's diaries. Osbert Sitwell portrayed him cruelly in a short story as still living in an Edwardian era. My favourite story told by Malcolm about himself involved arriving early for luncheon with the Queen Mother. At the entrance gates of Royal Lodge in Windsor Great Park, he was taken short. There was just time for a quick pee. At the very moment, in full view, the Queen's car and police escort swept by.

One night out at the theatre, we had settled in when a handsome young American took the seat next to me. Afterwards, Malcolm told everyone: "William spent the whole performance with his legs twisted around his neck!"

As an ex-First World War army officer, he was one of the first to go to the Theatre Royal Stratford East to see Joan Littlewood's *O What a Lovely War*. Every music hall song mocked his fellow officers, and he loved it. Yet he had lost his closest friends in the conflict. It was just the sort of thing that appealed to his subversive nature.

He took me on social calls in Cambridgeshire and Suffolk. On the way to lunch with Angus Wilson and Tony Garrett at their Felsham Woodside retreat, he let slip he had had a brief fling with young Tony, unknown to Angus. Another time, we were expected at Binkie Beaumont and John Perry's Knots Fosse cottage, only to find Binkie (HM Tennant's *soigné* West End producer) up a cherry tree cutting down a branch. The effort was affecting his composure. Other guests included two famous actresses, who were "resting", and a young Italian. The latter was introduced as Binkie and John's language tutor. After lunch, finding myself alone in the garden, I was accosted by the Italian with the suggestion we should meet up in London.

It was typical of Malcolm's hospitality to invite my parents to lunch at Great Shelford, when they came up for my graduation in the summer of 1963. As ever the perfect host, careful not to tease, nothing was said to cause embarrassment. I need not have worried.

My second year was spent out of college, lodging with a famous Cambridge landlady, Mrs Dench, in Green Street, which is no longer there. Charles and I were together again. I was best man at Eddie's wedding, and we were at the reception afterward. The circumstances were similar to Eddie's twenty-first birthday the previous year, and we picked up where we had left off. All sense of rejection was forgotten, yet I was jealous of the life he was living without me. Jealousy is a terrible vice, and does not help a relationship. He came up to see me often enough, but he had so many other interests. Not only had he a practical knowledge of anything electronic, he was also busy running a pop group. He had natural authority, which Eddie noticed in the army, and included a maverick streak, differentiating him from the other officers. All this made him enormously attractive to younger people. Amongst those attaching themselves to him was a young Swede, who was first cousin to the future King of Sweden. Haakon thought Charles would be good for his cousin, and arranged to have him invited to Balmoral when Carl Gustav was staying. Charles declined, and, in so doing, revealed the diffidence Eddie noticed he displayed in army life. I should have been proud he had so much success.

For my third year, I was back in college, this time in M4 Great Court, my father's old rooms. One day, looking out of the window, I speculated pensively on what might have been.

My choice to read English Literature had been inspired by Raef Payne, David Cornwell and Richard Bull. But at Cambridge I failed to find their equal. My first supervisor had been as old and stale as the pipe smoke that filled his stuffy and overcrowded rooms, situated away from the centre of town. The other undergraduates were unin-spiring and self-satisfied. I even recognised one from my prep school days. I was able to scrape through the first year without attending su-pervisions in these surroundings.

Harry Williams, crossing Trinity College Great Court

In my second year, I was supervised by a tutor in New Hall. She was not exactly what I was looking for, but had beautiful rooms in an old house overlooking the Cam. This was temporary accommodation, before New College moved into its new buildings.

Finally, in my third year, my supervisor was young and was based in Trinity Great Court, so I had no distance to go for tutorials. He shared rooms with another young Eng. Lit. supervisor, who strolled around Great Court whilst supervising his pupils. Watching from my window, I felt this was a mockery. What I was witnessing was exactly how I imagined "reading English" would be. But I was excluded.

My own supervisor, Keith Walker, was a New Zealander. Coming from a provincial background he lacked personality, despite his undoubted ability. Visiting Wellington, NZ a few years later, I heard mention of him as "local boy makes good", but also as a bit of a bore.

The paragon was Simon Gray, the playwright and novelist. My heart would beat faster as I observed this tall, slim, athletic, godlike figure deep in conversation, oblivious to his surroundings. Here was the ideal way to blow fresh air into the Tripos syllabus, the personification of my expectations. This was confirmed two years later when I was visiting his old university in Halifax, Nova Scotia, which claimed him as its star graduate. If only I too could have claimed his acquaintance. He depicts himself in his play *Butley* as a subversive university tutor. Disillusioned and bored, he was brilliantly played by Alan Bates. Richard O'Callaghan had the part of his neurotic and gay supervisee, who might have been based on me, but, of course, was not. In real life I saw Simon Gray in the National Theatre foyer shortly before his early death. Ravaged by drink and cigarettes, he was no longer recognisable as the Trinity Apollo.

As the end of my final term drew near, I was invited to a drinks party given jointly by the Pitt Club and The True Blue Society in the Fellows' Garden on the Backs. More like a park than a garden, with mature trees and shrubs, one was encouraged to drink, circulate and enjoy the warm summer evening. It was like joining fellow guests at a weekend house party in the country. As I explored the footpaths between high hedges, away from the generously sweeping lawn, I was set upon. All eyes were on the very drunk guest who had been following me. Not until he was practically on top of me did I recognise the stumbling, bleary-eyed figure as Keith Walker. It was obvious to onlookers what amorous intentions he had in mind. Yet I had no warning of his inclinations, nor had I given him any encouragement.

I left Cambridge as marquees were being erected for May Balls at the end of term.

Graduation Day, with my parents

City Again

Nothing turned up during the three years I was away from the City to prevent renewal of my articles with the firm. I decided to seek fun and adventure before becoming an articled clerk again, and committed to accountancy exams for another three years.

Choosing the South of France turned out to be not such a good idea. I should have learnt better from a painful experience I had the previous year in Paris, when I visited the Turkish baths in the Rue de Penthièvre, a gay attraction at that time. I moved for refuge from the very public gaze of staring Arabs in the showers, to the comparative privacy of the brightly-lit locker room, piled high with freshly laundered soft white towels. The time spent in the steam and dry heat rooms introduced a glowing sensation of relaxation, and, as it turned out, vulnerability. I was followed by a Frenchman, who gave me no time to resist as he had his way with me. It was a new experience. It was not unpleasant. As I made my escape from the establishment, walking on air, I realised that, technically, I had been raped. He gave me his name and phone number.

I called the next day. He was unenthusiastic, complaining his partner was "Lourd", and he was tired. I delayed departure one more day. I followed the directions to his apartment, with warnings to ignore the concierge and to avoid his "directeur". He was a dancer at the Folies-Bergère just across the street. His "partner" was heavy to lift. We were interrupted by his girlfriend. I had noticed high-heeled shoes under the bed. It was not a success. I returned to London with an excruciating pain in my backside. Our family doctor was mystified, and returned with a "bottoms specialist", who questioned me bluntly: "Have you been putting a rusty nail up your bottom?"

I took a cheap night flight to Nice in August. Dining with friends who were familiar with Cannes before setting off, I was provided with details of beaches and bars, but no warning about travelling alone or the need to book a hotel in advance. "Are you going in that?" one commented on my John Michael suit.

Hours were wasted looking for a room. At last I was the new face on the beach. There was no difficulty in making friends. One character, impossible to avoid as he cruised the sunbathing bodies, was Bill Taub, an American lawyer. Small, dark and ageing, he was frequently mistaken for the French recording artist Charles Aznavour. He was so attentive and helpful, I was prepared to ignore the indecent bikini and the dyed hair. He insisted I move to the Martinez Hotel, where he had influence. It was certainly an improvement, and I gladly accepted. Settling in, I sent my mother a postcard:

> Arrived at 5 a.m. to find there was not a spare bed in Cannes. Spent five desperate hours looking and at last found this, it costs a fortune (but free sun lotion and white bathrobe go with the room – gratis). The elegant rate of life is an eye-opener. I can't get used to the luxurious sights. I hope to be back on Tuesday, but unless there is a cancellation on the 'plane I will have to wait until Wednesday. Very glad I came – but I wasn't for those five hours.
>
> Love, Bin.

What followed was a horror story. I dined with BT and friends, who took me to a bar where I was served a drink. They left, as I was now able to look after myself. Finding myself alone and in unfamiliar surroundings, I decided not to linger, and set off back to the hotel. On the way, a man attached himself to me. He was importunate. I wanted to throw him off. Reaching the Martinez entrance, I made the decision I was to regret. Rather than going in and revealing where I was staying, I kept going. In the darkness, the man steered me down to the beach-front rocks, and forced me to commit an indecent act. Lights sprang from all directions, spotlighting our lowered trousers. Gendarmes must have been waiting for just such a moment. Left alone in a Cannes prison cell for an age, I made a full confession to a young plain-clothes detective in the early hours. He said I spoke good French, which was certainly not the case. I heard the man screaming at me to deny everything. We were taken to Nice police station. Horrified my mother would learn of this, I gave a false name. I did not have my passport or room key with me. I was transferred to the notorious prison in Grasse, where dangerous criminals are rescued by helicopter from the roof-top exercise yard. I was made to share a cell with my co-defendant, as an extra punishment. He became suicidal. Why had I confessed? Why had I ruined his life? He would lose his wife, his children and his job as Madame Cinzano's butler in Menton. Why had I got us into this mess?

The situation was partly alleviated when we were joined by a respectable Englishman, who had been caught "cottaging", an expression that needed explaining. His bad luck was to be the only one caught when the police raided the public lavatories. He explained that the police crackdown resulted from Madame de Gaulle's crusade to stamp out immorality in France. I was in no position to disapprove of this urbane and supportive cell-mate's way of life. We exchanged addresses and planned to meet in London.

After four days of detention, it was clear the only way out was to reveal my identity. My passport was retrieved and I was assigned a female attorney. I was allowed a pen and paper, and wrote to my mother full of remorse, concerned she would learn of my shame. I assumed the letter was posted. The matter was never mentioned, and I imagined she was being circumspect and supportive. As she kept all my letters, but not this one (I found the postcard later), perhaps she never received it.

I was convicted of "scandale de pudeur", and instructed to leave France immediately. Should I re-offend within two years, I could expect to receive a severe sentence. My initial reaction at the fact I had a criminal record was that I would not be able to marry Princess Anne.

I had been treated well in prison. Even whilst exercising with rough Algerians and Moroccans on the rooftop yard, I was able to retain my dignity. I paid the hotel bill for the unslept-in room. The receipt, which I kept and which helped me out of a future difficulty, revealed I had been four days in prison.

I returned home on the intended Wednesday flight. The early morning airport bus into London had one other passenger. He was an airline employee in uniform, and engaged me in conversation. I revealed nothing about myself. He told me he knew Martin Parsons. Had a new shiftiness in my appearance made my demeanour reflect a similarity to that notorious character, who kept turning up?

On the way to Yorkshire for a Deb Dance, I called on Harry in Cambridge. He said my experience had traumatised me, but I had not had a breakdown. This was reassuring, as he had had one himself, and knew how to deal with neurotic undergraduates.

I resumed life in the City as though I had never been away. On the first day back, I encountered office gossip reminiscent of the Martin Parsons scandal three years before, on my first day at Abacas House. "Was I anything to do with Nick Cavendish?" Nothing, apart from the fact we were at school together. Why? What had he done now? I was unable to learn the circumstances of his dramatic departure. His career was unaffected, and he became a Whip in the House of Lords.

Accountancy is not everyone's cup of tea. It is more of a culture shock to some than to others. Into the articled clerks' room that first day back came someone I recognised. We had originally joined on the same day. We took our luncheon vouchers to a restaurant, where tables were reserved exclusively for the company chairman. Now I was ignored, as he confidently rounded up a team to set off on an audit. He was now my superior. All rather depressing.

I was sent to Newcastle. The hotel was grim. The client's office was Dickensian. And there was another scandal. The clerk I was replacing did not return to the hotel one night. Asked how he had got on, his response caused a sensation: "It was great! He was wonderful!"

Excused preliminary exams, I was to take the important Part 1 Accountancy examination in May. One was permitted two months' study leave, with the option of attending a crammer's course for those who could afford the fees. Cooper Brothers were amenable to my making another departure. I paid a deposit on a residential course at a hotel in Hampshire, and looked forward to returning at weekends to the flat I was lent by my aunt. Living alone, at last, suited me. Sharing bedrooms with future accountants in March and April, the lack of privacy, the visits to local pubs after lectures, were not a great prospect, but guaranteed a pass in the exams. London was only an hour and a half's drive away.

When in London, Harry stayed nearby in Brompton Square with his friend, and My Tutor's "brilliant History specialist", Simon Stuart. There I met Michael Ricketts, who lived with Tom Goff, the harpsichord maker. This led to an invitation to a private George Malcolm recital at Tom's house in Pont Street on Tuesday, 14th January 1964. "You might as well come! It's black tie for nine p.m." Michael condescended. Perhaps he felt I was moving up too rapidly in his social circle.

The audience was provided with small, hard gilt chairs, the sort one expects to find at such occasions. Among the guests were some Directors of Sotheby's, where Michael's brother Howard was armour expert. My bottom was pinched repeatedly by an American picture expert seated behind me during the recital. I might have been back at Eton. After the applause died down, something quite unexpected happened. We moved into various reception rooms for refreshments. I found myself chatting with someone who seemed to know me, but I did not recognise. I was then ushered to a quieter place, away from the general melée. Standing alone, with his back to the large fireplace, was a tall elderly man (he was fifty-nine), smoking a pipe and wearing his dinner jacket comfortably as if it was his usual evening wear. This was Joseph Lockwood. Here was a man relaxed, and totally at home in his surroundings. His manner would put anyone at their ease. We were introduced, and I was absorbed into his aura.

"You must know my personal assistant, BC," were his first words. So much could be read into my reactions; as to what I replied, regardless of what I said, or left unsaid, it was significant. I now realised I had been speaking to BC in the other room. I may not have spoken the words, but my eyes revealed my reaction: "That was the boy sacked from Eton for buggery!" Whether or not they crossed my lips was never discussed in the years that followed.

There were further questions. What did I do? Where was I working? My replies provided a string of coincidences. I was working for his business accountants. I was based at 9 Manchester Square. His office was at 20 Manchester Square. Something passed between us. It was difficult to put a finger on what it was. He disliked public schools, universities and chartered accountants. Yet that was all I had on offer.

The next morning, Sir Joseph Lockwood descended from the 6th floor Chairman's Suite of EMI House and crossed Manchester Square and knocked on No. 9. But I was no longer there.

PART 3

Sir Joe and Me

(1964 – 1991)

Sir Joseph Lockwood

1964

A Proposal and "Meet the Beatles"

Had he not phoned the next evening, I would not have given that first meeting a second thought.

Now, it was clear: the imposing pipe, the dinner jacket, the deep voice, the apparent interest, the encouraging manner, expectant, instant rapport of two people alone together. He was reading me like a book.

Joe strolled across Manchester Square the next morning. How did he know I was working in an office a couple of doors away? I must have told him. And if I had been there, and not reassigned to another client, how would I have reacted? Someone is sure to have said: "Who was that old man?"

He knew me; but I am not sure I knew who or what he was when I went to his flat. He told me the reason for inviting me was to tell me he wanted me to be his personal assistant. Nothing could have been a greater surprise. My reasons for refusing were dismissed. Yet they were rock solid. I was two years short of completing my articles, and – pause here – I had a criminal record. He was undeterred. And here I was telling him things my employers, who were *his* accountants, did not know. Would it not serve us best if I returned in two years' time, as a qualified chartered accountant?

He made light of objections. A word with the senior partner of Cooper Brothers would suffice. Interest in my early misdemeanours was nil. It was: "Join me, and see the world!" One subject was not discussed. Why did he need a new PA? And, "Why me?" He usually got his way.

I see from the office diary that we had dinner with Julian Gibbs the following Sunday. Julian had supplied my phone number, and, no doubt, let Joe know about me. Listening to the litany of complaints about BC, I soon realised Joe needed me more than I needed him. BC was driving him to distraction. Joe was clearly in love with him. The expression on my face when his name came up at Tom Goff's must have penetrated deep into suppressed emotions.

This unexpected offer found me at sea. My parents and the senior partners at Cooper Brothers (later PwC) galvanised into action. My father tore round to White's, and consulted *The Directory of Directors*, *Burke's Peerage* and *Who's Who*. My mother enlisted her sister's husband, who was a director of German and British companies. Kleinwort Benson Ltd wrote on 21st February:

Dear Prince Wittgenstein,

Sir Joseph is known to one of our Directors and is regarded as being pleasant to work with, although fully aware that he is very much the leader of his company. He can be quite tough when the occasion demands it, but apparently he is always quite straight and fair in his dealings. He is highly regarded in the industry and is considered to be very able, having successfully reorganised his Group from scratch and set it on an extremely prosperous road. The company itself is extremely sound and a leader in its field.

My employers were being difficult. A cable went to Senior Partner Henry Benson, who was abroad: "Do we release Cavendish?" To which came the reply: "Who is Cavendish?"

A letter from Cooper Brothers reached me at the accountancy crammers in Hampshire, where I was spending three months preparing for the chartered accountancy exams. David Corsan, who had interviewed me in 1959 with Benson, wrote:

Sir Joseph Lockwood spoke to me the other day about the possibility of your joining him as a personal assistant. You will remember from our last conversation that I told you I thought you would be very unwise to break your articles in order to take up this appointment. I still think that your own interests would best be served by going on to become a Chartered Accountant, but this decision must be yours. I suggest you discuss the matter with your father. The Staff Committee discussed this matter and decided we would be prepared to agree to cancelling your articles if you wish to take up this appointment with Sir Joseph Lockwood, but we would not be willing to offer you fresh articles if at a later date you wished to return to us.

From day one, I treated Joe's proposal as a fling. I was the "intended", and it was for me to accept or reject. In preparation for the "wedding", the only person I consulted was the Dean of Westminster, whom I met through Harry Williams. Eric Abbott wrote on 24th February: "Best wished for your work for the Accountancy examinations, and for a brave decision about your future plans."

Cancellation of my articles was registered at the Institute of Chartered Accountants in England and Wales on 20th May.

Joe snuffed out my contract and brushed aside other ambitions. In return, I was to cure the obsession that was destroying him. Criticisms of BC came fast and furious. He was lazy, incompetent, unpunctual, badly dressed, always forgetting his passport and never having any money. If he did have any money, his father would take it. Worse still, his father, who bullied him for being sacked from Eton, was just a mere stipendiary magistrate, a paid position. His sisters came in for criticism. One, a secretary, was a snob. Another asked to meet Cliff Richard, when Joe was making a gold disc presentation. She deliberately used the occasion to insult Cliff and embarrass everyone at the ceremony.

I remember how flattering it was to receive these confidences. At the same time, they left scars of jealousy. The slightest thing made me jealous. Joe went to see *Who's Afraid of Virginia Woolf?* at the Old Vic with a companion, something planned before I met him. He loathed the play and derided it for years. It was mentioned as a butt for his enduring scorn and I wondered who the companion was, and what had been so disagreeable about that evening. Was it only the play that made his so angry? I knew better than to ask. Years later, I deduced that the companion was a friend of Julian's. There was no need to be jealous. One thing was clear: when Joe was angry, he was not to be questioned. He told me to be circumspect at all times, but I already was.

A problem arose that I never solved. What should I call Joe? Should it be Joseph, Joe, Sir Joe, or plain "you"? Employees called him "Chairman" or "Sir Joseph", friends and colleagues called him "Joe". As both employee and companion, I called his nothing. I was "William". Strange, in what became a lifetime's partnership, that there was no "Dear" or "Darling" for me, when I had so many diminutives: Bill, Billy, Pussy Cat Willum, and Bin.

The first months of 1964 were full of significant events. The Beatles' 'I Want to Hold Your Hand' climbed to the number one position in America's Cash Box Singles charts on 16th January, two days after I met Joe. Great news for the group, who were performing in Paris. They were waiting to go to the United States, for this moment to arrive. It was inconceivable to reach America without a recording contract with Capitol Records. Having passed over the first two hits, the company at last released this US single, which rapidly sold a million copies. The group's world sales in 1964 would exceed 4,500,000.

Brian Epstein planned the trip the previous November. His boys were to arrive in New York on 7th February. Joe decided that Capitol should offer its own separate contract without any pressure from London. To date, Capitol had free rein whether to take EMI artists or not, to avoid accusations of Anti-Trust. The Justice Department in Washington would love to make EMI sell Capitol.

Three days before the Beatles' sensational arrival at J. F. Kennedy International Airport, Joe set off on a secret mission. Little evidence survives. Traveller's cheques were delivered to the office on 28th January for "the Chairman's overseas trip". Accompanied by his PA and a copy of the Beatles' EMI contract, he took off for a week's stay in Nassau. The British Bahamas are outside American jurisdiction, easily accessible via Miami for Capitol executives, as well as American holidaymakers who felt they were still in the States. Reporting to Joe, and benefiting from a less demanding time differential, were Alan Livingston in Los Angeles, Roland Rennie, EMI's licensing manager, in New York, and LG in London. Livingston was to spend $50,000 on promoting the Beatles' arrival with local radio stations. Rennie's role was to stifle the two small companies, Swan and V. J. Records, licensed to issue the group's earlier singles.

Apart from photographs in Joe's album, the only record of those five "lost days" is my postcard from the British Bahamas: "This place is jammed tight with the idle masses searching happiness and we can hardly find a quiet place in the open to discuss business. However, it is a pleasant change in midwinter from London. Wish you were here with us; Joe." The photos depict an extremely bored and disgruntled PA standing with a Capitol lawyer outside the British Colonial Hotel.

Back home on 10th February, return delayed until mission accomplished, Joe was content to read of Alan Livingston handing out gold discs to his newly signed artists as though he had had them for years. And EMI's share price, recently depressed by poor results from Capitol, rose 20% to $6.38 in New York. Not unreasonably, the Beatles never warmed to the company that had rejected them for so long.

During the early weeks of our acquaintance, Joe held meetings with the Prime Minister, the Leader of the Opposition and the President of the Board of Trade: Alec Douglas Home, Harold Wilson and Edward Heath. And he was entertaining Maria Callas, Tito Gobbi and Walter Legge. At the same time, he was making me feel important.

Walter Legge dined at Joe's flat on 24th January, and left EMI whilst Joe was in Nassau. Knowing his volatile nature, one might form a connection between the two events, and even contribute them to Joe's state of mind, possibly even involving me in some way. Nothing could be further from the truth. Joe had recently bumped into "Ted" Heath at lunch with Roy Thompson, who owned the *Times* newspaper. He liked Thompson, who, when they were attending the same evening engagement, asked Joe whether he was keeping on his chauffeur so that he could send his home. Such economy on the part of a multi-millionaire was particularly appealing to Joe.

Heath was a "groupie" after anyone to do with classical music. He wanted to meet Walter Legge, and Joe arranged a quiet dinner for the three of them. Legge's departure from EMI came suddenly and shocked many. Although his reason was not so surprising when looked at later. He uprooted, moved to Switzerland, and sold his white Jaguar to his assistant, Suvi Grubb. William Mann, the music critic, claimed the unthinkable had happened, and that EMI had sacked their great recording producer. Joe did not sack people. Apparently, unknown to EMI, Legge owned the Philharmonia Orchestra, and the rights to its name. If this came out, he could have been in great trouble. Apart from sending someone "downstairs", to see if there was anything incriminating, Joe decided not to pursue the matter. Having previously eliminated the self-defeating rivalries between HMV and Columbia, he blandly stated that David Bicknell, "a good HMV man", was now in charge. No longer would Legge keep a taxi waiting for hours with the meter ticking away in Manchester Square. No longer would Legge take the Philharmonia to Vienna, when Abbey Road was perfectly adequate for recording.

On 29th January, Joe dined at 10 Downing Street. The next night he was on television with Harold Wilson in the BBC's *Gallery* programme, questioning the Leader of the Opposition. Next day's *Daily Telegraph* exclaimed: "Beatles safe under Labour, says Wilson". Joe had wanted a straight answer. Was Labour intending to impose stringent currency restrictions, forced repatriation and taxation of Beatles record sales in America? "Of course not," replied Wilson. "There is no suggestion over what you record. I know the Beatles very well. They are in my constituency."

The new production of *Tosca* by Franco Zeffirelli at Covent Garden on 21st January brought Maria Callas back to the opera stage after an absence of eighteen months. Her performance with Tito Gobbi was sensational. Her fame matched Anna Pavlova, Vaslav Nijinski, Margot Fonteyn, Rudolf Nureyev, Paul Scofield as King Lear, as someone one should see once in a lifetime. *Tosca* was sold out, but I managed to book tickets for a performance. Cooper Brothers decided to send me to Newcastle for two weeks. Joe said he could get me seats for another evening. Numerous requests for tickets appeared in *The Times*'s personal column. A box number took me to a house in Fulham, where a banker handed me cash on the doorstep: "You're mad to give up your seats!" Joe was in Nassau when I rang his office about tickets. Not a word had been mentioned. Perhaps I should be more careful in future about expensive offers and promises coming from that direction, where nothing appears impossible. Had I known then that I was missing my only opportunity to see Callas, would I have acted differently? Possibly. At the time, it never occurred to me to ask for a day off work. Fate stepped in again the following year. Callas returned for five further performances. After the first night, a Royal Gala Performance, she was taken ill. That evening was the last time she sang at Covent Garden. The production was filmed in 1964 and the rights devolved to EMI. Some years later, the Victoria and Albert Museum mounted an exhibition about the Royal Opera House. It would have been incomplete without screening the famous Tosca/Scarpia scene. Paul Findlay, assistant to the General Manager of the Royal Opera House, invited me to accompany him to Elstree Studios. He obtained the necessary permission from EMI Films to feature an extract from the film.

On returning from Nassau, Joe came to stay the weekend at my aunt's house in North Yorkshire. As I was still based in Newcastle, I met him at Darlington Station. He was given "The Middle Tower Room". As a child, this had been my bedroom for afternoon naps. He was an instant hit with the family. My grandmother shared views he expressed on television. She subscribed to Joe's friend Stephen King-Hall's monthly newsletter, and remained abreast of current affairs. Joe told her I had excellent business sense, whatever that meant. Most impressed of all was my great-aunt's cook, Mrs Pat, who saw him on this occasion, and on another brief visit to Mortham. Like so often, he had worked his magic, and Mrs Pat became a fan.

A couple of weeks later, Joe invited me to Manchester Square, "to see how we operate". An EMI DEC 1100 computer proudly churned the staff payroll on tape decks in the entrance hall, to prove this was not just a music business. The secretaries in the lift appeared impressed when I pressed the button for the sixth floor. Somewhat facetiously, as it turned out: the lift was generally vacated for the chairman and his guests. "We are honoured," exclaimed the sensibly dressed girls. I sat in on a meeting with the manager from Chile.

Then it was off to the crammers to prepare for the accountancy exams in May. Andover was a mere two hours away, and weekends were spent in London. I joined Joe for long walks through familiar streets. Entering Chelsea, we would pass through the street where BC lived, knowing he was away for the weekend. The pretty little house had been bought with Joe's money. Joe was strangled with emotion as we passed it without stopping. He was imagining the parties he had heard described that did not include him. I felt the importance of being the confidant, who makes no comment and retains a respectful silence.

One day, walking in Holland Park, we were accosted by a slight acquaintance who approached Joe purposefully. Dr Francis Singer's company, Chesham Amalgamations, had made a successful business merging companies. He was out for EMI to buy MECCA, the bingo and dance hall empire. I was impressed by the effortless way Joe brushed aside this importunate man without any hint of rudeness.

Charles Selby and I were drifting apart, but the end came as a shock. There had been 156 typewritten letters arriving with scarcely a break over the last four years. The final one, dated 7th April, arrived at the crammer's without any hint it was to be the last. Reading it again after all those years, I see how small a part I was playing in his life. If there was such a thing as a mid-twenties-life crisis, this was it. He wrote:

Dear Bin; I always leave work at about 4.00 pm on Fridays, as there is so much to do at home, so that is why you couldn't reach me. I am going on a week's holiday, starting tomorrow – I didn't know you would be at Constantine at the time – but I am arranged for the week now. I think that May would be too early to take my main holiday, but I have one week owing that I could possibly take then. I will have to see. Very sad yes, but I have little time see anybody. Even Spae is being neglected, which is not good for his ego. I expect that the "boys" are interested in impresarios/ agents but I am great difficulty in staving off bookings at

the moment. They want to work during the week as well as all weekend – and unless I change my job – I just can't do it. When our "demo
disc" is out I will send it to you! Then you can get us on everything. Life
is very hectic and people at EIL (Electronic Instruments Ltd) seem to
object to my sleeping all day Monday, trying to catch up for the weekend. I must stop now and WORK; Write from Constantine, Love,

Charles.

He came to see me, hair lank, suit shiny. He looked exhausted. His
letter described his life as an electro-chemical engineer by day, and a
manager/player in a pop group at nights. He was in a hurry and
refused to stay. We exchanged neckties at his request. His was
polyester and nondescript. I kept it. Mention was made of "older
men", perhaps with a note of reproof. He was off to see Mrs Mathew,
who liked him because he was "such a good influence on her sons!" I
was jealous and unsettled.

Charles emigrated to America. His boss told my father, who had
found him the EIL job, that he wanted to keep him, but it was his own
decision to go.

Rather than return to London at weekends, as studying intensified
and exams approached, I headed for Cornwall. Constantine is my
holiday home. Charles had been a regular visitor. But now, on 10th
April, I was at Bodmin station, meeting Joe and Julian Gibbs. Already
staying with me was a young surfer I had met on the beach. This must
have caused tension, but nothing was mentioned. Perhaps this, or that
he was catching a cold, irritated Joe.

Inevitably Phyllis, our dear Cornish housekeeper, fell for Sir
Joseph. She said he reminded her of Mr Stokes. In him she saw a big
man, with a big voice, who enjoyed the company of young men. Dick
Stokes MP was Managing Director of Ransome and Rapier, and
Cabinet Minister in Attlee's Labour Government. He enjoyed playing
backgammon with my great-aunt. He did not bother with a beach
towel when removing his wet swimming trunks. People could think
what they liked.

A massive anger attack arose from that weekend visit. This was the first I heard described. To be a witness of cause and effect was still to come. Joe and Julian found their train compartment on the return journey to London occupied by drunken merchant seamen. At Plymouth, Joe demanded their removal before allowing the train to continue. At Paddington, he marched to the front of the long queue and claimed the first taxi. Julian said he was "very impressed". I know now how he felt. One stands aside, eyes averted, pretending to be invisible, totally ignored, silently sympathising with his victim, but at the same time admiring Joe's bombast. He retired to bed having found it hard to tolerate the least inconvenience, such as a cold in the head. And this attitude was tested when he fainted a week or two later at a reception at the Royal Festival Hall before a London Symphony Orchestra concert. Shocked onlookers thought they were witnessing a guest suffering a fatal heart attack. Luckily, Joe had been talking to a retired Field Marshal who was familiar with soldiers fainting on the parade ground. The cause was a combination of low blood pressure, stifling atmosphere and crowding bodies. He was rushed to hospital for observation, checked himself out still in his dinner jacket, laughing the incident off to me on a phone call the next morning. Nothing further was said.

Joe and me with Jack Hylton

Joe took me along when he called on his show-business friends Jack and Beverley Hylton, who had an apartment across Grosvenor Square. Jack was seventy, and ex-Australian beauty queen Beverley was thirty-one. We were fifty-nine and twenty-four, and we behaved as any similarly matched couples would behave. Jack got out his new Polaroid camera. We all posed together as a souvenir of the occasion and were given copies. A band leader and impresario, Jack Hylton was Joe's favourite because he sold more records for HMV and Columbia than anyone else. In addition, Joe found him amusing in the same way he found Jules Thorn and Roy Thompson amusing. He was also an astute businessman. A recent history of EMI claimed "the company had not had an act of the magnitude of the Beatles since the days of Jack Hylton in the 1920's". A Northerner, born in Bolton, he had the simple warmth and humour that reminded Joe of Stockport and Manchester, and addicted him to the new Granada TV series *Coronation Street*. The thirteen-year-old "Singing Mill Boy" in music halls became the "Happy Days Are Here Again" band leader. With success, he became an impresario owning theatres and commercial television companies. Musical comedies imported from Broadway and backed by EMI would most likely be in one of his theatres, and Joe would be at the first nights.

Jack and Beverley had recently married. I do not know how serious Jack was when he blamed Joe for making them marry, but the circumstances sound familiar enough to make it probable.

Taking the lead from Buckingham Palace court protocol on Joe's instructions, invitations to EMI's annual dinners were for married couples and single guests. The term "And Partner" was yet unminted and unembossed. The company secretary, who prepared the list on behalf of "The Chairman and Directors of EMI Limited" made no exception. That we were in "show business" made no difference. Executives in EMI Records had greater reason for dissatisfaction than those in Electronics, who were less likely to be divorced, separated or single. The embarrassing and inevitable moment duly arrived. Jack was taking his seat at the dinner in December, only to find no place was laid for Beverley, who was humiliated and made a scene. As a result, "I had to marry her!" Jack claimed. Until recently he had been a regularly philandering husband, but his wife died, and he no longer had an excuse for failing to commit himself. Fortunately, Beverley genuinely adored him and their marriage was happy.

Joe found the whole thing hilarious and no immediate plans were made to change the rules. Norman Newell, who was relied on to provide artists for the cabaret at the dinner, complained bitterly to me that he had to come alone.

Another Northern favourite was Stanley Holloway and his broad Lancashire monologue: "The Lion and Albert". Joe never tired of young Albert's unfortunate encounter with a lion in the Blackpool Tower menagerie. In the same vein was "Pick up tha' Musket". Holloway is best known now as Eliza Doolittle's cockney father in *My Fair Lady*.

My first encounter with EMI people was at a party given by Norrie Paramor. I do not recall the occasion, but Ken East, an EMI executive, said it was where he saw me first, and I made a favourable impression.

Whilst sitting Part 1 of the accountancy exams in the Central Methodist Hall, Joe was away in Greece with BC, attending the blessing of Columbia's new studios by the Metropolitan Bishop. Joe had laid the foundation stone on a previous visit to Athens. At Delphi, he was photographed posing wistfully, as he contemplated our future partnership.

In Milan, on their return, they encountered an American music publisher, Bobby Mellin, who Joe liked. He was the spitting image of Edward G. Robinson, and I never understood his appeal. It must have shown, as I did not get the presents he sent BC. Joe had difficulty in appearing to appreciate the chunky cufflinks arriving each Christmas. Mellin would invite us to dine and smoke cigars at the Café Royal to watch and bet on boxing matches. Mellin Music published The Beach Boys' songs, and Paul Anka's 'Diana'. EMI bought the company some years later.

In June, Joe lobbied the Permanent Private Secretary to the Postmaster General to ban pirate radio ships. I sat on a dais in a House of Commons committee room, facing ten Conservative MPs. Major

*Joe in Delphi,
as I sit for exams*

Morrison (later Lord Margadale) quipped he was expecting the Beatles. It remained for the next Government to bring in the Marine Offences Bill, and for Harold Wilson to have the credit for ridding the high seas of ships illegally broadcasting pop records off-shore.

I was in Cornwall when Joe was reported for driving dangerously on the M1, visiting his mother in Southwell. He spent a weekend with the Vernons at their 1930s waterside house on the Solent. I collected him in my Mini Cooper. Nancy Vernon greeted me warmly. We moved on to spend the night at Julian's weekend cottage at Beaulieu. I was impressed at how smoothly Joe moved between his straight and gay friends.

I started work at EMI on 1st July, and was sent to Hayes for a two-day inductory tour to see over one hundred and fifty acres of factory. A basic tour was prepared for the time available. I was shown Centurion tanks, Green Archer mortar-locating radar, rocket fuses, top secret projects in the Central Research Laboratories, and everything that goes into producing and testing LP records. I remarked on the number of American companies forming joint ventures with EMI: Raytheon, Varian, Hughes Tool and Cossor.

EMI Head Office at Hayes

Joe's ten-year presence was felt in all corners of the site, raising enormous amounts of respect wherever I went. The Philips-EMI magnetic tape factory manager's admiration was nothing short of worship. Security staff and uniformed gatekeepers at each location would salute the chairman's car, and ring ahead to alert their colleagues as it followed its daily route from Farnham Royal or London. Head office commissionaires would be outside the entrance to greet the chairman. Joe, presenting Sergeant "Mick" Grant of the works police with his twenty-five-years-service wristwatch quipped: "I've seen you around quite a lot!"

Luckily, I was already familiar with ear-blasting factory tours where noise wipes out every word of explanation. Otherwise those two days would have been overwhelming.

I got to know the secretary Joe shared with John Wall. Jean Hemson showed me the small room allocated to the chairman's PA, next to her office. Mrs Hemson, a senior secretary for twenty years, and aware of her status, was promoted from the largest typing pool of any company I had ever audited. Living locally, her husband George was superintendent of the power plant supplying the site and surplus electricity to the National Grid. Two sons worked at Heathrow, one as a pilot, the other in the kitchens. Beneath that battle-axe exterior lay a human heart. Mrs Hemson was no prude. She remarked on Joe's obvious relationship with BC. I was struck by her perceptive "take" on the situation. It was not so much that BC did not admit to the affair, he failed to deny it. Anyone loyal to Joe should outright refute and dismiss such talk. That was her objection. Jean Hemson thought that was what Joe deserved and expected.

Things were not turning out as I expected at Manchester Square. For a start, BC was still there and showing no sign of moving. I had agreed to replace him in January, and we were now in July. He was perfectly amenable as we went around together. He had no particular role and I had nothing to learn from him. He was quite open about the perks that went with the job. He warned me "not to worry about Ann (our London secretary). She's OK. Her boyfriend picks her up in his Jaguar after work." He had more privileges than Ann, who was jealous.

On Saturday 11th July, Joe and I went down to Chichester for a matinée performance at the Festival Theatre. He pointed out John Hansard's country home. He was impressed that all his "non-execs" had grand houses in the country as well as in London. My mind was elsewhere. I was struck by something he said as he sat beside me in my Mini Cooper: he was still seeing BC outside office hours! I was devastated, dumbfounded, shocked, totally taken aback, and, of course, jealous. I sulked. Nothing, but nothing, could have been worse, yet I received a massive reprimand. My shock was compounded by Joe's angry reaction. I was experiencing for the first time the violence that erupts out of nowhere so often. It was horrible. The day was a disaster. Joe said it was "the most depressing day of his life". That is how I learnt never to sulk again. There were three of us in the relationship. The honeymoon was over.

A letter came from Cooper Brothers, congratulating me on passing my exams. But I had made a terrible mistake. I had burnt my boats. I had to face up to things, but things were to get worse. BC told Joe I would be suitable "in the job", but added that I wore make-up! Angus Wilson had suggested I should try it, but it was so incredibly untrue. That was not all. Judy Lockhart Smith, down in George Martin's office, told BC, who told Joe: "He's OK, but of course he's a woman!" Judy was very insecure until she married George, and made scathing remarks about his artists' shortcomings. Shirley Bassey had scrawny hair, terrible skin and pocky complexion. Better forgotten! It was a compliment to be the subject of one of Judy's comments. We would become great friends when we discovered our parents knew each other.

I appreciated the attributes that made BC generally popular with the staff. Leading an active social life on the golf course and at the Garrick Club, where he was on the wine committee, he also played the cello and had a wide knowledge of classical music. All this fed my sense of inferiority. Strangely, EMI Records appeared reluctant to offer him a job in one of their departments. He seemed to be so well suited. Peter Andry, the athletic and handsome manager of the Classical Artists Department, was his ideal. Never short of exaggeration, Joe claimed BC was in love with Peter. But no offer was forthcoming from his hero.

Raymond Leppard told me about Peter, when I went up to Trinity to dine in March. He had heard I was joining EMI. Ray was fond of

David Bicknell, "a lovely teddy bear", but Peter, he said, was less sympathetic and unpopular with artists. EMI had issued Ray's Glyndbourne production of *L'Incoronazione Di Poppea* in a handsome two-album box set with libretto, but had abridged it without approval. He now favoured Decca's specialist label *L'Oiseau Lyre*. To elaborate on our conversation, Ray said Peter was fucking his secretary.

This information was still in my mind when Joe sent me down to the Classics Department on some quest. Sitting at her desk outside Peter's office was Diana Chapman, quiet, efficient and conservatively dressed, not at all as I had been expecting. This was definitely not the secretary that Peter was fucking.

One morning, encountering Peter in the Manchester Square garage, on his return from an overseas trip, I asked how it had gone. "You PAs are all the same," he snapped. "You can't keep anything to yourselves!" How was I to know the chairman checked his expenses? Now I was a sneak, and Peter was definitely no teddy bear, as Ray had warned.

Joe thought up chores to occupy my time in the small room I shared with BC. A copy of the 1956 Copyright Act was produced for comment. I noted statutory record royalties were calculated to the nearest farthing in pre-decimal days. Asked to check EMI's share price I was stumped, never having turned to the City pages previously. At Cooper Brothers, my supervisor who had looked after EMI – asked by me, before I left, for tips – reported poor stock control in the Electronics Division. At Cambridge, I took a vacation job in London at Opus 20: Opera Ballet Limited, selling HMV and Columbia records. I overlooked the small print on each label: "Manufactured by EMI Records (The Gramophone Company Ltd, Hayes, Middlesex, England)." And I ignored publicity material: "The Greatest Recording Organisation in the World!" My small knowledge of classical repertoire was plain. Asked for "anything by Couperin" by a tall plain girl in glasses and duffle coat, I realised the enthusiastic Couperin customer was Vanessa Redgrave. Unbelievably, I had not heard of the composer.

August came, and at last my predicament was resolved. I was to accompany Joe on a week's tour of four Scandinavian counties, and, on our return, BC would be gone. The promise "to see the world" had been genuine. Each manager in each country competed to provide the best hotel, the best restaurant and the best sightseeing tour. The Finns proudly displayed cannons directed at Communist Estonia. Our hosts laid on the epitome of entertainment, an evening in the sauna, an *entente cordiale* devoid of all clothing.

Travelling with the Chairman

As a novice, I was accorded special attention. My diploma, signed by The Scourge Master, Chief Assessor and Chairman of the Bath, indicated I did not disgrace myself in such proximity: "He did without constraint or undue persuasion, be it from the Sprites or Spirits, undergo the Purgatory of the Finnish Sauna, passing stark naked through all the stages, from the Lowest to the Highest, to attain the Transcendental State, having given proofs of Maturity, Endurance, and Moral and Physical Hardness."

Told to make a comparison of the companies we visited, I noted that Norway pressed more records than Sweden, and Denmark owned a music publisher: Imudico. This, alongside small publishing companies in the US, Britain, and Italy, was a mere toehold in the Industry EMI was to dominate.

Joe was summoned to attend the Magistrate's Court in Newport Pagnell on 19th August. He was required to make a statement to Northamptonshire Police about the motorway incident in June. I went with him. Although overtaking someone hogging the outside lane is not an offence, the solicitor supplied by the AA advised Joe to plead guilty, as he was accused of dangerous driving, and his license was due for renewal in September. There was no need to appear in person, but he was interested in all court procedures. He felt he was being victimised for driving a Silver Cloud Rolls Royce with the distinctive "EMI 1" number plate. The headlines in papers reporting the case the next morning supported his claim: "How not to get ahead – even in a tycoon Rolls", and "M 1 driver shook his fist at EMI Chief in Rolls". I could easily imagine Joe's seething anger at the driver's refusal to get out of the way, despite blasts on the horn as he swept past at 90 mph. The Cooper Brothers boys I encountered at Hayes showed little sympathy for my boss, who "quite rightly" had his license endorsed.

So far I had felt isolated. But things were to change. With BC out of the way, no one had a good word for him. I felt like the heroine when Daphne du Maurier's ideal wife "Rebecca" was finally exposed. BC could now be my "Rebecca"! BC was lazy, unreliable, an embarrassment to the chairman. He had left his desk uncleared alongside piles of factory-sample records submitted for his approval.

These were all classical records. A couple of executives informed me of their particular tastes, chamber music for example, should I continue to pass on copies I no longer wanted. Joe soon stopped all this. The "white labels" were sent back to the factory to be broken up.

People began to take me into their confidence with hints of discontent. The Group Treasurer's wife said Joe was driving her husband too hard and he couldn't go on like that. He soon left the company. A friend from Cambridge days described observing a member of his Club crying over his drink. The member attributed his breakdown to being overworked by Joe. Colonel "Kit" Dawnay wanted Joe to retire: "Everyone should retire at 60!" he declared, almost talking me out of my new job.

Had he known of these murmurs, Joe would have been amused. He frequently told of the train journey he took soon after joining EMI. A fellow passenger, learning where he worked, told him a friend was a director: "He says they have a new chairman – he's a real bastard!"

Criticism of Joe stretched to his personal appearance. The company secretary's wife preferred him before he used hair gel to hide his bald patch. I believe it was called Gomina, available at his local chemists. Admittedly it did look a bit grungy when too much was applied. This was beyond my remit. I was able to suggest small changes to his attire with gentle hints. His tie clip was abandoned, as was the handkerchief he kept in his sleeve. This old-fashioned habit can be seen peeking out in the 1962 Nicholas Egon portrait.

Joe reciprocated. Perhaps I should have been grateful to be told I had bad breath! I acted on the advice. Criticism of the cut of my trousers was surprisingly harder to take. I ordered new suits from Blades, the gentleman's outfitters recommended by Julian Gibbs.

Unlike Daphne du Maurier's anti-heroine who disappeared mysteriously, my "Rebecca" was still around. BC continued to appear in the chairman's desk diary, at weekly intervals, blocking out other evening engagements. Not being in an exclusive relationship gave me freedom I was not seeking. For I was to be "circumspect at all times", and not do anything that would affect Joe's reputation. Yet I found I was more sensitive to guarding Joe's reputation than he was himself.

Joe loved gay parties. I didn't. We were invited one evening by Edward Montagu, who kept a flat in London. There would be boys and drink and possibly drugs. I was reluctant to go, but Joe insisted. It was late night when we got there, and found we had come to the wrong address. We never made the party. We went to Montagu Square, whereas Edward lived in nearby Bryanston Square. Joe was furious, certain that I had deliberately made the error.

Less inhibited before assuming this self-imposed responsibility, I went to a gay bar with Joe and Robert Stigwood. We were amused by Robert's claim he could take a boy from the street and make him a pop star. One such was "Simon Scott", a good-looking boy, who Robert promoted even before his first disc was issued. A miniature plaster bust of the singer was distributed to all the radio stations and record stores. The marketing people in EMI had not been consulted, and were not surprised when the record failed to sell. Simon Scott was soon forgotten.

Real showmanship and celebrity were on display when the Hyltons invited us to a performance of Lerner and Loewe's *Camelot*, their import from Broadway. The Theatre Royal, Drury Lane, retained all the tradition of a Royal Box, with plush décor and flunkeys attired in velvet breeches and powdered wigs standing behind our chairs. Alan Jay Lerner looked in during the interval but declined a seat, declaring he "had already seen the show"! Lerner was devoted to Hylton, not least for showing confidence in his show, and was devastated when he died suddenly in 1965. He revealed this in his autobiography *The Street Where I Live*, the title taken from his song in *My Fair Lady*.

We went backstage after the show. Beverley Hylton was popular with Sir Lancelot and the Knights of the Round Table. Laurence Harvey, King Arthur, insisted on taking us all to dinner at the Mirabelle, although we had previously booked at the White Elephant further up Curzon Street. No one was more flamboyant and consistently generous than Laurence Harvey. After the meal, he toured the kitchens and greeted the chef. I have seen other stars perform this ritual. None compared with the sincerity of his praise. Ever the showman, he had embraces and kisses for everyone, as we took our departure in Curzon Street. Formal photographs of Joe in City papers overlooked the fact that artists found Joe very kissable.

I was unprepared for my first contact with celebrity. When an American voice came through on my office phone – "Hi, this is Frankie Day!" – I knew immediately this was Frances Day, American star of pre-war West End musicals, popular with my parents and famous for Cole Porter's 'It's delightful, is de' lovely, it's delicious', issued on HMV before I was born. "I've won the raffle! How about it? Let's get together, you boys!" Joe, or rather EMI, had donated a fridge made by Morphy Richards to the Cancer Research Charity Ball raffle. Frances Day was keen for the publicity. Joe was dismissive: "Put that on to Staff Sales," he instructed. Humphrey Tilling reprovingly told me the staff sales manager came to him for a float to pay for taking Miss Day out to lunch! This was no way to treat a West End star. Tilling invited her to dine with the senior executives. Joe was not prepared to humour self-important ex-stars with red carpet treatment. He was simply not interested. There was a rather sad outcome. Maybe, I was a little bit responsible. Frances Day had re-invented herself as "her daughter" Frankie Day, on TV panel games. Her comeback was short lived. After this episode with EMI, and its unfriendly chairman, she withdrew from public life and died a recluse.

Joe involved himself thoroughly in another fundraising campaign for Cancer Research which he recalled frequently, choking with laughter. The Duchess of Bedford and Mrs Gerald Legge (later better known as Lady Lewisham) came to Abbey Road to record a disc for Norman Newell. The song Norman wrote for the Duchess was 'Luck's in Love with Me', and for Mrs Legge 'I'm in Love'. They lasted 2.21 minutes on each side of a 45-rpm record, with proceeds going to the Charity. Norman said both ladies were quite drunk, but "it had helped".

Life in the chairman's office varied. On 24th September, I was summoning extra chairs for the boardroom: Joe had invited twenty shop stewards to tea. With Mr Grosch, the group industrial relations officer and myself in attendance, but otherwise quite alone, Joe addressed the trades union representatives gathered round the table. He reported and discussed the year's results to be published the next morning. This was privileged information, yet to be issued to the City, the press and the shareholders. He showed faith in his listeners, resisting the temptation to speculate. Poor Grosch was in a permanent state of agitation. Catching my eye, he implored me to share his distress. Headlines in the newspapers the next morning shouted "EMI Profits Soar 80% to Peak £9 Million". Joe was sharing success with his workers. This was the last time these informal gatherings with the chairman took place.

Following the Beatles' sensational first visit to the West Coast of America, their record company presented each of the boys with a souvenir. Capitol could have given them Thunderbird sports cars, but instead chose the latest recording device invented by Ampex., the cam-corder. Unfortunately, no one checked that these video recorders recorded on a different frequency and were useless in the UK. Guess who had to send all four models to CRL for modification? By the time they were ready, their novelty had worn off. I wrote to Wendy Hanson, personal assistant to Mr Brian Epstein, on 28th July 1966: "The boys are naturally impatient and fed up at having to wait all this time, when they were led to expect their presents, first of all at Christmas, and then at Easter."

I was reminded of this mess thirty years later, when HM Customs put on display a collection of unclaimed items. Among them were the Beatles' gold discs, sent by Capitol in 1964. Those were exciting times. My first visit to America with the company followed soon after the Beatles tour.

But first, we were in Holland visiting our record licensee, Bovema. Bovema did not represent Parlophone, and consolation was required "for not having the Beatles". Time was set aside to tour Verkade, the famous Dutch biscuit manufacturer. The company was known to Joe from his flour-milling days. EMI Electronics had been awarded the contract to automate their new factory. To Joe, there was no such thing as unmanned "automation". Even EMI's driverless Robotugs feeding the assembly lines were man-operated. It was clear EMI had taken on a contract at a huge loss, and Joe was furious. Heads would roll when we returned to Hayes.

I was to be the innocent cause of Joe's next anger attack, during that visit to America in October. It was exciting seeing New York and Los Angeles again after five years. I was still inclined to play as an eighteen-year-old during the few moments of release from the busy schedule laid on by Capitol. Glenn Wallichs met the plane. I was squeezed into a front seat of the limousine, my face confronted by a freezing blast from the air-conditioning. As we crossed the East River, the Manhattan Skyline unfolded before us. Glenn asked whether I had seen anything like it in my life. Circumspect as usual, I took care not to mention I had been here before, on a Greyhound bus.

The general idea was for the non-executive directors to see America and hold a board meeting at Capitol's headquarters. Travelling with us were Lord Mills, Ian Jacob, Dawnay, Hansard, Wall, Tilling, Richard Dawes, veteran EMI executive, and some wives. The wives had been Wall's idea. We were assigned suites permanently owned by Jack Wrather, a Capitol director and friend of Wallichs's, in the Pierre Hotel on 5th Avenue. Wrather owned TV rights to *Lassie* and *The Lone Ranger*, and was married to Bonita Granville, the 1930s film star. We arrived to news that Labour had won the general election. Joe gave me an important role, as our distinguished party assembled in a state of dejection. "William, read out what the press are saying!" He described Harold Wilson as "a canny little Yorkshireman", who had the potential to be a successful Prime Minister. The newspaper article concurred with his view.

Evenings were spent on Broadway, watching musicals sponsored by Capitol, *Ben Franklin in Paris*, *Funny Girl* and *Golden Boy*, all of which failed to transfer to London. We sat with Sammy Davis Junior, recording the *Golden Boy* original cast album. Barbra Streisand, the "funny girl", was a big hit with Joe. Her seduction scene, with Ziegfield, was the funniest thing he had ever seen. It had him in hysterics.

Richard Dawes, still barely recovered from Joe's arrival at EMI, received a call on the Pierre's internal system: "I am staying in the hotel, and I think it is about time I met your chairman," announced Richard Armitage, whose Noel Gay Agency represented a number of EMI artists, including Paul Jones and Manfred Mann. Armitage, a formidable character, was not prepared for rebuff from Dawes. Joe liked successful, aggressive and even pushy people, provided they shared a common purpose, and Richard was all of these. We found he was unusual for an agent, even more complex than his artists. His father wrote the musical *Me And My Girl* at a time when publishing was more important than gramophone recording. Richard had become a successful promoter of pop stars by inheriting his father's music publishing company.

Stimulated by all the razzmatazz and socialising with celebrities, I did something I was to regret later. With a free afternoon to do what I liked, I paid Bill Taub, my South of France friend, a visit. Why I had remained in contact I have no idea. Taub's apartment was crammed with signed photographs of famous people. He was a high-class New York show-business lawyer. His pride-and-joy was a filing system in the form of a carousel, which he revolved to obtain immediate access to his contact details. I was impressed.

The heightened atmosphere I was experiencing repeated itself in California. The Beatles had left recently, and anything or anyone to do with them caused excitement. Parties were given for them at the Wallichs's and Livingston's Beverly Hills homes. When our group spent the weekend in Palm Springs, the *Desert Sands News* pictured Glenn Wallichs's daughter Susan "learning all about the Beatles from William Cavendish the young Englishman currently visiting here".

At a reception for Nat King Cole in Hollywood, the seven EMI Directors were guests of honour. The Capitol artist died soon after. Capitol's vice-president assigned his PA to look after me. I was immediately attracted to Roger Kunz. The feeling was reciprocated.

l. Glenn Wallichs fits Joe's Beatle wig

R. Lord Mills in Beatle wig

Roger's crew cut reminded me of The Kingston Trio, the 1950s All-American college boy folk-singing group. This was frustrating, as Susan Wallichs also had a crush on me.

Somehow it came to Joe's attention that whilst in New York, John Hansard had "used me" to get theatre tickets for his two nieces. Joe was infuriated. He considered Hansard was treating the trip as a joyride, and sacked him from the EMI Board on the spot. This did seem a little extreme. Perhaps he had been looking for a convenient excuse. Hansard had left Joe to sort out the liquidation of Rio Flour Holdings, which was still dragging on. Tilling was available to carry out the formalities. Nothing was said.

Tilling was a popular after-dinner speaker, making frequent and witty reference to the toils of being a Number Two carrying out Number One's orders. Number One, i.e. the chairman, could move on without further thought, leaving Number Two to carry the can. The chairman would be invigorated, whereas he, the company secretary, was left careworn and looking forward to retirement. The handling of Hansard's departure was discreetly executed. I was uncomfortable about the episode and my part in it.

Among the friends I made on my first visit to America were Jim Bollmeyer and his girlfriend Monica, daughter of the Swedish Consul. Jim was a scriptwriter and had shown me round TV studios. Jim and Monica were now married. I rang Jim one evening from my Beverly Hills hotel room. Monica answered, and asked me over. It was late, and no way was I prepared to take a taxi to their beach house in Malibu. She persisted, and eventually explained why she wanted to see me urgently. It could have been easier to explain that Jim was dead. I was deeply shocked. As a teenager, I had witnessed Jim in a drunken fight with a jealous husband, but this was a bit extreme. Apparently he had gone scuba diving and not returned. His body was not recovered. The police treated Monica as a suspect. Had there been a row? She had no explanation. She was now living alone in that beach house. And, even though I was no longer the eighteen-year-old she once knew, I was not sufficiently adult to bring consolation. Instead, I cried myself to sleep, drained and exhausted. Real life replaced the fantasy make-believe world of Tinsel-town and Disneyland, and it was a raw experience.

The greatest excitement came, not from music and entertainment, but from our interest in electronics. High above the beach at Malibu we were taken to a laboratory at night. We witnessed the arrival of a beam of light. We were told we were witnessing the first laser beam. It emanated from the Hughes Aircraft headquarters down the coast at Long Beach.

General Shoop was Chairman of EMIHUS, EMI Electronics' joint company with Hughes Tool based in Long Beach. "Shoopy" gave the last of the Hollywood-style balls, bringing together Howard Hughes's two worlds of entertainment and technology. Our visit was the excuse for him to lay on a party. I was introduced to a dowager who had been a friend of Lord Charles Cavendish. "Charlie," she said, with a knowing look, "had been great fun!" I had not the faintest idea whom she meant. He was in fact the Duke of Devonshire's younger son, who married Adele Astaire, Fred Astaire's sister, and died of drink.

Joe's party partner was Ann Miller, star of the MGM movies *On the Town* and *Kiss me Kate*, where she burst through the 3D screen, high-kicking and singing 'It's too Darn Hot!' Like Joe, she was tall and long-legged. Dancing the foxtrot together they drew gasps of admiration. Escorting her home at the end of the party, they snuggled together in the back seat of the Cadillac. I huddled in the front overcome with jealousy (of her!).

Lord Mills, Chairman of EMI Electronics, wanted to visit EMI-Cossor, our company in Canada, on his way home. This was well off the route, in remote Halifax, Nova Scotia, and Joe had reluctantly agreed to accompany the seventy-four-year-old. For me, the highlight was to be shown round Dalhousie University, where Simon Gray, the famous novelist, had graduated. Dearly would I like to claim this glamorous celebrity as my English Literature supervisor; but I had merely admired him from afar, as he strode under my window in Trinity Great Court, tutoring some other lucky pupil. Back in London, I was surprised to receive a letter from the viscount to thank me for looking after him during that part of the tour.

Joe became Chairman of the Governors of the Central School of Speech and Drama in November. This was the first of many posts he took on whilst I was with him. Equal in prestige to RADA, the School was short of funds, and Joe treated this as another chore, whereas to me, who had actually heard of the School, this was all very exciting. Pressure had been mounted to accept, led by John Davis, Chairman of Ranks, who was bored with the job, as was Sir Michael Balcon, their Appeal Chairman. We were visited by Gwynneth Thurburn, the Principal of the School. She brought along Dame Edith Evans. Baroness Stocks, Lord Simon's friend, invited Joe to dinner to meet Dame Sybil Thorndike and Sir Lewis Casson. On that occasion Joe was sick and fainted during the course of the meal. Fortunately, Feather was on hand to drive him home.

Joe made one condition on accepting the chairmanship. That was that I should sit in on governors' meetings. The School occupied the old Embassy Theatre in Swiss Cottage. We went to productions together, but eventually I was going on my own. The students were anxious to show they could sing as well as act. One boy I found particularly attractive was heard to say, behind my back, "Who does one have to sleep with around here to get a recording contract?"

Joe's real love was the Royal Ballet School, and in particular its Christmas party. EMI's CRL installed a temporary sound system in the large studio. I acted as disc jockey, bringing a suitable selection of LPs which also provided prizes for charades. Norman Newell brought his recording artists, and looked forward to the party even more than Joe.

Arnold Haskell wrote in *Balletomane at Large* how Joe:

brought a group of pop artists to our Christmas Party, providing our students with a concert that it would have been impossible to arrange commercially. I did not always enjoy the noise, apart from the exuberant Mrs Mills, a survival of the old music hall and the late lamented Alma Cogan who would put across a song with perfect timing and great personality, but the end-of-term atmosphere was electric – so were the guitars – and Lockwood's contact with singers and dancers a treat to watch.

At EMI's dinner on 10th December, at the Europa Hotel, it was Norman's turn to provide the cabaret. Students were invited to perform. Joe's favourite, Wayne Sleep, had already graduated to the Royal Ballet Company in September, but came especially to dance for him.

Joe was in demand for Christmas and New Year parties, attending more than two on the same evening, so as not to disappoint. He had found "Rebecca" a job at Morphy Richards and looked forward to their party, but he was not there. According to a member of staff "he was useless", and shortly afterwards found his way back to Manchester Square in the Marketing Department. Never short of an apt repartee, the story went around EMI House that a colleague returning to the shared office after lunch was greeted with: "Would you turn out that light, some of us are trying to sleep here!"

The Beatles were at Norman's New Year's Eve party. Paul McCartney wanted to exchange Joe's Rolls with the EMI 1 number plate for his Ford Anglia. Joe told George Harrison that Sir Arnold Hall's daughter wanted to meet him. In case George had not heard of the Chairman of Hawker Siddeley, Joe explained that he was famous for discovering the cause of the Comet disasters. "The droiver I sup'pose," retorted George.

We saw the Beatles again the next night, when Alma Cogan took us backstage at the Hammersmith Odeon. It was their second Christmas season and the atmosphere in the dressing room was bad. John Lennon was moaning and counting the days for the shows to be over.

Looking back on the year's achievers, the *Sunday Express* City Editor listed the Governor of the Bank of England and the Chairman of the Stock Exchange first and second. Next came:

A Beatle wig for Sir Joseph Lockwood of EMI for being a top pop in the lounge and the kitchen. His team picked the Beatles two years ago. He sold nearly 7 million of their discs last year, and the current one is expected to exceed that. With fridges and irons going well no wonder there was a record in Sir Joe's profits too.

Half-year profits announced on 28th January increased by 40%. Joe was now sixty. Take no notice of the Dawnays of this world. His every intention was to retire not a day before he was seventy. Pensions were non-transferable. This meant his twenty-five years with Henry Simon were frozen. A fresh plan at fifty required twenty years of service. The date he would work towards was clearly stated: 14th November 1974.

Rather than rest on his laurels, he now brought a fresh impetus to the company. He concentrated on the records side, which many thought had already received enough of his attention. Even in this pre-digital age there were always improvements to be made in analogue recording. Compansion, record-groove control and ambiophony, unfamiliar words today, were areas where Joe concentrated his mind unrelentingly. And sound equipment improvement came second only to cost-cutting. There must be a more efficient way of distributing records. A bold plan was hatching in his mind to close long-established depots in Birmingham, Manchester and Glasgow, to be replaced by a single super-store at Hayes.

1965

A Security Risk

The Executive Directors of EMI worked from the head office building on the Hayes site, now a listed building. Each was provided with an office connected to a room for his secretary. All rooms led off one long first-floor corridor. There was no need for directors or their secretaries to use the corridor to reach each other. Likewise, directors could access colleagues through connecting doors via their secretaries' rooms. In this way my office, Mrs Hemson's room, Joe's and John Wall's offices were all interconnected. Wall would pass through Joe's to reach their shared secretary, as Joe was spending most of his time in London.

One morning, early in the new year, Joe came into my room with the message: "Wall wants to see you." To this was added, with a wry smile of warning: "You've been a naughty boy!"

I went into the corridor and knocked on the managing director's door. Wall told me he had been visited by Interpol and informed of my criminal record. It was a complete shock. I explained that Joe knew of the circumstances. Fortunately, Wall was always compliant in all matters relating to Joe, and he acted similarly in this matter. There was no interrogation. Instead, he asked how I got on with Mrs Hemson. Perhaps he was referring to her strong sense of propriety and expectation of respect for her senior position. Fortunately, he could see I really liked her. I had met many Mrs Hemsons in my accountancy days.

No further mention was made of this little matter, but it was not completely forgotten. As Joe, Wall and I stepped off the plane at Charles de Gaulle Airport on March 31st, Wall turned to me and quietly suggested I keep out of trouble. We were in Paris for a board meeting of Pathé Marconi, our French subsidiary. There was no need for the warning. Nevertheless, as we booked into the Royal Monceau, a hotel guest crossing the foyer stopped suddenly. Was he attracted by my looks? Not for the first time I appeared to have a certain "je ne sais quoi" for Frenchmen. It was not to be the last.

The Government was a major EMI client, and we were well covered for national security. We employed officers for military security. We employed officers for civilian security. McMichael, head of military security, came from the military police. He commiserated with me, of all people, about Joe's lax attitude to his advice. Our files must be kept in stronger cabinets, with combination locks known only to ourselves. Joe disclaimed knowledge of any form of classified or sensitive information. At the end of parent company board meetings, he left all his papers on the table. Nothing was retained. I locked the boardroom when these meetings at Manchester Square dispersed to the Connaught Hotel, awaiting Tilling's return from lunch for their removal. Joe was amused at LG's (Len Wood's) devotion to retaining so much paperwork.

I also got on well with Mr Gourd, the surly ex-Metropolitan Police inspector who looked after civilian security. One good turn deserved another. Gourd helped retrieve my car when it was stolen. In return, I had information for him. A boy I met in a pub boasted that his EMI friend was removing quantities of LPs from the Hayes stores at night, and flogging them around Brentford Market. Gourd was intrigued at the society I moved in, but admired my discretion when I declined to reveal my source.

Joe kept a part of his life private. Those "Xs" marked in the office diary, meaning "Keep free of appointments", continued to appear at regular intervals. I took this to mean I was not exclusive, and was free to get up to whatever I liked. I should have liked to be exclusive. Nevertheless, this worked to both our advantages; for had it been so, it would have been difficult to disguise. As it was, no one questioned whether our relationship was anything other than professional.

Joe did not ask about my own private life. He was ambivalent. He knew I was still sleeping with Robin (my Eton friend). He approved. He was amused. Yet when BC received phone calls at the office from his former school admirer, Joe seethed with suppressed jealousy. He was not interested in how I came to meet a young French diplomat or the son of a Prime Minister. Rather than complimenting my discretion at handling these two brief affairs, he gained prestige. He wanted them to know "he knew", such was his insensitivity. My loyalty was total, and I soon found myself in an impossible situation. When Gérard André, Monsieur Le Ministre at the French Embassy, asked me: "Is there anyone else?", I had to say "No". From then on, I was out of my depth. For my affair with Gérard depended on his not knowing my true relationship with Joe.

I rarely caused Joe to be angry. But anger was never far from the surface. Even though I was not the cause, I was frequently the sole witness. In March, Princess Margaret paid Hayes an official visit accompanied by her husband, Lord Snowdon. Feathers were ruffled behind the scenes. Tony Snowdon had come alone a few weeks previously. As adviser to the Council of Industrial Design, he was interested in a new type of stereo record player. We were no longer making gramophones, and this was something Morphy Richards had come up with. It was suggested Snowdon should be presented with the prototype. "Absolutely not," exploded Joe, and had it installed in his own office. However, Snowdon was impressed with his reception at Hayes, and the Royal visit followed at his suggestion.

I was to make arrangements with Kensington Palace. The Private Secretary advised: "Normally Princess Margaret likes only a three-course lunch … On the drinks side, a dry hock or a claret is most acceptable but not champagne. Before lunch, the Princess normally has a gin and tonic with ice and lemon, and Lord Snowdon drinks whiskey and ginger ale. The name of the chauffeur who will be driving the Princess to your factory is Mr Larkin."

The Lord-Lieutenant of the County of Middlesex announced he would be receiving HRH and introducing Joe to her. "Absolutely not!"

Princess Margaret at EMI

fumed Joe. "I already know Margaret". Tilling attempted to explain protocol, but was left to sort out things, as usual. The Lord-Lieutenant was told he would not be required.

Princess Margaret arrived with a large vanity case, and retired to Joe's private lavatory for some time to freshen up. This was a great privilege. Joe kept a lavatory for his exclusive use at Hayes, at Manchester Square and, previously, Henry Simons. It was noticed he was anxious to wash his hands after Margaret's departure. He need not have worried, as the Royal hand was gloved when shaking hands. Some assumed Joe did not like women. In fact, his hand-washing discipline went back to those five years in South America, where he found habits did not compare with Southwell.

Our chauffeur was ready with EMI 1 to drive the Royal couple around the site after lunch. Princess Margaret's preference was to go in her own car, which was larger. Snowdon intervened and directed her into the back of Joe's Rolls. On departure, the Snowdons signed the Gramophone Company Golden Book.

We saw Robert Stigwood regularly, generally at his request, during the first weeks of the year. We three dined together on Saturday, 6th February, little realising we would not see him again. Word filtered back to Manchester Square as to what happened.

Stigwood was in New York on 12th February, arranging a UK tour of American artists. He called at the office of Transglobal, our company set up to license artists in America. He asked Roland Rennie, LG's former PA, to lend him $20,000 to tide him over the weekend as the banks were closed. On Monday, 15th February, Stigwood declared himself bankrupt. He never intended to return the money. Back in London, Rennie was summoned to a meeting with a furious Joe at 9.30 a.m. on Friday, 19th February. One can only assume Stigwood used his friendship with Joe as a means of influencing Rennie. But this betrayal was compounded when John Leyton and Stephen Komlosy, Stigwood's young business partner, came to Joe with similar tales of how they had been deceived. The funds Komlosy's father provided to set him up in business were all gone. There was no forgiveness for someone who had cheated his friends in such a way as far as Joe was concerned. Nothing would sway Joe from his principles, but these were to be sorely tested. For no one knew better than Joe, Stigwood's ability, which he had been the first to recognise. Years later Bernard Delfont and David Land, two great impresarios, attempted a reconciliation, but Joe was implacable. Stigwood joined Fred Lockwood in oblivion.

Rennie soon left EMI to run Polydor Records. Stigwood was back in business and assigning his artists to the Polydor label. The most successful of these were the Bee Gees, whose contract should have been with EMI. No one dared tell Joe that Stigwood had gone into partnership with Brian Epstein, whom he had met late-night gambling at the 21 Club in Curzon Street. In 1967, the Bee Gees' father would send Brian Epstein a demo tape from Australia, and Stigwood auditioned the four boys when they arrived in England. Something far worse could have happened. There was no intention to repay the $20,000, and the Beatles' contract was under discussion with EMI. Could Stigwood take them away?

While Stigwood was away in New York, things were carrying on as normal at Manchester Square. EMI Records was hosting a reception in the ground floor theatre for Joe Meek, the independent producer. It was at Meek's Holloway Road flat that John Leyton recorded 'Johnny Remember Me' in 1962, before Stigwood took over the actor's management. Now, Meek was hoping for similar success with Heinz, the blond member of The Tornados, who was going solo with 'Diggin' My Potatoes'. Arthur Muxlow, EMI's artists promotions manager, devoted much time to this release, but to no avail. Muxlow was an insignificant individual with a Walter Mitty personality. He produced a regular programme of new releases for Radio Luxembourg. Donning a huge pair of earphones, he mentally doubled in size as he took command of the session. He was the only person to make disparaging remarks about Joe: "Everyone knows the chairman prefers boy singers to girls." As a matter of course, Joe chatted with Meek and his protégé. I noted Meek's shy and respectful manner towards him. Pale faced, looking younger than his thirty-two years, wearing a grey suit and white shirt, I had the impression he lacked the personality of a successful producer. He was grateful Joe showed any interest in him. I believe this was the only time they met, apart from the appointment he requested shortly before he shot himself.

Joe now found himself devoting more time to Brian Epstein. The dozen or more times they met in 1965 proved beneficial. Under discussion was the 1962 contract George Martin had signed the Beatles to for five years. Starting at the much-publicised "penny-a-track", with adjustments, it now stood at 5% royalty rate.

Whilst attending a recording session at Abbey Road on 16th February, Joe took it into his head to invite all the Beatles and their partners to dinner the following Friday evening. His flat was too small, and I reserved the dining room at the Connaught Hotel in nearby Carlos Place, where the EMI Board lunched regularly. This was fortunate, as the numbers grew rapidly to eighteen. George Martin and Judy were naturally included, and I added Shirley Spence, who shared Judy's office, to the list. I was summoned by George, who addressed me sharply. Did I not realise that Shirley was Ron Richards' secretary? Ron was George's assistant, and hugely successful in his own right, recording the Hollies. Although not mentioned by George, it was Ron, and not George, who was initially in charge at the Beatles audition. He was added to the invitation list, which already included LG and Carol, Joe's London-based secretary. Arrangements were left in the capable hands of Mr Rose, the banqueting manager. Dinner was to be 7.30 p.m. for 8.15 p.m.

Late that afternoon, Joe was at Rediffusion's TV studios for a "live" performance of *Ready Steady Go*. Elkan Allen, the producer, banned artists miming on the show. This came as a blow, as it diminished the aural impact of the recordings. The Beatles mimed at all their TV appearances. The press expected a big row. Instead, Joe and Elkan expressed mutual respect, agreed to disagree, and reached a form of compromise.

We arrived punctually at the Connaught at 7.30, to find all the Beatles and their wives and partners sitting waiting patiently. The meal went smoothly. No one thought to circulate the menu for signatures. And no speeches were proposed, until Ringo rose to his feet. We were regaled with stories of his experiences working as a steward on the Mersey pleasure boats. As the oldest Beatle, it became him to toast his host.

News of who was dining in the Carlos Suite had spread rapidly among the hotel guests. It was impossible to escape. They crowded both sides of the corridor for our exit. One guest, introduced as head of the New York Fire Department, requested autographs for his daughters back home. LG claims that John Lennon hailed Joe to "Get your chauffeur to move your ruddy car!"True to form, Feather would have parked in the best place. Was he still on duty that evening, to offer guests a lift home? Joe's flat was just round the corner.

Mr Rose stood silently to watch the confusion. To him, the whole thing had been a disaster. He had not been told who Joe was entertaining. These were not our normal guests! He brushed aside my offer of thanks: "Never again!" I felt I had betrayed a dutiful friend.

Joe decided Epstein was getting bad advice from his accountants. He introduced Messrs Graham and Kelly from our own Tax Department. Epstein invited Joe to dine at the Belfry, a restaurant near his flat in Belgravia. Over dinner, Joe expounded on the danger of providing successful artists with excessive wealth from disproportionately high royalty rates. As an example, he cited Frank Sinatra's ingratitude to Capitol Records, who "had picked him up out of the gutter!"

Learning that Brian was a keen racegoer, Joe invited him to Ascot, where Smiths Industries took a box each season. This year, Ralph and Beryl Gordon-Smith were entertaining in a top-tier box in the brand-new grandstand. As Gold Cup day approached, Joe had another engagement. I was delegated to escort Brian. We met in Belgravia and set off in his maroon Rolls Royce. His grey top hat matched the fetching lavender-grey gloves.

My father frequently remarked approvingly on Brian's immaculate appearance and well-cut suits. As we drove up to the course, another good dresser greeted Brian: Frankie Vaughan's stage appearance was the top-hatted, white tie and tails, cane-strutting boulevardier. Brian, the rookie, fitted perfectly into the Ascot scene. He was already

Ready for Ascot

planning his own box and tickets for the Royal Enclosure next year. He had "a good day". We learnt on return to London that his chauffeur had also "made some money on the horses". The Gordon-Smiths were very easy hosts to get on with, and Joe knew I would have no difficulty.

Brian brought an associate to a meeting on 8th June. We were introduced to Geoffrey Ellis, Brian's Liverpool friend who had given up a career in insurance to run his artists management company. Something happened to Geoffrey as he sat across the table from me in the boardroom that afternoon. A relationship was born that day, to endure until Brian died two years later. Joe said that despite many meetings, he scarcely knew Brian. Geoffrey and I had much more in common, having been respectively at Oxford and Cambridge. Geoffrey's Oxford friends were amused that someone with a good law degree should end up running pop stars. Staid and conservative, Geoffrey was someone Brian could rely on completely. When Geoffrey was formally appointed to the Board of Directors of Nems Enterprises Ltd, Brian's family company, and of Nems Presentations Ltd, Brian wrote: "Dear Bill, I am anxious to mark the occasion by gathering together a few close friends and business associates. I hope very much that you will be able to join us at Brown's Hotel."

Looking back, I am sure our affair played a big part in Brian's decision in 1967 to re-sign the Beatles, collectively and individually, to a further nine-year world-breaking exclusive golden contract with EMI. We were so respectable! Geoffrey claims not to have been consulted: "Brian just did it!" No doubt there was enormous input from Joe and LG over the three years the Beatles were recording, with contractual arrangements still in the air. Circumspection was paramount. I think Joe and LG were unaware of the affair, although they had reason to suspect. I slipped up once and was made to eat humble pie for an indiscretion. Not realising that "penny returns" were a well-kept secret, I mentioned their existence to Geoffrey. It was standard practice to make an arbitrary deduction from artists' royalties, based on an estimated number of returned records. I was not to receive recognition for my part in the most lucrative deal in the history of popular music, which was signed in 1967.

Nems Presentations included ownership of the Saville Theatre and sponsorship of stage shows. Joe, aware of Brian's theatre interest, proposed making him a Governor of the Central School of Speech and Drama. He put forward this suggestion at the first of the board meetings it was agreed I should attend. It was held at 5.30 p.m., followed promptly at "7 pm Poetry Recital – leave by 8 pm". Philippa, Lady Astor was amused at my attendance, and added a light touch of her own: "Do I detect that the new principal has a speech impediment?" she remarked endearingly at the man's unmistakable stutter. Another governor, Lady Kilmuir, impressed Joe less: "That woman's husband was a bigot," he hissed in my ear. She was married to the Conservative Home Secretary, David Maxwell Fife, who made an example of Edward Montagu, and delayed implementation of the 1957 Wolfenden Report's recommendation on Consulting Adults in Private until 1967. Elderly governor Dame Edith Evans graciously accepted a lift in the Rolls after boasting she usually walked back to Piccadilly from Swiss Cottage.

Mixing with luminaries of pop and stage did not mean we were neglecting our classical recording artists. Classic music also had its show business stars.

To celebrate Sir Malcolm Sargent's seventieth birthday in April, a luncheon was given in the Pinafore Room at the Savoy. David Bicknell was instructed "to invite a few of my close personal friends". These included Prince Philip, Lord Mountbatten and Lord Zuckerman. Those regretting a previous engagement included the Duke of Kent, Sir Laurence Olivier and Sir Thomas Armstrong. Archbishop of

Canterbury, Lord Fisher, was heard to whisper on arrival: "Can anyone tell me why I'm here?" Bicknell kindly invited me "to make up the numbers", and distribute the seating place cards. The card for Prince Philip was left blank with "Reserved" in place of a name: he was coming incognito. Unfortunately, the card remained on the table, and HRH was amused, insulted and baffled as he took his seat. He added an exclamation mark when asked to sign the table plan later. He was in great form. Joe was presenting Sir Malcolm with a special volume of his recordings and listing his honours and achievements. He was surprised to add Fellowship of the Royal Zoological Society. "Yes," interrupted Philip, "there's a Sir Malcolm Sargent House."

Sir Malcolm Sargent's 70th Birthday Lunch

Prince Philip had something he wanted to ask Joe, which had to wait for another occasion. Invited to a garden party at Buckingham Palace in July, Joe was instructed: "Please be in the Bow Room by 3.30 p.m. and ask one of the footmen to contact Mr Orr or Admiral Bonham Carter to let them know you have arrived." Joe's letter to Prince Philip's secretary the next day explains the reason for this special treatment:

Yesterday at Buckingham Palace, HRH The Duke of Edinburgh asked me whether the picture was finished, and you will remember that I could not think what he was talking about. I feel terribly guilty on reflection. Of course, he obviously meant the painting made of him, with me, which hangs in our Boardroom. I had, of course, forgotten that the picture was made after his Hayes visit. His memory is obviously much better than mine, and I hope you will apologise on a suitable occasion.

Joe shows Prince Philip record presses at Hayes

The picture in question was an amateur effort, based on a photograph taken of Joe showing Philip around the factory the previous year. Joe, not realising the Royal visitor had granted the artist an extra sitting, had refused a similar request. Luckily, Prince Philip had not asked to see the picture, which remained incomplete and hangs inconspicuously in a remote corner.

David Bicknell had a motive in including me in the Malcolm Sargent lunch: "to make up the numbers", as he put it. He needed an ally when dealing with the chairman. Each year he had to make a case for spending £500 on a full-page advertisement in the Glyndebourne Festival programme. This was too large a sum to come out of EMI Records' budget and was not treated as a charitable donation. The programme was a beautiful souvenir of the whole season. For a reward, each advertiser was offered four seats for one evening of their choice. As the exclusive producer of Glyndebourne Opera recordings, there was no way EMI could not be included. Nevertheless, Bicknell was made to grovel for the money every year. There must have been a row in the past.

On numerous occasions Bicknell's diplomacy was required when dealing with artists, involving the chairman. One of many memos addressed to me is my favourite. It is headed "Re: TITO GOBBI":

11th October, 1967

CONFIDENTIAL

_____

Mr W. Cavendish.

Re: TITO GOBBI

Reference Tito Gobbi's letter to the Chairman dated 4th October.

1. I am sorry that Tito Gobbi is upset as I engaged him 20 years ago, he is an old friend and has rendered great service to the Company, but is now approaching the end of his career.

2. He is furious because we have engaged Dietrich Fischer-Dieskau (with Sir John Barbirolli's full approval) to sing the baritone part in Verdi's "Otello" next September, and he would dearly like to sing the role.

3. Barbirolli has asked me to keep his name out of it as they are both Venetians!; and, therefore, Gobbi's displeasure is directed against this Department. But we are used to this and he will get over it.

4. He talks of compensation – but this is ridiculous – we do not pay compensation to artists for NOT singing a role for which they were NEVER engaged!

5. I attach a conciliatory draft letter for the Chairman in reply.

J. D. Bicknell.

One might think such sensitive situations were confined to the classic world. Not so. The pop world was no less convoluted.

George Martin was negotiating to leave EMI. LG drew up a new contract to continue recording the Beatles. George insisted on being photographed with Joe signing the contract. No one was more keen to get away than Judy. She had virtually been living with George, a married man, for fifteen years. This was quite public, and she was resentful. It came out in disparaging remarks made about staff and artists alike. Staff photographer John Dove was overheard by George referring to Judy as "That bloody bitch!" Yet, Brian Epstein claimed Judy was the first friendly face he met at EMI. It was Judy who invited him over to Manchester Square from the HMV store in Oxford Street, where he had been transferring a Beatles demo tape to disc. Judy liked Brian, and made the appointment for the Beatles to audition at Abbey Road. I received less favourable treatment when friends of mine bypassed her to get to George with their "terrible demo".

George and Judy needed someone to share the great emotion they experienced the day they left EMI, and I was that person. They took me to dine at their favourite local restaurant, Genevieve, in Thayer Street.

From that moment, Judy became a different person. This was the Lockhart Smiths' little girl, my mother told me, who had seen me in my pram, presumably in 1941! My mother assumed we were friends, and now we were. George and Judy were also free in another respect. They married soon after, and started a family the following summer. Their wedding reception was held in the Fellows Garden of the Royal Zoological Society, home to the London Zoo in Regent's Park, halfway between Manchester Square and Abbey Road.

George represented a new trend in pop music. The three A&R managers remaining at Manchester Square were unaffected. Wally Ridley, at HMV, the complete professional, continued to record his "popular", as opposed to pop, artists, Joe Loss, George Melachrino, Semprini, George Mitchell and the Black and White Minstrels. Joe Loss prided himself on being EMI's longest-serving artist.

Norrie Paramor, at Columbia, fared less well. I was dispatched to the fourth floor to discuss Joe's latest brainwave. He proposed putting together four boys, any four boys "off the streets", to "manufacture" what was later to be called "a boy band". Norrie rejected the idea as impractical. His own group, The Shadows, best known as Cliff Richard's backing group, with five Number 1 singles, including 'Apache', had grown up and developed as musicians together. A similar argument could be made for Capitol's Beach Boys, who were virtually a band of brothers. Unfortunately for Norrie, The Monkees, a previously unheard-of group, appeared at the top of the American charts. All four of its members came from different backgrounds, but with one thing in common: they had answered an advertisement worded in the very way Joe was suggesting a few weeks before.

Norman Newell, also at Columbia, was later to blame the 1960s pop scene for destroying his world of well-written songs and compositions. Yet he was continuing to be successful. Ken Dodd, the comedian, unexpectedly had a huge hit with 'Tears'. Joe presented him with a gold disc for selling a million singles. Norman failed to get Ken Dodd to sign a contract. This was an unusual situation. The artist's failure to accept convention was later exposed. The Inland Revenue took him to court for refusing to pay tax on his earnings.

Johnny Mathis, the mellow-voiced young American crooner, was a particular favourite among the artists Norman knew Joe enjoyed meeting. A letter kept by Joe showed the enjoyment was mutual: "Sir Joseph – Besides being sincere I often try to immulate (sic) a gentleman in all ways, you are very generous with your most presious (sic) posession (sic) – Your Time! You are also a VERY KIND MAN. Thank you and God Bless, Johnny."

Mathis had been under the control of a harsh and dominating manager, Helen Noga, from a very, very young age. Joe played a part in removing him from her clutches.

One evening, Norman invited Joe to dine at the Empress Restaurant. Mathis was staying nearby at the Mayfair Hotel, and Joe offered to collect him. Ushered up to his room, Joe was greeted by a completely naked Mathis. Joe told me: "He was a very naughty boy!"

I experienced a similar unexpected lack of inhibition in the artist. Mike Regan joined EMI to look after artists relations. He came from managing Russ Conway, another of Norman's artists, who had two Number 1 singles: 'Side Saddle' and 'Roulette'. Before that he was a Butlin's Holiday Camp Red Coat entertainer. Small, quiet, unassuming, he was a perfect foil to the egos of the artists put in his charge. Our friendship dated from the morning I phoned down to his office to say "The chairman wants to meet you." Possibly because he had not heard my voice before, and being a natural joker, he assumed it was a hoax. Why should someone so low down be summoned up to the sixth floor?

Some years after his stay at the Mayfair Hotel, Johnny Mathis, now a very big star, had a large luxury apartment placed at his disposal when appearing in London. Mike noted from the address that it was across the road from where I lived. I have no idea who decided the star should meet Edward Montagu at my flat. The two obviously knew each other very well. My flat was a ground-floor bedsit, with the bed only partly disguised. Oblivious to my existence, ignoring any form of introduction, the two flew fully clothed to the bed. However much they enjoyed their encounter, it certainly enhanced my prestige. A neighbour, seeing Johnny Mathis leave my flat, never fails to tell me how impressed he was. Mike also made use of my Mini Cooper. We collected teenage Liza Minnelli from a luxury flat in Chelsea. She had been invited to the Variety Club of Great Britain luncheon and wanted Mike's reassurance "that the event was important enough" for her to attend. We also drove Alan Freeman to Hever Castle to compere the disco at a charity ball. "Fluff", as he was nicknamed, treated the upper classes to the same treatment he gave his "pop pickers". The DJ slept soundly in the back of the car on the way down to Kent, as he did on the return to London at dawn.

Joe showed no interest in my escapades. He had plenty of his own. For example, his appointments diary for 10th May stated baldly: "6 pm Scotland Yard. Meet in saloon bar of Red Lion. Ask for Pinkerton." It was customary for the police to invite VIPs to tour the Black Museum.

For overseas trips, it was more acceptable for a boss to be seen around with his PA, and on such occasions we were inseparable. We went abroad regularly. In August, we flew from our West German headquarters in Cologne to Berlin. We looked into the Eastern Sector at buildings formerly owned by our company. We were reminded of a similar situation after the First World War when the Gramophone Company's original foothold in Europe was confiscated. This was Hanover, the birthplace of Emile Berliner.

Dr Veder put us into a taxi, instructing the driver to take us through Checkpoint Charlie. He did not accompany us. It was the only period in Joe's long life spent on Communist soil. Apart from the contrast between East and West, he was even less impressed when forced to exchange good Marks for bad, with nothing to purchase but a box of matches. Sightseeing lasted less than thirty minutes.

Later that month we were staying at the Baur au Lac in Zurich. I came down to breakfast in my brand-new John Michael suit, on which our area supervisor remarked approvingly. The look on Joe's face confirmed he did not agree. After the meal, I went back to my room and put on something different. We had companies registered in the tax-free Canton of Zug, but no staff. A Swiss lawyer acted as our host. For the second time that day, I met with disapproval. Intrigued at Zurich's reputation as the drug capital of Europe, in such a law-abiding country as Switzerland, I admitted I had been out the previous evening exploring the hippy areas. Nor was Joe too thrilled when our lawyer drove us up to a chateau where the EMI International Classical Artists Committee was "conferring", to be greeted by Peter Andry in crisp white tennis shorts.

From Zurich we flew to Portugal, where we spent the weekend at Estoril. Whenever we left the hotel, Joe was mobbed by street urchins drawn to him like a magnet. They could tell he enjoyed the experience. When he proceeded to photograph them, they posed provocatively.

From the Ritz Hotel in Lisbon, next was the Ritz in Madrid. Then by train to Barcelona. This was an overnight journey, made memorable by an unscheduled stop at dawn in the middle of nowhere. Orson

A light for a street vendor in Portugal

Welles disembarked. He was joining his film crew on location with *Chimes at Midnight*, which he was directing.

Two new directors joined the EMI Board during the year. Former Attorney General and President of the Board of Trade, Lord Shawcross had abandoned the law, politics and public life to take on a string of remunerative directorships, including an office and secretary provided by Shell. One reason for the career change was the new ruling to tax the pension pool that barristers had been able to build up from fees. Hartley Shawcross, ex-Labour minister, and member of White's, with an expensive way of life, had a young wife, three children, and his wife's horses to support. I was instructed to await his arrival for his first board meeting. We ascended in the lift which had been held in readiness on the ground floor. I noticed that Joe's ex-wartime boss was visibly trembling in anticipation.

John Read, an Englishman, came as an executive director from the Ford Motor Corporation, where top jobs were reserved for Americans. "He put his name with headhunters!" Joe was heard to remark disparagingly. He was interviewed by Lord Mills and Kit Dawnay. But it was Dawnay who must take responsibility for grooming Read to succeed Joe, and eventually bankrupt EMI, ten years later. Joe never looked on him as his heir-apparent, but when the time came to hand over he deigned to observe "he may grow into the job." From day one, he criticised Read's judgement: "That man is gullible." This early comment followed Read agreeing to see Fritz Philips's son-in-law, who Joe had brushed off at the AGM: "They're after him to join Moral Re-Armament." MRA was a well-intentioned but discredited Christian organisation.

Joe never expressed a view on Read's wife, Dorothy. I had difficulty. Quite simply, her ambitions for her husband spelt death for the company. Her arrival on the scene took place in October, when the board was entertaining the Directors of Capitol Records at the Garrick Club. Humphrey Tilling, a Garrick member, arranged the dinner to impress the Americans. Centre of attraction was the weighing machine in the club's entrance hall, for the use of jockeys and Byronian figures in Regency times. The Californians took it in turn to sit in the machine. Wives were included in the social occasion, and that meant Mrs Read. From the moment that large, coarse, vulgar woman opened her mouth – "Ever so pleased ter meet yer" – there was no way those first impressions could ever change. If only she had been at the job interview with Dawnay, Mills (or was it Gordon-Smith?) things might have turned out differently. I am sure she was waiting outside the door.

A tall, somewhat dour and colourless, American frequently found his way to our office that autumn. Edward Roth was forming a secret consortium to bid for the Yorkshire-based regional commercial television station. In so doing, he was to bring Joe into the larger-than-life sphere of the very large Lord Goodman. For the next twenty years, Joe and the famous solicitor were barely apart in what can only be called a mutual admiration society.

The first meeting of the consortium was held at the offices of the *Daily Telegraph* in Fleet Street. We were shown into the boardroom by the proprietor's butler, who was more formally attired than our own James. Despite finding ourselves at penthouse level, we looked out of the boardroom window on to a swathe of neatly mown lawn. Our hosts were Michael Berry, the Editor-in-Chief, and his older brother, Lord Camrose, the chairman. This relationship was made clear when

Berry addressed the meeting sharply at one point: "Would you please keep quiet, my brother is trying to say something!" Lord Goodman arrived late. He was a notorious timekeeper. Joe recognised him as the grossly overweight figure he saw regularly at first nights, sitting alone. I compared Arnold Goodman to Samuel Johnson, for wit, and to Alfred Hitchcock and Francis L. Sullivan, for looks.

The consortium made an impressive and entertaining group, and it was sad when EMI had to withdraw. The North was represented by newspaper publishers and Lady Crathorne, who was noted for restoring the Georgian Theatre in Richmond. Nancy Crathorne bewailed the loss of Joe. He gave her lifts in his car, and hospitality at Manchester Square. The Independent Television Authority (ITA) ruled EMI out of the consortium for owning the Grade Organisation. EMI's takeover of the publicly-listed talent agency had been done in a hurry. The Grade Organisation represented many EMI recording artists. It was run by Leslie Grade, whose two older brothers had interests: Lew Grade at ATV, the commercial station, and Bernard Delfont, with several theatres. When Leslie had a stroke, the family decided to sell. The ITA ruled there was a conflict of interest for an artists' agency to hold a stake in a TV company. When EMI eventually took control of a commercial station, it meant goodbye to Grade as well.

Edward Roth would have found satisfaction at his match-making had he taken his seat in the stalls at Covent Garden on 14th December. Looking up at the Grand Tier boxes, his eyes would have rested on Lord Goodman with his guests, for a performance of *Simon Boccanegra*. Seated on either side, in evening dress, were Joe and the Minister for the Arts, Jennie Lee, who was responsible for Goodman's appointment as Chairman of the Arts Council of Great Britain.

Access to one's own private box during opera performances proved ideal for poor timekeepers such as Lord Goodman. Joe recalled sitting quite alone for the whole first act of Richard Strauss's *Die Frau ohne Schatten*, or, as he called it when repeating the story of that excruciating ordeal "Die Frau ohne Schlatten".

Towards the end of the year, my position as PA became more intimate. Deprived of my offices at Hayes and Manchester Square, I was now working in Joe's room. Not only in his room, but sharing his desk to save on space, as he put it. When my presence was not required, I moved into the boardroom until summoned. For ten years, I sat beneath the original HMV picture. Inevitably I overheard many unexpected phone conversations, especially as Joe was amused to keep the speaker on. Lord Boothby, who could only claim a casual acquaintanceship, came on once: "Joe, I'm not a rich man. I have some EMI shares. Is it a good time to sell?" Joe was unlikely to be drawn on a subject so close to his heart as our share price. He would complain we were undervalued, as would any company chairman. Yet he maintained the market was generally right, and prices eventually settled at their true value.

But I was never allowed to feel totally secure, as I jealously retained my position. Sir David Webster rang from the Royal Opera House one day: "Joe, I know you like to change your assistants from time to time. I have a young man I should like you to see." Of course, Joe was pleased to oblige. The only comment I received on the interview was "the boy had on rather a lot of scent." The General Administrator of the Opera House apologised to me later for not realising sooner that Joe had a permanent attachment.

That Joe could take me for granted became evident when we set out to look for a country house retreat. Whether or not it was in his mind that I should share weekends with him, that was to be the outcome. At the time I was in a relationship with a Frenchman, which lasted five years, and which I kept secret from Joe. Joe and I toured Buckinghamshire, Berkshire and Hertfordshire looking for a suitable property near London, until we found the ideal location on the Bucks/Berks border early in the new year.

After my previous experiences in France, I should have been more cautious about overtures from a young diplomat at the French Embassy. At a dinner party, the sort of party one is still invited to up to the age of thirty, as the saying goes (I was still twenty-four), Z began to flirt outrageously. He said Malcolm Bullock had invited him for the weekend. Wasn't it shameful Malcolm hadn't invited us for the same weekend? I knew exactly what Z meant. He also seemed to know about me. We met a couple of times. I was one of many conquests. When Z returned to Paris, he qualified for Thackeray's perceptive description: "For who ever yet met a Frenchman, come out of England, that has not left half a dozen families miserable, and brought away as many hearts in his pocket book?"

He invited me to lunch at the Angus Steak House in Knightsbridge, close to the French Embassy. He was sitting in a corner alone, nursing a bottle of burgundy when I arrived. We were joined by a small middle-aged and slightly bald man with glasses, who was introduced as Monsieur Le Ministre Gérard André. At the end of the meal, when Z had already left, Gérard asked, "Is there anyone else?" The truthful answer to this direct question should, of course, been: "Yes – Joe". But there was no way I was going to admit this to someone I had just met. After all, it was as if a perfect stranger had asked me in the street whether I was available! In fact, a customer at Harrods, when I once worked behind the counter one Christmas, had done just that. This was different. Gérard was very respectable and respected by Z. And this began a clandestine affair.

The challenge was to keep secret my feelings for Joe from Gérard, and at the same time to conceal the existence of Gérard from Joe.

Years later, I remembered a Saturday matinée when Joe and I were sitting behind a little man in a half-empty theatre. As the performance began, a tall youth joined him. The couple must have been Gérard and his former companion of the time, Billy McCarty. What a strange world. Memory plays interesting tricks.

Gérard's and Joe's worlds overlapped. Yet only twice did my heart leap at the prospect of having to account for myself. After dining with Julian Gibbs, as we were making our farewells, Lord Moncell called across to me: "Give my love to Gérard!" We were already in the street and luckily Joe did not catch what Gérard's friend was saying. And the second occasion occurred in 1982, when Peter Heyworth, the music critic, and another friend of Gérard, came to Joe's flat. Joe agreed to give his views on Walter Legge for the biography Heyworth was writing, *Otto Klemperer: His Life and Times*. He recognised me as I was seeing him out. The door was already open, and I bundled him out. Joe was standing in the hallway. "What was that about?" he asked.

That Christmas, Norman Newell brought a starry group of artists to entertain the Royal Ballet School students. Once more, I was in charge of the disco. Our friend David Frost "dropped in" on his commute between Heathrow and J. F. Kennedy airports. Mr Fergyson, the prim bursar, dispensed drinks in his small office. Dora Bryan took charge, with the memorable comment "That's what I call a dirty glass!" as she upped the measures. This was to be the last of our traditional Royal Ballet School Christmas parties. In future, the students decided to plan their own — or that was how it was put across. Norman was devastated. I knew the true story, when Fergyson confided in me "that man's a terrible pansy", and, as such, was not welcome on the premises. For years Norman asked me how something that had been so appreciated and so much enjoyed, especially by Joe, had been stopped. I could not possibly tell him. He was angry and the hurt festered throughout our friendship. Lord Hastings, Chairman of the Royal Ballet Benevolent Fund, and Sir David Webster from the Royal Opera House were Joe's guests at that last party. David Webster wrote: "What I saw of you party at the School was marvellous; thank you so much for inviting me".

Norman was on duty that Christmas. He took it in turns with Norrie Paramor to provide the cabaret for the annual dinner. EMI Electronics and EMI Records executives attended in equal numbers. Joe's speech covered both branches. They did not mix comfortably. Lord Mills leant across on one occasion, when Adam Faith was singing, to remark: "That man's wearing make-up!" Norman excelled himself. He squeezed the cast of *Hello Dolly!*, led by Beryl Reid accompanied by Geoff Love and his orchestra, on to the Royal Garden Hotel Ballroom floor. As an added touch to please Joe, he included students from the Royal Ballet and Central Schools, performing pieces especially devised for the occasion. Eight Central School of Speech and Drama students wrote to thank Joe for some LPs: "Thank you for allowing us to appear before such a professional audience. It was quite an experience, and although our contribution was rather different from the rest of the programme, we hope it was entertaining in its own particular way."

The Chairman's Dinner, as it was called, later became a "Dinner Dance". No cabaret, but entertainment as usual from that well-known after-dinner speaker Humphrey Tilling.

EMI's "Top Brass" (LG Wood second row on left)

In conference

1966

Mountbatten Commands, Goodman Requests, The Chairman Instructs

David Frost started the new year with a trend imported from America: the breakfast meeting. On 7th January, he invited the Prime Minister to breakfast at the Connaught Hotel. David's manager, Richard Armitage, described Joe in the corridor, doing a double-take on seeing Harold Wilson and retreating rapidly, on the assumption he had come to the wrong meeting. *Private Eye* depicted the PM, Frost, Lord Longford, Joe and others, surveying a bare tablecloth with overturned HP sauce bottle (the PM's favourite) and cornflakes packet. A bête-noire of the magazine, Captain Robert "Bob" Maxwell MP, was another guest.

For Joe, the trend was not particularly novel. Invited to Goodman's flat in December, he was greeted by the solicitor in pyjamas and dressing-gown. The same month he was breakfasting with Jules Thorn at 9.30 a.m. on a Saturday morning.

Apart from Goodman and Thorn, Joe also found time for Lord Mountbatten, who invited him to stay at Broadlands. Recently retired as Chief of the Defence Staff, and at a loose end, Mountbatten had rediscovered his early interest in radio. He was a qualified wireless operator and instructor. To raise radio's profile, he created the Institution of Electronic and Radio Engineers, in direct competition to established Institution of Electrical Engineers. Already a companion of the IEE, and now a companion of the IERE, Joe did the usual, and delegated such matters to Percy Allaway at EMI Electronics. Yet Mountbatten was in the habit of dealing with the top man. "Always go to the top" was a motto Joe shared with this distinguished suitor, whom he had hoped – but failed – to evade. Joe would not have included himself among hero-worshippers of Mountbatten, but something happened in January to earn his unqualified admiration.

Joe invited Mountbatten and Graham Clifford from the IERE to dine at his flat, just the three of them. During the course of the meal, Clifford asked to be excused. Absent for a considerable time, he was discovered slumped on the lavatory floor, covered in vomit and diarrhoea. He had been too scared to admit to being allergic to oysters. It was evident he would take time to recover. Yet Mountbatten insisted on remaining until he was satisfied that his factotum was well enough, however long it took. Joe considered this the sign of a great man. Conversation was continued the following week over dinner at the Royal Thames Yacht Club, conveniently situated near Mountbatten's mews house in Knightsbridge.

An invitation to attend the Trooping of the Colour on Horse Guards Parade in June, as guest of the Colonel of the Life Guards, was initially declined. We had already planned to visit the Morphy Richards factories in Scotland, staying with my ex-Housemaster at Glenalmond School and with my family in Yorkshire. The refusal to attend the parade was not permitted. It was a command. The colonel was Mountbatten, who was also Gold Stick, which, barring royalty, is the most important figure at the ceremony. Reluctantly, donning tails on a blazing Saturday morning and holding a signed letter from Mountbatten, "please give the bearer every facility", promising speedy departure, we reported for duty. Despite this delay, we were able to set off for the north in normal clothes. The formality and spectacle of the Trooping does not compare to the Combined Services' Annual Royal Tournament at Earls Court, a far more theatrical and exciting event.

An invitation from Goodman was also something not to be declined. His wit was second-to-none, endearing him to his wide circle of listeners, and making them forget how ugly he was. Brilliant though it was, his wit was quite impossible to convey. There were gems that convulsed Joe in the retelling. Whether it was an informal supper at 10 p.m. with philosopher Sir Isaiah Berlin, or a black-tie do at 8 p.m. with Sir Allen Lane, founder of Penguin paperbacks, there were never less than eight for dinner. Goodman's main interest was music – for example, Berlin was on the board of the Royal Opera House. Making up the numbers would be his brother Theo, who, to Joe's secret amusement, was a musicologist, which seemed a strange profession.

Goodman was asked by the Labour Government to report on the state of London orchestras in 1964. He concluded that all five (including the BBC Symphony) should be retained. Joe maintained "London has far too many orchestras". Despite this and other views on which they differed, the two batted together and supported each other. Jennie Lee appointed Goodman Chairman of the Arts Council in 1965. Joe became a member in 1967, purely as a favour to Goodman.

Goodman, who had brought Allen Lane into the Yorkshire TV bid consortium, had the novel idea that EMI should buy Penguin Books. A proposal to merge the two companies' up-to-date storage facilities for books and records in West London seemed feasible. Negotiations were top secret and only known four people, i.e. Goodman, Lane, Joe and me, or so I was led to believe. Imagine my shock when a car screeched to a halt outside South Kensington tube station, and hailed me as I was crossing the road: "EMI's taking over Penguin!" I recognised the driver as someone I hardly knew and who worked in the City. Laughing hilariously at the expression on my face, he re-wound the car window and drove off at speed. Shortly afterwards, Penguin was taken over by another company, without the newspapers being aware of EMI's dalliance. I began to wonder whether I had been imagining that encounter in South Ken.

At the time, I avoided an indiscretion as the result of a misunderstanding. Visiting Harry Williams, who was recovering in hospital, I bumped into his ex-pupil and lover, James Mitchell, whose publishing company Mitchell Beazley had brought out *The Joy of Gay Sex* and the *Pocket Wine* booklets. I must have mentioned I knew Allen Lane socially, and this would have been of interest to James. I declined

James's dinner invitation, as I did not fancy what it might entail. Rather than sex, I realised later he was anxious to pursue the subject of Penguin Books. He went on to produce a series of Pocket Guides, which would have fitted in well with the paperback publisher.

Jennie Lee, the Minister for the Arts, came to our office at 9.15 a.m. one day. She was sent by Goodman. Aneurin Bevan's widow was given responsibility by Harold Wilson to set up his brainchild, the University of the Air. This was something he had thought up during a holiday in the Scilly Isles. Joe criticised the Government's estimate of £20 million, suggesting that sharing transmitters with the BBC and the IBA, the new station would only cost £6.5 million to set up. He noted that its advisory council consisted of twenty academics, and not a single expert on telecommunications.

The small, rotund, elderly Scottish woman threw off her heavy fur coat, knelt on the floor, spreading her papers on the carpet, where Joe joined her.

Harold Wilson claimed the success of the University of the Air (the Open University) as his proudest achievement during his time as Prime Minister. Joe presented Jennie Lee with a privately pressed LP of Bevan's speeches, selected from the BBC Sound Archives. "Nye" Bevan was reputed to be the best speaker in the House of Commons, after Winston Churchill.

Ever since that visit to *The Times*, watching the next day's edition come off the presses, Joe had hammered on about his plan: "If newspapers can be on the breakfast table, why can't gramophone records?" The answer was the railways. W. H. Smith and Sons had exclusive rights to British Rail's overnight freight trains, "The Newspaper Trains". And, Peter Bennett, Managing Director of W. H. Smith, owed Joe a favour. When Joe joined EMI, records were only sold through record shops. Bennett made the case for W. H. Smith to stock EMI records in his stores, which Joe saw no reason to refuse. It mirrored the tradition he had already quashed of HMV records being limited for sale through HMV assigned stores exclusively.

Joe took EMI's sales manager to lunch at W. H. Smith's headquarters in the Strand. John Fruin, under Joe's leadership, was equally dedicated to make a success of his brainwave. With thanks to Bennett and Fruin, Joe gained fame for revolutionising record distribution and outmanoeuvring the competition. The Board of British Railways invited Joe to lunch at their Marylebone headquarters, to "thank him for showing confidence in the railways".

Another important event occurring during the early part of the year was the purchase of Hatchet Wood. Charmed by the location, Joe was determined to rebuild the house on the site. Situated in an "Area of Outstanding Natural Beauty", planning permission was difficult to achieve and required all the resources of EMI's Legal Department. In a way, it was Joe's final achievement: "Everyone wants to build one house for themselves in their lifetime." And it was to be modern: "not some Georgian pastiche".

Julian Gibbs's friend Michael Raymond, of Colefax and Fowler, decorated Joe's flat and our offices, and now had the commission for Hatchet Wood. But an architect was needed, and Michael recommended his friend Tony Cloughley's firm, Garnett Cloughley Blakemore Partnership. Sir Charles Forté had chosen GCB to design the first motorway service station on the M1 at Toddington, which shared similarities with Joe's proposed new house. Large glass double doors led into a glazed corridor linking four pavilions. It gave the impression one could see right through the single-storey house, so as not to break up the steep contour of the land. Taking this one stage further, the sitting room had swatches of green and yellow wool sewn into the thick carpet to give the impression of a grass lawn swamping the room. Although the idea of verdure was suggested by John Fowler himself, it did not meet everyone's approval. Bette Davis frightened everyone by pretending to trip on the protruding swatches. When the house was demolished years later, the new owners told me they were keeping a sample as a memento.

Hatchet Wood was less than fifteen miles from Hayes. With EMI's Works Engineers and Building Services Department taking a supervisory role, and EMI's chief fire officer installing sixty metres of fire hose and carrying out regular inspections, construction was also carried out by an EMI-approved firm of builders. Bills would be scrutinised by EMI's

Purchasing Department before being passed, in trepidation, to Joe for closer scrutiny.

By the end of February we were able to set off, slightly later than usual, for two months of overseas travels. This was to be a world trip for EMI Directors and their wives. Joan Shawcross effortlessly stood out among the latter, as she made last-minute phone calls from Heathrow's VIP departure lounge. The welfare of her horses was her main concern.

Hatchet Wood at time of purchase

Five mile view

In Southern California, we were taken by charabanc to inspect Capitol's investment in orange groves. Stepping down between the rows of fruit trees that stretched to the horizon at the Valencia Orange Farm, where the coach had deposited us, we were greeted by an enormous sign: "Welcome To The Lord Mills Ranch". Lord Mills had objected to this use of surplus funds, as too far removed from our normal business. Capitol knew he would be amused. It was a play on *Welcome to the LBJ Ranch*, Capitol's hugely successful comedy album issued the previous August. Actual interviews with Lyndon Johnson, Lady Bird Johnson, Eisenhower, Nixon, Robert Kennedy etc. were taken out of context, giving answers, "but NEVER EVER EVER TO THESE QUESTIONS", posed by The Robin Dowd Comedy Interviewers.

Lunching at the home of Capitol's vice-president, Joe was very taken by a young fair-haired house guest, who was introduced as Lou Rawls's brother. This was somewhat confusing, as Capitol's mellow-voiced, soul-singing recording star was black. Crew-cut Roger Kunz made a brief reappearance. Joe and I were descending from the Capitol penthouse, when the lift stopped at a floor and Roger got in carrying papers. Joe glared at him. Not a word was said. I learnt Roger was moved later to represent Capitol in Allentown, PA. It must have been a small outpost, as we were not to visit Pennsylvania on our future travels.

By the time we reached New Zealand, the Shawcrosses were established as the star attraction of our party. This was not surprising, as they were a good-looking couple. Hartley, anxious to keep his figure, stuck to a diet of Complan throughout the trip. Hardy Amies clad, Joan travelled with a large number of suitcases and hatboxes. An HMV executive assigned to greet us in Auckland exclaimed: "Aw, Laidy Shawcross, where DID YOU get that hat?" Rumour spread they were aiming for the governor-generalship of Australia or Hong Kong, both on our itinerary. Hartley did in fact pick up lucrative consultancy work with Hong Kong tycoon Run Run Shaw.

We travelled the length of the North Island by coach, stopping for the night in Rotorua. Our energetic young HMV guide took me to bathe in the foul-smelling sulphur springs before breakfast. Perhaps the spa had some beneficial effect, as I was the only member of the party not to have flu when we reached Wellington. To make up numbers, I was included in the invitation to take tea with the Prime Minister, Keith Holyoake. Assigned to escort Sir Ian Jacob for sightseeing, I was warned by Joe to be circumspect about his family connection with BC. This was rare for him to show sensitivity on that subject.

In Australia, we were the guests of honour at the Coogee Beach Metropolitan Surf Life Saving Carnival. Escorted by police motorcyclists, our convoy passed the half-built Sydney Opera House. Whilst Lady Shawcross presented medals to the winning clubs, I was able to slip away with a camera lent by Ken East, who was a former lifeguard. Ken could see I was dying to photograph the hordes of suntanned humanity crowding the golden sand at the water's edge.

Lady Shawcross presents trophies at Coogee Beach

As Glenn Wallichs was with us, and John Burnett, Chairman of EMI Australia, who was also a director, it was possible to have a fully-attended board meeting. After all, this was the intended purpose of the tour. And Humphrey Tilling was there to take the minutes. His fame had preceded him, as a speech he made to the 40 Club had been issued locally on an LP. The Club was an exclusive Cricketing Club, and some very famous names called on him at our hotel.

I lunched with JC, now a mining company executive, in the commercial district of Sydney. He was affable, and I was as infatuated as ever, not least because he was wearing fetching shorts, considered normal office wear. I felt rejected when he did not invite me to visit his home. Joe received a less than wholehearted welcome at the routine press conference arranged for financial journalists. They were unexpectedly hostile. Rather than praise Joe, the interviewers tended to resent our success, preferring to attribute everything to the Beatles. We felt a long way from home. The City Editors would have had a less blinkered perspective had they known of our next destination. This was the secret rocket testing site at Woomera in South Australia, where EMI Electronics maintained a large establishment. Our hotel was in Adelaide, but the site was remote from any town and surrounded with massive security. Those MI5 officers from Interpol who came to see John Wall might have considered this as my intended destination.

In Hong Kong, we were entertained by the colony's two famous taipans, the chairmen of Jardine Matheson and J. D. Hutchinson. Both were our trading partners. As a special privilege, we were taken to the Fanling mainland and invited to observe Communist China from a police observation tower. Hong Kong was the Shawcrosses' final destination, and they left the party when we went on to Tokyo.

Run Run Shaw, Wall, Shawcross, Joe, me, Wallichs, Ted Insley in Hong Kong

Here, as in Hong Kong, Glenn Wallichs, who had developed a passion for travel, was our guide. In Hong Kong it had been shopping, in Japan it was Kobe beef, tea ceremony, geisha hostesses and something he was determined we should experience, the sauna with its tiny masseuses who walked up and down our spines. Capitol was responsible for the area and licensed Toshiba to distribute its repertoire, including the Odeon and Angel labels. By a lucky coincidence, Kyu Sakomoto, who welcomed us in Tokyo, was not only having a massive hit with his pop song 'Sukiaki', but could boast that his record-breaking sales were on the Capitol label.

Back home, we were soon off again, this time to Greece and Turkey. In Greece, we inspected our olive groves along the coast from Athens. These were another novel form of investment for surplus company money, as an alternative to repatriating funds to head office to be heavily taxed at a poor rate of exchange. The purpose of the visit was to attend a gathering of the overseas managing directors, but beforehand we spent a week aboard the *Stella Solaris* touring the Greek Islands. Joe was not the usual tourist, firmly remaining on board when we docked in the Cretan port of Heraklion and at Kusadasi on the Turkish mainland. I missed guided tours of Knossos and Ephesus. Instead, we befriended two young Oxford undergraduates, who "picked us up" on the quayside in Crete. At Kusadasi we stretched our legs on a hillside overlooking the bay, and observed a Biblical scene of a peasant ploughing his fields.

Relaxing in Greece

We stayed at the Hilton in Athens, where something occurred barely worth mentioning, except for having a significant outcome. Using an automatic exposure camera, we took photographs of ourselves relaxing on the balcony of our suite. Copies went to my grandmother, to add to the annual albums she made for me. Her second husband, Alexis, was bisexual, but sexual orientation was not generally discussed between grandmothers and grandsons. We never touched on the subject. She said those pictures of Joe and me "were a revelation" to her. I had never questioned in my own mind how she has coped when Alexis left her to live with Hardy Amies. She was someone who was so perceptive and quick to judge personality. For example, she described the suffragette Emily Davison, her governess in 1900, as "a brilliant teacher, and a good woman, rather unbalanced and strange". Examining a suitcase containing some of my grandmother's belongings after she died, I came upon a handwritten extract she made from W. Somerset Maugham's *Don Fernando*: "Now it cannot be denied that the homosexual has a narrower outlook on the World than the normal man ... I should say that a distinctive trait of the homosexual is a lack of deep seriousness over certain things that normal men take seriously." It was a strange book, in which Maugham revealed his fascination for the Cretan artist El Greco, whom he described as gay. Incidentally, Alexis and Somerset Maugham both fathered daughters and left their wives for men.

From Athens, we moved to Istanbul, our final destination. The manager of our Turkish company, Gramofon Limitet Sirketi, asked whether this was my first visit to Turkey. "No," I replied, "I was only here a couple of weeks ago!" It was unworthy of me to make such a dismissive remark, which I immediately regretted. I vowed to be more gracious in future. The port of Kusadasi barely counted.

Back at Heathrow, Ken East, who was accompanying us, was met by his future wife. We were not introduced as they hurried away. Ken and Dolly married soon after. Before joining Peter Gormley, Cliff Richard's agent Dolly had worked at EMI. Judy Martin and Dolly became my closest friends.

Joe was to take on many new jobs, which meant frequent absence from the office. The offers flowed in, but the most important descended on 2nd May 1966. Summoned to the Secretary of State for Economic Affairs' office, he was invited by the Rt. Hon. George Brown to accept a two-year directorship on the board of the newly-created Industrial Reorganisation Corporation. With a Government loan of £150 million, the IRC had the task of encouraging large companies to put differences aside and to merge, to create greater efficiency for the nation, without involving the much-hated threat of "nationalisation". Dr Francis Singer, the aforementioned pushy Managing Director of Chesham Amalgamations, wrote to congratulate Joe on his appointment: "I hope when you are handling the £150 million cash you will think of your poorer acquaintances!"

Sir Frank Kearton, Chairman of Courtaulds, the single socialist among the "Group of Ten" dining club who met at Joe's flat, was to be chairman, with Ronnie Grierson, seconded from Warburgs as managing director, reporting to a board of distinguished industrialists. There was no indication at the time that Kearton and Grierson would soon resign and leave Joe to bear the burden.

Firmly establishing the IRC as independent of the Government and civil servants, Grierson set his own rules. Staff was not to exceed twenty. Seven executives, in their early thirties, chosen for entrepreneurial flair, from Industry, the City, and even from the Civil Service, would be given equal status to stir things up. Known as "Young Turks", they were brilliantly selected by Grierson with Joe's assistance. During the four short years of the IRC's existence, there was not one dud among those selected, and all went on to senior posts with their careers enhanced. Needless to say, it was their youthfulness that gave Joe the stimulus he needed when he unexpectedly found himself chairman. For this selection he could be grateful to Grierson, his volatile maverick investment banker friend.

This appointment coincided with an invitation from the opposition party to spend the weekend at the Conservative-run Swinton College, to discuss employment and the economy. Joe was amused to find himself among industrialists accused by a Conservative MP and Edward Heath of accepting jobs from Labour. He responded: "It is certainly a new thought in Britain that anyone not agreeing with the Government of the day should never try to serve it." Only recently he had a private meeting with the Chancellor of the Exchequer, at the Treasury. He failed to convince the Rt. Hon. James Callaghan of the inequity of charging 40% corporation tax on the overseas earnings of companies, which, for example, in EMI's case provided 68% of the company's profit. The newly appointed board of the IRC was invited to dine at 10 Downing Street, and Joe was able to raise this, and other problems, with the PM. Harold Wilson listened to a string of complaints about trades unions, about devaluation, but most of all about pirate radio stations, which Joe claimed: "Should be scuttled without trace!" Eventually, Wilson was able to claim passing the Marine Offences Bill as one of the major achievements of his premiership, alongside the Open University, despite becoming a hated figure in the process among less reputable elements of the record industry.

Our tour in June took us to the Turnberry Hotel in Ayrshire. Joe had been invited to the National Association of British and Irish Millers dinners annually. This time he made a special effort to attend. Wilfred and Nancy Vernon's son, Michael, was taking over the presidency. At table, I explained to my neighbour that I was the former Chairman of Simon's PA. "No, he was not chairman!" he contradicted. For it was well known in the milling world that Joe's departure rested firmly on Lord Simon's plate, for not offering him the chairmanship of the parent company. The Industry felt the loss deeply. This was the first time I met Highley Sugden, a conventional bachelor. According to Joe, he liked young girls. The convention lasted three days, and during most of the time Sir Charles Dodds, the immensely eminent biochemist and Milling Industry Consultant, was drunk. It is a fact of life that someone, whose advice Joe was to value in the future, was an alcoholic.

After visiting our factory in Dundee, we spent the night with My Tutor in Perthshire. David Graham-Campbell left Eton early, when offered the Headship of Trinity College Glenalmond in his beloved Scotland. This unexpected move pre-empted Raef's expectation of taking on his Eton House. Raef reacted badly at not inheriting the boys he had cultivated.

Joe was a great hit with David, and I felt very welcome. David's status was enhanced when the Glenalmond boys, seeing the Rolls, the chauffeur, and the EMI 1 number plate, thought he was entertaining the Beatles. Less popular were his previous guests, a ballet company,

who gave him a sleep-
less night. His bed-
room must have been
close to the laundry.
The washing machines
and tumble driers
were in permanent
motion, cycling the
dancers' sweat-stained
practice costumes. We

*David and Joan
Graham-Campbell
and Feather in
Scotland*

rather avoided mentioning that we had been visiting a washing
machine factory that day.

Returning south, Joe inspected modern flour milling machinery
at Simon's, and stayed with Tommy Russell near Manchester. This was
where Tommy moved on leaving the home he shared with Joe. A
household full of his wife and four grown-up children was witness to
where the time had gone. The same age as the oldest child, I was quite
moved by the deep affection Joe and Tommy still shared.

Returning to London, I realised I had met all the important people
in Joe's former life, apart from his family. I also saw Yew Tree Cottage
in Combs. And Hill House in Mobberley, Feather standing patiently
beside the car. Where Feather found accommodation on overnight
stops, I never asked. His experience as a van driver delivering
gramophone records around the country helped, and it also made him
a master route-finder.

Joe's anger was unpredictable. Nothing could be taken for granted.
I suffered as a result of a well-intentioned initiative. We followed a
fairly relaxed policy at Manchester Square, where "the chairman's
door is always open". Joe set an example by wandering around the
building, looking in on people unannounced. This meant our floor
was accessible to anyone. Gordon Waller, of the Peter and Gordon
duo, came up one day when I was alone. It was not immediately
obvious he was drunk, although his black leather and rocker-style
bomber jacket added an air of menace. It soon became clear this was
not a social visit. I felt cornered. The duo's follow-up to their number

one single, 'World Without Love', was not selling. Gordon could not find a copy on sale in the HMV store, and he marched over from Oxford Street to "have it out", with me of all people. Fortunately, word got around that he was in the building, and I was rescued. Gordon was a good-looking boy, very attractive to both sexes, who adopted a tough guy image to play down his Westminster schoolboy education.

In May, Joe and I were introduced to a young German artist by an agent looking for a recording contract. Without our help, they managed to get a meeting at the office with one of our producers in July. The boy arrived at our floor unannounced, and I sent him away as Joe was busy. When I mentioned this, Joe was furious: "Get him back!" The building was searched, but the boy was gone. "Make an appointment for him to come!" I was instructed. What right had I to stand in the way of youthful talent? The fact was, the boy was obviously gay, Joe was interested, and I was jealous and ultimately humiliated.

We were soon off abroad again, this time for two weeks in South Africa. Seated in first class, a few seats in front on the flight, was ex-Cabinet Minister for Aviation, Julian Amery, now in opposition. Joe asked for a copy of the *Financial Times*. A steward explained that there was only one copy, and it was reserved for Mr Amery. Joe exploded, fortunately out of earshot. He despised politicians, however eminent, but for some reason he cared even less for Mr Amery, who admittedly had a very affected and irritating upper-class voice, exuding self-importance.

A weekend was spent in the Kruger National Park. Senior game rangers took us at daybreak, off the beaten track, ensuring we were guaranteed sight of every sort of wild animal. Bill Stanford, EMI's Overseas Director, was with us, and we had the local manager's black chauffeur, Nicholas, to drive us. Bill was uncomfortable about apartheid. Taking advantage of having Nicholas on his own, Bill was keen to hear his views on the situation, away from his boss.

The powerful Afrikaans Bruderbund ran the South African Broadcasting Company. Unbelievably, television was banned in the country, considered too subversive. Compounding this, the Beatles' records were not being played on the radio. This was John Lennon's punishment for claiming to be more famous that Jesus Christ. Popular music was strong here, and sales were favourable despite the lack of promotion. Unable to hear their music played, Beatles fans had no alternative other than to go out and buy their records. Joe pointed out to SABC that the Vatican acknowledged Lennon's claim to be genuine.

The day of departure from South Africa coincided with the assassination of the prime minister, Dr Verwoerd, in Cape Town.

In September, it was announced that Joe, who never looked for directorships, had joined the board of the Beecham Group Limited. Len Smith, an old EMI Records man who recorded Thomas Beecham in the 1930s, wrote:

> It is a great honour, particularly as EMI have been associated so many years with Beechams. Sir Thomas told me that his first job was in the Advertising Department. He wrote a slogan:
>
> Mary had a little watch
> She swallowed it one day
> And now she's taking Beechams pills
> To pass the time away.
>
> Sir Thomas said it was never used but he could not think why! Soon after his father, Sir Joseph, said it was better for Thomas to start an opera company, and so was born The Beecham Opera Company.

The fact was that Joe was a personal friend of Henry Lazell, the chairman, who lived in the same block of flats and had been after him to join his board for some time. Joe considered Lazell to be outstandingly the best and most progressive company chairman he had ever known. They both used pencil and paper to analyse statistics. In Joe's case it was gramophone record sales, and a formula for a cut-off point when ordering more pressings to avoid bad stock. With Lazell, it was to study marketing methods in America. He was the first in this country to use this knowledge, to promote Beechams' consumer products. Everyone knew about Horlicks, Lucozade, Ribena, Brylcreem and Maclean's toothpaste. And, with pharmaceuticals, he expanded the company from pills and powder to penicillin-based antibiotics.

In 1961, Joe had bought 800 Beechams shares for £2000. Now, he had no need to add to his holding, which was a respectable enough sum to appear in Beechams' annual report. These were the shares that were valued at £300,000 when Joe died. Joe explained that he was making time to spend half a day per month at Beecham House down the Great West Road, by resigning from ECGD, BECC and NRDC.

Lazell was prepared to put into effect an innovative proposal which Joe had brought to him. This was the introduction of a pension scheme for non-executive directors. It was a more attractive incentive than fees or salary. Smiths and Hawker Siddeley followed suit. Group pensions managers must have cursed Joe for the headache of setting up a scheme for a sixty-year-old. Hartley Shawcross soon caught on.

Joe and Lazell belonged to the "Club of Ten" company chairmen, including ICI, Unilever, Courtaulds, and Marks and Spencer, who met regularly to dine at one of their homes. Their shared aim was to act as a lobby group to put pressure on leading politicians of the day. On 4th November, it was Joe's turn to act as host. Invited to dine at his flat that evening as the club's guest was Edward Heath, recently elected Leader of the Opposition.

A few days later, Heath was being honoured by another club. This was the Carlton in St James's Street. Joe belonged to the Carlton, which he rarely used. This was a party-political event, and he did not attend. However, I was there. As an all-male event, hosted by the United and Cecil Club, any suggestion this was a camp occasion was misleading. Cecil was the family name of Lord Salisbury, and the evening reception was a regular fixture in the right-wing Conservative Party's calendar. Admittedly, the Carlton Club secretary invited his young, good-looking friends to meet the older members. As one of that category, I was introduced to Edward Heath. If this was intended for our mutual enjoyment, it failed dramatically. I said I gathered he had dined with Joe recently. He responded: "The most depressing evening of my life!" as he moved on. At the dinner, each guest, led by Joe, had turned on Heath, in a single concerted effort to commit him to tackle the Unions. He made no attempt to respond. Instead, he remained silent and left in a major sulk.

Beechams and Unions were a minor distraction from the main event in Joe's life, for which there was no competition. This was, of course, EMI with its unending supply of Beatles recordings. Even Joe was unaware of the impact the group's music was having, until he dined with Lady Ashcombe one evening in November at her large house in Charles Street, Mayfair. After dinner, the hostess asked her guests, who were in full evening dress, to sit on the floor as she put on an LP. It was the just-released *Revolver*, the Beatles' latest album. So Joe, with merchant banker Kenneth Keith, and others, reclined on the carpet and listened to Paul's 'Eleanor Rigby', Lennon's 'I'm Only Sleeping', George's 'I Want to Tell You', and Ringo's 'Yellow Submarine'. Both sides of the LP were played to a spellbound and silent audience. It was an experience for Joe: Beatles music had penetrated high society. But Ghislaine Ashcombe wanted more. It was getting late, but to Joe's disgust, she insisted the Chairman of EMI and the Chairman of Hill Samuel escort her to Annabel's, the exclusive nightclub in nearby Berkeley Square. Another dinner invitation the same week did not drag on into the early hours. Ex-banker Leo d'Erlanger's invitations to dine in Upper Grosvenor Street were always for 8 p.m. prompt. At 10 p.m. he always got up, saying "I'm going to bed now", leaving his guests to entertain themselves. Leo was famed for eccentricity, not least as President of the non-functioning British Channel Tunnel Co. Ltd. Joe sparkled at his table in mixed company. Leo would ring the office with an invitation: "A certain lady will be disappointed if he is not there on the evening." The lady was Mary, Dowager Duchess of Devonshire, daughter of the Marquess of Salisbury.

In October, John Wall left EMI temporarily to became Chairman of the Post Office. The invitation came from Edward Short, the Postmaster General. The £12,500 salary was less than Wall was getting, but EMI made up the difference. Joe boasted loudly: "We've lent Wall to the Government!" Read and Stanford became deputy managing directors, with Joe retaining control.

This was a significant moment in the company's history. It was when Joe showed the meaning of "control" in its most blatant form. He completely reshaped the company he inherited, cutting staff and costs. The resulting success must not allow a lessening of his strict regime.

His target was EMI Records. His attention to day-to-day matters would have come as no surprise. Rather than leaving it to the Purchasing Department, he personally renegotiated the price of that essential raw material – vinyl. This meant an annual phone call to the Chairman of ICI. As possibly the sole source of the product, ICI was in a strong position. Nevertheless, EMI was their main customer, and Joe never failed to get a reduction.

On 29th September, everyone entering Manchester Square was directed to read the noticeboards. Under the heading TO ALL MEMBERS OF THE STAFF, and over the signature of G. N. BRIDGE, MANAGING DIRECTOR, EMI RECORDS, was the following message:

On the Chairman's instructions, resulting from members of the staff failing to arrive by the agreed times, EVERY member of staff is required in future to be at EMI House by 9 am each morning. Arrangements which have previously existed in certain cases for alternative hours are cancelled.

Members of staff who normally clock on will continue to do so; all other staff will, if they arrive later than 9 am, sign a book which will be kept at the Reception Desk.

The Chairman is quite determined – and rightly so – that in order to meet the Government's call for increased productivity and efficiency, the poor timekeeping of the past must be eliminated.

This notice applies to all EMI staff employed in EMI House.

Geoffrey Bridge had succeeded LG, and his tenure was short-lived. He had compromised his authority by invoking Joe's name in the instruction. A young trainee, Peter Jamieson, swore that if ever he became managing director, he would never endure such humiliation. His resentment stemmed from being turned out of the lift to make way for the chairman.

If this notice appears over-the-top to modern eyes, another, even more mind-boggling memo went out, this time over Joe's signature, on 19th December. Marked PRIVATE and addressed to Mr J. E. Read, with a copy to Mr J. G. Stanford, it read:

I have given instructions to William that no more of the internal press-button intercom telephones should be installed without the written authority of a Director of the Main Board.

The reason is that I am horrified to find that Mr Paramor has now had one installed at Manchester Square – costing something like £40 a year to rent. Mr Paramor will thus be able to save dialling on the ordinary 'phone when he wants to speak to me, Mr LG. Wood and Mr Bridge. As he only speaks to me once every three years and he is now in the office next to Mr Wood, it seems an unnecessary extravagance.

When I first installed this system for myself so that I could speak to Mr Wood and Mr Bridge I did, in fact, delay seven years in making the decision until I felt the Company could afford it.

We did, some seven years ago, spend £100,000 in introducing what was supposed to be the latest inter-communication system in the world, i.e. the dialling telephone, so that anyone of the 2,000 people on the staff of EMI could be dialled directly by each other.

The installation of expensive internal intercom press-button telephones should, therefore, be strictly limited to people who are absolutely the top of the business or who want to communicate with a certain person at least 40 or 50 times a day, and are able to save much time in avoiding dialling.

This memo, which cannot exactly have increased my popularity, was not the raving of a Luddite. We were still living in an analogue pre-digital age. Joe's only electronic aid was a battery-operated Casio desktop calculator, and he still used the slide rule he kept from his milling days. Made in Japan by Casio Computer Co. Ltd, I still use that adding machine today.

On 7th December, Joe received a letter from Jennie Lee which had been drafted by that great solicitor Arnold Goodman:

> I believe that you already know that a vacancy will arise on the Arts Council at the end of the year, and I am writing to say that the Secretary of State [Anthony Crossland] and I would be most glad if you would be willing to accept an invitation to serve as a Member of the Council. I feel sure that the Council would benefit greatly from your wide knowledge and experience of the Arts.

The Arts Council Board Meeting

> If you are willing to accept this invitation, the proposal would be that you would be appointed for a period of four years commencing 1st January, 1967.

So, a self-proclaimed philistine replaced the Earl of Snowdon, to join the country's most powerful charitable fund. Angus Wilson was also called on to replace Henry Moore in this elitist organisation.

*John Lennon's
cartoon for
Christmas Card*

*Brian Epstein's last
Christmas Card*

Christmas Greetings

NEMS ENTERPRISES LIMITED · LONDON

1967

The PM is Libelled
and I am Blackmailed

EMI made the most profitable deal in its history during 1967: a personal triumph for Joe. Another deal in the same year was to set the company on a downward path.

In 1967, Leslie Grade had a stroke, aged fifty, Joe Meek shot himself, aged thirty-seven, and Brian Epstein died, aged thirty-two. It was the year I was subjected to a nasty attempt at blackmail.

On 27th January, EMI Records signed the Beatles, as a group and individually, to a nine-year contract with no advance payment. LG signed for EMI, Brian for NEMS; Paul, John, Ringo and George individually. Joe was not present at the historic occasion. For a year, the boys had recorded without a contract. Everything depended on Joe's meetings with Brian, but these had dwindled in 1966. Throughout, Geoffrey Ellis and I were seeing each other regularly.

For two years, there were moments when it looked as though we would lose the Beatles. Much rested on Brian's unstable condition, which was hinted at in a handwritten note on 5th December 1965:

Dear Joe,

It occurred to me in a moment of contemplation yesterday that I had made a fairly serious omission in that I should have apologised to you for not being able to attend the meeting which I was so keen to convene between yourselves, Capitol and us. You may have heard that I have recently been unwell and in fact just over the two weeks ago ordered to rest by my doctor. And it is because I was not too well at the time that I did not attend. I am very sorry about this although I hear that the meeting went quite well. Now I am feeling much better and stronger and after a brief trip to New York during this week I hope to return to routine normally. I hope that we will soon meet again socially. From a business point of view I am of course most anxious to finally settle the new agreement as I'm sure you are at EMI – this I hope will not take very long. In the meantime kind regards and renewed apologies,

Sincerely, Brian Epstein.

A temporary contract expired the previous June. Brian and Geoffrey came to the office to discuss the situation with Joe and LG. We were joined by the grim-faced Managing Director and Chairman of Northern Songs, the Beatles' music publishers. Dick James and Charles Silver claimed to have evidence that EMI was cheating their artists. A comparison between copyright royalties from Beatles overseas sales paid to Northern Songs as songwriters, compared with royalties paid to NEMS as recording artists, showed a discrepancy. EMI was paying royalties on fewer sales. We had no explanation, and the meeting ended on a sour note. But LG was back from his office in no time. The sales figures were identical. Might not James and Silver have been aware that the standard copyright rate in Continental Europe was 8%, compared to 6.25% in the UK? Problem solved.

And in July it was Brian's turn to be incensed. He wrote to Joe: "I cannot say how appalled I am that EMI should allow this to happen". (Issuing a cover version of the Beatles' 'Yellow Submarine' song.) "It seems to me to be quite ridiculous to put out another version of a Beatles single to compete against it. How am I going to explain this to the boys I do not know, but it does seem to me a case of lack of loyalty and co-ordination. Personally I am rather disappointed." Joe's reply reassured Brian that EMI never used advance information. Donovan, the artist who made the cover version, had told Mickie Most, his recording manager, about the song. "It is, of course, impossible to prevent by copyright law an artist recording one of the Beatles' songs and selling it on the day following publication of a Beatles record." He hinted that the more cover versions of a song sold, the more Northern Songs, where Brian and Geoffrey were directors, would benefit.

Between them, Joe and LG did amazingly well to keep things on the rails. No doubt LG had the harder job. Ridiculous as it may sound, his biggest problem was to convince Brian, who had experience as a retailer, that Beatles royalties, rumoured at the time to be 10%, were normally based on sale price, and not wholesale price as Brian insisted, based on his experience as a Liverpool shop owner.

Geoffrey told me Brian was much more relaxed after the contract was signed. It was to Brian's credit that he so trusted EMI that he had not bothered with lawyers. Geoffrey, a trained solicitor, was not consulted. Goodman Derrick was the firm acting for NEMS, but Joe and Lord Goodman never discussed the matter.

Kept secret from Joe was the arrival of Robert Stigwood at NEMS. Brian had taken Robert into partnership with the intention that he should take over. Robert boasted to Geoffrey he had cooked dinner for me soon after I met Joe. I recall there was a whole turkey between the two of us, and the flat in Regent's Park was fitted from floor to ceiling with white fur.

Brian and Robert were late-night gambling partners at the 21 Club. Brian had been mad about Robert's John Leyton, boasting of ordering 300 copies of 'Johnny Remember Me' before it became a hit. Had he listened to Robert's advice, at worst there would have been no contract, at best he would have insisted on imposing a new royalty rate to act retrospectively on previous record sales. In fact, Joe's suggestion of a sliding scale on future sales was adopted. Royalties started at a modest rate, but increased steeply as sales grew.

Brian spent ten days drying out at the Priory Clinic in Roehampton in September 1966. His management contract with the Beatles was due to expire in September 1967. Allen Klein, the American agent who already represented some EMI artists, had wind of the Beatles' EMI contract expiring "some time in 1967 or 1968".

In February, released at last from business pressures, Brian bought a place in the country. Kingsley Hill, situated near Heathfield in East Sussex, had six bedrooms, a barn ready for conversion into a cinema, an oast house, a five-acre garden, and a housekeeper/gardener couple to look after him. Twelve miles away as the crow flies was Glyndebourne. Brian was already deeply in love with the Glyndebourne Festival opera season. His friend, John Pritchard, was principal conductor.

On Friday 9th June, Geoffrey and I drove down to Glyndebourne to see *L'Elisir d'Amore*. Striding across the lawns in the interval came Brian, beaming and carrying an enormous wicker picnic hamper, the contents provided by his housekeeper.

AT BRIAN EPSTEIN'S
KINGSLEY HILL
HEATHFIELD
SUSSEX.

MAY 1967.

Brian

Geoffrey
Ellis
Brian's partner

After visiting Glyndebourne

Brian Epstein's country retreat

Very much later we all went back to Kingsley Hill for the night. The house was lit by candles and smelt strongly of incense to hide the scent of drugs. Sadly, the pleasure of weekends in the country was soon to pall. Brian died during the night of Sunday, 27th August at his London home, while his long-term friends, Peter Brown and Geoffrey, were left to entertain themselves down at Kingsley Hill. I was probably the last person in EMI to see him alive.

Brian had overdosed and possibly died peacefully in his sleep. Joe Meek, the first independent record producer, had ended his life far more dramatically the previous February. Meek was becoming increasingly unstable during 1966. He was having money problems. A claim of plagiarism, that was settled after his death, had frozen royalties from 'Telstar', the hit single he made back in 1962 with the Tornados. Record-breaking world sales for the instrumental number, much loved by Mrs Thatcher, would have meant financial security. Without it, it was enough to turn anyone's mind. Among people in the Industry, he approached Joe and LG. Tilling instructed EMI's Legal Department to study his contracts in October. Joe and LG met with his solicitor in November. There was a final meeting with Meek on 17th January. It was clear he was unfit to join a large organisation. He was a mixed-up loner whose idiosyncratic recording techniques were laughed at in the Industry. His very success as an "independent" made him incompatible.

One morning, a week after the meeting, Joe came into the office in a towering rage, clutching a letter. It was difficult to tell what had made him more furious, the way the letter was delivered or its contents. Somehow, a boy had managed to get past the hall porter in the night to ring Joe's bell. This was bad enough, but what could have merited such urgency? The boy must have belonged to Meek, because the letter was from him, and it was the work of a lunatic. LG was summoned, and he and Joe examined eight pages of perverted obscenities. Was Meek making sexual overtures to Joe? The letter never left the room. It was immediately torn up in my presence. Joe and LG alone had read the contents. "Filth," snorted Joe. The matter was closed. On 3rd February, Meek shot himself and his landlady.

Over the years, a myth grew about a mystery letter, which was in some way connected with Meek's death. Had he been offered a job by EMI? No one at EMI could throw light on the matter. No contract had been discussed.

In 1985, when we had moved permanently to the country, Joe began to receive calls on the ex-directory number at Hatchet Wood. The caller was John Repsch, who rang repeatedly each 14th November to wish Joe a happy birthday and to ask about "a letter". Joe was quite capable of being civil and dismissive at the same time. I did not speak to the man, but made a note of his name. It was unusual.

In 1989 came an explanation. *The Legendary Joe Meek the Telstar Man* was published. The author was John Repsch. The book describes a mysterious letter being delivered to Sir Joseph Lockwood by eighteen-year-old Patrick Pink. Meek accused EMI of bugging him "with listening devices. They're watching and listening. They're watching us through the walls."

Repsch persisted. The last call came on 27th January 1991. He did not seem surprised when I, rather than Joe, answered the phone, for the first and last time.

After Leslie Grade had a stroke early in the year, older brother Bernard Delfont moved in rapidly to manage the Grade Organisation. As a publicly-owned company since 1964, it was a price-sensitive situation. The group had expanded into cinemas, and had mopped up smaller talent agencies representing Laurence Olivier, Roger Moore and Franco Zeffirelli. Now they were joined by Bernard Delfont Limited, the theatre management company. Joe had been a frequent visitor to Bernie's office above the Prince of Wales Theatre. He liked all three Grade brothers individually. Lew (later Lord) Grade, the eldest, was boss of ATV and Pye Records. Someone who knew them collectively was the stockbroker friend of my father. Jamie Drummond had advised Lou, Bernard and Leslie on how to get listed on the stock exchange. He said they were great fun to work with. Once their shares were quoted, they no longer needed him. Plans to move into expensive new offices in Park Street, Mayfair were cancelled. The Grade Organisation was now in trouble.

Joe had introduced John Read to Delfont. Read was ambitious to expand, and already relished the prestige that resulted from taking over electronics companies. Here was a perfect opportunity to expand into entertainment. By acquiring the Grade Organisation, EMI would be buying into a whole new industry, bringing with it the perfect person to run it. It did not occur to Read that Bernie might also have ambitions. The share price was always going to be the issue. On the one side was Joe, standing up for EMI shareholders. Against him was the formidable Grade family, which significantly included Leslie's son Michael Grade. Rather than look to EMI as their saviour, the Grades were out for the best price they could get. The City loved it.

Negotiations dragged on for six weeks. It was time for Joe to visit Capitol, still with nothing resolved. We would be away for three weeks. Before driving down to Southampton to board the *Queen Mary*, Joe formed a committee of Read, Stanford and Dawnay to continue negotiations with Grade's advisers. We would be back for the Easter weekend.

After Wall's departure, Joe would meet Read and Stanford every week. Monday mornings were reserved for "The Chairman's Policy Meeting", followed by lunch. I kept the minutes. Joe's views were well known inside the company. Dawnay's outlook down in the City at Lazards was different.

Aboard the liner, on one of its final Atlantic crossings, was Hermione Gingold. Remaining aloof initially, complaining of seasickness, the celebrity eventually joined our table and inevitably bonded with Joe. They discovered a mutual interest in ping-pong, which neither played very well. Hermione Gingold had a lot of film work in America, but was well known for never flying. One experience had been enough. She described setting off, and the horror of being strapped into a seat, and finally the unanticipated descent into Boston, where she abandoned the plane. She removed herself and her luggage, taking the train back to New York. There she sat on the docks with her suitcases, prepared to take the next boat back home, "even in a maid's cabin".

Glenn Wallichs arranged for Joe to be made a temporary member of the exclusive New York Athletic Club. Knowing it would please Glenn, we decided to explore the club's facilities. It was a short walk from our hotel. We absorbed the Edwardian all-male atmosphere of the gymnasium, the boxing ring, the fencing room, and then discovered an enormous swimming pool situated way up in the large building. Joe decided to go in. As the club only provided towels, I declined. You would not expect to come across waves in an indoor pool, but its depth and size caused turbulence. Joe, struggling to the high-sided edge, was in trouble, but no one was paying attention. He admitted later, had I not come to the rescue, he would have drowned. Years later I was tempted to revisit the scene, but admittance is only permitted to members.

We broke the journey to LA by visiting Capitol's remote manufacturing facilities in Jacksonville, Illinois. This was the Midwest, and St Louis was the nearest airport.

We were guests at "The Nat King Cole Birthday Ball" at the new Century Plaza Hotel in Hollywood, where we were staying. His widow, Maria Cole, had place of honour, and it seemed strange singing "Happy birthday to you" to the deceased.

I was with Joe the next evening when he answered the phone. It was his fellow guest at the ball. She was staying in the hotel. Would Joe join her in her comfortable suite? Her husband had gone back to New York, and she was alone. Her husband, a typical Madison Avenue advertising agency "Mad Man", had bid for the million-dollar Capitol Record Club account. This was a breath-taking and unprecedented sum. Ever chivalrous, Joe might have fallen into a trap, had I not been there to advise against accepting. (He did ask me after all!) I smelt blackmail, compromise, divorce; but, basically, I was being my jealous possessive self.

We flew into Mexico City to visit Discos Capitol de Mexico, when Joe's mood changed. He had not forgotten the border-crossing incident from his flour milling days. By the time we reached the El Presidente Hotel, he was determined to have a row. Anything after the Century Plaza in Hollywood would compare badly. We waited in the dismal foyer, which was like the set of a Tennessee Williams play, and no one was on hand to collect our bags. Mexico City is situated high above sea level, and the air is thin, causing fatigue. Added to travel weariness, this may have increased Joe's impatience. The Royal Ballet declined an invitation to perform at that altitude, and the ambassador pleaded with Joe to use his influence to make them reconsider. Returning to Mexico City three years later, we would be booked into the brand-new Camino Real Hotel.

It was a long flight home, setting off at lunchtime, arriving for breakfast. So we were jet-lagged at Heathrow at 9.40 a.m. when met by Read and Stanford. Good Friday, 24th March, is a date the pair would not forget easily. Expecting praise for taking over the Grade Organisation, they received a sharp ticking-off. *The Times* of 21st March said it all: "Grade shares leap 6s 9d on EMI bid ... EMI bid several times before eventually giving in yesterday morning and agreeing to pay Grade's price of over £7 million or virtually 40/- a share against the market price of 26/9 a week ago. EMI's shares lost 1/1½." It was noted that the deal was done during Joe's absence abroad. Grade had refused 35/-, and the 40/- offer was made from Colonel Dawnay's office at Lazards. It was way over the odds. Joe fumed, he had never overpaid for a company. He rejected MECCA when they asked too much. Years later, Michael Grade was able to write with relish that EMI had overpaid by four times.

Read and Dawnay rushed through the deal four days before Joe's return, and EMI was damaged. Dawnay found he could manipulate Read. Delfont, overnight EMI's largest shareholder, proved Read to be an easy touch, or in other words, as Joe put it, gullible. EMI was going soft.

The Grade Organisation brought with it two major problems, and its final dissolution. Ownership of a talent agency forced EMI to drop out of bidding for Yorkshire Television on the instructions of the Independent Television Authority. Ironically, it was the ITA that later forced EMI to disband the Grade Organisation in return for control of the larger and more prestigious Thames Television. Seven million pounds was written off, as the agencies swallowed up to form the Grade Organisation were returned to their managers.

Joe promoted the positive outcome of acquiring Delfont to the board of directors. He admired Delfont's drive and ambition. At the same time, he knew that "Mr Showbusiness", the country's great showman, must be kept in harness. Delfont had plans: he proposed EMI should merge with his friend Charles Forté's empire. Joe was wined and dined at Forté's Café Royal. When their overture failed, Delfont produced Cyril Stein, the young head of Ladbrokes. Stein was looking for the respectability that merging with EMI would bring to his casinos and betting shops.

In each case, it was stressed Joe would remain chairman, but Read and Stanford must go. Despite everything, Joe had no intention of dumping them.

In May, Joe was back in more familiar territory when a Beatles problem arose. In contention was the cover of the *Sgt. Pepper's Lonely Hearts Club Band* double album. The boys and Epstein produced the artwork, but EMI had overall approval. Many views were expressed, but the decision remained with Joe, who went to Goodman and Shawcross for advice. The wisdom of Solomon was required.

Joe reported: "The artwork alone has cost fifty times more than the artwork on a normal LP, but it's their best ever record and I hope we'll sell about seven million." The cover depicted many familiar figures, both living and dead. According to Shawcross, a claim by any single objector could cost EMI thousands of pounds in damages. Without hesitation Joe removed Shirley Temple, whose views on drugs and morality were well known. Gandhi had to go too. "There are millions of people in India who might be offended," Joe explained to the *Sunday Times*. Joe claimed he also removed Leonard Bernstein.

It was agreed that Wendy Hanson, Brian's PA, should write to everyone in the picture for written approval. No one objected, and the historic double album was released on 1st June. Less than three months later another record was released in even more controversial circumstances, but by then we were in North America.

Joe and I travelled to Montreal and Toronto on 21st August to visit Capitol and Hawker Siddeley's operations in Canada. Sir Arnold Hall came over from London to show us around the de Havilland plant. He used the occasion to tackle the subject of the Hawker Siddeley chairmanship. To put it bluntly, he asked Joe to be a good non-executive director, and sack seventy-six-year-old Sir Roy Dobson. This was achieved with efficiency on our return. I waited in the Rolls outside Sir Roy's flat in Eaton Square. Joe was only gone for five minutes.

On 25th August, the day the "controversial" record came out, we were staying at the Beverly Hills Hotel. Elmo Williams, Glenn Wallichs's film producer friend, gave us a tour of Twentieth Century Fox Studios, where he was head of production. He was preparing for the Pearl Harbour epic *Tora! Tora! Tora!*. We found ourselves on a set recreating the Ivy Restaurant (where Joe lunched with Jules Thorn). We were introduced to the cast of *Star*, the film biography of Gertrude Lawrence, Noel Coward's favourite musical partner. Joe was struck by the perfection of "Gertrude's" English accent, and hastened to compliment the "American" actress for her achievement. This came as a surprise to Julie Andrews. Joe was unaware she was the very English star of *My Fair Lady* and *The Sound of Music*, not that it mattered to him. Of greater interest was the youthful Ryan O'Neal, who Elmo Williams brought over from the set of *Peyton Place*, the TV soap opera.

I was brought down to earth by a very real-life drama of my own there in Hollywood itself. We were with the Directors of Capitol on the top floor of the Capitol Tower when Alan Livingston handed Joe a cable: "Sir Joseph Lockwood has approved a million-dollar investment in a musical based on the Rothchilds; signed William Taub". It was clear Joe had absolutely no idea what this was about. The matter was dismissed. Like so many things, not another word was said. I was dumbfounded. No one seemed to notice.

My big mistake was to keep in touch with Taub on his infrequent visits to London after such a casual acquaintanceship in Cannes and New York. We would dine amiably, until one evening in 1966 he became too interested in what I did. We were at the Hungry Horse, an expensive restaurant in Fulham, when his manner became malicious at my failure to respond. I recall being expected to pay for the meal. I was not to see him again, and was determined to forget all about him. A year went by, when I received a phone call at the office. It was John, one of Jack Hylton's many children, saying he was with someone who would like to speak to me. Taub's voice came on with a "long time no see" greeting, and I promptly replaced the receiver. He would have sensed my fear. That should have been the end of the matter, but that Capitol cable showed Taub had other intentions.

Taking the overnight flight from LA, we arrived back early on 31st August, having set off at noon the previous day. Joe went to bed early, taking a sleeping pill. I had dinner with Gérard André. That night, Joe received an urgent phone call summoning him to 10 Downing Street. "I am in Canada. I have taken a sleeping pill," Joe mumbled and hung up. The phone went again. This time it was Goodman: "The Downing Street switchboard is to be congratulated on finding you in Canada!" This time Joe was awake, and agreed to meet at Goodman's flat at 9 a.m. Arriving late at the office, Joe demanded "Get me the postcard". The Prime Minister had been libelled, and EMI was implicated. The incriminating item was retrieved from downstairs. Postmarked 22nd August 1967 on one side, addressed to "Colin Burn, EMI, 20 Manchester Square, W1", the reverse depicted Harold Wilson in bed with his secretary observed by Mary Wilson. The unknown artist had clearly been influenced by the political lampoons of James Gillray and the erotica of Aubry Beardsley. It was a clever caricature that had no obvious connection with a record it was promoting. Nevertheless, it had arrived at the desk of the head of EMI Records Promotion Department to advertise The Move's new single 'Flowers in the Rain'. However, the wording accompanying the cartoon was clearly libellous: "Disgusting Depraved Despicable though Harold may be Beautiful is the only word to describe Flowers in the Rain by The Move Released Aug 25". Rumours, but nothing more, about "Mrs Williams, Harold's Very Personal Secretary" were based on Downing Street chauffeurs' room gossip. Joe impounded the postcard. All knowledge of its existence must be denied. It was important that EMI had nothing to do with it. Fortunately, it was the only copy sent to us (it is now mine). Released by, but not produced by EMI, the record was intended to coincide with the launch of BBC Radio 1 and was expected to sell well. Radio 1 was the BBC's answer to the pirate radio station closed down by the Wilson Government's Marine Offences Bill. It was a publicity stunt concocted by The Move's agent, Tony Secunda.

Not only was Goodman the PM 's solicitor, he was also the supreme libel lawyer. In 1957, he won £7,500 damages against *The Spectator* for libelling three Labour politicians, who were described as "Drunk in Venice" at a Socialist Party Conference. Now Goodman smelt money. On 29th September, Joe wrote to him that royalties from the offensively marketed record would be considerable:

> In the UK we have to date sold about 115,000 records, for which the royalty payment would be about £3,200. Our estimate is that the record will probably sell about 300,000, in which case the royalty we pay would be over £9,000. If the sale by chance should go over 500,000 then the royalty rate is increased to a higher rate on the extra sales and the figure would soar. In addition to sales in the UK there are, of course, sales abroad which I think it reasonable to expect would equal the sales in the UK, so that the above figures would therefore on that estimate be doubled.

Left out, but later netted by Goodman, were the songwriters' and music publishers' royalties. Artists' income continues for fifty years, and songwriters' for longer.

This letter gives one a rare insight into the Beatles' contract, where royalty rates escalated as sales exceeded 500,000. Such information was designed to divert blame and was successful in exonerating EMI. Wilson wrote later:

> I much appreciate the sentiments expressed in your letter of September 4th [a letter drafted by Goodman for Joe] and would like you to convey my thanks to the members of your staff who expressed regret at the postcard. With regard to a public announcement, Lord Goodman no doubt will be in touch with you further if this becomes a practical possibility.

Roy Wood, The Move's lead, was allowed to keep his royalties as writer of the song, after a plea was made on his behalf. But no exception was made for the group, who were totally out of pocket, and relied on their manager for subsistence. In 1997, the *Sunday Telegraph* reported on their plight:

> Sixties naughty boys lose £1 million in Royalties ... For thirty decades, members of The Move have watched up to £200,000 in royalty payments – probably £1 million in current terms – being distributed to charities nominated by the late Prime Minister Lord Wilson. They are paying the price for a libel case arising from a publicity stunt to promote the single that went on to become a symbol of the "summer of love" of 1967 ... The anniversary next month of Radio 1 has again made the song a valuable property.

Goodman wrote to Joe on 13th September: "How kind of you to remember the colour television." One of the first HMV colour television sets to be manufactured was installed in Goodman's flat. It was a present.

A letter marked PRIVATE & PERSONAL arrived on my desk at the end of September. *I was being blackmailed*. Anyone who has not been subject to blackmail will not understand the feelings of shock, sickness and fright engendered. But those are the intended symptoms of blackmail:

> Dear William,
>
> I act for Mr William Taub and he has consulted me in connection with a loan of $350.00 which he made to you. I shall be obliged if you will let me know when it is convenient for you to repay this sum, and if you like to see me so as to deal this matter personally I should be pleased to keep any appointment convenient to yourself.
>
> Kind Regards, Your sincerely,
>
> David.

David was David Jacobs, the society and show-business solicitor. Even better known than Goodman, he was another first-nighter, frequently escorting glamorous actresses at premieres. Tall, handsome, flamboyant, dyed black hair and eye mascara, he had something of a reputation. It was said he was first at the house when Brian died, before the Epstein family solicitor arrived from Liverpool. We had known each other socially for three years. Geoffrey took me to one of his parties in Hove where Sir David Webster gave his famous impressions of the Queen Mother and Margot Fonteyn. He was previously the subject of an amusing mix-up at the office. We expected him one morning for an appointment with Joe, when a secretary rang to say Mr Jacobs would be delayed as he had suffered a riding accident in Richmond Park. Our surprise was short-lived when David Jacobs, the disc jockey, limped in.

Despite all this, it was with some trepidation I attended David's office in Pall Mall. The previous night in tears, I told my parents I was being blackmailed. "Is it Lockwood?" was my father's reaction. "Absolutely not!" That did not help much.

The meeting was formal. David listened. I was distraught. I explained there had been no loan. By luck, I had kept the receipts for the three nights that the Martinez Hotel in Cannes had charged me for the single room I had not used in August 1963.

This was Taub's vindictive way at getting at me, by exposing my time in a French prison. He had failed to receive a response to his August cable to Capitol.

David explained that he did not know Taub, who had come to him on the recommendation of Dame Anna Neagle and her film producer husband Herbert Wilcox. The once-famous couple were behind the musical based on the Rothschilds, mentioned in the cable. The matter was closed. David must have given me some sort of reassurance. He committed suicide the following year, totally unexpectedly. The reason given was depression. I hope he wasn't being blackmailed too.

Taub was gone. But I saw him one more time. It was a TV news item. The House Committee for Un-American Activities was sitting in Washington DC, to investigate Mafia control of the Teamsters

Union. Taub was appearing as a character witness for a union member. Was it Jimmy Hoffa, the notorious union boss who disappeared in 1975, to be declared dead in 1982? Whether or not it was Hoffa was of little concern. It did not take much to imagine Taub and the Mafia as bedfellows. Luckily, their stranglehold did not reach our shores.

Joe effortlessly mixed pop and politics in his daily life. Daytime he would relax on a sofa with his pipe, chatting to Gene Pitney, Stevie Wonder, the Beach Boys, Diana Ross or Pink Floyd. Once he came back from the A&R floor, after seeing Lou Rawls: "Would you believe it, that fellow just suggested the two of us, just him and me, should go on holiday together to the South of France!"

Lou Rawls over from Los Angeles (me on the left)

Greater attention was paid to politicians than to pop stars. Despite accepting a Government post, Joe was again well in with the Tories. He felt forgiven when Edward Heath invited him to a black-tie musical soirée at his set in Albany, W1. The next morning Joe sent round a thank you present of gramophone records, classical of course, and Heath accepted an invitation to lunch at the IRC.

Joe was openly angry with the Chancellor's tax increases:

> This year I am due to pay £28,000 in tax, based on the fact I have a private income and 12 or 13 Directorships. But all my EMI income is taxed at 19/3 in the Pound. I am left with less than £2,000 p.a., for being Chairman of EMI. I could keep the easy money, go to monthly Director's meetings, say yes or no to important decisions and give up the Chairmanship of EMI, and I would lose only £2,000. Yet the EMI Chairmanship is extremely harassing. I get up at 6.30 every morning, and am booked up all day and evenings. Last week I had to have a very important meeting with Lord Goodman, and the only time we could manage was at midnight. I also had three breakfast appointments. I do it because it is my life. I enjoy responsibility, and the power, I suppose.

There was a group of twenty-four industrialists all increasingly anxious about the economy. Joe was a member. The Industrial Policy Group's aims were to study the cause of the country's malaise: "The Government's mishandling of the situation caused devaluation. It is no good blaming the British people for the crisis," said Joe. James Callaghan, the Chancellor, had had enough, calling the IPG members "potentially sinister men, and some rather dubious people". Joe responded: "It sounds as if he has gone off his rocker."

The press got excited: Lord Robens, Chairman of British Coal, should be put in charge of the country to run "Great Britain Ltd", with Joe as Minister of Technology. Cecil King, the newspaper tycoon, proposed a similar body with Lord Mountbatten in charge. Joe openly criticised the Government of the time when interviewed by Bernard Braden the following year. Callaghan had asked how he would get workers to invest in National Savings. Joe said they would be cheated, as devaluation meant they would be getting back less than they put in. Callaghan agreed inflation was the problem, but did nothing about it. Roy Jenkins, who succeeded him, was tackling the situation; "but there will always be lunatics like Michael Foot" in government, said Joe. Callaghan went on to become Prime Minister, and, as one might have guessed, "lunatic" Michael Foot followed as Leader of the Opposition.

Cinemas, Television and a Dramatic Phone Call in Milan

The year began with my promotion to "Administrative Assistant (or AA) to the Chairman". It brought no increase in responsibility, but gave Personnel an excuse to raise my salary. In this new capacity, I wrote to the managing directors of our overseas companies. They were requested to be less indulgent when receiving the chairman. No longer should hotel suites be reserved. Meetings with local dignitaries were not necessary. Only those closely connected to the business should be invited. Parties should be avoided, unless expressly requested by the artists. It was well known that Joe enjoyed samba parties in Rio de Janeiro, and that South America had been where his career began. Most important of all, the managers' annual reports, which were traditionally addressed to Joe, were in future to be sent to Stanford. These were detailed documents, not confined to profits and loss, but covering local political and economic situations, all of which would influence the company's business plans. The thirty or so managers knew what Joe was looking for: is our money safe if we increase their capital? Reports formerly consisted of basic accounts submitted to the Gramophone Company at Hayes, a tradition still followed, for twenty years after the Communist Revolution, by the Chinese subsidiary from its office on the Bund in Shanghai.

The managers resented having to report to Stanford. Even a basic acknowledgement of their efforts from Joe, drafted by me, had been appreciated. As a compromise, we continued to receive copies. They must now provide a "Five Year Plan" for Read. This, for companies depending on the volatile music industry, barely able to see one year ahead, must have made them wonder what was going on at head office.

Joe was actively delegating more. This extended to his profile with artists. Introduced to Pink Floyd and Deep Purple, he did not "get" the psychedelia portrayed by the former or the heavy metal by the latter group. Their offbeat attire and attitude belied the fact they were ex-college boys and talented musicians. Drummer Nick Mason published a memoir in 2004 called *Inside Out: A Personal History of Pink Floyd*, in which he recalled a meeting at Manchester Square:

> I clearly remember riding up in the lift with Sir Joseph Lockwood, the Chairman who was in his sixties, but seemed a nonegarian to our eyes. He seemed unflappable at yet another quirk of the music industry. He did rather alarm Derek Nice, the director of our "Arnold Layne" promo, when he suggested that they should install a backdrop of the Tower of London upstairs, and then the bands would come and simply mime their hits to a camera before sending them out world-wide. Sir Joseph was years ahead of his time.

The last time Joe posed with artists signing a recording contract was in July 1969. It was with Deep Purple.

Bernard Delfont had quietly set about building EMI's new Entertainments Division, with the modest £4.5 million purchase of the original 1891 Blackpool Tower and Leisure Complex. But something bigger was afoot. On 1st February, all seven national newspapers ran the headlines: "EMI BID FOR ABC: TV-CINEMA £38 M. PLAN. BEATLES DISC FIRM IN BIG BID FOR CINEMAS."

Delfont bought Warner Brothers' 25% stake in Associated British Picture Corporation for £9.5 million, aiming to swallow the whole company's 276-cinema chain and half of Thames Television. In what became an acrimonious takeover battle, Read and Delfont expected Joe to negotiate with the Independent Television Authority and the outside shareholders. He had already spent so much time at the ITA over Yorkshire, and was well thought of there. But this was to go on for a year, and he must have come to hate those ABPC initials. He and the Chairman of ABPC remained aloof of the proceedings. Over lunch at the Carlton Club, Sir Philip Warter asked whether it was so important to make such a fuss and excitement over his company, which had a consistently steady but predictable profits record. The Industry was controlled by just two companies, ABPC and the Rank Organisation's matching chain of Odeon cinemas. As Warter's Chief Executive, Robert Clark, put it: "Why could not EMI keep out of the way and let a well-run business continue to run itself?"

A half-share in London's commercial TV station was ABPC's crown jewel. Run in partnership with Rediffusion, it was essential to retain a controlling stake, let alone face having it confiscated. Joe spent day-long meetings at ITA headquarters in Brompton Road. He did not particularly like Sir Robert Fraser, the Australian Director General. When Fraser admiringly whispered "What a good-looking man your John Read is!", Joe realised the whole thing rested on personalities. Luckily, Rediffusion's pompous chairman, Sir John Spencer Wills, was actively disliked by the authority. Fraser would come down on EMI's side should its bid succeed. Rediffusion would retain 49.9%, but 50.1% would go to EMI with the essential "controlling vote", giving it the statutory right as a major shareholder to run Thames Television.

But control of ABPC was proving elusive. By the end of the year, the 25% stake had reached 45%, valuing the whole company at £45 million. Without another 5%, failure was inevitable. Joe had the task, and Warter was complaining about his methods as ungentlemanly. Only Joe could do it. He put through a call to the Chairman of Norwich Union, who were sitting on 5%, and remained unpersuaded after twelve months. Somehow it worked. Joe was able to tell Read and Delfont that the country's largest insurance company was accepting the offer at last. Victory came on 30th January 1969, previously noted in my pocket diary as the day "EMI offer closes at 3 pm if 50% not achieved". The announcement was made from the boardroom in Manchester Square, with the press present. I looked after Gerald Seymour from ITN, who was the first reporter to hear the news. Rushing to the lift in his hurry to leave the building, he wanted EMI's masthead logo to take back to the studio for the 6 p.m. news screening. We had no press or public affairs office (Joe did not see the need) and I knew we had nothing. In desperation, we stopped the lift at the Record Sleeve Design Department. Luckily, George Freshwater, the manager, was able to rustle up a board depicting the "EMI The Greatest Recording Company in the World" motif to appease the reporter. Gerald Seymour became famous as the author of popular crime thriller novels.

The takeover of ABPC was seen as a success for Read. I was dining at the Carlton with its secretary and his young friends a few nights later. Leaving the club at midnight, a fellow guest asked for a lift in my car. Between St James's Street and Hyde Park Corner, where he asked to be let out, my passenger turned out to be a financial journalist. This was a relief, as I thought he wanted to go home with me. He prophesied there would be difficulties between Read and Delfont. It was certainly a novel and slightly disconcerting speculation that did not invite comment. This perceptive young reporter went on to become the City Editor of his paper.

Joe decided to save the company money by giving up having a full-time chauffeur. It was an extravagance, and he wanted to set an example. It was such a waste of time for Feather to sit around all day when he was off duty. Feather was now to be available to drive other directors. The faithful Feather, who had driven Joe since the East Burnham Well days, refused, and was put back on to driving vans. He died soon after.

In March, Hatchet Wood was nearly ready for occupation, when Joe's London housekeeper died unexpectedly. She had planned to accompany him at weekends. She was a country lover and looked forward to pulling up blackthorn bushes in the fields. One bedroom suite was earmarked for her. It was even installed with a servant's bell, at which she objected. The other two bedrooms were for Joe and for his guests. No one had considered where I was to sleep. The guest room was too superior, but that was where I slept, moving into the sauna when there were visitors. An annexe was added later, and the caretakers had their own cottage. Having no room I could call my own, I had little input in the Colefax and Fowler décor. Guests were not expected to need television. I missed not having a TV aerial socket. That was just one of Joe's many economies. Colefax and

Fowler claimed that when it came to approving costs, Joe was second only to Sir Arnold Weinstock as their meanest client. Joe took it as a compliment. The suggestion for a landscape gardener was rejected: "What is the need? I already have an uninterrupted five-mile landscaped view down the Hambleden Valley!" A large Ben Nicholson abstract relief, painted on board, was installed in the sitting room. Joe saw how much I admired it, but it had to go: "I'm not having a piece of wreck!" Instead, he chose a life-size portrait of Patrick Procktor's boyfriend, Gervase. This was displayed for a time in Colefax and Fowler's shop window. Joe selected it at Patrick's studio in Manchester Street. Each morning a car with darkened windows would pause outside the shop. It was rumoured to be Mick Jagger, stopping to admire what he took to be a portrait of himself.

During construction, frequent visits were made to the site to see architect, builders and decorators. But on some weekends, we went down when the place was empty, and had lunch at a pub in Skirmett. Very early one Sunday morning, Joe rang to say he was in the mood to slip down there. I did not answer, as I was not at home. For a number of weeks I had been having an affair with Nick Eden (the ex-Prime Minister's son), but this was the only time I spent a whole night at his flat. We had met playing Bridge at Gérard's. I was swept off my feet. We were in a relationship which was totally discrete. No one would have heard about it, especially Joe, had he not phoned that morning. I had been caught out, and, of course, I confessed, and never saw Nick again. Joe forgave this one indiscretion, and, in the process, possibly saved my life. Nick, despite a distinguished career in the House of Lords (as the Earl of Avon) and in government, was extremely promiscuous. It was through the decadence of his demands that I was still in bed with him that morning. He was vain, with reason, very handsome, and particularly proud of his hair. He was planning to take me down to the South of France in his open-top Rolls. Perhaps that is where he caught AIDS, the cause of his death. Had our passion persisted I may have suffered the same fate. Joe had given me credit for saving his life in a swimming pool. By stopping a promiscuous relationship and keeping me clear of infection, I am sure he saved mine.

Hatchet Wood was complete, and I would be away from London temptations at weekends. Our first morning I was woken early by a strange noise, and went out to investigate. It was a youth in army fatigues hovering in the outbuildings. He claimed he was scavenging for food. It somehow reminded me of Eton Cadet Corps on field days, and I sent him away. In fact, he was from the nearby borstal institution. Joe was furious at breakfast. Why hadn't I got him up? It never occurred to me he wanted to see the boy!

Hatchet Wood rebuilt

Joe relaxing

Me relaxing

We had visitors every weekend to admire the house. Somehow I prepared lunch for the Vernons, the Jefferys, the Wallichs, the Reads and the Martins with baby Lucie. Tommy and Penny Russell came to stay for the Henley Regatta in July, which meant fresh sheets for "my/guest" bedroom. The unexpected death of Percy Mills prevented Joe having to disappoint his Sunday invitations. Their regular dinners together would have had to end.

Our well-planned weekends went badly wrong one Saturday in May. On the way to the country, we stopped for lunch at Reigate Cricket Ground. It was the annual Cooper Brothers v. EMI match, which articled clerks, such as myself of old, were expected to attend. The fresh-faced among us would be chatted up by gay managers. Now I was the uncomfortable guest of my former employers. It was a blazing hot afternoon, and when we got home, the large bulk stock of frozen sirloin steaks in the boot of the Rolls had thawed out. Frozen steak is cheaper than fresh. Joe was furious. "Don't you know you can't re-freeze them! You've wasted everything!" Country life had not tamed that temper.

These outbursts were uncomfortable for those present when made in public. We walked out of a concert given by The Who. Joe found the noise insufferable. EMI executives at the performance sympathised with him the next day. It was not for nothing that the group had the reputation of being the loudest and most destructive of their poor instruments.

In July, on another hot summer afternoon, a ceremony took place to mark the opening of Brunel University, previously a technical college. EMI Electronics was one of the sponsors. A marquee was erected for the installation of the first chancellor. This was the Earl of Halsbury, Tony Halsbury, Joe's fifteen-year colleague on NRDC. Not long into the speeches, Joe got up: "Come on, we're leaving!" He had obviously had enough. The dramatic effect of our exit was intended. Anyone knowing him would have recognised what was on his mind. He hated pompous occasions in Latin, hated universities, had resigned from NRDC, and simply decided we had better ways of spending the afternoon. No apology was felt necessary.

I was unaware that five years before my time, Halsbury had made an appointment to introduce Joe to Dr Elliot Jaques, the psychiatrist and Social Sciences Director of Brunel College. This was to outline their plans. Dr Jaques and his actress wife Kay Walsh were my London neighbours. The only time we had met was over a wrongly delivered parcel; apart from which, we were unaware of each other's existence. I was passing their window some days after the opening ceremony. "He was feeling faint." I realised Dr Jaques was addressing me. For a moment I couldn't think who "he" was. Dr Jaques's analysis of Joe was impercipient.

The Honorary Degree intended for Joe was quietly withdrawn, and transferred to Percy Allaway.

We were seeing more of the Beatles, now that they had formed themselves into a company, called Apple. One night in May, Paul McCartney introduced us to Mick Jagger of the Rolling Stones. It was unplanned. We had gone backstage at the Lewisham Granada during a concert. Earlier that evening we dined at the Savoy with Richard Armitage, his wife, Paul, and his girlfriend Jane Asher. It was typical of Richard to book a private room, the Patience Room, for a party of six. Richard's top group, Manfred Mann, with lead singer Paul Jones, were performing at the Granada, and we got there at about 10 p.m.

Jagger was already ensconced, whisky glass in hand, and cigarette firmly in mouth, making the meeting fairly fleeting. We gave Paul and Jane a lift back into town, dropping them off at the Saddle Room nightclub in Park Lane. For them the night was still young.

The Beatles opened a boutique in Baker Street which they called Apple. Here they installed The Fool, a group of way-out designers, whose clothes they admired and wore. We were invited to the launch of their collection. The fashion show took place in the trendy King's Road, Chelsea. I remember the occasion as fairly chaotic, but worth recording, as it was here that the rumour first circulated that John Lennon "had a new girlfriend". The couple was briefly glimpsed.

On 5th June, the Beatles came to lunch at Manchester Square. The lift door opened and five creatures emerged. We were expecting four. Lennon and his companion were identically clad in white collarless trouser suits. They were photographed later that day dressed in this way at Robert Fraser's art gallery. Robert was the son of Joe's merchant banker friend, Lionel Fraser, who once congratulated Joe's knighthood with that Cole Porter song. Robert championed avant-garde artists who are now household names. He dealt in drugs, was famously arrested with Mick Jagger and Marianne Faithful, and died of AIDS. Lennon's partner, introduced to us as "my secretary", was of undefinable sex. A tiny figure in trousers, shaggy black hair obscuring its face — it might have been a golliwog. It was something Lennon realised required clarification when he signed the butler's visitors book: "Yoko Ono (female)". All was revealed. This was the conceptual artist who sought notoriety with her *Bottoms* film. Joe was impressed with my knowledge as I whispered the identity of our guest. In fact, it was a movie devoted exclusively to naked male bottoms, something even Andy Warhol had not attempted, which established Yoko Ono in my mind. One might say I was the first person in EMI to accept her. She sat in my lap, as she squeezed beside Lennon at the dining table where no place was laid for her. That is how I saw the concealed Philips cassette tape recorder that she was having trouble adjusting. She would not have made a very good spy. Her wires were tangled.

So. when Paul, John and Yoko came to see Joe in September, he was able to show no surprise at what they wanted to discuss. Rather, surprise came from their quarter, when Joe failed to react at the nude photo of John and Yoko intended for a record sleeve. "You would sell more copies with Paul. He is prettier!" EMI objected, and there was need to compromise. EMI agreed to press the *Two Virgins* LP, "in which two artists meditate and philosophise to electronic sounds". EMI would deliver it in plain white bags, but would "not handle the covers at all."

Paul was the Beatle most receptive to suggestion. He and Joe lunched with the Chairman of Lazards in July. It was Joe's idea that Lord Poole should give Paul some good financial advice. The day was scorching. As they arrived in the City, scaffolders on a nearby building site, who were stripped to their shorts, wolf-whistled Paul as he got out of the Rolls. Oliver Poole, former Conservative Party Chairman, entered the spirit as he greeted his guests, by removing his jacket and revealing his braces. Writing to thank Poole, Joe told his host that Paul had described the lunch as "Great!" – "this phrase in his language is the highest praise he can give."

When John and Yoko were arrested in October, it was Paul who contacted Joe for support. The best thing was to speak to John, who seemed unaware of the serious situation he was in. Joe put a call through and John was brought to the phone: "This is Sergeant Lennon of Marylebone Police Station!" The next day an emergency meeting was held at Paul's home. A pair of long, slender bare legs were seen descending the stairs. They belonged to his new girlfriend, Linda Eastman, who was not introduced. Joe reached for his teacup, which he had placed carefully beside him on the floor, only to discover Martha, the old English sheepdog, had been there before him. That Christmas, Joe received a card from John and Yoko, signed "Two Virgins 4 ever".

In September, "Top of the Bill", Engelbert Humperdink, produced a bottle of champagne for Joe in his dressing room at the Blackpool Grand Theatre, following a tradition kept alive by Ken Dodd and Tommy Cooper. We were touring EMI's "amazing amount of entertainments" put on by Bernard Delfont, the showman.

In November, Joe was invited to act as a witness at the Farm Street wedding of adolescent Peter Noone, lead singer of Herman's Hermits.

EMI's classical companies could be of use in the most unlikely circumstances. Step forward John Coveney, the urbane manager of Capitol's Angel label in New York. Instructed by Glenn Wallichs, he obtained two tickets for the sold-out rock musical *Hair*, which had transferred to packed houses on Broadway in July. This was not for my benefit, although I was keen to see this nude, anti-Vietnam show. Joe was there officially to represent the board of EMI. Delfont was anxious to bring this long-running show to the Shaftesbury Theatre, which was going through a lean patch. Up against him was Sir Ian Jacob, who was implacably against EMI endorsing this anti-establishment, pro-drug, nude show. It was agreed that Joe should see a performance and mediate. Sure enough, he enjoyed it as much as anyone, and we were at the (un)dress rehearsal when it opened in London on 24th September. It was a sensation. Audiences joined the cast on stage at the end of performances. Even Princess Anne was caught up in the throng. As co-owner of the theatre with Charles Clore, our four house seats per night were much in demand. The show's producer was none other than Robert Stigwood, now a successful theatre impresario. Joe was kept uninformed and Robert lurked unseen at the back of his box.

We continued our journey from New York to Los Angeles for a regular Capitol Board Meeting, after which there was a party for directors and their wives. Mike and Lorena Nidorf made a great fuss of us. He was the contact man who had bought the Warner shares in ABPC. Joe was furious later when he discovered Nidorf had demanded and been paid a finder's fee. Lorena was the widow of MGM's Louis B. Mayer. Mike was previously unmarried. Lorena was very attractive and I was embraced by her warmth, until she spoilt things: "You must see *The Boys in the Band* when you are in New York," she enthused. "You particularly will love it!" When I found out this was a gay play, I realised she had me weighed up.

Mike drove us to Universal Studios. His purpose was to introduce Joe to Lew Wasserman. "You wait here!" Nidorf instructed me, when we reached the President's penthouse. I found myself pushed unceremoniously behind a pillar. On the other side, I could hear another visitor chatting up the President's high-powered secretary. Their fast talk was straight out of a Hollywood movie.

That evening, back at the Beverly Hills Hotel, I ran into a couple: "Hello, Billum! I want you to meet my husband!" It was Mei Mei, my childhood friend, the little Chinese girl I shared a governess with. Her mother was Han Suyin, the novelist. And her husband was Sydney Glazier, the fast-talking, tough, hard-nosed producer I had overheard earlier that day at Universal.

A figure who dominated the classical world would re-surface after a five-year absence. Walter Legge wrote from his home in Geneva, inviting Joe to lunch, "now that our differences of opinion have been amicably solved". Dismissing the suggestion that he should meet Read and Stanford, his wit was as sharp as ever: "If one has an audience with the Pope, one willingly sacrifices the presence of the most eminent cardinals. So if it is agreeable to you, I suggest we meet at the Mirabelle on September 16th at 1 pm. There is a saying – If the Mountain does not come to Mahomet, it behoves Mahomet to go to the Mountain." Beside the familiar wit was the extravagance that so offended Joe. Mumm champagne and Bolivar cigars were ordered. Elizabeth Schwarzkopf, Legge's wife, joined them for coffee after the meal.

During the year, Joe resigned as Chairman of the Central School, remaining a governor and on the Finance Committee. Something bigger had cropped up. As a member of the Arts Council, he felt under an obligation to help Goodman and Jennie Lee build a National Theatre, on the site next to the Royal Festival Hall. The South Bank Theatre Board was set up in 1962, to supervise construction and commissioning of the building. Membership comprised half and half GLC and Government, to reflect its ownership. The Government actually controlled the budget through the Arts Council. Jennie Lee now put Goodman and Joe on the board to safeguard her interests. Joe was officially appointed by the Secretary of State at the Department of Education and Science, Patrick Gordon Walker, on 8th March.

Goodman and Joe looked at the figures and told Miss Lee what she wanted to hear: the project cost estimates were feasible. This was the green light she needed. Joe told me he and Goodman kept their hands firmly behind their backs, fingers crossed, tongue in cheek, when endorsing a budget based on one per cent annual inflation.

Eventually, on 3rd November of the following year, Jennie Lee, wearing her familiar fur coat, dug the first sod from the South Bank site. A celebratory reception was held at County Hall, that lumbering "white elephant", so hated by Joe.

Joe's appointment was for two years. Inevitably, as with so many bodies he joined involving monthly board meetings, he was to become chairman. He was reappointed every two years by successive Secretaries of State from each party. The Conservatives were Mrs Thatcher, Paul Channon and Lord Gowrie. The Labour ministers were Hugh Jenkins and Lord Donaldson. The board remained in existence long after the theatre opened. Joe was chairman for eight years and resigned in 1985, aged eighty, leaving the Arts Council to tie up the never-ending loose ends.

The National Theatre was a political football. This struck me once whilst waiting for Joe outside County Hall. The Conservatives were in power, but the GLC was under Labour control. This meant the leader of the GLC was a socialist, and his chauffeur, with whom I was having a friendly conversation, was a communist. He informed me that the City was controlled by Old Etonians belonging to Free Masonries. Familiar OE names were mentioned. In addition, I learnt that citizens of Moscow were provided with commodious flats and supplied with all their needs. I wondered what was keeping him here.

We visited Switzerland and Italy. From the moment we registered at the Baur au Lac in October, not a moment was to be wasted. "How are our record prices being undercut?" Joe insisted on an answer. To date, no satisfactory reason had been forthcoming. He was assured export prices to Switzerland from all our sources were identical. That night, we sat closeted in Joe's bedroom with two executives. He was not leaving until they produced the answer. Phone calls were made to managing directors all over Europe, which produced identical answers. Midnight approached. "Try and try again!" Joe instructed. Eventually, the trail led to a small importer in south-east France who was re-exporting records to Switzerland on which he had been given a discretionary discount to cover his remote location. I was immensely impressed by how Joe refused to budge, as he sat on the bed, in mounting anger, until he got a satisfactory answer. He was reduced to threats. Stanford's Overseas Division must pull up its socks.

Checking quality control in Milan

EMI's Voce del Padrone offices were in the Piazza Cavour, close to Milan's Duomo and La Scala. Untouched since Edwardian days, dark and dingy, HMV's Fred Gaisberg would have still felt at home. Out of the blue, Joe was summoned to the phone. There was a call from London. It was Charles Villiers, the new IRC MD: Frank Kearton was resigning, and would Joe be Chairman of the IRC? The young executives would not accept anyone else. Various board members had applied. There had been a vote.

It is true Joe felt comfortable with the staff. He enjoyed giving the thirty-year-olds allocated to him free rein. He supervised areas of industry where he had no conflict of interest. British ball-bearing manufacture was in danger of becoming foreign controlled, unless something was done. The solution was to strengthen the Industry by merging three British manufacturers to become Ransome Hoffman Pollard. The Chairman of Pollard, John King, had another plan – to accept an offer from Skefco, the larger Swedish company, for his controlling shareholding. Personalities were involved. The IRC boy on the job was quoted in a French magazine to the effect that King, a hard-nosed North Country businessman, was "pas assez costaud" to

Joe and Charles Villiers at the IRC's office

run the £400 million turnover merged RHP. This was the same John King who went on to save British Airways and the Concorde, Mrs Thatcher's favourite businessman.

Villiers had recently succeeded Ronnie Grierson, who was inclined to go off the handle. On one occasion, he was reputed to have flung the telephone out of the window. This was at Warburgs, where Siegmund Warburg recoiled at the size of Grierson's phone bills. Things had run smoothly at IRC, but its methods of reorganising industry had a hint of nationalisation, enough for Grierson to decide to leave. Later suspicions were raised when two specialist instrument manufacturers were merged. IRC was accused of using its own resources to favour George Kent's bid for Cambridge Instruments, in preference to an earlier approach from the Rank Organisation.

Back in London, Joe visited IRC's offices on 21st October, "to view the executives". He reluctantly agreed to serve one year, aware that Villiers, another volatile ex-banker, would require a restraining influence. *The Times* reported on 21st December: "Of the three most likely candidates the successful one seemed, on the face of it, the most unlikely ... Sir Joseph has pursued a somewhat eccentrically independent political line, attacking the Government about spending; proposing Parliament should only sit twice a year."

Villiers, ex-Schroder Wagg, was hyper-active, having recovered from the terrible war injury which smashed up his face. Taking the ball-bearings bull by the horns, he made a direct approach to the Chairman of Skefco, Marcus Wallenberg, head of Sweden's great Enskilda banking family. Wallenberg put the matter in his solicitor's hands. "Who is this man Villiers?" he asked Goodman, whom Joe had added to the IRC board.

"Next time you see Villiers check whether he is wearing the diamond necklace King James I gave his ancestor!" Goodman wrote Joe privately, and, more publicly: "You know talking to Mr Villiers is like teaching Mah-jong to a mule!"

Christmas Day was spent with the Vernons for the last time. In future, we would be at Hatchet Wood. The break was inevitable, but Nancy Vernon misjudged Joe, provoking an anger attack. Her crime was to try and introduce him to the local county set. Someone rang, claiming to be her friend, to solicit a donation for church funds. I took the call, relaying the caller's hint that failure to contribute would not go down well with the community. Joe was furious. How dare she give his phone number! In fact, the caller got it from poor Mrs Hemson at the office. One hot summer day, Nancy arrived unannounced with the wife of the Chairman of H. Samuel, the jewellers, and caught us sunbathing. That was the last straw. It would be many years before he saw his oldest and most devoted friend again.

Boxing Day showed Joe in a more charitable light. A large turkey would arrive each Christmas from the farmer who rented his fields. Unable to eat it alone – I was still with my family in Yorkshire – he invited the family of the President of the Electrical Trades Union to attack the carcase. Les Cannon was on the IRC board as the acceptable face of TUC. An ex-communist and married to a Czech, he and Joe agreed on many matters. Les, Olga and the two boys polished off the bird, anticipating that this was to be annual event. This gesture of entertaining a unionist was a familiar routine for Joe, who belonged to the Foundation on Automation, a body bringing together industrialists and unionists over a large expensive meal. When Joe was the host, lunch was at the Connaught. He took Ken East along. Ken described the scene, and how Mr Rose, the banqueting manager, as usual outlined the additional specialities of the day that were not included on the already extensive menu. Vic Feather, general secretary of the TUC, another friend of Joe, remarked they all sounded interesting and he "would have some of those". "Those" he proceeded to consume, watched by an open-mouthed East.

Les Cannon died unexpectedly in 1970. Olga and the boys had one further feast at Hatchet Wood, but Joe made it clear there would be no more invitations.

The morning of New Year's Eve was spent at IRC's office, with Goodman and Skefco representatives. Joe had entered his sixty-fifth year anticipating greater leisure. He now found himself in even greater demand than when he came to EMI.

*Our office at
Manchester Square*

1969

Oh Dear! Another Blackmail and Joe Hands Over Executive Duties at EMI

1969 was a year of wall-to-wall press cuttings and imposing headlines. There were also to be surprises. The Beatles began to split up. Joe became a Director of the Derby racecourse. I was offered a job in films. There was another mention of blackmail. Most compelling of all was the addition of a dachshund to the household.

Witnessing the devastation of Germany, during the final stages of the war, Joe was entranced by the sight of a very special dog. It was a standard long-haired dachshund with a bright red coat. He would love to have it. The prospect of more leisure meant time to have a dog again. Those pre-war rambles in the Peak District with Rufus could become walks through the Hambleden Valley. And the Chilterns were less daunting than the Pennines for someone getting on.

We found a perfect puppy also called Rufus, because of his red coat. Re-named Maximilian, he arrived at Hatchet Wood one cold snowy day, and captivated everyone. He was soon joined by Caesar, a black Labrador. Caesar was a house-warming gift from Hawker Siddeley, or rather from the company secretary who bred shooting dogs for Sir Thomas Sopwith. He was unsettled, and something had happened to him as a puppy. No use as a shooting dog, he needed a home, and he was delivered to our office, collarless and tied with a rope. Labradors are a one-man dog. Joe was to be that man. Max was more liberal in his affections. Caesar's unusual arrival at Manchester Square would have been frightening for any dog, and we were unaware of his condition. But Nanette Newman, Bryan Forbes's wife, immediately saw something was wrong: "That dog's mother sat on him when he was a puppy."

Bryan and Nanette were dining at Hatchet Wood. Bernard Delfont had put the actor-director in charge of ABPC's Elstree Film Studios on a £30,000 salary. Delfont boasted to Read: "The Industry was something of a sleeping giant with tremendous concealed reserves of business power." This phrase was used again some years later, preliminary to EMI's decline. Bryan claimed he would restore Britain's film industry to its former glory. Successful as actor and director (*The L-Shaped Room* was outstanding, and *King Rat* was my father's favourite film), he was confident he had what was needed to run Elstree. His recently completed *The Madwoman of Chaillot* was a disappointment, but he was already established at the studios when it flopped.

The challenge overwhelmed him: "I started my first day being handed 37 full length scripts," he boasted. "In the first 48 hours I have read nine of them". I was flattered to be asked to read some for him. He wrote to me in May:

> I cannot tell you how grateful I am for your quick and intelligent comments on the "Ned Kelly" script … It occurred to me the possibility you might care to read selected scripts for me from time to time. I know your opinion would be valuable to me and it is my intention to try and solicit reports from people such as yourself. With the Chairman's permission, therefore, may I send you things from time to time?

Flattery was followed by a proposal, when Bryan asked me to be *his* PA: "You should be moving on, at your age. Time is running out!" It cost him nothing and, fortunately, he did not press the offer. Joe remained silent. It hurt to be told I was in a rut with a chance of escape. It helped that I never considered it as such.

Joe, so careful to avoid influencing my decision (in fact, he considered Delfont had picked the wrong man for the film job), was soon to spring an ultimatum of even greater surprise. I returned from a brief holiday in Cornwall to be greeted by that black look that preceded an unsuppressed anger attack. I knew it so well, but it was all the more shocking this time, as it was aimed at me.

My absence coincided with the final visit of the decorators to Hatchet Wood. Colefax and Fowler sent their expert painter, Joe called him Picasso, to glaze the walls with one more coat. Admittedly, Joe had to cope, and curse, on his own, as each room was turned upside down again. He put it to me simply: "If you plan to go off again, I'll sell the house!" That was to be the end of holidays for me. Now I was a fly trapped in amber. The result was a beautifully decorated house, displayed on two occasions in the pages of *House and Garden* magazine. It eventually became my property.

Interior showing Patrick Procktor's portrait of Gervase

"More photographs for your 1969 book, please," my grandmother requested. The truth was, the albums she made me every year were getting thinner, as the press cuttings book I kept at the office was getting thicker.

Bryan was not exactly desolate at rejection. Joe and I were invited to Elstree regularly. Determined to keep the workforce fully employed, he turned the studios into a conveyor belt for films, of varied quality. The carpenters were running up aviaries designed by his friend Lord Snowdon, initially for the Queen Mother's homing budgerigars. But the one on display at the Chelsea Flower Show, Joe agreed to take for Hatchet Wood.

Bryan was unable to resist the temptation to direct films himself. With *The Raging Moon* he chose an uncommercial subject, considered too sensitive to tackle. Nowadays the story of two paraplegics falling in love is perfectly acceptable, but at the time it was untested. Leading roles were taken by Nanette and a young actor, Malcolm McDowell, who we had befriended after seeing him in *If*. We were Malcolm's guests when he was working on his own *O Lucky Man*, which came out in 1972. Joe gave Bryan his full support on *The Raging Moon*. This was appreciated when things began to go wrong. Bryan's role did not extend to distribution of the films he had commissioned. They were not even guaranteed a showing in the ABC chain, and some indeed were not shown. After three years, he had had enough. Before he left, he told me to: "Keep an eye on the remaining projects for me. They will need a lot of support." Joe remarked: "Do you know, they never managed to get that man to sign his contract the whole time he was there!"

Although the Beatles broke up officially in 1970, Joe could see the way things were going from the moment Paul, John and Yoko came to see him in September 1968. That October, George sent him his solo album, *Wonderwall*, issued on the Apple label. In November, he was invited to Apple's Savile Row offices to meet John's protégé, "Magic" Alex, Alexis Mardas, a young Greek inventor, now running Apple Electronics Ltd, and introducing new techniques in the basement recording studio. We took Mr A. B. Logan of EMI's Patent

Department to look at Alex's "five light and sound patent specifications". EMI Electronics Research Department reported: "There is no reason to fear that the activities of EMI would be adversely affected by the grant of patents on any of the applications, and no commercial benefit is likely to be obtained from licenses to use the inventions."

Possibly because of his knowledge of these new developments at Apple, Joe found himself invited by the Arts Council to join fellow members Angus Wilson and Sir Edward Boyle MP on a New Activities Subcommittee set up to report on arts laboratories, happenings and psychedelic light shows. A leading alternative society figure advocating Arts Council support was Jeff Nuttall, author of *The Exploding Foetus* and collaborator with Yoko Ono on her naked men's bottoms film *Film No: 4*, who described the Arts Council members as fat and middle-aged. Joe responded that at twenty-one stone he was aptly describing himself.

On 29th January 1969, Joe received a letter signed by George and Ringo, with John's approval: "This is to inform you that Allen Klein is also acting on our behalf and request you to give him all information and co-operation concerning our business affairs." Significantly, Paul's name was not included. Klein was the notorious American agent, "the toughest wheeler-dealer in the pop jungle", who once threatened to replace Epstein. Confrontation came at 4 p.m. on 24th February, when he marched the Beatles into our boardroom to confront Joe and LG. Klein said he wanted changes made to the EMI contract. Joe replied he would also like changes. The meeting was short, so sudden, that I was swept aside as the visitors stormed to the exit. LG was in shock. Joe was non-committal: "Don't worry he'll be back." Sure enough, Klein rang LG to apologise that very afternoon. He hoped he had not offended Joe. In an interview with *Playboy* magazine, asked for his views on the people in the pop world, Klein had one word: "Shit!" Asked about Joe, he made an exception: "A great guy!" That was the sort of flattery Joe liked.

It was hard to refuse a request from Goodman, even when it involved horse racing. Harold Wilson had appointed George Wigg, ex-Labour MP, as Chairman of the Horserace Betting Levy Board, set up to oversee the country's major racecourses. Lord Wigg, dour, mean and irascible scourge of John Profumo in 1962, was now making trouble for the Jockey Board. To prove he was in charge, he confiscated the commentator's microphone during a race meeting to make an announcement. Joe agreed to join Goodman as the two Government representatives on the boards of the racecourses reporting to Wigg. The other directors were Jockey Club members. That is how Joe, who was trying to cut back, became a Director of Racecourse Holdings Trust Ltd, Metropolitan and County Racecourse Management and Holdings Ltd, United Racecourses Ltd, plus the more interesting-sounding Epsom Grandstand Association Ltd, and Sandown Park Ltd.

At the Royal Ballet School, the IRC and the South Bank Theatre, Joe had become chairman by default. Determined for it not to happen again, he was generally spared. The United Racecourses Board met to decide who would succeed Sir Brian Mountain as chairman. Mountain diplomatically absented himself through ill health, and Joe was asked to take the chair. The choice was between the heads of two great banking families, Jocelyn Hambro and Evelyn de Rothschild. Prestige was involved, as the chairman traditionally acted as host to the Queen at the Derby. Having to make a decision, Joe chose the younger man, de Rothschild. Hambro was gracious in defeat, but could not resist a comment: "Evelyn doesn't even know the date of Derby Week".

Joe was subjected to late-night telephone calls from Wigg, the ramblings of a lonely old man. When the Levy Board expired, Wigg was rewarded with chairmanship of the Tote. Joe resigned his racing directorships in 1983. Goodman stayed on.

It was difficult to drop out of anything, and required great resolve. Sir John Russell, the honorary registrar of the Imperial Society of Knights Bachelor, wrote:

> Please don't resign. I personally will never forget that it was in your office, on that day when you were our host, that the fateful decision was taken to proceed with the Dedication, and I well remember how

interested the Queen was to meeting you at our Party last year. I mentioned you to her and the Knight Principal, and she at once said; "Oh yes, EMI." It is of paramount importance that we should have men like you who are known to all to be pre-eminent. Please stay.

I enjoyed seeing famous sporting knights and actors out of context, such as Donald Wolfit and Laurence Olivier in plain business suits when the society met at our office.

"Lockwood's IRC" was time-consuming. In 1969, he attended 136 meetings or meals, involving "69 mergers in 20 industries". When Villiers was on holiday, Joe went to their offices in Pall Mall at 9.15 a.m. before coming on to Manchester Square. Our desk was loaded with private Government-business reports and documents. No one asked me to sign the Official Secrets Act. Seven young executives reported to Joe individually or collectively. Roger Brooke, ex-Foreign Office, was "bright, unlike any civil servant I have known". Alistair Morton had to be reminded not to be superior: he was among equals. Geoffrey Robinson was assigned Rotary Hoes, and John Gardiner, Rolls Royce.

Brooke went on to create Candover, the first venture capital fund. Morton saw the Channel Tunnel built, Robinson became an MP and Paymaster General in a Labour Government, and Gardiner became Chairman of Tesco.

In June, the IRC reported a surplus on its Government loan. A £750,000 dividend was paid to the Secretary of State for Economic Affairs, which silenced its critics. In May, Villiers made much of this at a London conference of international bankers, and invited the delegates and wives to a weekend lunch at his home in the country, followed by a tour of the Saville Gardens at Windsor. He cleared this with Joe, who reluctantly agreed IRC would pay the cost.

Joe rarely gave up a moment of his weekends. But here was an opportunity to see Villiers's new house on the edge of Windsor Great Park, which was not far out of his route back to London on the Sunday. He accepted the invitation, which meant I went with him. I would not have given the occasion much thought in retrospect, had not something unpleasant occurred the following September.

I arrived for that September weekend separately. Joe was already at Hatchet Wood, and he looked grim. "I need to speak to you!" This was an unusual form of greeting. Something important must have happened. He explained he had been to see Goodman at his request. Nothing unusual about that, but this time it was different. Goodman told Joe that Villiers had been to see him, to tell him that he, Joe, was being blackmailed and it was a very serious matter. Joe was incredulous: no one was less likely to be blackmailed, anyone would know that. Where did this come from? Goodman said Villiers had absolutely refused to reveal his source. Considering that Joe saw Villiers practically every day, this made it all the more shocking. There was mention of a young man, money, and even a house.

I was even more shocked than Joe. Neither of us had the least idea of what had got into Villiers. I was a young man, but Villiers could not possibly have been thinking of me, who had his cine films transferred to videotape, and did him other favours. He would greet my father across Swinley golf course, "How's William?", and other such jovialities. The only other young man was BC, whom Joe had lent money to buy a house and mortgage. But that was seven years ago.

The matter was dropped. There was no confrontation, no apologies asked or given. Nothing more was said. But I felt differently. The word "blackmail" had been used, and that stuck. Even if no one else demanded an explanation, I did. Slowly, I arrived at one, and it is worth recording how a trivial conversation can be worked up into something out of all proportion. It is so trivial yet it is the only solution. Old Etonians gossiping in St James's Street Clubland could so easily damage a reputation beyond repair.

Villiers's nineteen-year-old daughter, Diana, was helping with guests at the lunch that weekend in May. We chatted until she moved on to discuss matters with more important visitors. She was not particularly impressed to learn I had been to school with her brother: Not surprising, as he was ten years older and only a half-brother. I gathered afterwards that she felt my presence had spoilt the occasion: I should not have been included. Nick Villiers was a contemporary of

BC, who was publicly thrown out of Eton. Joe's loan to buy a house was fully disclosed.

Whether or not Diana was a scandal-monger is neither here nor there, no damage was done. After dining with the Villiers sometime later, Joe ventured: "Diana seems to be more settled these days." In 1972, half-Belgian Diana came to Manchester Square wearing a jaunty beret. Her appointment "was with Mr Cavendish". Her mission was to seek EMI's sponsorship for "Europalia", the bi-annual European arts festival, held that year in Brussels. Considered a prestigious event, Britain was represented by opera, ballet, theatre companies and orchestras. The Royal Ballet boys told me it had been a "Europhalia".

Did Villiers ever think about his mistake? He might have seen the irony when faced with a predicament of his own, ten years later. A newspaper ran a critical article on the British Steel Corporation, where he was chairman. The information could only have come from an insider, and Villiers demanded to know the source. The paper was intransigent. By going to court, Villiers failed to get disclosure, but he persisted. BSC was looking ridiculous. Villiers was invited to explain his actions to a House of Commons committee. He refused to go, and was fetched by the Government tipstaff, which was unprecedented.

I was cause for further ruffled feathers two months later. We were in Japan to launch Capitol and Toshiba's joint company. At breakfast on the first morning, things got off to a bad start. I ordered strawberries, which were on the menu, as a novelty. Joe's face went black: "I have never had strawberries for breakfast in my whole life!" Our manager, who was with us, turned white: "I've ordered strawberries for the reception," he muttered. An invitation came from the British Embassy for Joe to lunch with our ambassador's wife the next day. Joe declined as I was not included. The manager was unable to cope with the situation. Lady Pilcher was not to be snubbed. Joe sat on his bed and would not be persuaded. It was put to him that it was undiplomatic to disrupt the seating plan by bringing an assistant. Eventually the embassy relented, to the manager's immense relief.

The purpose of the lunch was revealed when Sir John and Lady

Pilcher, the pompous couple, asked Joe to persuade the Beatles to visit Tokyo for British Week. Joe thought John Lennon, whose wife was Japanese, might be interested; "I'll get William onto that." Seated at the bottom of the magnificent dining table, I felt the eyes of all the guests turn in my direction.

This was before one of John and Yoko's famous "Happenings", when they promoted 'Give Peace a Chance' very publicly in their Montreal hotel bedroom. Some months later we received an urgent plea from the embassy to dissuade the couple from coming to Japan.

Asked by the Hong Kong Festival organisers to persuade Margot Fonteyn and Rudolf Nureyev to grace the Territory, Joe had to explain that the couple no longer danced together. Likewise, in Tokyo, he revealed it was three years since the Beatles had last performed before a paying audience.

In contrast to the formal social occasion at the embassy, lunch with Akio Morita, the cosmopolitan founder of Sony, was a relaxed yet highly significant meeting. It was just the three of us at Maxim's, an exact copy of the Paris restaurant, but this one was owned by Morita. Sony was not in music, and Morita wanted to know everything about EMI's links with Toshiba. Joe's enthusiasm was all he needed to turn Sony on to recording and record production. Twenty years later, Sony bought CBS Records and become the world leader in music.

In October, Harold Wilson lunched at the IRC, and added his seal of approval to the body conceived by George Brown. The PM warned the Conservatives would abolish the IRC if they came to power, despite the French Government's interest in creating a similar organisation. *Private Eye*, the satirical magazine, ran a spoof article headed:

THE FEW WHO SAVED BRITAIN

Night after night, the fleets of German Salesmen flew in from their bases on the Continent. But the "Few" were waiting for them. They didn't look much like heroes, men such as Arnold "Buffy" Weinstock, Joseph "Ginger" Lockwood, Lew "Jumbo" Grade, Donald "Taffy" Stokes. From his underground HQ in Downing Street the master-mind of the Royal Export Force, Harold "Crafty" Wilson snapped out the order they had all been waiting for: "Scramble Lads!"

How could anyone call Joe "Ginger", cockney slang for ginger beer – queer? No need to be touchy: in Captain W. E. Johns's Biggles books, Air Detective Inspector Bigglesworth has an accomplice affectionately termed Air Constable "Ginger" Hebblethwaite. No schoolboy would make the connection.

Joe was approaching his sixty-fifth birthday. He was to give up executive control of EMI. The IRC was taking up so much of his time. Read and Stanford welcomed his frequent absence from the office. Things did not run smoothly at Capitol when Glenn Wallichs loosened his reins at about the same time.

Capitol Records Inc. celebrated its twenty-fifth anniversary in 1967, with an LP entitled *The Silver Years 25*. In the sleeve notes, Alan Livingston, the President, reaffirmed "the extraordinary leadership of the Company's Chairman of the Board and Chief Executive Officer, Glenn E. Wallichs". Receiving a Humanitarian Award from the National Conference of Christians and Jews the following year, Glenn was introduced as Chairman of the Board and President of Capitol Industries, Inc. Capitol Records had become Capitol Industries, and were now quoted on the New York Stock Exchange, separately from EMMIES, by taking over a small tape manufacturer and its share listing on Wall Street. There were rumours of Capitol breaking away from EMI. Alan Livingston boasted that Capitol "was growing and maturing, for the best years ahead". Wallichs did not like the sound of this. The overambitious Livingston was brutally removed and replaced as President by Stan Gortikov, boss of my friend Roger Kunz. The full impact of this coup was revealed some time later, when Nancy Livingston cut Dorothy Wallichs dead in the street. Ten years later I witnessed Joe involved in a similar situation with a humiliated wife.

Joe had announced, back in mid-year, that he would be giving up executive control of EMI on his birthday, but would remain chairman, the post he had held for fifteen years. I was away the day it was announced. Apparently, the *Evening News* rang our office to ask: "But what is going to happen to Mr Cavendish?"

Read and Stanford arranged a surprise "retirement" birthday lunch at the Dorchester Hotel penthouse. Guests were purely business colleagues, including Ted Lewis, Jules Thorn and Henry Lazell. Guest of honour was Tony Benn, newly appointed Minister of Technology, who was delighted Joe had agreed to extend his term at the IRC for a further six months: "I am looking forward to working with the IRC," he enthused. Read and Stanford, now appointed joint chief-executives, secretly hoped Joe's term would be extended indefinitely.

65th Birthday Lunch. Tony Benn, Technology Minister the main guest

For once, Joe personally drafted the chairman's statement in EMI's annual report: "£100 invested in the Company's ordinary stock in May 1954 would be worth £1,240 at September 30th 1969. This is seven times the 162% improvement shown by the F.T. Index over the same period. Sales have grown from £32.1 million to £176.3 million and pre-tax profits are up from £1.1 million to £117.6 million." He added that profits and sales in the year under review were up 50%.

Amongst telegrams of congratulation came one from the Beatles: "Very many Happy Returns on such a big birthday and you are as young as ever, love John, Paul, George, Ringo, Neil, Peter and all the other Apple gang." Charles Forté wrote: "I would like to take this opportunity to tell you that when we were discussing matters with Bernard and John Read I made a particular point of saying to Bernard – and I'm sure he must have repeated to you – that one of the main conditions I would make was that you personally should remain as

Chairman for a minimum of 3 to 5 years, and longer of it suited you. I have always had in mind that I would tell you this one day, and now I have the opportunity to do so." Forté enclosed a letter from his henchman, David Karr, "which I hope you do not find too flattering!" – as if!

> Today, I received my copy of the Annual Report of EMI containing a very excellent statement by Sir Joseph Lockwood who is retiring as Chief Executive Officer but continuing as Chairman. Sir Joseph has made remarkable contributions to the restructuring of EMI in recent years. In the 10 years that I have known him, I have found him to be one of the outstanding men in industry throughout the World. He took a somewhat dishevelled company and gave it structure, form, leadership and direction. To me, Sir Joseph is almost the epitome of relaxed perpetual motion and resilient mental youth. He continually goes on to greater challenges. I have just finished reading an article about his new work in the IRC in the important French magazine "L'Expansion". I thought you might like to pass this article on to Sir Joseph for his own justifiable edification.

Joe made no secret of enjoying this sort of flattery, something he shared with Jules Thorn. He kept the letter permanently in his briefcase and produced it whenever he wanted to impress.

David Karr was a secretive Russian who lived at the George V Hotel in Paris, at Forté's expense. No doubt there would have been a hefty finder's fee should Forté and EMI merge. He died a multi-millionaire, in suspicious circumstances, ten years later, reputedly at the hands of the KGB.

Joe spent Christmas Day with Michael Vernon. "Mr Michael", Wilfred and Nancy Vernon's son, who was appointed Chairman of Spillers in 1968. He was to be subjected to a hostile takeover.

Goodman's message on his New Year's greetings card summed up the closing year: "To our undimming agreeable association."

1970

Two Breakups: "I'm on Strike"

The next year saw the final breakup of the Beatles group, and the demise of the IRC.

Joe and Ken East, EMI Records MD, had high hopes of John Eastman, Paul McCartney's brother-in-law, bringing conformity to the group. This clean-cut young Ivy League American appealed to Joe. He studied Law, and was under the influence of his father, Lee Eastman, a successful music publisher and patron of modern art. But it was not to be. East received a letter from Apple dated March 31st, signed by John Ono Lennon, Director, and George Harrison, Director:

> We have considered very carefully indeed the position concerning the release of Paul McCartney's album on 17th April. In all circumstances, we have arrived at the conclusion that it would not be in the best interest of this company for the record to be released on that date and we have decided to re-schedule the release for the 4th June, to coincide with the Apple/Capitol Record Convention in Hawaii. The forthcoming Beatles' album will be released as scheduled on 24th April, to tie in with the film release date in mid-May.

Let It Be was the last Beatles album. Paul sent Joe a copy of his own album with a drawing by daughter Mary of a cherry tree: "Dear joe (sic) We hope you like it. Love Heather Mary Paul and Lindea (sic)".

As a tribute to their honorary godfather, each of the "boys" would send "Sir Joe" copies of their solo records: sixteen from Paul, two from John, six from George and two from Ringo. Their contract retained their services to EMI individually for a further six years.

The row over release dates had been the final straw for Paul. He tore a sheet from a foolscap pad, and wrote by hand:

To E.M.I.

Dear Sir Joe and Stan Gortikov,

No matter what anybody tells you, The Beatles are no more (John and I, at least are pursuing our own careers.)

I think that the only thing to do in the circumstances is to dissolve the partnership, and the money and artistic control to go to each of us individually.

I hope you can do something to help, because until this is cleared up, I'm on strike

Paul McCartney.

Two letters from Tony Benn on 8th and 25th June indicated the change of Government. On Ministry of Technology paper, Benn reappointed Joe Chairman of IRC for another six months; and then, on plain Commons notepaper:

Dear Joe

How very nice of you to have written. I never cared for the trappings of office, but I thought the job we were doing was worthwhile, and the people I worked with inside and outside Mintech were really great.

I particularly enjoyed working with you, and would like to wish you all success with the new Government.

Yours, Tony.

The IRC was not to let politics get in the way. It was working at full throttle. Through the year, Joe had attended 110 important meetings, one of which was held in the Talk of the Town nightclub.

Tony Jay, the BBC producer best known for his *Yes Minister* TV series, told Joe of a young man to look out for in ABPC who should be nurtured. Richard Dunn was making management training films for AB Pathe in Wardour Street. Joe agreed to sit in on one of Richard's afternoon seminars to launch the "Management By Objectives" series. Richard booked the Talk of the Town, jointly owned by Delfont and Forté, where Delfont put on floor shows and Forté did the catering.

During the film show – in which Rolls Royce, ironically as it turned out later, exemplified good management techniques – I took a call from IRC. John Gardiner needed to see Joe urgently about a crisis at Cammell Laird shipbuilders. The club manager made his office available for a 4.15 p.m. meeting, probably the only time the former London Hippodrome Theatre, and, later lap-dancing club, had been used for official Government business.

When the Conservative Government terminated the corporation, IRC boys were inevitably receiving tempting job offers. Gardiner was one of the first to go. His anti-establishment attitude appealed to Joe. His scorn towards the Chairman of Babcock and Wilcox, who were losing money, was evident: he "offered us the choice of three Rolls Royces for a lift back to the office."

IRC formed the Laird Group from the non-shipbuilding elements of Cammell Laird that were worth saving. Joe was attacked for putting in the young and inexperienced Gardiner as managing director: "John Gardiner is the best man for the job. There is nothing wrong with a financial journalist." (Gardiner had been LEX columnist for the *FT* for five years). Joe did not want to be chairman but agreed to sit on the board, which would meet every two months. There was an immediate row with the company secretary, who was indoctrinated: board meeting dates, times and places must be fixed a full year in advance. That was the correct way to treat non-executive directors.

Geoffrey Robinson, who accepted IRC board member Lord Stokes's offer to run Jaguar Motors, rang me reprovingly. He had heard Read was taking on Jon Chaplin, the IRC Company Secretary. "Why isn't he snapping up the real executives before it is too late?"

He had a point. They all went on to glittering careers. Five received knighthoods. Prospective candidates demurred at the prospect they would be working for Read and not Joe, quite a different proposition. Gardiner had already declined and was now accounted for. Joe never expressed what must have been on his mind in later years: had he and Gardiner been running EMI, the company might have had a very different history. As it was, Joe made himself available for weekly meetings with Read at EMI, and Gardiner at Laird. On Monday morning, Read came to consult, listen, and do nothing. On Friday mornings, it was Gardiner's turn. Here was the contrast: Gardiner did the talking, leaving Joe to concur or comment constructively on his actions.

The first member of the new Government that Joe was to hear from was Margaret Thatcher. (The fate of IRC had to wait until October.) With regard to the National Theatre, the new Secretary of State for Education and Science wrote in July. She was deeply concerned that the members of the South Bank Theatre Board, whose term was up in August, would all leave at the critical moment when "it will have to consider letting the contract for the second stage of the building. I share with my predecessors very real appreciation of all that the board has done in carrying the work so far towards completion of the new theatre building". Joe and Goodman, who never resigned from anything (including racecourses), agreed to stay on for a further five years.

By chance, a letter arrived at the office the previous month which led, unexpectedly, to EMI playing a role in Mrs Thatcher's route to 10 Downing Street, during her years as Leader of the Opposition. It was from Cliff Michelmore, the presenter of *Tonight*, BBCTV's topical news programme. Michelmore and Joe were friends, Michelmore frequently reminding Joe about the gramophone records he sent to his small son, Guy. The family had been driven mad by the boy's banging on his toy drum in time to the music. Michelmore wrote:

A small group of television and film producers and performers have got together to enter the field of producing programmes in the field of home television on cassette/disc/film. It seems to us that those of you in the hardware market could co-operate with those of us in the software market to our mutual advantage and benefit. If you are interested perhaps you would like to meet two or three of us for one day soon.

Joe invited Michelmore and his producer colleague, Gordon Reece, for lunch, to introduce Read. From then on it was out of his hands. Read said: "This is something we must do something about." In other words: "Keep out, I'll take credit for this if it's a success."

RM–EMI Ltd was formed and moved to a four-storey building, not far from where Richard Dunn's film unit operated on a shoestring, producing software not dissimilar to what Michelmore envisaged. Far too ambitious and extravagant to succeed, RM–EMI was soon in trouble. By 1975, Michelmore was gone, and the whole thing was nothing more than a vanity project for Gordon Reece, the original cuckoo in the nest. Reece was a hyperactive, jumpy little man who fed on champagne and cigars to create a larger-than-life image. Joe did not consider he knew him particularly well. So it came as a bit of a surprise when Reece asked him to put him up for membership of the Carlton Club. It soon became clear where his ambitions lay. He had followed the career of Christopher Chataway closely. Chataway, sports celebrity and TV personality, had moved from the BBC to become a Tory MP and Minister of Posts and Telecommunications in the Heath Government. Reece had moulded Chataway, the Olympic athlete, into "Chatabox", the viewer-friendly BBC TV interviewer. Who better than he to work his magic on Mrs Thatcher? Conservative Central Office was impressed and offered to take him on full-time. His brief was to improve the Leader of the Opposition's hair, clothes and voice. EMI jumped at being free of someone who had become an expensive embarrassment, and agreed to release him. Salary and large expense account were to be shared equally between EMI and the Conservative Party.

Gordon Reece gave a party at the Carlton Club in Mrs Thatcher's honour. Joe was invited. Mrs Thatcher congratulated Joe for his generous loan. Yet it was nothing to do with him, as he was no longer Chairman of EMI. For this was 1975. Most effusive in his praise was fellow guest Charles Forté, who knew the form: he had been a financial supporter of Edward Heath.

Back to 1970, Bernard Delfont was now based at ABPC's Golden Square headquarters, having temporarily abandoned his office in the Prince of Wales Theatre where I had first seen him.

One of Bryan Forbes's films not to get a cinema showing was *The Breaking of Bumbo*, starring Joanna Lumley and Richard Warwick. Based on Andrew Sinclair's 1958 novel about National Service and the London season, it was something I had been looking forward to seeing. Also keen to view it was ex-Life Guards officer Peter Lendrum at Ranks, who pressed me for a private screening. This was fixed for early one evening in April, at Golden Square. Joining Joe, me and Peter were Anthony Blond, the book's publisher, and various of his boyfriends. We assembled in the foyer. At that moment, the elegantly dressed Carole Delfont arrived to collect her husband. She greeted Joe warmly, ignoring everyone else, which was fortunate, as Anthony Blond's flies were undone.

Delfont must have learnt why we were there. "I couldn't possibly release it," he told me later. We both knew what he was referring to, but the reason he gave was a surprise. A scene was filmed at Madame Tussaud's, where the participants went mad and burnt an effigy of Winston Churchill, reducing it to liquid wax. "Quite unacceptable!"

I found Delfont very human, very approachable, as in this case, very patriotic, yet at the same time a terrible liar. In show business, hype becomes second nature to a wheeler-dealer. As a favour to a drama coach at the Central School, I wrote lobbying Delfont to transfer a play doing very well at the Theatre Royal, Stratford, East London to the West End. It was Joan Littlewood's production of *Marie Lloyd*, with Avis Bunnage brilliant in the leading role. I heard nothing. Sometime later he took me aside to explain how sorry he was not to realise the show I was writing about was already on, yet he must have known. He said, had he known, he would have sent someone to see it. In truth, he had a personal vendetta with Joan Littlewood, who had walked out of Lionel Bart's *Twang* musical when it was being tried out in the provinces, before failing at our Shaftesbury Theatre.

Bryan Forbes invited us to watch the Royal Ballet filming *The Tales of Beatrix Potter* at Elstree. As the dancers shared the Royal Ballet School's premises, Joe already knew Frederick Ashton, Wayne Sleep, Lesley Collier and the other dancers who were performing that day. I was captivated by Sir Fred, or Freddie, who was almost hidden in his Mrs Tiggywinkle costume. He did not want to be photographed as it would spoil the illusion. How different he was from the description given by the assistant stage manager at the Arts Theatre in Cambridge: "Frederick Ashton and Lesley Hurry, the two biggest queens in the business!" I had been backstage to collect two sketches I had bought at an exhibition of Leslie Hurry's designs for the Old Vic Company. Later, when I got to know Fred, I asked him what he thought of Gérard. Came the reply: "Gérard is the most musical person I have ever met. He listens in a trance, and you can almost see the music in his face!"

Bryan Forbes on the "Tales of Beatrix Potter" set at Elstree

Bryan feared *Beatrix Potter* was going the same way as some of his other films. Delfont was reported to have said: "Do you know, it's got no dialogue!" Bryan needed allies. He wrote after a preview: "Dear Willie, Bless you for being so sweet last night and for giving such generous support. I shan't forget." He need not have worried. The elderly Sir Ian Jacob revealed that he was brought up on the Peter Rabbit stories. The film's producers were Richard Goodwin and Lord Brabourne, Lord Mountbatten's son-in-law. The Queen was persuaded by Mountbatten to attend the premiere, and success was assured.

Sir Frederick Ashton at Beatrix Potter premiere

If a strain in relations between Read and Delfont was developing, it might have been noticed on a strange occasion. The whole board of EMI and their wives, me included, were invited to spend an evening with Hammer Films, of horror movies fame. We were shown the company's operations, and then taken to dine in a private room of the Mirabelle Restaurant as guests of Sir James and Lady Carreras. It emerged later that Hammer was insolvent. Had Jimmy Carreras been trying to get EMI to buy his company before the news got out? Finding

Delfont unresponsive, and Read an easier option, was he intending to go over Delfont's head? As it turned out, he failed. Anyone, Read in particular, would be expected to treat Carreras with caution in future. On the contrary, Read engaged him as a "consultant", reporting directly "as his most trusted adviser". At the same time, Lady Carreras formed a close relationship with Dorothy Read. Many of the new ventures EMI entered into were brought to the company by Carreras. These included Brighton Marina and the Angus Steak Houses, including one in Knightsbridge, where I was introduced to Gérard. Joe did not care for Carreras. And when a chain of hotels was added to the restaurants, they formed a division clearly outside Delfont's control. To compensate for exclusion from Brighton, Delfont was later to make a huge success of Chichester Marina, but that is another story.

There were minor rages that remained suppressed during the year. For example, Joe was furious with Princess Margaret for arriving late at the Royal Ballet School, keeping her mother waiting. And PM Edward Heath's failure to get stuck in, with so much to sort out, was a growing irritation. That came later. The big eruption was saved for our overseas tour that year, when we set off for Mexico, Barbados, Brazil, Argentina and South Africa in March. All went well until we reached Johannesburg.

Barbados was already a popular holiday destination for my parents. I looked forward to seeing them. It was a convenient stop between Mexico and Brazil. Nevertheless, Joe made no exception to a procedure approved by Joe Smith, his tax adviser at Cooper Brothers. The part of his salary paid from Interton, our Swiss company, was treated as "Overseas Earnings". Provided he was travelling on company business, the Inland Revenue allowed freedom from UK tax. Big-earning EMI artists Cliff Richard, Queen and Pink Floyd, even George Martin, took advantage of similar schemes, provided they lived abroad for a year, a condition the Beatles rejected. Originally set up to pay overseas-based executives, Interton was a valuable tax dodge, so valuable that Hartley Shawcross asked to be included.

Before setting off, Joe drafted a letter for EMI's taxation manager to sign:

My co-Directors in Interton have asked me to ask you to visit a number of associated companies at some time convenient to yourself. These particular companies are all giving problems at the moment, and need advice and decisions to be made which involve, in some cases, the management, and, in other cases, their method of operation. Barbados: The West Indies Recording Company has been left very much on its own. It appears to be making considerable profits in which we do not participate.

On our return, Joe reported to Interton: "March 5th and 6th, I spent in Barbados, much of the time with our licensees West Indies Recording Company. I dealt with a number of problems on copyright and the question of releasing Apple Records in Barbados and the surrounding islands."

Face obscured from the sun by a towel, he presented a comic figure on the island as he walked along the beach from the Sandy Lane Hotel. Was he hiding from the scorching heat? More likely he was avoiding conversations with tycoons, the Rothschilds, the Bernsteins, the Spencer Wills, even the Governor of the Bank of England, exposing their flesh along the shoreline.

Shortly before the trip, I took an unexpected call from the manager of our South African company: "Would the chairman like to see the Kimberley Diamond Mines?" As he had organised our previous visit to the Kruger National Park, this did not seem a particularly unusual request. "What was that all about?" Joe asked, with a strange look in his eyes. He had overheard the conversation. With that super-sharp instinct that served so well, he must have sensed that Stanford had given instructions to keep him away from day-to-day business affairs, now that he was non-executive chairman.

On arrival in Johannesburg, we kept to the schedule and took an early domestic flight to Kimberley. Joe was already tense that morning. His mouth was dry, and his tongue was making that clicking noise indicating there was something terribly wrong. The moment we arrived at De Beers Consolidated Mines offices he said he must go straight back to Johannesburg. There was no time to look at diamond mines. We were told there were no domestic flights until later. He persisted. As luck would have it, Harry Oppenheimer, Chairman of De Beers, calmly came to the rescue. He put his private plane at our disposal. Un-pressurised and limited to four passengers, including the Cape coloured pilot, it was not a craft Joe would normally contemplate. The return journey was terrifying.

Joe had discovered what he had already suspected, that our company was signing a contract that would have disastrous consequences. On a previous visit, the Manager of Teal Records impressed him as brighter than anyone at EMI. Now, that same manager had done a deal for EMI to press Teal's records at a substantial loss. It was a con. Joe reported to the Directors of Interton:

> Whilst there I dealt with a new agreement with Teal Records, which could have involved the Company in severe expense and losses. Although the Agreement had just been signed by the Chairman of the Company, it was necessary to re-negotiate it, and completely revise the Agreement on to a different basis. This was subsequently done.

As I was on duty both weekdays and weekends, I was never sure how people would respond to my status. That Sunday lunch at the Villiers' had been bruising. We attended Farnborough Air Display as guests of Hawker Siddeley, and had lunch in their marquee. The Air Minister, accompanied by his Private Secretary, arrived late and was escorted to a spare seat beside me. This was Sir Peter Emery, a long-serving MP, recently elevated with a Government job and very aware of his self-importance. Obviously he expected more knowledgeable company. Arnold Hall was at a Society of Aero-Manufacturers reception and unavailable. I failed to impress. The following years, Hawkers suggested directors treat their invitation as personal and only bring guests on Visitors Day. Emery was arrested on a driving charge sometime later. I was amused at the loss of dignity that entailed.

We went for long walks with the dogs at weekends. Arriving for Sunday lunch at the McAlpines' in Fawley, they could not believe that Joe had come all the way on foot. Fawley was at least halfway to Henley from Hatchet Wood. True, it was a little hard on Max with his short legs. We were *all* made to feel very welcome. During lunch, Lady McAlpine provided Max with the pen previously used by her own dachshunds. Sir Edwin praised Joe. He wanted to build more nuclear power stations: Joe alone could get the Government to make its mind up on whether they should be advanced gas or pressure water installations. His construction company heard rumours that Read planned to build a great new head office in London. We walked home after lunch declining the offer of a lift.

Brother Charles would bring his family to Hatchet Wood every year to see uncle Joe. Joe considered his nieces spoilt, their husbands not-up-to-much, but was very fond of their children. They all considered me part of the establishment, which was pleasantly reassuring, as they were a large family.

One of Joe's "Young Millers" from Henry Simon days brought his sixteen-year-old son to be introduced to his godfather. "What is he doing here?" the boy asked, looking in my direction. The parents were not invited again.

First news about IRC's future came from Sir Richard Clarke, Permanent Secretary at the Ministry of Technology, and, incidentally, father of future Labour Home Secretary, Charles Clarke. In a letter dated 14th October and marked PERSONAL AND CONFIDENTIAL, Sir "Otto" wrote:

"to give you a few hours advance warning of the changes of the machinery of Government which will be announced on Thursday afternoon ... There is to be a new Department of Trade and Industry." He went on to describe how IRC would be split between permanent secretaries and ministers. Two items were of great significance. Sir Antony Part was to be one secretary. Another would be responsible for the Ministry of Aviation Supply:

The work on Rolls Royce will of course be under that Department.

Finally, as to my own situation. I am 60 and will be retiring from the Civil Service early next year. Meanwhile, I shall be engaged on special duties in the Civil Service Department.

I would like to take this opportunity, as I shall not have time later, to say how much I have personally enjoyed working with the IRC during these years, and I know that this has been felt by very many of us in this Department. Governments change and policies change and the needs of situations change but I shall always look back upon this period with a great deal of warmth.

Joe invited Sir Otto to be a non-executive Director of EMI, the only civil servant on his board. In retirement, Sir Otto openly criticised Parliament for failing to control public expenditure.

On 30th October, John Davies, Secretary of State at the Department of Trade and Industry, wrote to tell Joe he would be making a statement in the House of Commons that afternoon proposing the dissolution of the IRC. He hoped Joe and the board would remain and keep things going into the new year. It was not to be the last time a minister asked Joe to extend his term. It was to become a regular occurrence.

Not a word from the new Prime Minister about dumping the IRC, just a note from Downing Street:

Dear Joe

I am writing to thank you very much for the magnificent selection of records which was delivered to No. 10 this morning. This really is most generous of you and I shall look forward to listening to them over Christmas.

With best wishes for Christmas and the New Year,

Yours ever,

Ted.

Goodman's year end card bore the message: "What SHALL we do next year with out the IRC?"

*Chairman poses
with original
HMV painting*

1971

"Sir Joseph's time is worth £500 a minute"

I was now thirty and living in a home of my own. My flat, which my mother bought for £8000, was in a new block beside her house in Cadogan Lane. We had adjoining front doors, with a party wall obscuring comings and goings. For the amount I saw my parents, we might have been worlds apart. My father complained about laundry left for collection at their address. In return, I pushed mail through their letter box when they were away. My mother went into my flat once and found my valet, who was on loan from the Carlton Club, lying in a coma. He had not told me he was diabetic. I did not see him again.

My London bedsit

I entertained Robin, Gérard and Harry Williams. Harry's close friends John Betjeman and Elizabeth Cavendish advised against his decision to retreat into a monastery, at Mirfield in Yorkshire. "You will miss William and David," referring to me and David Moore-Gwynne, his two former pupils.

When allowed out, Harry stayed in one of two houses Elizabeth owned in Chelsea. John called it "a sort of clergy house". One evening I was taken to meet Elizabeth and John, interrupting their dinner party. They were entertaining Anne Scott-James and Osbert Lancaster. Learning I lived in Cornwall, Anne, a keen gardener, asked about the clifftop spring squill, the little blue flowers. Elizabeth was not pleased at the intrusion and John took us into his study. Harry had been examining my Eton albums earlier. John, not to be outdone, produced photographs of prep-school boys in grey flannel shorts. John wrote to me: "Having Harry staying in this house has emboldened me to write to you about something dear to my heart and where I think you can help through your Chief and his firm." He wanted to record the Isle of Man poet, T. E. Brown. "If the only thing I can achieve as Poet Laureate is to have these poems read in the Manx dialect onto a gramophone record, I shall not have lived in vain … this noble cause might even be remunerative for there are many thousands of Manxmen throughout the World and every Manxman will want the record." I contacted Decca, the only company with a suitable spoken-word label. Fortunately, they were keen to follow up on Sir John's request.

Joe and I were off on another world tour, taking us the whole month of January. In Los Angeles, Joe was to see Glenn Wallichs for the last time, although he didn't know it. Capitol Industries' profits were down by three quarters. We flew on to New Zealand, where Joe was interviewed by a Wellington newspaper. He said Britain's entry into the European Community would present New Zealand with a fantastic killing. "Too small for self-sufficiency, give up manufacture of HMV refrigerators, become a County of England, and bring huge lamb exports to the Union: Otherwise I think that the Common Market countries will reduce the amount of produce they will take from New Zealand. The country will suffer and the standard of living will fall." By the time the press caught up with us, we were staying at a sheep station on the South Island. An NZ MP accused Joe of "showing a complete lack of appreciation of the character of New Zealand people". Ignoring the intrusion, Joe relished observing how one man and a dog could control immense flocks of sheep. We spent the day with a farmer whose five children, three boys and two girls, were quite spellbound by Joe. They had never seen anyone like him. They sat in awe, encouraging him to just go on talking.

Back home a few months later, I noticed the same effect on a group of management trainees at the Administrative Staff College in Henley. He received letters afterwards asking for jobs. I recorded the talk on the Sony tape recorder Akio Morita had given him. The Director of the College was put out when Joe declined future invitations to repeat his success.

In New Zealand with my cousin Paulette

"Managers do not go on training courses. They do not need to learn to understand human beings and common sense. They do not like to spend money – unless it is going to bring in more money."

In Canberra, Australia's capital, we took tea with the Governor General and his wife at Government House, breaking the new rule not to mix with dignitaries. In Sydney, Ken East, now Managing Director of EMI Australia, asked Joe to put in a word with the people back in London about fellow Australian Rolf Harris. Despite regularly topping the UK charts with 'Sun Arise', 'Tie Me Kangaroo Down' and 'Two Little Boys', Harris felt he deserved greater attention. Joe promised to talk to Delfont. Joe looked for standardisation among the overseas companies to produce savings. Efficient pressing of records received his attention, as did the printing of sleeves and, even, the little round paper labels attached to the discs. He was given a demonstration of a revolutionary new machine made by Multilith Addressograph for possible use in each territory.

L. Informal in Australia

R.With Dolly East

In April we were in Rome. This was unusual, as company business usually took us to Milan. But we were not visiting Voce Del Padrone. We attended the takeover of a TV set manufacturer. Bill Stanford had met Arnaldo Piccinini, the founder of Voxson, which manufactured those beautifully Italian-designed television sets, on a plane journey.

Voxson television demonstration

Stanford's instructions had been to expand by acquisition. Piccinini revealed he was considering disposing of the family's majority holding in the company. It was all so simple. After the deal was done, it emerged Piccinini was dying, and his son preferred to design racing cars. The TV sets did not work, the company was losing money and Italian unions made it impossible to sack workers. As neither Read nor Stanford spoke Italian, they had relied on an EMI executive, who impressed them with his multilingual talents rather than commercial sense. The British Consul had a word in my ear at the launch of the takeover. He was disgusted that "your people had not consulted my staff". Joe enjoyed the party, and was charmed by the Piccininis.

John Davies, who had reported the closure of IRC back in October, now wrote on 27th April:

> I have decided to make 1st May 1971 "the appointed day" for the repeal of the Industrial Reorganisation Corporation Act 1966 and for the transfer of the Corporation's property. This means that the dissolution of the Corporation should take place one month later and I am therefore enclosing a copy of the formal minute re-appointing you as Chairman until the 31st May 1971.
>
> Thank you for agreeing to serve for this further period.

He invited Joe and past and present members of the board to a small dinner party at the Oriental Club on 20th May. The *Sunday Telegraph* commented, "The Funeral wake took place in a private room of the Oriental Club." All the members wrote to Joe, including this from Goodman:

> You handled a mixed bag of people with extraordinary skill and discretion and even managed to keep our Managing Director – the Prince Rupert of Throgmorton Street – on the battlefield most of the time!

An embattled Villiers claimed that "If IRC had not existed Heath would probably have invented it!"

Villiers' own persistent lobbying had persuaded the obstinate Prime Minister to counter-react. Joe and Jules Thorn, who frequently lunched together, had experienced Heath's resistance to advice. This did not prevent Joe receiving an invitation to lunch at Chequers later in the year. Asked to remain after the other guests had left, Joe expected to be given the opportunity to discuss the Government's progress. Instead, Heath proudly demonstrated his new hi-fi system.

Joe was invited to give evidence to the Expenditure Committee of the House of Commons Trade and Industry Subcommittee on 23rd June. Reassured he was safeguarded by Erskine May on anything he said, he stated the IRC had told the previous Government that Rolls Royce was not only a lame duck, but bankrupt. He was thanked by the chairman and members of the subcommittee for the valuable help he gave the meeting. Nothing more was heard until 3rd August, when a transcript of Joe's evidence was published: "We certainly made it known to the Government that millions and millions would be required by Rolls Royce and that in our view Rolls Royce was not a viable entity." He did not believe the management knew what was happening financially. All hell broke out. The evening paper news-stands screamed "Rolls Royce shock!" The *Daily Mail*'s 4th August edition featured an enormous headline: "ROLLS: SHOCK REPORT WAS KEPT SECRET. Truth kept from Cabinet for fear of slander." The scandal remained newsworthy until the end of the year. Joe was recalled by the subcommittee creating further headlines: "Saving Rolls cheaper than bankruptcy, says ex-IRC chief," and: "Rolls could have been saved, say top IRC men." The IRC's confidential report was dated 22nd December 1969 and ran to 120 pages. Joe, who never retained business papers, kept a 60-page summary, "Just in case." I destroyed it later.

For many years, Villiers campaigned to publish a book about the IRC, but was regularly rebutted. The main objector was Antony Part, Otto Clarke's successor, who rightly considered it a vanity project, but gave Government confidentiality as the reason for refusals. Villiers persisted, and a non-controversial volume, *The IRC: An Experiment in Industrial Intervention*, was published in 1983.

Glenn Wallichs failed to attend the June board meeting. He died of cancer later in the year. I had taken Glenn and Dorothy antique-hunting in Portobello Road, and only recently had procured seats for Ken Tynan's notorious revue *Oh! Calcutta* at the Roundhouse. They had to see something that scandalised New York. In the 1960s, when UK taxes were penal, Glenn insisted on including a reluctant Joe in Capitol's Deferred Compensation Scheme. At $40,000 a year for seven years, this produced a tidy retirement lump sum in 1974, which Joe sheltered in a Channel Islands Investment Trust.

Urgent steps were being taken to restore Capitol Industries, where things had been going wrong. I picked out an article in an American magazine, where Allen Klein boasted a massive increase in Beatles earnings since taking over their management. "Go downstairs and get the Beatles' contract with Capitol," I was instructed. Assured there was no copy, I returned empty-handed. Joe instinctively knew something was being kept from him. I was sent back to the Legal Department a second time, and remained until a copy was found. "I took the contract home," Joe said, "and I wrapped a damp towel around my head and studied it and still found it unintelligible." Sure enough, Klein had re-negotiated the contract, making Capitol concede certain rights to his ABKO company. He had increased the Beatles' earnings at the expense of Capitol.

A young Indian was sent to run Capitol. This was Bhaskar Menon, head of EMI's Calcutta-based subsidiary. How Bhaskar came to join EMI in 1957 is explained in a letter Joe received from Dr Philip Andrews, Professor of Economics at Nuffield College, Oxford in March 1956:

Dear Mr Lockwood,

I mentioned to you while you were here that I had an extraordinary Indian pupil who was thinking he would go into industry in India. V. B. Menon is a nephew of Krishna Menon and so is well connected, but I should hasten to add that I found no trace of left wing nonsense. He is a very patriotic Indian but he has a long-run view and a wisdom which

I find surprising and encouraging … He is one of the most able people I have taught for about five years … I have no doubt that whoever would have to train him would benefit as much from the relationship as I did when I taught him … P.S. One tiny fact: He did not seem at all perturbed at the thought of Dum Dum. His only reaction was to say that he knew it and of course it was one of the areas of heavy industry. He did not follow my own lead on the subject of the aesthetic shock of working in such an environment.

After spending time as a trainee in George Martin's office, Bhaskar was sent to work at the Gramophone Company – in Dum Dum. He was to give Joe credit not just for employing him, but also for sending him to put Capitol right. This is untrue. Read and Stanford put him in charge of Capitol. Joe would have treated this as a short-term assignment, with ultimate instruction to return to the EMI fold. In fact, Bhaskar went native, not surprising considering the scale of salaries paid to top American executives. His initial two-year employment package included incentive compensation of $75,000 p.a., on top of his $100,000 salary. This doubled after Glenn's death. Joe's salary was £32,000. Bhaskar still lives in Beverly Hills.

On 10th March, the very week of his sudden resignation, Bryan Forbes invited us to a private screening at Golden Square of a film about Rudolf Nureyev. Kit Dawnay, revealing a secret passion for the dancer, demanded to be included. This was a good omen, corresponding as it did to Ian Jacob's love of the *Tales of Beatrix Potter*. What we saw was Nureyev in *La Sylphide* and *Marguerite et Armand*. What we had was too short for a film feature. With much cajoling of the reluctant dancer, there was eventually enough in the can to consider issuing it at the end of the year, entitled *I am a Dancer*. We were kept informed of the proceedings during the intervening months. Bryan put his trusted assistant John Hargreaves in charge, and we went to see him at Elstree Studios, unaware of the commotion this created. Read came to our room white-faced: "Bernie says you have been to Elstree!" he said, confronting Joe. The company was obviously seething with intrigue, of the sort Joe would never encompass, and we were now apparently involved. It was so childish. To make amends, we made a further visit to Elstree, at the invitation of the new manager. Joe was given yet another full tour of the studios, during which Hargreaves's department was ignored.

Two ballets were chosen to complete the film, Glen Tetley's *Field Figures* and a *pas de deux* from *Sleeping Beauty*. For the former, Nureyev refused to partner Monica Mason ("like dancing with a man!"). Performed in full-body practice leotards with Deanne Bergsma, it was hard to tell the sexes apart.

"I Am a Dancer"
premiere

MichaelWood,
Royal Ballet School
Director with
Rudolf Nureyev

Rudolf with
Charles Murland

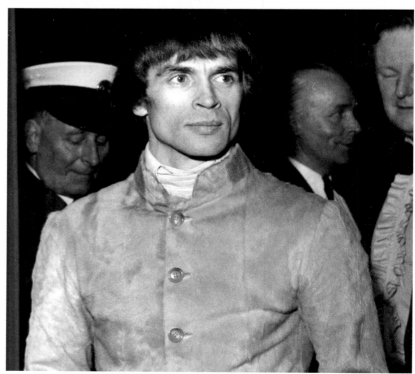

First choice for *Sleeping Beauty*, Merle Park, slammed down the telephone exclaiming: "That's Margot's thing!" referring to the Fonteyn/Nureyev *Marguerite et Armand* piece. Lynn Seymour accepted instead, and filming took place one cold November Sunday in the deserted Coliseum. Bryan Forbes directed the dancers to taped music, with curtain calls before an empty auditorium. He told me later, Nureyev was the most unpleasant artist he had worked with: "There is an inbred evil that he inflicts on others," this from a director who was known for his sensitive way with actors. "Rudi was impossible that day; brilliant, genius dancer, but a somewhat foul and flawed human being who came to a hideous end!"

Joe and I were in a film later that year; or rather, characters played us. Malcolm McDowell had impressed Joe when he saw *The Raging Moon*. Joe sent him a George Harrison LP, and received a letter recommending a "difficult novel. *A Clockwork Orange* by Burgess," later filmed with Malcolm in the lead. In April, he invited himself to the office to discuss a project. He planned to make a film using the same team from *If*, Lindsay Anderson's anti-establishment satire, another film Joe enjoyed. He brought his scriptwriter, David Sherwin. They wanted to see how a tycoon operated, and they liked what they saw. Joe, seated in his accustomed place at the boardroom table, pressed the concealed button to summon me. Here was the magic rapport between chairman and PA the filmmakers were after. In *O Lucky Man!*, the corrupt tycoon Sir James Burgess, played by Ralph Richardson, has a PA called William. The PA informs the chairman's visitor: "Sir James's time is worth £500 a minute." Lindsay Anderson's published diaries describe a meeting: "Today lunch at TV Centre with intention of soliciting patronage of Director General. I arrive first; a smooth young man – very reminiscent of Sir James's William in 'O Lucky Man' asked me if I'd like a drink, or would I wait for the others? ... I had a drink!"

Malcolm savoured Joe's aphorisms: "There's a thin line between Wormwood Scrubs and the House of Lords." David Sherwin wrote:

> Sir Joseph Lockwood sees us in his huge Boardroom. He tells us some of
> the truths of business ... "It's not a question of morals – it's waste. Once

you allow waste it goes right down the company. You end up ruined, be you the United States, or a fish and chip shop at the Battersea Funfair." I type out the speech. It's perfect for Sir James to say to Mick [Malcolm] in the back of the Rolls Royce. It is shot but cut out in the editing.

Richard Dunn of AB Pathe noticed the circles I was moving in, and invited me to lunch. He wanted something more challenging than documentary-making, and sounded me out about moving on to produce feature films for the big screen. It was a gratifying experience to be consulted by this attractive younger man. Richard went on to run Thames Television, which was nothing short of what Antony Jay anticipated when recommending him to Joe.

Derby Day at Epsom on 2nd June was the setting for a strange event, where the worlds of ballet, banking and music merged at the races.

Joe became a director of a "fringe" bank, where there were no board meetings. He did this as a favour to Charles Gordon, ex-financial journalist, who raised money for the Royal Ballet School from his contacts, including £50,000 from Max Rayne and £50 from Charles Clore's young daughter, "a charming girl", who became leading patron of the arts, Dame Vivien Duffield. Spey Investments competed with major merchant banks. Charles had persuaded the Electricity Board, Barclays, ICI, Royal Insurance and Unilever to put their pension funds at his disposal. Sir Paul Chambers of ICI was Chairman of Spey, Joe was Deputy Chairman, and Lord Chalfont, the former Foreign Minister, Chief Executive. The latter appointment caught the attention of the press. *Private Eye* made Charles out to be more of a "confidence" man than a "contact" man. Stung at comments that he lacked banking experience, and sensing Charles was not all he made himself out to be, Chalfont resigned. "The shortest City banking career I have heard of," commented the Men and Matters column in the *Financial Times*.

Charles Gordon was married to Nadia Nerina, Principal Ballerina with the Royal Ballet, recently retired to support her husband's business interests. Frederick Ashton created some of his best roles for Nadia, but did not like Charles, who had an affair with his boyfriend Alexander

Grant. So Charles had enemies in the ballet as well as the City. It was considered in the company that Nadia had "made a bad marriage".

Joe genuinely liked the couple, and, not surprisingly, Nadia, counting on his friendship, decided he should redeem Charles's reputation before the scandal broke. She would convince him Charles had done nothing wrong, even though their extravagant lifestyle was evidently underwritten by the pension funds. She had to see Joe immediately. That was impossible – he was off to the races. Joe explained it was Derby Day and he was entertaining guests. She was undeterred.

The guests were George and Judy Martin. The previous week, George finalised a deal with EMI to issue recordings from his independent company, exclusively for five years. He claimed he had "a new act coming along which will be a sensation … if they only sell one-twentieth of the records that the Beatles did, I shall make more money than I did out of the Beatles." Joe agreed to be photographed signing the contract with George.

There is nothing to beat watching the Derby from the privacy of the Directors' Box, and lunching high in the stands, away from the crowds. One had to admire Nadia's audacity for breaking up the scene, demanding to talk to Joe. As he guided her into a side room, Judy exclaimed: "What does that woman think she is doing here?" Charles and Nadia had another box.

In 1971, Joe became Chairman of the Royal Ballet. This was a simplification of the formal title of Chairman of the Governors of the Royal Ballet Companies. In 1956, Queen Elizabeth II granted the Sadler's Wells Ballet, Sadler's Wells Theatre Ballet and Sadler's Wells Ballet School a Royal Charter, and they became the Royal Ballet and the Royal Ballet School. This gave both the Company and the School a separate entity from the Opera House, something Joe did not fail to remind the Royal Opera House Board, who were inclined to forget. The Charter Body was required to meet occasionally, at what Joe referred to as a talking shop, where no great decisions were made. Nevertheless, it brought him prestige at Covent Garden, where he was to play an increasingly important role replacing the IRC and, ultimately, EMI in his portfolio. Following the unexpected death of

David Webster, he was reluctantly drawn into choosing the new General Manager for the Opera House. There were two candidates: John Tooley, Webster's long-term assistant manager, and the Earl of Harewood, a cousin of the Queen and authority on opera, who had worked at Covent Garden. Harewood had the backing of Goodman, still Chairman of the Arts Council, and whose choice should have been critical. Lord Drogheda, as Chairman of the Opera House, was desperate to appoint Tooley, whom he could control, at the same time jealous of Harewood. Someone had to have the casting vote, and the lot fell to Joe. He did not know Harewood, and his dealings with Tooley exposed shortcomings of a non-commercial nature. There was the tonic water episode, when Beechams' offer to stock the bars with two years' free supply of Whites tonic water was rejected on the grounds that operagoers preferred Schweppes. Joe gave this as an example of Opera House extravagance at an Arts Council meeting. Closer to Joe's heart was the failure to record live performances of the ballet at Covent Garden, made impossible by musicians' union demands which should have been challenged. Although brought in by Drogheda to arbitrate, Joe owed him no favours, but decided on balance Tooley should have the job.

This was the only occasion when Joe and Goodman failed to back each other. They continued in opposite camps. When Harewood went to run the English National Opera, Goodman joined him, severing ties with Covent Garden despite retaining his box. There were too many links between the two to let this affect their relationship.

Joe received a handwritten letter on Kensington Palace notepaper, dated 28th May, from Princess Margaret:

Thank you so much for sending me news of the Royal Ballet. I have always wanted to receive regular news ever since I became President, but it never seemed to transpire! Now I am most grateful and delighted that you have become Chairman.

The performance last night was exquisite and I had a very good liaison talk with Kenneth MacMillan and Peter Wright and John Tooley so I hope to be able to take a close interest in the Ballet's affairs which is very close to my heart.

Yours very sincerely,

Margaret.

Joe avoided his President that evening, accepting an invitation from Sir Thomas Sopwith to come fishing, remembering to take a dinner jacket.

It was not so easy to avoid the seventy-three-year-old Founder. Dame Ninette de Valois continued to put in an almost daily visit at the School, even though she was officially retired. Finding Madam's presence an interference, the staff decided on a solution, which was to give her a leaving party and present. Joe was to make the presentation. The *Daily Telegraph* reported: "When Sir Joseph bravely attempted the impossible and made a moving speech about Ballet's debt to her, she almost managed to turn the occasion into a public expression of thanks for all Sir Joseph's achievements as Chairman of the School, which although considerable, were not really what the occasion was about." Needless to say, her visits continued.

Where did I fit in with all this? Was I becoming isolated? With no overseas trips to plan, I was more involved in domestic matters. Joe decided to make changes to his town and country staff. Rather than hard-to-find elderly housekeepers, we were to look for young males. Four came and went, each worse than the previous one. They were interviewed, engaged, and almost immediately dismissed. A tedious process. Joe reverted to a middle-aged married couple for the country and an elderly spinster for London.

I had an operation in November, which kept me away from the office for a couple of weeks. I could not help noticing whenever I was away, which was not often, that Joe had a much jollier time without me. There was the Ball Paul and Linda McCartney gave at the Empire Ballroom, Leicester Square from 8 p.m. to midnight, which Joe attended with Elton John and his partner John Reid, with drinks at the flat beforehand. The next night it was dinner with Peter Lendrum, "to meet a young man" from Hambros Bank. I knew that "young" meant "youthful and attractive". Joe was susceptible and offered the youth a lift home afterwards.

It was always EMI's ambition to have the number one record in the charts at Christmas, when the sales were at their highest. For seventeen years, Joe made a point of calling at the HMV store in Oxford Street a week before Christmas. The manager of the store would be waiting for him in the street, ready to show him round even though this was its busiest period. This year, I noticed the manager was somewhat less deferential. It was as though a new level of executive management had grown up between him and Joe in recent months.

George Martin signs a new contract with EMI in 1971

With Judy Martin at a wedding

1972

Intrigue: Invention of the Brain Scanner

In one single year, two quite separate issues – one involving a person, the other a product – were to combine and to ultimately determine the sad fate of EMI. The catalyst was Joe's inevitable retirement in November 1974.

The person was Dorothy Read, whose ambitions for her husband outshone Lady Macbeth. Joe had opportunities to quash her. Instead, he delayed announcing her husband as his successor until a mere five months before relinquishing the post.

It began when Joan Shawcross told her that her husband had let out that Read would never be chairman. Read raised this with Joe, who made no comment. Thereupon Dorothy decided she would play an active role in company matters. Joe showed no objection, and even encouraged her in a neutral sort of way. With Stanford retired from ill health, she was now wife of *the* Chief Executive and Deputy Chairman, a further title Read had wrangled for himself.

The Reads moved to a flat close to Manchester Square and bought a house from a speculative builder in Brighton, the town where Dorothy grew up and was reputed to have been the town's first woman police officer (in the War?). Dorothy told Joe they were finding it impossible to get the Brighton house insured. Joe asked Julian Gibbs, his insurance adviser, to help. It was "jerry-built", yet Julian still managed to sort it out. "John's not very good at that sort of thing," Dorothy confided to Joe, uncharacteristically admitting that her husband was not infallible, possibly hinting that she was the one with the business brain.

I sat next to her at a private preview of *Cabaret* starring Liza

Minnelli and Michael York. Turning to me after the screening, she let fly: "Absolutely shocking! I have never seen anything so revolting and disgusting! It shouldn't be shown!" *Cabaret* was to be nominated for eight Oscars and won five. York screams at "divinely decadent" Minnelli: "Screw Max!" Minnelli responds: "I do!" "So do I!" retorts the naïve Englishman. All too much for Dorothy, who modified her tone as we left: "After all I suppose we are all basically beasts."

Hartley Shawcross, now Chairman of Thames Television, circulated his concern at the growth of violence on our screens. A "Morals Committee" was set up to discuss permissiveness, made up of Thames and EMI Directors. Jeremy Isaacs, MD of Thames, expressed surprise to LG at the inclusion of the Chief Executive's wife on the committee.

Bernard Delfont opened the first theatre to be built in the West End for many years. It was on the site of the old Winter Garden Theatre in Drury Lane. Many nostalgic actors came to the launch party, including Dame Anna Neagle, Jack Hawkins, Tony Britton and Bernie's wife, Carole Lynne, who had sung on the Winter Garden stage with Richard Tauber. To general disappointment Arnold Goodman announced: "I hereby name this theatre The New London Theatre." It was absurd not to keep the original name, everyone thought. But Dorothy Read had interfered. To her, Winter Gardens were commonplace places that the hoi polloi visited in native Brighton and Blackpool. No one dared to tell this vulgar woman the single "Winter Garden" had a charm she would not appreciate. Nor did she realise the problem she created for London taxi drivers. The New Theatre, long-established in St Martin's Lane, wartime home of Laurence Olivier and Ralph Richardson's Old Vic Theatre Company, felt obliged to change its name to the Albery Theatre.

Joe was gracious in acknowledging Dorothy's status. Invited to join Dame Joan Hammond for tea in the chairman's office, she arrived dressed as for a garden party at Buckingham Palace in hat and long white gloves. By contrast, the Australian opera diva chose a tweed suit and sensible shoes, in tune with her passion for golf.

On 8th May, Joe accepted a lunch invitation from Sir Charles Dodds, the eminent biochemist, the same Sir Charles Dodds who drank himself under the table at the Millers Convention in Scotland. Sir Charles introduced Dr James Bull, a radiologist, recently returned from an American conference. They wanted to tell Joe that EMI had invented the Brain Scanner. What a way to learn that EMI Electronics had made a discovery equalling, if not exceeding, the importance of EMI Records' discovery of the Beatles. Dr Bull had attended the congress where Godfrey Hounsfield revealed to the world how to examine the brain in three dimensions. It was the biggest discovery since the invention of X-rays. It was beyond a radiologist's dreams. To Joe it was gratifying. He had often watched Hounsfield, the Newark Magnus schoolboy, experimenting in the CRL. It was explained to him, in language he could understand, how "computerised axiomatic tomography" (CAT) was used to build up the internal image of a pig's head, slice by slice on a screen, from multiple X-ray photographs.

The next morning, at their regular weekly policy meeting, Joe broke the news to Read. This was the biggest thing in medical electronics, and he had learnt it from someone outside the company. Its significance was being felt in America, this British invention, even before reaching our shores. Events were already tumbling upon each other. Neville Hart, Emmie's long-term and loyal official stockbroker on the New York Stock Exchange, was arriving in London demanding to have his brain scanned.

All along, Joe held the impression he had learnt of Hounsfield's discovery before the news reached Read's ears. Nothing was done or said to change this view. The truth is different, as I learnt when I was helping on a biography of Hounsfield in 2012. Two internal memos were produced dated 21st and 25th April 1972, from the archives filed away at Hayes.

The first was sent to Read by Bill Ingham, CRL Director, and headed "EMI Computer X-Ray System":

This new system was announced yesterday to the Medical World in a paper read by Mr Hounsfield of Central Research Laboratories and Dr Ambrose of Atkinson Morley Hospital at the Congress of Radiologists. I expect you will have seen the press cover, but this was the result of a press conference organised before the meeting and embargoed until after the event. You may therefore like to hear about the re-action of the Congress to this invention.

The new EMI System allows cysts, haemorrhages and tissues to be seen for the first time and I think it would be fair to say that when the pictures were shown they created quite a sensation. The session Chairman, in fact, referred to privilege at being in the Chair at the meeting in which this important paper was read.

There was quite a sense of occasion and I am sure you will be glad to know that, in addition to its commercial prospects, this invention of Mr Hounsfield is regarded as a significant scientific achievement!

Read responded briefly on 25th April:

I was extremely pleased to receive your note of 21st April regarding the paper read by Mr Hounsfield at the Congress of Radiologists.

It is very gratifying to know that we have in this Department a project of such acceptance and I am very pleased to learn of the commercial prospects which this scientific achievement offers.

I am also writing to Mr Hounsfield direct on this.

Why Joe was not shown this correspondence can be interpreted two ways. Either Read jealously wanted to claim credit for the scanner himself, or he genuinely did not realise its importance, until told by Joe, by which time it was too late to admit he had already been told something of significance which he was incapable of comprehending. He was either too deceitful or too embarrassed. I tend to go with the second view. He had congratulated Hounsfield for his "Computer X-Ray system".

Copies of these memos had gone to John Kuipers and Dr John Powell. Both were main board directors based at Hayes, and members, with Percy Allaway, of EMI Electronics Ltd, a subsidiary board. Kuipers came from Ford, where he had held a role senior to Read. He was responsible for closing the Hayes Gramophone Company's museum and listening room to make way for a conference room. He did tell me beforehand, as he knew Joe might need appeasing. Also sad was the disappearance of the illuminated EMI sign on the Hayes water tower. This was visible from the arrivals and departures lounges at Heathrow at night, shining its clear red lettering. Apart from being a great advertisement, it was a reassuring something one had become accustomed to. Kuipers said the new EMI logo shape could not be accommodated. Henry Ford II, President of Ford, lived near Hatchet Wood. He came over one weekend. Looking at Joe quizzically, he enquired: "EMI – didn't you take one of our people?" "Yes," said Joe. "You must mean Read." "No," replied Ford, "that name's not familiar. I remember now, the fellow was called Kuipers. He did a good job re-siting our works." Shawcross was irritated at board meetings by Kuipers' unintentionally supercilious manner according to LG.

Dr Powell was younger and a new arrival. He came from Texas Instruments, where he had been managing director of their UK company. His capability was proved, quite by chance, not long after he had been with us. I got a call from my German industrialist uncle. He had a colleague who would like to meet Joe, and would I arrange it. Casimir did not tell me his friend was a headhunter. Texas Instruments wanted Powell back, and his meeting with Joe, naturally, proved fruitless. This track record made Powell the ideal person to run the EMI scanner project. Unfortunately, that is not how it turned out. It started well. He accompanied Joe, John Gardiner and me to see Dr Ambrose demonstrate the scanner at Atkinson Morley Hospital. Dr Ambrose recalled using the machine for the very first time, discovering a previously hidden tumour, and saving the patient's life. The Government provided no funding for the scanner project, and Joe was furious with Barbara Castle, the Health Minister, for her decision. Instead, Bill Ingham did a deal with the NHS to build four machines. The NHS would pay the cost, but allow EMI to keep two.

Ambrose's scanner was an NHS model, basically still under test, and he alone would choose the patients. Neville Hart could do better in America, as an EMI model went to the Mayo Clinic.

Leaving the demonstration, Powell summed up the visit with a familiar remark: "We must do something about this." As before, I took this to mean: "Keep out Sir Joseph, we can manage very well on our own!" With no Lord Mills around to preside, Joe allowed EMI Electronics to do their own thing. The vital decision to build the scanner rather than license it was never discussed at the main board. Kuipers, Powell and Allaway knew that Read was incapable of making the case cogently. They risked being shot down, determined as they were to manufacture in-house. They missed hearing Joe's advice to Malcolm McDowell on the subject of music cassettes: "By all means innovate. But let someone else manufacture first. It takes time to standardise, and it is very costly."

The Reads' ambitions to use the scanner success story for their own purposes dates from the evening Joe invited them to dine at his flat to meet Sir Charles and Lady Dodds, on 1st August. They could sit back and begin to bask in its glory, and Dorothy would be all ears. Her husband's prestige would be enormous, and it would all come from this one thing. The Brain Scanner was to be their meal ticket.

Godfrey Hounsfield awarded for inventing the Brain Scanner

On 22nd November, at the Savoy Hotel, Prince Philip presented Godfrey Hounsfield with the first of what were to be numerous awards from all over the world. It was the MacRobert Gold Medal (and £25,000) awarded in "recognition of the technology innovation contributing most significantly to the prestige and prosperity of the UK". Judging the award, Lord Hinton, Chairman of the Atomic Energy Authority, stated: "No comparable discovery had been made in this field since Röntgen discovered X-Rays in 1895. The EMI Scanner was as much a one-man invention as anything can be these days." He added the calculations used by Hounsfield were beyond his own comprehension.

Dorothy Read was photographed at the reception with Prince Philip. By November, orders for the machine totalled £600,000, the majority coming from America. Philips, Toshiba, Siemens, GE and Picker happily paying "100% with order".

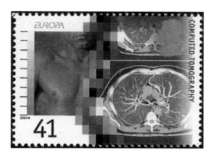

Royal Mail Brain Scanner commemoration stamp

In May, Joe and I went to the House of Lords with passes issued by Black Rod to watch the Bootlegging Bill debate. This led to a law making it illegal to sell recorded music without the owners' permission. Lord Goodman, supported by Jennie Lee and Lord Limerick, introduced the bill, and commented later: "I was pleased to play a small part in introducing a highly benevolent measure. No doubt when malefactors are now removed in Black Marias for long sentences they will hurl imprecations at the name of Goodman." His involvement came as a favour to Joe who had helped him elsewhere.

Goodman was Chairman of the Sir John Barbirolli Memorial Foundation, and, as such, wrote to Joe ominously: "It may even be a surprise to you that you are a member of the Appeal Committee – but this you are and there is evidence that it was of your own free will!" Elizabeth Schwarzkopf had agreed to perform with the Halle Orchestra, Barbirolli's orchestra, at a memorial concert. However, she had decided to donate her fee to the Musicians' Benevolent Fund, and not to the Barbirolli Foundation. This was taken as a snub to Lady Barbirolli. Could Joe do something? Joe wrote to Walter Legge, who replied: "You are the one person who can effect the most elegant solution – to induce the Halle Committee to allow my wife to cancel. I am delighted that you have some new transferring equipment producing the results which spur you to such enthusiasm. What a pity you didn't have it when I made the original recording!" (EMI released the original 1957 mono recording of Rosenkavalier in stereo.) Joe wrote apologetically to Goodman: "I always knew Walter Legge was difficult, but I hardly expected him to be quite as difficult as his reply suggests."

Ill will continued to dog the appeal, and toes were to be trodden on again. Another Barbirolli memorial concert was given, this time to an invited audience at St James's Palace, in the presence of the Queen Mother. Those who had attended received a letter from Goodman hoping they had enjoyed the concert, and inviting them to make a donation to the Foundation. John Sainsbury, the millionaire boss of Sainsbury's, replied pompously that he had attended as the personal guest of the Queen Mother and, therefore, had no intention of contributing. Goodman told Joe he would have nothing more to do with the man. That was OK for him, but not so easy for Joe: Sainsbury was a Director of the Royal Opera House, Chairman of Friends of Covent Garden and a Governor of the Royal Ballet School. Perhaps it was fortunate that Goodman's influence would lessen, now his long term as Chairman of the Arts Council was over. It was something *Private Eye* frequently probed, under such headings as "Friends of Lord Goodman" and "Why Everyone sends for Lord X". Jules Thorn was listed as a friend of Goodman. Joe was a friend of both. He became involved in a project that involved all three.

Joe was amused at the efforts that Hambros Bank made to find new interests to occupy Jules, who was seventy-two and showing no signs of retiring. Their anxiety grew as he failed to appoint a successor at Thorn Electric. "Life is short. The sooner that a man begins to enjoy his wealth the better," quoth Dr Johnson, but Jules was not interested.

He bought a flat in the South of France, which was soon sold at a profit. Farmland in Lincolnshire doubled in value, but he never visited it. A racehorse inevitably won the Gold Cup at Doncaster, engendering no interest in racing. Jules did acquire a valuable painting by Camille Pissarro at Christie's, but only with Joe sitting beside him, encouraging him to go on bidding. It was for his large apartment in a grand terrace overlooking Regent's Park. Here he engaged a butler, previously employed at Buckingham Palace, who he caught having sex in the kitchen. "It was with Selwyn Lloyd's nephew," Jules told Joe, giving the occurrence a superior tone.

Jules was tempted by a proposal made by Goodman. It was to set up his own investment company. Using his capital, Ohm Investments Limited was registered. Jules, Arnold and Joe were joint directors, and Jonathan Stone, Arnold's solicitor nephew, was appointed manager. Meetings were held at Stone's Berkeley Square office, away from Thorn House. The initial plan was to find and take over a publicly listed company worth £5 million, and I was told to compile a list. Stanley Gibbons, the stamp dealers, appeared a possibility, but as the Crown Agents owned 30% it was ruled out. Its share price fell dramatically when the management was exposed as corrupt. As usual, luck was on Jules's side. Likewise, he declined to become a Member of Lloyds of London, shortly before the Crash.

Ohm Investments Limited was wound up after less than a year, and I asked Joe why. "Jules didn't care for Stone," came the reply. More likely, he had just lost interest.

We were abroad between July and November. The Chairman visited Holland, Belgium, Denmark, Sweden, North America, Peru, Argentina and Brazil. In Los Angeles, recently widowed Dorothy Wallichs took us out for a meal. Joe was impressed when she made it clear *she* was paying the bill, without palaver. Whilst in Peru, we received a request from our Chilean company to cancel the planned visit. The country was in chaos under President Allende. Food and petrol were in short supply, the wine industry had dried up, and it would be impossible to entertain the chairman without attracting criticism. The elected communist government was eventually overthrown by the army. That situation must have been desperate. Joe recalled that President Frei and previous presidents had run the country without requiring the support of the army. I missed seeing Chile through Joe's eye, and visiting the site where his flour mill once stood. We were with Charles Lockwood in Argentina, little knowing he was to suffer kidnap and ransom before we would see him again. In Brazil, our exuberant musicians gave Joe a samba party, which he and the ambassador enjoyed, but our consul hated.

Samba party in Rio with British Ambassador

On the flight to New York, my pocket knife was confiscated by Caracas Airport Police, and handed to the pilot, who returned it on arrival. The overnight journey from New York to London is always tiring, and we had been travelling for three weeks. Not being able to sleep does not help. Joe decided to exercise, walking up and down the aisle and through the curtain separating the next compartment. Just when I thought he had been gone rather a long time, the curtain stirred and billowed abruptly. It was caused by Joe falling in a faint. The reduced lighting added to the drama. Cabin staff administered oxygen routinely, and we reached our destination without further incident. It was not the first time Joe had succumbed to a combination of low blood pressure and lack of oxygen.

Luckily, the incident on the plane went no further. Read had been intriguing during our absence. Joe must remain steadfast. Read was seeing Kit Dawnay. I was able to establish through my own channels what he had been scheming. Dawnay's official line was that the City still needed reassuring that EMI was secure, should anything happen to Joe, even though he was "non-executive" chairman.

Titles were of little interest to Joe, and, to make Dawnay and Read happy, he agreed to Read having three! These were duly listed in the next report as "Deputy Chairman, Chief Executive, and Managing Director". People could think what they like, but, as far as Read was concerned, should anything happen to Joe, he, Read, was to be chairman. All he lacked was an endorsement from Joe.

My EMI friends Brian Jeffery and Robert Ascott invited me to join them for lunch at a restaurant behind Manchester Square. Joe had known Brian as a boy, and Robert was an ex-Harry Williams pupil at Cambridge. They were both doing well in EMI, managing overseas subsidiaries by the time they were thirty. What I thought was a pre-Christmas get-together turned out to have another motive. I was regaled with an out-flowing of discontent, created by Joe, who was "preventing Read from running the company". Read was inhibited by the presence of this overbearing chairman, who was not prepared to delegate. Someone had been brainwashing them. What was I supposed to do about it? I retreated to the security of the 6th floor, where reality prevailed.

Joe had chaired board meetings for decades, and it did not take much for him to work out what was going on. Obviously the executive directors would be summoned to a meeting with Read preceding the full board meeting, which they would attend with decisions already taken. But on one occasion, Joe's instinct sensed a lack of unanimity. The intention was for EMI to buy the Mirabelle Restaurant by taking over the de Vere Group, which also owned the Grand Hotel in Brighton. Joe decided to put the matter to the vote, going round the board table asking each director one by one. Delfont voted against, as did the non-execs, and the proposal was dropped. Joe said it was the only time he could be accused of influencing a board decision in five years as non-executive chairman.

Apart from the Brain Scanner excitement that dominated 1972, another equally significant advance was made during the year. For as long as I had known him, and for years before I knew him, Joe had banged on about antiquated publishers of sheet music, "a tight association consisting of many old men, now living off record sales." They kept 50% of their songwriter's copyright royalties. If he could break the monopoly, he was prepared to handle the copyright of any composer at a more fairly-based division of 15%. Chappells had overpriced themselves, and Warner Records had paid too much for them. But that was ten years ago. Recording artists were now composing, recording and publishing their own songs. The companies that previously resisted takeover were at last prepared to sell out, taking as much as they could for their rich catalogues. In November, EMI Music Publishing Ltd bought Affiliated Music Publishers Ltd for £3.3 million, to join Francis Day & Hunter, Feldmans and Robbins Music, and "Securing for us a leading position in World music publishing". By 1974, EMI was the largest music publisher in the country. By 1976 it was the most profitable part of the company. In 2003, profits exceeded £100 million, 40% of the Group's total. Joe could reminisce about the attempt to establish Ardmore and Beechwood in 1962 with the Beatles.

Postcard from John Lennon in New York

1973

More Intrigue Plus a Kidnap in Argentina

Arriving at Hatchet Wood one weekend early in the new year, I was met by Joe, white in the face and apoplectic. I soon learnt what had brought on this massive anger attack. Rather than blackmail, this time it was double-cross, deceit and disloyalty.

The previous November, Joe circulated the non-executive directors with a confidential memo headed "The Board of EMI". It was to consider the board's future composition, and he raised his own position:

> As regards the Chairmanship, I complete my contract at the end of 1974 – then 70 years old and 20 years as Chairman. Though I have no great desire to retire completely, it is, I feel, desirable that we should appoint a new Chairman then. It is my present view that John Read should be appointed, but I think the Company should have a separate Chairman and Chief Executive (or Managing Director). I feel, therefore, that John Read should produce a candidate suitable to be appointed as Managing Director, and he (then nearly 57 years old) should become Chairman with perhaps rather more executive powers than I exercise now. If he fails to do this by 1974, I should be willing if wanted, and if in good health, to continue as Chairman on a month by month basis until this was achieved. I think it would be a mistake to appoint him as Chairman and Chief Executive without some condition of this kind, as the Company would be too much under the control of one man.

Joe anticipated exactly what was to transpire. The memo was written when the Economy was facing a bleak period, experiencing a short working week and the OPEC embargo on oil exports. Industry needed strong leadership and secure reserves.

Sir Otto Clarke responded: "I am entirely happy to go along with what you and your colleagues think." Joe should not reduce his salary to increase Read's. The number of Electronics Directors on the Board should be reduced to one. He suggested replacements for the non-executives. Unfortunately, this undoubted ally died of cancer in 1975. He was already failing in health.

Then Shawcross dropped the bomb. He told Joe, Dawnay had been to see him in confidence, having already called on Ralph Gordon-Smith and Ian Jacob to discuss the memo. He told Joe he was being asked to join them in declaring outright for Read unconditionally. Non-executive directors' loyalty rests with the chairman of a company. Dawnay had broken the rule.

Joe could not believe Ralph's and Ian's behaviour. Had Ralph not asked him to save him from a similar situation? I remember the humbled non-executive directors of Smiths meeting in our office in a very subdued and embarrassed fashion, about who was to succeed Mr Ralph. And Ian was such a good judge of a man's character. He saw Ken East's potential when Read and LG Wood dismissed him as "too abrasive". Now, Ian was calling Read "such a nice person!"

Joe's reaction was immediate. The first thing he did after the weekend was to go and see Oliver Poole, Dawnay's boss at Lazards. Dawnay had exceeded his responsibility as a non-executive director, and, in the process, endangered Lazards influential position as EMI's bankers, the very thing he wished to avoid. He was thinking of himself as much as of Read. Poole was subjected to the mother of all tirades. Dawnay offered to resign, but as usual Joe's anger attack subsided as suddenly as it had erupted. I am inclined to believe it had its effect. A year later, Oliver Poole died from a life-threatening brain tumour. Did Joe aggravate it? Poole's young wife had demanded a "scan", and appealed to Arnold Weinstock at GEC, who in turn rang Joe in the country. Read's problem was that Joe would always be the one to appeal to, so long as he was around.

Shawcross wrote to Read: "My own feeling has been that you, if I may say so, have come to a period where you really have to make a choice between remaining a full-time Chief Executive of EMI, or becoming a part-time Non-Executive Chairman, the post being designated simply as that of Chairman since the title of Executive Chairman now really involves a direct conflict with the current philosophy." This was not what Dorothy had in mind.

The extremes Dawnay had gone to were revealed: He had given Read a copy of Joe's confidential memo. His actions had brought anger to Joe, but, in Read's case, they led to raw hysteria. With his office only a floor apart and in regular contact, I knew what was up when Read came through on the intercom demanding to see Joe immediately. He screamed at me when I said the chairman had left the building. He might talk to his people like that, but I was not having it. Joe was in the lift, the car was waiting outside, and there was an urgent meeting about the National Theatre awaiting him. I could have got Joe back, but why should I? Read's state was quite frightening. Just as I kept my conversation with Brian Jeffery and Robert Ascott to myself, I did not tell Joe of the verbal onslaught I had been subjected to over the intercom.

Things were progressing slowly with the building of the National Theatre. There had been a topping out ceremony. A Protocol Committee was formed to discuss Royal Opening plans. The South Bank Theatre Board met frequently to discuss delays rather than progress. Halfway through Heath's premiership, the country deep in recession, and suppliers failing to meet targets, Max Rayne, the NT Chairman, called in that pair of troubleshooters, Lockwood and Goodman, to get things moving. Peter Hall, the NT Director's diary described the situation:

This new pressure group of Rayne's first met only last week, and already it has started to show some results. The technique is very simple. Having discovered which supplier is holding up the contract, Rayne looks up the Chairman of the Company, and then either he or Joseph Lockwood or Goodman or some other heavy-weight rings him up, and says, surely the firm doesn't want to be the one that stops the National Theatre opening as planned, on Shakespeare's birth day 1975? After all, the Queen's booked and you can't put off a Royal Personage.

The Queen opened the Theatre in October 1976.

Joe obtained cables from BICC and electric motors from GEC. He knew the companies from IRC days and went direct to the factory floor rather than to the chairman. British Steel turned over a whole factory to meet the NT's special requirements within three weeks. Rayne wrote to Joe: "I am delighted by the tremendous success you have achieved in resolving the steel problem for the National Theatre ... How about running for Prime Minister? For what it is worth, you would be assured of my unqualified support ... With renewed thanks ..."

Time-consuming demands such as these prevented the Read situation festering during the year. Only once did Joe boil over, and this time the cause was inanimate. Arriving for the Royal Ballet School's open day at White Lodge in Richmond Park, his new Rolls Royce boiled over. It was a scorching day and Joe was furious. The new model, which no longer looked like the traditional Rolls, was giving problems, and now water penetration had damaged the air-conditioning. Joe refused to pay the high cost of repair, and we endured the very hot summer without air-conditioning. Abandoning the Rolls for the first time since Manchester days, Joe ordered a German BMW, much to the disapproval of EMI's Purchasing Department.

Wayne Eagling at White Lodge re-union

I was left to feel miserable that day at White Lodge. Joe enjoyed the event immensely. Old boys, now at the Senior School and in the Company, had been invited, and Joe was quickly surrounded, his car forgotten.

Boys from the School were to perform in Benjamin Britten's new opera, *Death in Venice*, with choreography by Frederick Ashton. We went up to Aldeburgh for a performance. Returning to the Snape Maltings car park in semi-darkness after the show, someone was brought over to meet Joe. It was Walter Annenberg, the newly arrived American ambassador who wished to express his sympathy about his brother Charles who had been kidnapped in Argentina. On 7th June, Charles had been abducted by Marxist revolutionary guerrillas from outside his house in the suburbs of Buenos Aires. A two-million-dollar ransom was demanded, and nothing was to be heard from him for two months. All the papers ran headlines: "Gang Kidnap Brother of EMI Chief".

The Press called Joe whilst he was dressing to dine with the Board of Beechams at Claridge's: "As far as I know he's never had any threats to his life. I have. I get one every few months, people threatening to kill me. This has come as a shock of course." His mother was equally nonchalant: "Mr Lockwood's 92 year old mother said last night she was convinced everything would work out all right. She is staying at the Elston, Notts., farm of another son, 72 year old Mr Frank Lockwood. He said: 'Mother was not at all alarmed when I told her Charles had been kidnapped'". The family noted Joe was not offering to help with the ransom money. Joe had no intention of encouraging kidnappers, nor was he inclined to cancel dining with Beechams or altering his plans.

Fortunately, John Morgan, a cultivated and urbane diplomat, was on the duty desk at the Foreign Office when the news from Argentina first came through. Despite total silence from the Montaneros guerrillas, he reassured Joe that he would be kept informed. I heard our secretary in the next office chatting regularly with the press, who were forever ringing. I asked her what on earth there was to talk about: "You can't just put the phone down on them," she explained.

John Morgan had a request for Joe. Would he ask the BBC to rein in one of their investigative journalists, who was compromising the police in their own clandestine enquiries? Huw Wheldon, Managing Director of BBC TV, refused point-blank to give John Humphrys, his youngest reporter, who was covering America, North and South, any such instruction. When it was made clear life was being endangered, Wheldon revoked his stubborn, ill-judged decision.

Charles was found abandoned and confused on 29th July. A ransom had been paid by his daughters and business contacts. On 15th August, his younger daughter, who was in London, rang to say he was arriving at Heathrow, and instructed us to send a car to meet him, and keep it secret. It was impossible to explain her uncle no longer kept a car and chauffeur at his disposal. I had no alternative but to send a pool chauffeur, and the secret was out. Joe suggested his brother put in a word for the BBC who had been helpful. Not knowing the difference, Charles gave an interview to ITN.

That brief introduction to the American ambassador during Charles's imprisonment had a positive outcome. Paul McCartney faced a flat refusal for a visa permitting his entry into the United States. He was the first Beatle publicly involved with drugs, admitting in a *Life* magazine interview to taking LSD, and John Lennon's presence in America did not help. Impressed with Annenberg's sympathetic manner, Joe approached him on Paul's behalf. In his mind they had a bond, as his Grosvenor Square study window looked directly into the embassy across the street, and on to the visa applicants forming long queues. Of course, that was pure nonsense. The ambassador apologised that the one area over which he had no influence was the US Immigration Department. Nevertheless, by the end of the year Paul's visa came through. His father-in-law, Lee Eastman, wrote gratefully: "I want to thank you for your kindness and assistance in helping Paul secure his Visa." Joe graciously accepted credit.

John and Dorothy Read's son was engaged to marry the Chairman of Blackpool Tower's daughter on 2nd June. It was being treated as a royal occasion, which I felt was rather tawdry. Joe had accepted an invitation, which meant I had to go too. The day before setting off for Blackpool, I bumped into Joan Shawcross in Belgravia. She was so friendly and effusive I knew she would have sympathised with my lack of enthusiasm at the prospect, but I resisted any temptation to tell her. In my mind was something she had confided to Joe. She appreciated he was "on the wavelength of the young today" and needed advice. Her younger son had absconded from school, severed all connections, changed his name, gone abroad and simply disappeared. Joe was inclined to reassure her it was a temporary phase, not to be taken seriously. He was wrong. When Joan was killed in a riding accident years later, the prodigal had not returned. She never saw him again. Later, he was to become reconciled with Hartley, which made her death all the more tragic.

We booked into the Savoy Hotel in Blackpool and watched the Blackpool Tower Ballroom Championship finals that evening. At the wedding lunch, Bernie Delfont hailed Joe from a neighbouring table. His loud comment, "You're never going to retire, Joe!" did not go down well in certain areas.

We spent much of the summer in the country. In July, John Boyden invited us to Glyndebourne. John was a young maverick producer, who made inexpensive original recordings for our budget label, Classics for Pleasure. In the process, he upset the musicians' union and EMI's Classical Department, but Joe approved of his efforts. He used his charm with the pianist Moura Lympany, and impressed us with a rousing rendition on the newly restored organ in the Royal Albert Hall. He collected us for the 5.10 p.m. performance of *Le Nozze di Figaro*, leaving little time to get from Oxfordshire to East Sussex. John's driving was terrifying, but the invitation to join Brian Epstein's friend John Prichard, the director, on the Opera House roof terrace after the performance, proved a tonic.

In August, Dolly East brought Elton John, John Reid and Tony King to dinner. John Reid, one of EMI Records' young label managers, was now Elton John's full-time manager and partner. Tony King was with Apple Records. Elton did not like soup, but soon recovered when we adjourned to Hatchet Wood's newly built pavilion annexe. With sliding glass panels and electric curtains, it was just what Elton and Tony needed for a game of their version of Charades.

The previous week we had dined with Elton and John at their new home in Virginia Water. The subject of age came up, and Joe challenged fellow guest, poor Alan Freeman, to touch his toes. The disc jockey proved less capable. Joe did not consider himself old. What he resented was sharing his birth date with Michael Ramsey, the Archbishop of Canterbury, "who has always looked a hundred!"

On 7th September, Joe announced publicly his intention to retire at seventy. The *Evening Standard* produced the headline "Sir Joseph to quit EMI", but learnt he was unlikely to vegetate. "I'm considering the chairmanship of a new Theatre Company," he revealed.

The Young Vic Theatre Company was the offspring of the Old Vic, the home of the National Theatre Company, before the move to the new building on the South Bank. With its own premises, director and board, all it needed was an independent chairman. Max Rayne asked Joe to take on the role. As we had not heard of the Young Vic, I went to look at it one evening, whilst a show was in progress. A couple of blocks along The Cut, SE1, from the Victorian Old Vic, I came to a plain building, clearly erected with limited budget, housing offices, canteen and an open stage. A "House Full" sign was a good omen.

Max Rayne made a proviso: Joe would have to get on with Frank Dunlop, the theatre's abrasive and unorthodox director and creator. Or was it the other way round? This proved no problem. Frank arrived at our office for his first meeting driven by Barry Evans, the Swinging Sixties film star and heartthrob. He must be OK! We soon learnt he appealed to young audiences by putting popular idols such as Jim Dale, Cliff Richard and David Essex in his "pop" productions. It was not a mere gimmick. The Young Vic was a company of young actors. The first production we saw was Terence Rattigan's *French Without Tears* with Ian Charleson, who became famous later. Someone with Frank's strong personality was bound not to get on with everyone. We were warned he did not like Peter Hall. Yet Ian Charleson's later success would be at the National Theatre. Theatre people are good at burying differences.

The Young Vic discovered Joe was a useful chairman. The company was keen to put on a show based on John Lennon's jottings, *In My Own Write*, to be called *An Outburp of Hysteriffs*. John lived in New York, and Joe knew where to get in touch. The management committee of the

Dakota Building had requested a reference from Joe regarding the Lennons acquiring an apartment, which LG drafted: "Whilst neither I nor the Company can accept any responsibility for Mr and Mrs Lennon I can say that through the Company's relationship with Mr Lennon that I would not expect him to enter into any obligation, which he does not reasonably think he can meet."

"Thank you for your letter which I can't find for the moment," John wrote, "I remember what it was about tho'. Yes, it's fine by me – I'm sure the Young Vickers will do a good job, all the best good luck, love, j.l. (one virgin)."

Quite aware that the Lennons would be refused re-entry should they leave the States, Joe teasingly responded: "It is about time that you came over to see us here in London, though I am sure you will have to be given a United Nations passport to make you more mobile. It would be very nice to see you."

After dining one evening in Fulham, Frank Dunlop took us to see a friend who lived nearby. Joe might have recognised the mews cottage as a former home of Lionel Bart from the loo seat, originally the throne from the set of his musical *Twang*. Frank's friend was David Shaw, disgraced director of City company Jessel Securities, former advisor to Brian Epstein, and now, unknown to Joe, a Director of the Robert Stigwood Group. There was a druggy party going on, and one of the young men introduced himself to Joe: "I am a great friend of your mother!" Obviously some explanation was needed. The tall, unprepossessing youth was Colin Stone, the "Gnome Millionaire". From the age of fourteen, this Southwell lad had made a fortune selling garden gnomes around the world. Companies doing business with him were unaware they were dealing with little more than a child. Fame and success did not last. By the time he met Joe he was bankrupt, and he died soon after in strange circumstances.

In September, Joe became a salaried Technical Consultant to Gérard's French Government. The appointment came at Charles Villiers' suggestion. The French were planning their own version of the IRC. All Joe's British Government jobs had previously been unpaid. I realised how close I had come to being in really deep water.

Gérard was based at the Embassy in Stanhope Gate for twenty-five years. Now Joe was going there to meet French ministers and commercial counsellors. A young embassy-based French diplomat was assigned to assist him.

Luckily, the French had decided the previous year that Gérard had been far too long in one post, and appointed him ambassador in Finland. I had not realised the depth of his affection for me. He insisted I visit him, and offered to pay my airfare. He knew I had relations in Helsinki. But our six-year affair was over. He became ambassador to Thailand, where he died in 1996. A mutual friend eventually told him about Joe and me. They never met.

EMI celebrated its 75th Anniversary with a gala concert at the Royal Festival Hall on 29th November. Joe was in his element. The press reported: "EMI celebrates 75th Anniversary with New Peaks in Earnings and Progress Worldwide". But there was a tense atmosphere during preparations, caused by Joe's reluctance to name a successor. Bryan Samain, the Director of Public Affairs, brought in by Read from Ford Motors to boost his image, was put in charge over Peter Andry, who had devised the whole programme.

*Maria Callas and
P.M. Edward Heath
at the concert*

Sir William Walton wrote a special fanfare. Sir Adrian Boult and André Previn conducted the London Symphony Orchestra and Yehudi Menuhin performed. The Queen sent a message of congratulation. Joe was joined in the Principal Box by the Prime Minister and Maria Callas, whose entry confused my ex-EMI neighbour in the stalls, who had just signed her to Polydor Records.

Behind the scenes, Read was asserting himself. The Managing Director of EMI Records and his wife, of all people, were not included in the VIP reception. Guests were allowed two tickets for the performance. When Patrick Sergeant of the *Daily Mail* was declined a third seat for his daughter, he complained strongly to Joe, who had to intervene. At the banquet afterwards, Samain left me off the seating plan, but Peter Andry asked me to join his table. A solicitor from the legal firm advising Read scrutinised me. Were they concocting a plan to oust Joe based on our relationship? Was I being paranoid? Joe complimented Edward Heath for his HMV Elgar Cockaigne Overture recording, produced by Andry. Shouldn't the Prime Minister have confined his talents to music rather than politics? "There goes the chairman's peerage!" someone whispered. Andry, forgetting I was near, impatiently mimicked Joe's slow delivery: "Slower and slower and slower." "There goes Andry's knighthood," I might have responded. And indeed, when Heath put Peter up for an honour, and asked Joe to support him, Joe did not reply.

Patrick Sergeant wrote how much he had enjoyed the gala, "and the marvellous speeches from Heath and yourself. If only our Prime Minister could speak as well as you, I think many of our problems would be solved."

Sir Edward Lewis's wife wrote: "We enjoyed the concert enormously ... I am looking forward with great pleasure to seeing you on Saturday, and inspecting the mole hills personally. Hope we don't get lost in the wilds of the country! Lots of love, Jeanie."

1974

"Retirement?"

My grandmother died in March, and Joe's mother died in September. As neither had been to Hatchet Wood, the two events would combine to close a chapter. My grandmother complained how little I came to Yorkshire. Joe "went home" every June for his mother's birthday, sometimes just for the day, by train or car. This year, with a Hawker Siddeley aircraft at his disposal, he stayed the night. He was flown from Hatfield to Tollerton, the airfield closest to Southwell. The pilot's father was Mr Cherry Downs, Chairman of Gilstraps, the Newark Maltsters that could be smelt for miles around. Joe told young Cherry Downs that the Mrs Lockwood who once worked as his father's secretary was his mother.

Mabel Lockwood fell in the street and died in hospital. There was a post-mortem, as she had shown no warning symptoms despite being ninety-three. Joe attended the funeral, and was very moved at the turnout of the townsfolk, including the entire local police force, all of whom his mother had known individually. Brother Frank was inconsolable. Brother Charles was unable to attend. Fred was not in evidence. Mabel Lockwood was buried in the plot retained for her by Southwell Minster's North Door, where Joe's father was laid to rest in 1910.

To add to the sadness, Maximilian was run over. We were desperate to replace him. Luckily, I found another puppy of similar pedigree. I brought Max Mark II from the New Forest to Hatchet Wood one weekend, and he quickly settled in. He lived a long life, avoiding the tragic circumstances of his predecessor.

As a reward for the support we gave him on *The Tales of Beatrix Potter*, Richard Goodwin invited us back to Elstree Studios in May, when he was producing Agatha Christie's *Murder on the Orient Express*.

Naturally, Joe asked Bernard Delfont's permission before accepting! All the cast was present that day. John Gielgud and Wendy Hiller graciously acknowledged Joe. Albert Finney and Sean Connery were more preoccupied with their moustaches.

Sometime later, I got a very angry call from Richard at the office. He was unhappy with EMI. He had commissioned the film music from Richard Rodney Bennett and engaged an orchestra, booking Abbey Road Studios, but EMI had failed to produce someone to record the session. Wasn't it important enough? Joe said he had never heard anything so ridiculous. "Send Charles Rodier!" he instructed, referring to his godson working in EMI's Classical Division. Of course, the Classical Department was not going to put up with the chairman's interference, and sent Christopher Bishop, their senior recording manager, to take the session. The music received an Academy Award nomination the following year. We were given a private showing of the film in November, followed by lunch at The Ivy. Lauren Bacall, in urgent need of a cigarette, hurried us to the restaurant: "Come along, you boys!" she chivvied, in the voice I had heard her addressing the Beverly Hills Hotel staff.

Christopher Bishop may have been bruised, but Joe was appreciated elsewhere in EMI's Classical Division. Suvi Grubb had worked with Walter Legge on the Klemperer mono recordings. He was now refurbishing them: "Apart from making the violins sound brighter and the lower brass instruments warmer, all I did was to add top on one channel and bass on the other – this was to make the set 'Stereo' within the meaning of the Act!" In sending Joe a set, he thanked him "for your interest in this aspect of my work which has always been an encouragement to me". The recordings would eventually be digitally re-mastered.

Despite nearing retirement, Joe's prestige was unaffected. In May, he was invited to "LUNCHEON in honour of Her Majesty The Queen of Denmark and his Royal Highness The Prince of Denmark" at Hampton Court Palace. Introduced to the Queen's French consort, Joe claimed their eyes met, in mutual recognition of their shared experience, namely myself. I dismissed it as a flight of fancy on Joe's part.

Reminders of just how long he had been chairman surfaced, when he received visits from figures dating back to the 1950s. John Leyton came to his flat for drinks. Roger Nelhams, Adam Faith's problem younger brother, who was around when Adam had a number one single in 1959, counting on past favours, came to see Joe at the office.

Ralph Reader invited us to the final performance of the *Gang Show*, which he had produced for the Boy Scouts regularly since 1942 and which EMI recorded. It was October, and Harold Wilson was three weeks back in office. As we set off for the Gaumont State Theatre in Kilburn, the Prime Minister was leaving 10 Downing Street for the same destination at the same time. His was a spur of the moment decision to spend the evening reviving his memories as a former Scout. During the interval, we were ushered by uniformed scouts to a private room, where seventy-year-old Reader and Chief Scout Willie Gladstone, former Eton master, were entertaining their surprise guest. On view was not the familiar pipe-and-pint PM. Wilson was drinking brandy and smoking a cigar. In the flesh he was not the sallow and slouching figure I had expected. He presented a perfectly normal human being, noticeably stimulated by the appreciative and attentive company.

A young Austrian professor came to lunch in the country one weekend. Ivo Brunner was studying English Literature for a thesis. He was thrilled that we were, at last, to have a National Theatre, and was impressed at the important role Joe played in its building. He listened intently as Joe described the problems he was having with Denys Lasdun, the architect, and Peter Hall, the Director. As a member of the Protocol, Finance and General Purposes Committee, Joe had to visit the site to "choose the chairs for the National Theatre", such detail for a building that was to have annual running costs of £5 million. The builders, McAlpine's, were quite out of control. With no project director appointed to oversee the development, it was left to the Rayne, Goodman, Lockwood "pressure group" to deal with suppliers of untested technical stage equipment. Ivo made Joe promise to invite him to the first performance. Whenever it happened to be, however long it took, he was determined to be there.

Read was appointed to succeed Joe at a board meeting of the EMI non-executive directors on 6th June. Present were Shawcross, Gordon-Smith, Dawnay and Michael Vernon, Wilfred and Nancy's son, who Joe had watched grow up and succeed his father at Spillers. Despite warnings that he would be too powerful, Read wangled it. Challenged to find an able deputy, he had failed to tempt Bhaskar Menon back from America. Bhaskar simply rejected him. Dr Powell was given the role instead, weakly promoted from deputy managing director to managing director. The title of Chief Executive, which Read had invented for himself, was dropped. He was now, all but in name, executive chairman.

It was a triumph for Dorothy Read, who would not envisage any challenge to her husband. From the day Powell arrived, she schemed against him, sensing rivalry. Why wouldn't the Powells sell their home in Bedford and move to London, as she and John had from Luton? She discovered the Powells' two children were adopted, whereas hers were legitimate. Wasn't that unhealthy? What a bigot! When Read mentioned this to Joe, he seemed to share his wife's disapproval. And Powell was toeing the line, boasting that EMI was "a sleeping giant", with reference to the body scanner, now joining the Brain Scanner as EMI Medical's weapon for dominating the world market.

Read announced to the press that he didn't "believe in running a company through fear". I wonder what he meant! In fact, his acolytes were afraid of him; as I discovered when he called me down to discuss his plans for running the EMI Charities Committee. He discovered EMI Electronics ran a separate budget for charitable donations. He failed to understand how this was so, despite a simple explanation. EMI Electronics shared the cost of the company's regular seats in the stalls and box at Covent Garden as a way of entertaining Defence Ministry generals and admirals with opera and ballet evenings. In doing so, it was supporting the Opera House while gaining military contracts. This was how EMI's commitment to Covent Garden originated, yet Read decided to handle these privileges centrally in future. I felt he was being very sharp with his staff, myself included. This reaction was confirmed by the Human Resources manager, who whispered: "I wish he was less hyper!" an opinion unlikely to have been expressed before Read was safely ensconced. The whole thing had been so trivial.

Dorothy Read's euphoria ("I thought he was never going to get it!") was deflated by the announcement of Bernard Delfont's knighthood in the Birthday Honours List. Bernie had previously turned down a CBE, which potentially ruined his chances of a knighthood. Also, he was unpopular with the Royal Family for "trying too hard". Princess Margaret hated him. I had seen him at a charity function instructing the organiser: "Make sure I am introduced to Prince Philip!" this when he had met the Prince countless times, and when more humble workers had one chance to meet a member of the Royal Family. A letter drafted by Goodman for Joe to sign in support of his own proposal to the PM on Delfont's behalf did the trick. Joe described Bernie as a family man, happily married to Carole since 1946 with three grown-up children. This was the real man, not the "Mr Showman" surrounded by a bevy of scantily-clad showgirls. Joe was warned the request would fail, just as approaches made by variety artists' charities had. More recently, the Cinema and Television Benevolent Fund's charities had a similar lack of success. Joe must have been tempted to tell Read and Delfont of his part in achieving the impossible at the celebration lunches and dinners that followed the announcement. But he thought it unwise to stir up more trouble.

Joe was to keep an office with access to a secretary and a chauffeur. In August, we were shown Carlton House, a building in Duke Street behind Manchester Square, opposite the staff entrance to Selfridges and the Selfridge Hotel which EMI owned. It was Max Rayne's first headquarters and gave its name to his company: Carlton Industries. EMI gained it notoriety as the dumping ground for "consultants", the hangers-on Read accumulated. These included a retired Admiral of the Fleet, who Mountbatten passed on to Read. Some took a look at the accommodation and were not seen again. Tilling, who was also retiring, had a room on one side of us. On the other was the admiral, who, finding his advice to EMI Electronics on defence matters rejected, became an "expert" on film and music matters instead.

Three significant dates remained in the chairman's diary. The 4th of November was the day we moved to Duke Street. The 14th of November was his seventieth birthday, and 28th November was the last EMI AGM at which he addressed the shareholders as chairman. Manchester Square was not exactly in turmoil about our eventual departure. Joe's door was always open. One day, when he was out, the Group Treasurer wandered into the room, forgetting I was still around. Finding me at my desk, he silently withdrew. Dorothy Read intended to install red curtains, "to brighten the place up"; purely a temporary measure. Plans were already afoot to create a grand new headquarters worthy of what she and John were already considering their own personal fiefdom.

Joe had pencilled in his diary "Dinner?" for Thursday 14th November. As the day approached, I penned in "7.45 for 8.15 p.m. Quaglino's Ballroom, Bury Street, black tie". The birthday dinner and presentation was a well-kept secret from both of us. The previous day, Joe went to see Boris Christoff at the Savoy Hotel. He was accompanied by Charles Rodier as chaperone, in case the Bulgarian bass had contract issues. Joe boasted afterwards he was hugged and kissed on both cheeks, whereas Charles was ignored. Poor Charles (I

Retirement Dinner. Dorothy Wallichs, Bernard Delfont and Arnold Goodman

know the feeling) discreet as ever, was careful not to mention he was included on the list of the wide circle invited to dinner the next evening. Dorothy Wallichs was Joe's surprise partner.

Vera Lynn sang "Happy Birthday to You Dear Joe". The "presentation" was a large portrait, painted in secret from an old photograph by an admirer in EMI Records. It failed for not being done from a sitting, and was a poor substitute for a Graham Sutherland commission Lord Brabazon felt was Joe's due in 1960. Messages were read out. Yehudi Menuhin's telegram praised Joe for "effectively furthering the cause of music". Paul and Linda were "very sorry we cannot be with you … but we are present at the other heart of EMI, Abbey Road, making, we hope, a new record for you". John Lennon cabled: "Dear Sir Joe due to the wonderful twentieth century postal system I was informed rather late about your birthday party." Ringo Starr sent an incongruous plaque advertising "Rooms by the hour 2/- each – complete night with attendant female staff 7/6". Speeches at such occasions were customarily recorded on to a presentation disc, but not this time. Boys came from White Lodge to add a much-needed touch to a rather predictable occasion. Their performance of traditional morris dances never failed to please. Speeches were made by Shawcross, Villiers, LG, Read and the Director of the Royal Ballet School. But what I enjoyed most was an interview Ken East gave to *Music Week* magazine in a special issue for the occasion:

> It was in 1963 when I came to Britain and I was something of an innocent in the ways of EMI. At the meeting of Senior Executives, one overseas company was under scrutiny, having recently lost its manager. The area supervisor was in temporary control. Sir Joseph enquired quite reasonably of the whereabouts of the supervisor and was told he was on holiday in Spain. I have never seen a man change so fast – his eyes were like razor blades. This was on a Thursday and Sir Joseph said: "If he's not back at his desk by Monday he's fired". The poor man was located and instructed by cable to return immediately. I learnt later he had jumped straight into his car and when it broke down near the French Border he just left it where it was and hitched rides the rest of the way."

Ken East pays tribute to Joe

The AGM was held at the New London Theatre. Kit Dawnay complained profusely to me afterwards about having to endure the blinding stage lighting. As if I was to blame!

Without putting it in so many words, Joe told shareholders they were losing a safe pair of hands as chairman, when the outlook was stormy:

> For the financial year under review we have encountered many difficulties in our International trading from political or economic causes. This year unhappily proved no exception … In the UK the year was marked by further taxation, sustained price restrictions, a national emergency during the winter months and a decline in business confidence – due largely to the uncertain course of Government economic policy. In spite of such difficulties the Group produced increased earnings per ordinary stock unit of 17.8p against 14.8p for the previous year.

As share prices on the UK stock market fell by a record 55% that year, to boast an increase in P/E was no mean achievement. Joe warned 1975 promised little sign of growth. The press praised EMI's resilience. Bryan Samain produced an aide-memoire for Read, listing seventy questions likely to be raised by shareholders at the meeting, with suggested replies. Joe did not receive a copy. Nevertheless, in a tour de force, he fielded every single question without referring to Read once. Years of practice trained him to refer anything he did not know "to the company secretary to look into after the meeting". With a knowledge of the record industry second to none, his explanations tended to be lengthy. This was unusual for AGMs, and Dawnay was visibly irritated at the delay in proceedings.

I was looking forward to Joe retiring as chairman. There had been too much intrigue behind the succession involving Dawnay. I knew Joe felt the same. I expected our days at EMI would be over. Nothing could have surprised me more when Read asked Joe to remain on the board as a non-executive director (no mention of President), and Joe accepted. There was no question of my leaving him. My rather unusual position was to become even more unusual. Was I with or was I not with EMI?

In December, we spent a week visiting Pathe-Marconi. As usual in Paris, we stayed at the Hotel Royal Monceau. On one day, we went to the factory and studios in the suburbs at Boulogne-Billancourt. Another afternoon, we attended a session at the Salle Wagram, where Rostropovitch was recording an album for La Voix de Son Maître label. Left to our own devices in the evenings, I took Joe on a tour of the gay bars I frequented ten years before. We looked for the Fiacre, the Festival, the Carousel and Mme Artur's, but stayed clear of the Turkish baths in the Rue de Penthièvre.

1975

No Plans for "Retirement"

Something to be grateful to the Heath Government for was the abolishment of Purchase Tax. Imposed on classical recordings in a discriminatory manner, this tax had been one of Joe's bête noires. Value Added Tax, or VAT, which replaced it, was a fairer all-encompassing tax set at 8%. In addition to products such as records, it also applied to services, such as the provision of professional advice. One had to register with Customs and Excise to be issued with a VAT number. Joe was one of the first to apply. He was in the perfect position to set himself up as a consultant. Hawker Siddeley, Laird and Smiths had dismissed his offer to retire at seventy. Non-executive directors' fees were now treated as consultancy fees. These companies, along with EMI, were happy to receive regular invoices from Joe with VAT added. The French Government, who were already paying Joe as a consultant, were exempt from VAT. Despite triggering the various pensions that were automatically age-activated, Joe had absolutely not retired at seventy.

I left EMI and was now dependent on Joe for employ. Clearly, I should also register for VAT as a consultant and invoice Joe for my services. He would pay my fee out of his consultancy fees as a business expense, and deduct the VAT I charged him from the VAT he passed on to the Exchequer. It was too good to be true, and my accountants assured me the tax man would never accept the scheme, as it was quite obvious I only had one employer.

Having gone to so much trouble to get his own situation accepted by the Inland Revenue, and advised Lord Shawcross, and anyone else who was interested, to do the same, Joe was not prepared to give up. As usual, he went to the top. An agreement was reached which required me to call myself a Technical Consultant, available to Joe, but also to other clients. For example, I would be able to charge for selling advertising in the annual Royal Ballet Gala programme. Joe and I kept this arrangement going for ten years without any questions asked. I was able to withdraw from the EMI Group Pension Scheme – neither of us had any confidence in the company's future – and start a self-employed scheme.

Joe showed little interest in the Royal Opera House at that time. He made sure it did not interfere with the School, mounted at least as many ballet performances as opera, and did not waste its Arts Council grant. He made it reserve one night every year for the Royal Ballet Gala in aid of the School and retired dancers. He found someone to chair the gala committees held at our office, but did not attend the galas himself. Harriet Carruthers, the gala secretary and I were left to liaise with Covent Garden and know what was going on. We reported Drogheda's curtain speech at his retirement gala in 1974: "The House is bankrupt and the building in danger of falling down," Joe laughed. This was the Garrett Drogheda who once wrote to him:

My Dear Joe,

If you have occasion to criticise anything in the running of Covent Garden, you would be doing me a kindness to talk to me first about the particular aspect criticised. If the criticism is justified, I should like to know about it. If it is not, then I am sure that you would prefer to be told before drawing false conclusions.

Yours, Garrett.

This was the Garrett Drogheda who asked Joe to arrange a recording session for his wife Joan Moore, the pianist. I booked the session with Vera Samwell at Abbey Road Studios. Drogheda assumed Joe would be there to lend support. Learning Joe had no such intention, he cancelled the booking.

Galas were grand occasions, attended by Princess Margaret and the Queen Mother. Some years the programme consisted of a mixed bill of new short pieces by Frederick Ashton and Jerome Robbins. Others marked the premiere of three-act ballets by Kenneth MacMillan. *Manon* and *Mayerling* were to remain permanently in the repertoire, and much acclaimed, despite receiving mixed reviews at their first performances. Drogheda and Tooley, without Joe present to see fair play, were inclined to snub the Gala Committee, leaving them out of Royal introductions. Lady Hastings, Committee Chairman for many years, and wife of the Royal Ballet Benevolent Fund Chairman, took this in her stride. But when Lord Erroll of Hale succeeded her, Harriet made sure that he and his wife were included in the Royal line-up. Our list of companies and benefactors who were interested in ballet and prepared to take advertising in the souvenir programme was to prove invaluable, when the Opera House eventually had to face up to mounting an official appeal for money. Lord Hastings chivvied Floris, the Jermyn Street parfumier, to take a quarter page, and Harriet persuaded Martell Cognac to reserve the back cover. Alfred Dunhill, Gallahers, and Benson and Hedges all expected preferential treatment.

Rather than attend the Royal Gala in March, Joe and I went to the rehearsal in the morning. It was for a new MacMillan ballet. The stalls were occupied by the Friends of Covent Garden, and the Grand Tier was empty. Sergeant Martin, the formidable linkman, who was in awe of Joe, conducted us to the Royal Box. Scarcely had we sat down when Trevor Jones, the pompous House Manager, stormed in: "You cannot stay here! This is reserved for Mrs Davis the Music Director's wife." Joe exploded: "I'm not moving for anyone!" and we stayed put. Possibly it did not help that Mrs Davis was the wife of Colin Davis, who the EMI Classical Department had rejected. "A clarinet bandsman, a Sadler's Wells conductor, of the second rank, and more suitable for a lesser record company such as Philips."

With the Opera House closed for repairs during the summer, the Royal Ballet moved to a circus tent in Battersea Park. The workmen erecting the tent watched dancers rehearsing and sweating in the heatwave. One reported admiringly: "I've never seen ballet, but watching those dancers, I'm definitely bringing my children to a performance!" Joe was thrilled as it underlined his drive to bring ballet to wider audiences.

The School's annual performance took place in the tent. It was Frederick Ashton's *The Two Pigeons*. He was there to see Stephen Beagley, Joe's favourite, triumph as "The Young Man". Joe brought the Thorns, ever hopeful for a donation from Jules. Jean reminded Freddie they had worked together in Whitehall during the war. Driving them back through Central London was an experience I was glad never to repeat. The little man sat on the edge of his seat, giving instructions that made an accident almost inevitable. I believe it was his normal behaviour.

Princess Margaret came to see the main company one evening. In the interval, Joe's stature as Chairman of the Royal Ballet was evident, and my existence was even recognised by the Droghedas. Norman St John-Stevas, the Opposition spokesman on the Arts, bore down on me. He was doing Desert Island Discs on the BBC, and was desperate to get a copy of one of the eight records he had chosen. It was Elizabeth Schumann's *In der Frühe*, a Hugo Wolf lied on HMV. As Joe was Vice-President of the British Institute of Recorded Sound, and Norman was a very important ex-minister, the BIRS was happy to oblige. Norman was overwhelmed and wrote to thank Joe for being so very kind "to think of this in your busy life".

Joe's status in the record industry remained unaffected. He presented Sir Adrian Boult with a golden disc for selling a million stereo LP records. He presented *Music Week* magazine's annual awards. He attended the EMI Records sales conference dinner at the Heathrow Hotel.

Inevitably, attitude towards him in EMI was changing. As I was still around, I felt it more, and on one occasion in particular it was rather painful. The April board was held in Paris. A man came from Barclays Bank with travellers cheques for Joe to sign before the trip. These were mostly unused, as Pathé Marconi paid the bills. Following his normal custom on returning, Joe endorsed the unused cheques, which turned them into cash, made out a receipt for EMI to sign and sent me over to head office. There had been no difficulty in the old days finding someone in authority either at Hayes or Manchester Square. A gulf had opened up between Duke Street and Manchester Square. I was directed to a conference room where Peter Hayman, the pushy Group Treasurer, was holding a meeting. "Hello William, what can I do for you?" he greeted me affably despite the interruption. Learning of my mission, the tone changed dramatically: "No, that's not important enough!" I was dismissed and had to look elsewhere. Pennies no longer counted. Joe once showed Hayman up in front of the board, and this may have been his revenge. That circumstance involved EMI taking control of Columbia's Screen Gems Music Publishing for a massive $15 million, but retaining the key executives. Joe mildly enquired whether we were well covered should they leave. "Yes, they are well insured," Hayman responded, giving the impression that they, rather than EMI, would benefit should they abandon ship.

Paul and Linda McCartney with Denny Laine (Wings) presentation

Joe returned from Paris with misgivings. EMI's Manager for European Operations had taken up residence in Zug. "There is no justification for running Europe from Switzerland!" This same manager had continued to send Joe payments from Interton, which ceased on his retirement. The money was returned with difficulty. Was the man incompetent, or was he trying to bribe Joe? What was going on in the company?

Joe had time to think about EMI's future whilst recuperating from a prostate operation in the London Clinic during July. Board meetings were his only window on the company. Always aiming for the top man, he made a note suggesting that the Government Chief Scientist, Sir Hermann Bondi, might be a suitable non-executive director. I conveyed the note personally to Read, but no more was heard of it. Whilst still Chairman of EMI, Joe was tipped by Ralph Harris of the Institute of Economic Affairs that Geoffrey Howe, ex-Trade and Industry Minister, was looking for a directorship. Read was not interested; yet within a year of becoming chairman, he was able to take credit for appointing Howe. Otto Clarke died in June, and after a respectable gap was replaced by Antony Part, the mandarin responsible for closing the IRC and actively campaigning to have Villiers' book banned. And when Dawnay retired, he was tidily replaced by Ian Fraser of Lazards.

Joe's regime at Duke Street was frugal. Lunch consisted of a crusty ham or cheese roll from a sandwich shop and coffee made by a secretary. Come mid-Friday morning, we fetched the BMW from Manchester Square and set off for the country on the new M40. It was exactly 35.8 miles, and the BMW did 33 miles to the gallon. Joe noted the mileage. We always filled up at the same place. He was convinced on the one occasion his calculations showed a discrepancy that the pumps had been tampered with. We stopped for our cheese roll at a pub at Northolt. By chance, the pub lay on the direct route between Hayes and Harrow. EMI was installing the first whole body scanner at Northwick Park Hospital between the two. An EMI Electronics engineer recognised us, and introduced himself. Rather than encouragement, he received short shrift. Joe failed to relax until we reached the country. He was able to bask in the glory of the scanner story, but was suspicious of the number of high-paid American technicians on the payroll, with their frequent trips back and forth across the Atlantic. He had to share cars and chauffeurs with them, and heard their big talk.

On 31st July, Joe's brother Charles was kidnapped in practically the same circumstances as before. Yet he had been reassured: "We never squeeze the same lemon twice." On 1st September, the *Daily Mail* reported: "Briton freed in gun battle". During the whole month we were at Hatchet Wood, not hearing a word from the Foreign Office, who had been so good previously. I mentioned this to our new London secretary, who exclaimed: "But I was kept informed!" I attribute this extraordinary behaviour to jealousy. The horrid woman knew that if she rang us, she would have to talk to me rather than Joe.

There was still much to enjoy despite our reduced circumstances. Little John Reid took us to watch Elton John's Watford football club play away at Reading. We were entertained in the Director's Box at the stadium. Reid gave Elton's team a pep talk at half-time. On another occasion, he brought his quiet friend Freddie Mercury to Hatchet Wood for dinner. It was as John Reid's friend that Joe got to know Freddie. 'Bohemian Rhapsody' was not released until November, when it topped the charts for nine weeks. He was still unknown when we attended John Reid's extravagant birthday party on the enormous Stage 8 at Elstree Studios. The *Daily Mirror* called it "Elton's Spectacular!" Paul, Ringo, Long John Baldry and Harry Nilsson were listed among the guests, but no mention of Freddie.

The following years, John Reid and Freddie co-hosted joint birthday parties which became increasingly wild, too wild for us.

After numerous approaches, Bette Davis agreed to make an album with Norman Newell. As someone she knew, Joe was invited to attend the session, by which time Norman had discovered she was quite unable to sing a note. By adding compositions of his own to pieces such as Liszt's 'Liebestraum' from *All About Eve*, he managed to put together an LP entitled *Miss Bette Davis*. This was issued as a double-fold album depicting *Whatever Happened to Baby Jane?*, where she "sang" 'I've Written a Letter to Daddy'. She came to dine at the flat with her travelling companion, Peggy Shannon. I asked Miss Shannon what Miss Davis would like to drink. Came the sharp reply: "You must ask Miss Davis!"

The Young Vic Theatre Company was flourishing as a separate entity from the National Theatre. Dollars were flowing in from Frank Dunlop's production of *Scapino* with Jim Dale on Broadway.

Joe set about finding a chairman to replace him by the end of the year. John Gardiner was not interested, but recommended the very ambitious Jeffrey Sterling, Chairman of Town and City Properties. "Over a spot of lunch" at Wilton's, Jeffrey jumped at the offer, but made it clear

Bette Davis visits

he aimed higher; there was no shame in being openly ambitious. He would like to be Chairman of the Royal Opera House. In the meantime, he would settle to be a Governor of the Royal Ballet School, another appointment Joe was delighted to throw in. The Young Vickers were not being abandoned. Joe stayed on the Board.

I had been welcome at the Central School. Now I felt equally at home with the Royal Ballet and the Young Vic. Unfortunately, my relationship with these two landed me in a situation. I still sweat with embarrassment to recall it.

Leslie Edwards' career as senior dancer with the Royal Ballet went back to its very earliest days. He was someone Margot Fonteyn trusted. He was a character dancer and Freddie Ashton created roles for him. He ran the R. B. Choreographic group. He was much respected, and Joe wrote to congratulate him when he was honoured with the OBE. He loved the old HMV and Columbia recordings of light music. His nickname in the company was "Lena", based on Lena Horne, the black singer. He was openly camp with his friends, and I was a friend. He regularly rang me about our repertoire of music hall singers, 1920s dance bands and 1930s stars. He needed songs for the Friends of Covent Garden annual Christmas Gala performance, when the dancers let their hair down and the opera singers did a knees-up. I watched in awe as he obsequiously begged Ashton and de Valois for permission to "borrow" extracts from their works for just the one night.

Leslie had an idea for the 1975 show. He heard an old variety hall song 'The Elephant's Bottom', and pictured this as a skit for Rudolf Nureyev. I found it on an album of music hall numbers by Roy Hudd, the comedian, who specialised in this period. Had I ordered a copy from the HMV store as in previous times, nothing would have happened. But things were different now. Our influence was gone. Joe would have been furious. I was frightened at incurring his wrath. By chance, Roy Hudd was appearing at the Young Vic, and, to my eternal regret, I rang my contacts at the theatre. They could ask his permission. I mentioned what I had in mind. Later that day, the *Evening Standard* ran an article: "Rudolf Nureyev to be the Elephant's Bottom". To this day I do not know how they got the story. I only spoke to Maureen the secretary, whom I could trust. Roy Hudd, I assumed to be professional and discreet. I can only conclude he was with a reporter from the paper, who overheard.

Leslie never forgave me. Nureyev was ballistic, and from then on treated Leslie with utmost scorn. It was too late to apologise. There was no way to make amends to Leslie. The damage was done, and I was not to be forgiven. As you enter the stalls for a performance by the Royal Ballet, you will see a bust of Leslie Edwards OBE by Austin Bennett. I contributed to this commission. I hate Roy Hudd.

After Joe's retirement, EMI's share price tripled, despite a rights issue, which usually dilutes a company's value. Emmies were the darling of the NY Stock Exchange. The scanner was the big story, with most of the sales made in America. *The Observer* ran a two-page feature on 2nd November: "Britain's billion-pound brain ... the most important advance in diagnostics since the discovery of the X-ray." EMI reported proudly there were 1000 UK staff employed in its manufacture. Dr Powell parroted Read's boast that EMI was a "sleeping giant". Not all the press was favourable. The *Daily Express* reported: "The City has gone wild for EMI ... It's time to sell ... the enthusiasm worries me. I would not buy EMI shares right now. If I had them I would sell them." And the *Investors Review* had news of a scanner "that takes five seconds against EMI's 20 seconds and ready for delivery by G.E, in 1976".

Under the Labour Government, inflation reached 26.9%. Joe predicted such an outcome, but the tripling of EMI's shares was quite another matter. He attended his first AGM as a non-executive director on 9th December, and heard Read announce profits would increase 50%.

Joe had accepted an invitation to address the London and South-East Milling Society that evening. The subject was leadership, and he asked me to prepare a speech. I knew how he revelled in the company of his "Young Millers", but things were not the same now. The meeting was held in the upstairs room of the East End pub The Old Miller of Mansfield, behind Guy's Hospital. The room was stuffy, crowded and stank of beer. Joe stuck to my script, which was embarrassingly poor, and failed to stimulate the audience. He lacked his former sparkle, and it was impossible to hide the general feeling of disappointment among his acolytes.

Japanese visitor at Hatchet Wood

*Joe displays his Dog
and Trumpet
cartoon collection*

The evening was a failure. Those four hours spent earlier in the day at a packed shareholders' meeting had drained him. There were the blinding stage lights of the New London Theatre to contend with. Then there were all those City Editors to feed with upbeat comments. He supposedly told one young reporter after the meeting that the scanners "are already bigger profit earners for EMI than the Beatles records ever were".

Master and hound

1976

EMI: "The Sleeping Giant"

Despite the isolation of Duke Street from Manchester Square, I was in a good position to observe the company in decline. This was because we shared a secretary and meetings room with non-executive director Humphrey Tilling. Read had put the former company secretary in charge of two enterprises destined for failure: the Brighton Marina Company and the EMI Centre. Had the Reads not chosen to live in Brighton, neither of these property developments, for that is what they were, should have been touched. Tilling knew nothing about property, and so was sent on a course.

From their Brighton windows, the Reads would have seen enormous caissons dumped into the sea to form an artificial harbour. Their friend and neighbour Jimmy Carreras "dropped in", to tell them how the yacht basin, plus clubhouse and cinema, would fit in perfectly with EMI's Leisure activities. Mention was made of a hovercraft service from Brighton to the Continent, but no word of the apartment blocks needed to fund the venture. The consortium required further capital. There were tax losses to be set against EMI's great profits. EMI undoubtedly had the expertise to run the marina, and the cinema would be an ABC.

Tilling was appointed Chairman of the Brighton Marina Company Limited, despite EMI being minority shareholders. Reporting to him were two brothers. David Hodges, the architect, who was responsible for the overall concept of the project. It was his baby. His younger brother, Dick, a solicitor, was managing director, and a shareholder in the company. As Tilling was an infrequent visitor to the office, I found myself taking calls from Mr Hodges, and being left to deduce which Mr Hodges. When the brothers fell out, the messages gained urgency, and one could tell things were not going to plan. By the time

EMI sold out for a reported £9 million, not a single apartment had been constructed.

Read had decided way back in 1970, as soon as he was Chief Executive, to bring all EMI's London activities under one roof. It was Carreras, again, who introduced him to his Brighton neighbour, Charles Hunnisett, the property developer. Hunnisett "happened to have available" a vast 156,000 square foot site at the southern end of Tottenham Court Road. The Gort Estate straddled Westminster City and Camden Councils, one Conservative, the other Labour, each with conflicting policies. The "New EMI Centre" was acquired for £5.8 million, significantly without planning approval, and Tilling was appointed Chairman of the Steering Committee. EMI was never to occupy the building, and so the rumour that Read and Delfont were to have separate entrances was never proved. "The day you commission a new building headquarters is the day before your business goes over the weir"; sentiments expressive of Joe's view were spoken by a fellow industrialist. There were grand plans to sell Abbey Road, create new recording studios and even include a cinema in the office complex. The fact that long-established light industrial activities were to be demolished, and provision made for affordable housing, was overlooked. Our shared secretary typed "New EMI Centre Steering Committee Meeting No. 12 – Chairman T. H. Tilling in 1977, No. 17 in 1978, and, finally, No. 32 in March 1980." No. 17 was held at Elstree. Were the film studios to be moved to Tottenham Court Road too? The contract to fit out the centre was awarded to an American company, Saphir Lerner Schindler Environetics Inc. Every detail, down to the last carpet, was planned by a revolutionary new technology. I could not resist the temptation to look at this design company's London office, conveniently situated near the GPO Tower. What I found was a nameplate and two occupied rooms in a nondescript, back-street block.

The National Theatre presented its first performance on 16th March. For the event, Peter Hall chose his already tested production of *Hamlet* with Albert Finney. In theatre history, it was rare for a new theatre "to open" with a new production. Of the three auditoriums, the Lyttelton was the first to be completed. The official opening of the Olivier Theatre by the Queen was fixed for the following October by the Protocol Committee. Ivo Brunner, our young Austrian professor, arrived from Innsbruck to remind Joe of the promise he made two years previously.

*The National
Theatre*

Luckily I was indisposed and he could use my ticket. Princess Margaret was guest of honour, and the audience included many celebrities, including Rudolf Nureyev, who came with banker and balletomane Charles Murland, a Governor of the Royal Ballet School. Charles involved himself in the lives of RB dancers, and was Nureyev's self-appointed PA. He hated the Opera House management for their treatment of the Company and its interference at the School. A bulky, florid, red-haired Irishman, he made an unusual figure. With his Ulster temper, he was quick to make enemies. He was also excessively generous. He invited Joe and Ivo to join him and Nureyev for dinner at the restaurant in Chelsea that he part-owned. Also in the party was Richard Buckle, the gay ballet critic, whose language, according to Joe afterwards, was "absolutely filthy". Leaving the restaurant in the early hours, Nureyev made a play for young Dr Brunner. Murland was ready to intervene: "In this country a gentleman is expected to leave with the partner he arrived with." Something was definitely going on, as Ivo confirmed to me in deepest confidence sometime later. He saw Nureyev again in Vienna, and was rewarded with an autographed photograph.

Norman Newell, having achieved his ambition to record Bette Davis, now wanted to make an album with none other than Rudolf Nureyev. For this he needed Joe's support, which inevitably meant Murland. I experienced, some years previously, Murland's enthusiasm for ballet projects that attracted him. He generously offered to lend Andrew Loog Oldham, the Rolling Stones' manager, a valuable collection of books on ballet that came with the house in Knightsbridge he bought from Robert Helpmann, who was returning to Australia. With success in creating the Stones, Oldham had delusions of succeeding another impresario, Serge Diaghilev. Mike Regan was humouring him, and we had the idea of lending Murland's rare editions, including biographies of Vaslav Nijinski. It was a disaster. Mike and I went to an address in Fulham with the books. Oldham, looking very strange, received us in a large artist's studio he was renting, and we never saw the books again. Requests for their return were met with blank disbelief, as if they had never existed. It was impossible to compensate Murland, and the fact he was so gracious about his loss may have meant that he was used to having his generosity abused.

From January to July, Murland, Newell, Joe and I were constantly in attendance on Nureyev. On 5th January, we dined at Nureyev's home in East Sheen, invited for 11 p.m. The next evening, we were at Covent Garden to see him partnering one of Fonteyn's last performances as Juliet to his Romeo. Newell brought his Scottish artist Moira Anderson along. On 13th January, Newell entertained us at The Talk of the Town.

On 18th March, we were back at Covent Garden for another Nureyev performance. On 7th June, he was dancing at the Royal Festival Hall with the London Festival Ballet. A couple of nights later the familiar quartet, minus Nureyev, were at the Albery Theatre to see *Equus*. On 1st July, we were at the Coliseum to see *Nureyev and*

Friends, followed by dinner. This was to be our last outing. Newell came to see Joe when we were back from the country on Sunday 29th August. There was to be no recording. Perhaps the Russian had never intended to sing.

Jules Thorn faced up to the inevitable and retired in June. He had been running his own company since 1928, when it was called the Electric Lamp Service Co. Ltd. He needed his hand holding as the day approached. The decision must have been made during January, when Joe dined with him three times. He produced a list of candidates that Hambros provided as potential chairmen of Thorn. The only name Joe recognised was Richard Cave, who had succeeded Ralph Gordon-Smith at Smiths Industries. Jules took this as an endorsement, and Cave was duly appointed successor, but not before Joe had been lobbied from unexpected quarters. Jeffrey Sterling saw himself running a large industrial company, as did someone else even better acquainted with Joe. Summoned unexpectedly to Goodman's flat, he was met by Villiers, who was there to make his case with Goodman's support.

Read and Cave were knighted in the June Queen's Birthday Honours List. There was a certain similarity in their appointments. Cave had been induced to accept the Thorn appointment with this reward. Read's wait had been longer, and Dorothy's impatience was plain to see. The EMI International Conference held in London in April culminated in a grand dinner, held in the ballroom of the Inn on the Park Hotel. Bryan Samain organised it as a "guest night" to which eminent people were invited. Attending a cocktail party at the Travellers Club in Pall Mall earlier in the evening with Lord and Lady Greenhill, Joe discovered many guests, such as Eric Korner, were going on to the dinner. Samain could have borrowed our address book. Seated next to Read at the top table was the Prime Minister, who was in the early stages of Alzheimer's disease. His memory was erratic. He boasted he had got John Wall a knighthood, but in his after-dinner speech he recalled his "old friend Joe Lockwood" as someone from the past. Sitting unobserved at a lower table, Joe could sense his neighbours averting their eyes and examining their menus.

Included in the June honours was a CBE for Godfrey Hounsfield. This was rapidly upgraded to a knighthood, no thanks to Samain. Hounsfield progressed to the Nobel Prize, whereas Read and Cave's careers were soon on downward paths.

All these honours were capped by the life peerages granted to Sir Lew Grade and Sir Bernard Delfont in Wilson's Resignation Honours List. *Private Eye* on 10th December ran a spoof "Today in Parliament – House of Lords" report:

Lord Longford:	I'm really here to tell you about Elizabeth's book. It's Byron …
Lord Delfont:	By Ron Who?
Lord Grade:	Don't speak ignorant, Bernie, I've told you a million times, you've gotta keep your mouth shut in this place or they'll tumble us.
Lord Clark:	What could be more disagreeable than these two late 19th Century Russian objets trouvés?"

With time on his hands, Jules Thorn was seeing more of Joe than ever. The same applied to another seventy-eight-year-old. Sir Halford Reddish remained Chairman of Rugby Portland Cement too long, leaving him aimless in retirement. He expected Joe to dine, and even breakfast, regularly with him in his permanent suite at the Dorchester Hotel. The two veterans hung on to Joe, the youthful seventy-one-year-old, filling Lord Mills' role in earlier times. An article in *The Economist* headed "It's so hard to go" referred to them as "the grand old entrepreneurs of British Industry who do not die". An exception was Ted Lewis, who died in office, and, to the end, had Joe to dinner regularly.

In July, Charles and Mabel persuaded Joe to join them on their annual visit to Southwell to see their cousins. He was reluctant to return to his childhood home since his mother's death. The

Lockwoods were, as usual, based in a rented flat in London for the summer months. They were delighted to be included as Jeffrey Sterling's guests at the Royal Tournament. Their host's property company owned Olympia and Earls Court stadiums, and they were impressed with his importance. They were seated in his box, and were joined at dinner after the performance by the general taking the salute that evening. Charles noticed Joe was less enthusiastic about his protégé than he deserved, attributing it to jealousy. How little he knew his brother. Sterling was already imposing himself on Garrett and Joan Drogheda, inviting them to "a spot of lunch at Wilton's", and grasping the prestigious appointment as deputy chairman to Drogheda on the London Celebrations Committee for the Queen's Silver Jubilee in 1977. Joe felt ambition's reward was to be asked rather than to ask: "I've never asked for anything!" And in July, he did receive such a request. LG asked him to represent the British Phonographic Industry at the Government-sponsored Performing Rights Tribunal's Statutory Royalty Inquiry, to be held in December. There was an air of desperation that reminded Joe of a similar approach in 1955 from the Copyright Department. This time, music publishers and composers were again audaciously claiming a bigger share of the income they already received from sales and public performances of records (e.g. on the radio). In the appropriate setting of the Savoy Hotel's Iolanthe Room, LG introduced Joe to Robert Abrahams, a young lawyer engaged on the Industry's behalf.

Abrahams was allocated a room and secretary in Duke Street, and for the next four months his meetings with Joe matched Read, Villiers and Gardiner for their intense regularity. Together, they went to see counsel in September, October and November. The tribunal sat for the whole of December, and they were expected to be available to attend. Joe must have wondered what could take a whole month. At last he was summoned to the witness stand by Roger Parker, the top QC, engaged to represent the Industry. He faced the three members of the tribunal, a QC and two advisers, seated on a raised dais. Reading the forty-page report published in May 1977, there is little doubt Joe was the star performer of those oral hearings. Launching into a virtuoso performance, he paused to enquire whether he was tiring the tribunal: "Please continue, Sir Joseph," the chairman reassured him, "we are enjoying listening to you!"

Joe was able to report that EMI's profits from music publishing now greatly exceeded record sales. Since the previous enquiry in 1955, 950 different artists had at least one disc in the UK Top Twenty. Of these, 49% were "one hit wonders, crowding the charts" for the performer's single moment of fame. But the published earnings of the song tended to continue longer than the original artist's version.

For me, Joe's tour-de-force was his outrageous attack on Dr Edmund Rubbra, the eminent composer, who was appealing on behalf of his fellow composers for an increase in their royalties. Listing his nine symphonies and fifty other works, covering half a page in *Who's Who*, Joe asked what commercial record company in their right mind would consider recording Rubbra. An increase of royalty rate would make little difference for him.

At the conclusion of proceedings, Dudley Perkins, one of the tribunal advisers, confessed he was a composer, and asked Joe whether he would assess his work as of recording potential. Joe was happy to oblige. Abrahams wrote to thank Joe on behalf of the BPI: "The Industry has been fortunate to have someone of your experience and eminence prepared to give so much time, and approach the task with such thoroughness as you have done. Moreover, in personal terms I found it invaluable to have your support throughout the case."

What was I doing these months? I was tied to Joe's desk, but attached to my own telephone line. On this I had calls which underlined my somewhat unusual position. Colin Wills, son of Sir John, the Chairman of Associated Rediffusion, confided that Geoffrey Ellis had asked him to look after his boyfriend while he was away on business. Barry Justice, the handsome young actor and caddish Burgo Fitzgerald in the BBC adaptation of *The Pallisers*, agonised over his unreciprocated love for Ian Charleson. "Do you think it is because of my hairy chest?" Cast together in a two-hander play, poor Barry was beyond frustration. Barry committed suicide and Ian Charleson was to die of AIDS.

There were danger warnings for EMI during the year, but it took the scandal of the Sex Pistols in November to indicate things were going badly for the company. As early as April, Kenneth Fleet, the *Daily Telegraph* City Editor, who had transferred his admiration for Joe to John Read, was questioning "Does EMI Have Muscles as well as Brains?" He referred to fears that American GE was launching a scanner that would swamp EMI. "It is conceivable that EMI is in the business of frittering away its leading position?" he asks, and yet concurs with the stockbrokers tipping the share price to exceed 300p "by the end of the year and beyond". Such bold words were to mean little when the country descended into financial crisis, and the Chancellor of the Exchequer appealed to the IMF for a loan. Dennis Healey had been sent records at Christmas when he was Defence Minister. Once cornered by Joe at a social gathering and challenged to reduce Purchase Tax, he responded: "Yes, thank you. I have a very good collection!"

In November, Bob Mercer, EMI Records Marketing Director, signed the Sex Pistols with a £40,000 advance. Even though it was not his own personal taste, he had spotted the commercial potential in the nascent punk-rock movement coming from New York. To launch their single 'Anarchy in the UK', the group replaced Freddie Mercury and Queen on an EMI-controlled Thames TV afternoon show. Challenged by the programme's presenter to do something punkish and anarchic on live television, the group spat out "Shit!" The expletive caused national pandemonium, and EMI panicked. Despite the fact that the group had been provoked, their behaviour was something from which John and Dorothy Read's EMI must, at all accounts, be disassociated. Standing over poor Bob Mercer was EMI Records' youngest managing director, Leslie Hill, a chartered accountant protégé of the couple, a square peg in a round hole. EMI's middle managers traditionally lived in the middle-class stockbroker belt town of Gerrards Cross. Leslie Hill, recently settled here with his wife and baby, had his windows smashed and his name abused locally and nationally. It was the nearest the Reads came to a personal attack. They made Hill sack the Sex Pistols. Instructed to write off

£40,000, EMI Records learnt it had lost the support of a chairman who lacked commercial sense, and interfered in a business he knew nothing about.

'Anarchy in the UK' and its B-side 'I Wanna Be Me' were deleted from the catalogue. Overlooked was information shown on the single's printed label: "EMI Music Publishing Ltd" shared ownership of the two songs with Rotten, Jones, Matlock and Cook. Bob Mercer had been canny enough to get the songs' future music publishing rights, despite the vinyl on which they were recorded being smashed and recycled. He survived the sack, but bitterly asked me: "What is the purpose of non-executive directors on the board?" He may equally ask what part did a managing director play? Dr John Powell did not appear to feature in this episode which concerned Mercer, Hill and Read in ascending order. Nevertheless, responsibility must rest with him. He attributed his late arrival for a meeting to discuss the prior Brain Scanner problems to the Sex Pistols. He must have discovered at last that he had entered a minefield. Outrageous behaviour by the Rolling Stones, The Who, even John and Yoko, had not damaged their record companies. A quiet word with Malcolm McLaren, the Sex Pistols' publicity-minded manager, would have restored sanity. Joe had managed to stop situations escalating by befriending managers.

An example of how he managed not to be drawn into controversy occurred in June 1977. Virgin Records issued the group's abusive single 'God Save the Queen'. At the time, the Country was celebrating her Silver Jubilee. Neville Trotter, a Conservative MP, wrote to Joe:

> It seems singularly inappropriate that you should have contributed to the Jubilee in this way. While you may feel it justifiable to earn money producing "punk" records, I would have thought that you could have made an exception in this case. Might I suggest that no further copies of this record are issued. Its production has certainly lowered my estimation of your Company and many members of the public share my view.

Joe informed Trotter that he had retired three years ago and "I have not in fact myself heard the record." No doubt EMI's reputation was tarnished by this episode. In 1996, *The Times* described the Sex Pistols in terms that vindicated Bob Mercer, if not EMI's reputation for spotting a trend, surely the essential ingredient of any pop record company: "In their time they were an outrageous symbol of youthful rebellion, whose brilliant singles and debut album administered a jolt that freed rock's wheel from a pretty muddy ditch."

The young male dancers in the Royal Ballet, coming up from the School, were always fascinated that their chairman also ran a great record company. Joe's favourites, Wayne Eagling, Julian Hosking and Steven Beagley, were rapidly rising through the ranks to become Principals and Soloists. Despite being surrounded by admirers, critics and fans of their own, they were envious of Joe for his access to the superstars of the pop industry. He had tried to interest Cliff Richard, the Beatles and Elton John in ballet, but they all thought "it was not quite their thing". This was now to change.

The boys were busy during the Autumn Season, noted for a number of new works entering the repertoire. The Royal Ballet Gala included no less than three original pieces, including Ashton's *Brahms Waltzes in the Manner of Isadora Duncan*, with Lynn Seymour as Isadora. Fonteyn and Rudolf Nureyev danced separately that evening. Fonteyn was partnered by David Wall, another favourite of Joe's. Wall was "taking my roles" remarked Nureyev, who was spending more time with the English National Ballet.

Most challenging for the boys that November was the arrival of Glen Tetley from Germany, with a ballet he had already mounted with the Stuttgart Ballet. *Voluntaries* was performed to Poulenc's 'Concerto for Organ, Strings and Percussion'. Tetley picked two RB School trained students, Richard Cragun and Maria Haydee, an American and a Brazilian. They, sadly denied UK employment, had gone to Stuttgart.

Joe and I watched our boys rehearsing at the company's studio. They were not happy: "We haven't been trained to do these lifts!" The situation needed dramatic attention, and compulsory back-strengthening exercises were added to their punishing routine.

Freddie Mercury had ambitions to become a dancer, and there was no better place for him to start than with the Royal Ballet. Joe invited him to the Box reserved for EMI in the Grand Tier at Covent Garden for a Nureyev performance. By lucky chance, Wayne Eagling replaced Nureyev as Romeo at short notice during the Christmas season. Edward Thorpe wrote in the *Evening Standard*: "Eagling has elegance, speed and elevation, and recently his partnering had gained assurance and strength." Wayne was a "laid back", easy-going, pop-loving, plugged-in Canadian, and the ideal partner to encourage Freddie's ambitions. They became instant friends.

Freddie wrote to Joe: "I'd like very much to thank you for that super evening at Covent Garden. It was quite an eye-opener and I enjoyed it immensely. I am having a little soiree for about 40 people at my place in Kensington on 23rd December this Thursday, and I'd like very much for you and William to come. I do hope you can make it." Freddie's "place" showed his passion for elaborate black and gold lacquered Oriental screens, decorated with rose bushes, pheasants and polychrome fruit. He was not a conventional pop star, and Wayne Eagling was not a conventional ballet dancer.

1977

A Helping Hand for our Two National Institutions:
Inside the NT and the ROH

Royal Opera House, Covent Garden

Joe had three of his public anger attacks during the year. His three great loves – the School, the Music Industry, and EMI itself – were subject to outbursts. Each was an isolated moment, and each stemmed from frustration at no longer being in charge. All he could do was spit and shout on the sidelines.

Joe rewarded Charles Murland with the Chairmanship of the Royal Ballet School Endowment Fund. He remained on the committee, and meetings were held in our office. Murland had proved his mettle in defending the School from the Opera House, when Mark Bonham-Carter, a director of both boards, suggested the endowment fund should bail out the Opera House's financial crisis. Murland had to be restrained with difficulty. He was easily provoked and volatile at the best of times. Unfortunately, Joe soon found he was unsuitable as chairman, but there was not much he could do. He was particularly irritated by a young stockbroker Murland had put in charge of the charity's share portfolio, who suggested Hawker Siddeley shares should be sold. This was tantamount to asking for inside information, or plain stupidity. Joe found his moment at a meeting with all the committee present and waiting to start the agenda. Murland had been in Paris with Nureyev, and was digressing on the exclusive inspiration he had from visiting the Opera Ballet School. Joe's impatience was tested, and he simply exploded. The Managing Director of Marks & Spencer's wife, who had recently joined the committee, asked at the end of the meeting: "Are we all sacked?" This was in fact the case, as Joe took the fund back into his own hands. It was badly handled. Mrs Sacher felt offended, as did the other members. Murland cut off his ties with the Royal Ballet. He took her and others with him when he raised his standard at the English National Ballet. It was a pity Joe made no attempt to carry the committee with him. He had no difficulty, once before, when he got impatient and called Mrs Strauss "a bloody bitch". Everyone agreed. But he was chairing the meeting. The lady was nit-picking over some procedural matter of little relevance.

Sir Claus Moser, who had succeeded Drogheda at the ROH, unexpectedly invited Joe to a meeting at Covent Garden on 8th

February. We parked in the special place Sergeant Martin reserved for us, and I waited in the car. Joe was not surprised to be told the Opera House was in crisis, but was amazed to learn that he was apparently the only person to save it; according to Moser, Drogheda, Goodman, Lord Sieff, Max Rayne and Prince Charles. Drogheda had unveiled an ambitious plan to redevelop the backstage with an extension on part of the fruit and vegetable market acquired for that purpose by the Government, at the cost of £1 million. Left to pay for it, without any further Government help, the Opera House Board, with no resources of their own, could forfeit the site. Marcus Sieff, the influential Chairman of Marks & Spencer, ran the £7 million redevelopment appeal. All hopes had been with him. He barely managed to raise £600,000, and threw in the towel; hence the meeting on 8th February. Back in the car, Joe told me he would only accept the poisoned chalice with my approval. His condition was that I should attend meetings, even Royal Opera House Board Meetings. It would be like raising money for the School, but on a vast scale.

Now we knew what had been going on, and why. Over lunch at Stone's Chop House, Jules Thorn described Sieff herding a group of tycoons around some derelict buildings in Covent Garden Market full of hippies, designers and artists, calling themselves "The Covent Garden Community Association". Sieff needed money to buy them out immediately. They threatened their intention to renew their leases. Jules and Joe had a good laugh, because they both knew Jules was not going to contribute. At the same time, I learnt from Harriet Carruthers that John Tooley's PA, Anthony Russell-Roberts, was fitting out a flat for his boss's wife's use. It was in one of the market buildings Jules had seen.

Joe owed the Opera House no favours. Although it was the home of the Royal Ballet, the Board's preference was always for opera. Admittedly, Drogheda was keen on Nureyev. But the only time I saw him talk to Kenneth MacMillan was to congratulate him for using music from Verdi's opera *Les Vêpres Siciliennes* in his new ballet *The Four Seasons*. Worse still was the choice of Lord Robbins, the seventy-eight-year-old oldest member of the board, to chair the Royal Opera House

Redevelopment Committee meetings which Joe would be expected to attend. It was Robbins who vetoed MacMillan's greatest work, *Requiem*, a "profoundly serious dance treatment of Fauré's beautiful score", as sacrilegious and not suitable for the Opera House. As a result, MacMillan took the ballet to Stuttgart and nearly went for good. *Requiem* joined the Royal Ballet repertoire some years later.

Joe was not boasting when he claimed he still knew everyone of importance in London, "but in five years I will be forgotten". He was the man for the job. He knew the industrialists, the reluctant patrons of the arts, many of whom disliked Drogheda and refused to support him on principle, or were reluctant to add to their existing contributions. Premium prices paid for tickets, produced additional money for running the theatre. Corporate membership of the Royal Opera House Trust, for £1000 per annum, went to a similar purpose. Both forms of support were treated as charitable gifts to the Opera House by the regularly solicited donors. Added to which were the Friends of Covent Garden and the American Friends of C.G. Joe took charge of operations in a professional manner. He adopted the title Executive Vice-Chairman. By chance, he had recently been asked for advice by Lord Shawcross who was fundraising for the Royal College of Obstetricians and Gynaecologists Appeal:

> I think your standard letter is very good but I do not think you will have too big a success if you have to send all the letters out yourself. You should have a Committee which will only need to meet about twice a year. I suggest you get hold of … who is a Director of the Prudential and several Investment Trusts. Once you have got hold of him you should then get him to draw in some of his business friends who have influence with those kind of people who have money to give, including the Chairmen of Public Companies, because in my experience they are the kind of people that always get a positive response, especially for those people who have overdrafts at the Bank. I can lend you a complete list of Companies and the contacts that are worth approaching, and also a list of Trusts. Each Committee member would mark those Companies or individuals who were personal friends or had business relationships.

An approach of that kind is worth 500 times more than an approach from a kind-hearted unknown person, however much influence he may have Nationally.

A similar appeal by the Royal Academy had failed, despite a committee of the great and the good headed by Prince Philip. Joe also had in mind the Westminster Abbey Restoration Appeal, which fell short of its target. The chairman, Sir John Davis of the Rank Organisation, took on everyone himself. He called on potential donors, placed his brochure on their desk, and departed.

Now Joe established the system outlined for Shawcross at the Opera House. He circulated his "Advisory Committees" with "Priority Approach Lists" (PALs) at regular intervals, writing:

I should greatly appreciate it if you will put a tick against those that you know, in column A, B, or C, as follows:

A   I know him VERY WELL, and would be happy to approach him personally.

B   I know him QUITE WELL, and would be prepared to approach him personally if no one else known him better

CI   know him ONLY SLIGHTLY (as an acquaintance), but would be prepared to approach him personally, if no one else knows him at all

We hope that no one member will be asked to make more than half a dozen approaches at this stage.

The first PAL listed 100 major Charitable Trusts. It went out in October after months of concentrated preparation. By then an "Executive Appeal Committee" of twenty members and a "General Council" of a further forty members were co-opted. The pressure was on. Eventual success meant everyone got in on the act, excited at the part the Royal Family, including Princess Margaret, Princess Anne and Lady Diana Spencer, on her engagement to its Patron, were playing, but Joe did not relax. When Prince Charles officially opened the completed development after five years in July 1982, with the target already exceeded, PAL No. 8 was still in circulation. The campaign concluded in 1983. By the time Joe set aside his begging bowl, he had become the most avoided person in London. He could empty a room, as occurred once at an exhibition at the Royal Academy, during a preview party, when fellow guests moved on quickly and we found ourselves left alone.

We were introduced to Polly Lansdowne, who had the double responsibility of coordinating the redevelopment for Lord Robbins, and raising the funds to pay for it. Under this burden, she was interviewing a firm of professional fundraisers when we arrived. We met in the canteen used by artists and staff, situated under the stage. Polly once appeared on *Jukebox Jury* as Polly Eccles. Now a Marchioness, although separated, and daughter of a Minister for the Arts, she was good PR for the House, and kept an evening dress permanently in her office. She had a strong personality. I took her down to the Royal Ballet School, as there were plans to include it in the redevelopment. Leaving White Lodge, she expressed horror at the restrictive conditions imposed on the children. It reminded her of her own schooldays. Coming to lunch in the country, she surprised Joe with her terror of dogs. She stood up to Drogheda, now joint chairman of the appeal with Moser. Drogheda brushed aside precedence. He was aware Marquesses precede Earls, but did not consider that it applied here. She felt that Prince Charles was not necessarily the most suitable Patron for the appeal. Perceptively, she noted the successful applicant to become Appeal Director was old, and would be hard to remove when no longer required. She stood up for me at an early Appeals Committee meeting. Looking down the table in the General Manager's office, Lord Robbins halted the proceedings: "Stranger in the House!" he exclaimed, meaning me. "But you know William, Sir Joseph's assistant," Polly intervened. In attendance also was the occasional presence of an Arts Council representative, sent to keep an eye on the Government's £1 million. The Opera House was sensitive to being spied on, but it depended on the Government for its annual grant.

Trevor Jones, the newly respectful and obsequious House Manager, was instructed to give Joe a complete tour of the theatre in March. Up in the roof we saw how a panel slid back in the false dome to reveal the spotlights. Crossing the scenery painting bay directly above the stage, we encountered Sir Geraint Evans, taking a short cut. Squeezed in a cupboard behind the Amphitheatre we came across a Reginald Goodall Wagnerian masterclass. Wherever we looked, we were made aware this building, which was re-built in a mere eight months after it burnt down in 1856, was no longer able to cope with modern requirements. Drogheda was not exaggerating when he warned he was leaving a doomed House.

The Opera House found it hard to concentrate on this major problem, when it was always "concentrating on the next production", to the exclusion of everything else. The ambitious plan to add new opera, ballet and orchestra rehearsal rooms at the back of the theatre required the removal of one of London's streets. I discovered by chance that Mart Street covered where the previous Opera House stood. A friend recalled how, as a child in a school party treated to a backstage tour, he was told how the great Polish Helden tenor Jean de Reszke's voice could be heard from deep behind the stage. This was when Hans Richter introduced Wagner's *Ring Cycle* to London. A photograph of the "beau idéal" in the ROH stalls corridor reveals Siegfried in his blond wig and pink tights. De Reszke was admired for his exceptionally high range and for his "Victorian good looks and charm of manner". The area to the rear of the stage would have been deep enough to allow the effect of de Reszke's distant approach. That area was cut through to make way for Mart Street, either when Sir Thomas Beecham's father, Sir Joseph, owned the theatre between 1910 and 1920, or when Sir Thomas returned in1934 with fresh financial backing to make "improvements". The Beechams sold the theatre in 1920 to repay debts. This was the area newly acquired for the Opera House.

Permission was required to remove Mart Street from London's A-to-Z map to allow the Opera House to expand.

Another problem facing the Opera House board came to light. The English Property Corporation had acquired the freehold of Covent Garden Market from the Duke of Bedford's estate. It was EPC who had agreed to sell the freehold of the land needed for the Opera House's expansion. However, it retained ownership of the Royal Opera House itself. Illustrating this, the Grand Tier Box next to the Royal Box, called "The Duke of Bedford's Box", was retained for the exclusive use of EPC Directors. "How can I ask people to pay for building on to a building we don't actually own?" Joe rightly asked. And that was only one aspect of the difficulty facing him. Contributors needed to know they were supporting a registered charity and their donations would be tax deductible. Many of the wealthiest Foundations he planned to approach ruled never to support "bricks and mortar". His power of persuasion was need to convince them they should make an exception. Their support was vital.

Inspired by vivid memories of de Reszke and Sir Thomas Beecham, Joe and I felt involved with a living organisation, and we were determined to make the appeal our crusade. In fact, Joe's first begging letter went to his friend Henry Lazell, former Chairman of Beechams's: "I don't know which way I would vote if you were not the supplicant," Lazell replied, "but I consider we owe you a lot for joining us when you did and for being so helpful. If I were on the Board therefore you would have my support." Beechams' £25,000 donation was a useful guide to other companies, who felt they owed Joe.

The request to close the Street was left to others. How to get hold of the freehold was another matter, and Joe soon found himself in a position with a unique advantage.

In July, Lord Donaldson, Labour Minister for the Arts, asked him to replace Lord Cottesloe as Chairman of the South Bank Theatre Board. In accepting the job for six months, Joe put the Government under an obligation. And when the six months were up, and when the inevitable request to continue came, Joe was ready with his plan. The

Tories had provided £1 million for the redevelopment. There was little chance of Labour matching them. Having secretly got EPC to agree to sell the freehold for a further £1 million, it was necessary to get the Government to change its mind. In December, with the appeal not yet sparking, surrounding buildings were already being demolished, and ROH working conditions deteriorated daily. Joe briefed Drogheda and Moser with his strategy. He fixed to take them to see Lord Donaldson in the House of Lords on 22nd December. Moser was in a panic, threatening to resign at the lack of progress. Joe wrote to him the day before:

> I hope you won't feel too disheartened but I am not nearly as depressed as you are about the attitude of the two Arnolds [Goodman thought the Government should pay for the re-development, and Weinstock offered to find a Japanese company to sponsor the whole project] at lunch at Drogheda's house. I never thought this Appeal was going to be easy and I think there is a reasonable chance we are going to succeed ... I hope you won't think it necessary to resign either from the Opera House Board or as Joint Chairman of the Appeal.

The meeting with Donaldson led to a further meeting at the House of Lords in February, to make the case to Shirley Williams, Secretary of State for Education and Science. By then EPC had done a valuation of the property, down to the last chandelier. Mrs Williams agreed to grant £1 million, spread over four years, provided the appeal reached its target.

Joe made a similar approach to the GLC, which shared responsibility with the Government to complete the National Theatre building. Again, Joe briefed Drogheda and Moser before taking them along to County Hall, to meet Horace Cutler. The Conservative Leader owed him a favour. "Are you German?" asked Cutler, meeting Moser. If he was taken aback, this was nothing to Moser's expression at Cutler's next comment: "Will £1 million be all right?" The GLC had not been an Opera House supporter, but was monitoring the whole area vacated by the fruit and vegetable market. The grant was also to be spread over four years. "Do you want indexing?" Cutler asked as an afterthought. GLC's support eventually totalled £1,145,000.

Joe took his position as executive vice-chairman seriously. He knew how much the Joint Chairmen disliked fundraising. It was now going to be a one-man job. In March, he and Drogheda interviewed the applicant for the post of Appeal Director, which would release Polly Lansdowne to concentrate on the planned development. Pat Spooner came with references from Salisbury and Canterbury cathedrals. He was obviously that dreaded thing, a professional fundraiser. He claimed he was not tied to the well-known fundraising firms. This seemed unlikely, but with this assurance, he was appointed. To quell any doubts, he was assigned an office and put on the staff, working from the building in Floral Street opposite the stage door. His room was close to the box office manager's, which facilitated subtle means of obtaining "impossible to obtain" opera tickets for potential major donors to the appeal.

Taking Spooner with him, Joe set out to activate the most prominent members of the Appeal Committee. All doors were open to him. By October, they had called on the Governor of the Bank of England, the former Governors of the Bank of England, the Chairmen of four major banks, and all the merchant banks, tobacco companies and insurance companies. This went to Spooner's head. Soon, feeling he had kudos enough, he decided to go on his own. This led to a sharp rebuff from Weinstock at GEC, who wrote to Moser: "Who is this man Spooner you sent to see me?!"

Neither the Salisbury nor the Canterbury appeal reached its target. Lord Astor of Hever's effusive reference, as Canterbury Appeal Chairman, was probably prompted by a wish to move Spooner on. There had been a recent altercation with its patron, Prince Charles, who was not amused at a poorly-attended film premiere of *Rolls hyphen Royce* for which Spooner took the blame.

It was now Spooner's ambition to redeem himself with the Prince of Wales. Obviously his thick skin, which could be an advantage for a fundraiser, failed in this respect. Prince Charles's Private Secretary,

Edward Adeane, wrote to Moser, politely requesting that Spooner should "not get too close to the Prince of Wales". Apparently he had offered to accompany Prince Charles's first visit to India "as a supernumerary". His service to his future sovereign was of greater importance than to the Opera House.

The Royal Opera House Development Executive Appeals Committee met for the first time on 2th October. Drogheda was agitated that no one was on hand to receive the important visitors at the Floral Street office entrance. I found myself adopting the role of formal greeter that I'd once held at Manchester Square. Joe knew Weinstock would bully the meeting. He admired the rough treatment he gave his staff at GEC, and was glad I could witness it now. Yet Weinstock was a passionate lover of opera, and took Peter Andry and his wife to Salzburg by private jet.

As Chairman of SBTB, Joe ruled that all bills relating to the construction of the National Theatre, as it dragged on, must come to him for approval. He was stricter still at Covent Garden. Cheques on the appeal required his signature. Shortcomings at the National Theatre emanated from failure to appoint a project manager. So as not to repeat this mistake, the National Building Agency produced Robin Dartington, a personable young architect, to relieve Polly. His success as project director on the redevelopment emphasised the mess Joe was left to sort out at the NT. Although Dartington worked exclusively for the Opera House, NBA charged for his services. This was an appeal expense too valuable to dispute. On the other hand, Spooner's ever-increasing expenses claims drove Joe mad at his extravagance.

Joe knew how bad EMI's Annual Results, due for announcement in November, were, when we went to an event on 18th October. The figures for the first quarter of the current year were worse. His diary appointment read "8.00pm Supper and presentation of awards to pop artists black tie". The event turned out to be a far grander event. The venue was the Wembley Conference Centre. It was organised by the British Phonographic Industry, to commemorate the Queen's 25th Anniversary with the inauguration of the Britannia Awards, or BRITS, for services to light music. Joe grew restless as LG addressed the audience, and presented George Martin with a "Lifetime Award". He knew the two disliked each other. Unable to suppress his disgust, he pushed forward to the "supper" as the proceedings reached their conclusion. Taking one look at the massive spread, to him a symbol of the growing waste and extravagance in the Industry, we walked out and made for our car, brushing aside all protests. Luckily, we were not observed by Judy Martin, sitting alone and embarrassed by the proceedings. Yet again, listening to speeches in a confined area kindled Joe's unbridled anger.

So what caused Joe's even greater eruption after EMI's AGM at the recently acquired Tower Hotel on 6th December? The accounts showed profits of £64.7 million against the market's expectation of £75 million. Net profit after deducting "extraordinary items" was down from £28 million to £7.7 million. The Chairman's Review was complacent:

> During the year the US Government stepped up measures to regulate expenditure on capital equipment by medical institutions, so leading to a marked decline in the rate of new orders being placed on the CT industry. Our World medical electronics business during 1977/78 is unlikely to show a greater volume than that of the past year.

Read visited Washington DC to harangue President Jimmy Carter, but to no avail. The truth was different. The American operation to manufacture whole body scanners, and avoid Anti-Trust law, had failed. In the words of McKinsey & Co, the management consultants, called in to report: "You could look around this colossal building and see the beginnings of say half a dozen scanners, that was all, over there, and you'd see two or three people working and we'd got orders for sixty scanners, there was something wrong somewhere." They reported it would take eighteen months to produce a machine costing hundreds of thousands, by which time the competition, Picker and GE, overtook them. They were still selling the 1973 UK-designed machine. Hounsfield, ignored by the EMI Board, summed up: "My feeling is that there were not enough people at the top getting their fingers dirty, going round the factory and seeing in America that is, that things were not going right. I'm now talking about the very top." The board had already decided to get out of medical electronics because of the mounting costs. No wonder the next day's headlines ran: "EMI's Scanner hopes turn sour" and "EMI's agony stuns City".

It was customary for AGMs to end with a tame shareholder getting up to congratulate the chairman. It was the turn of EMI's long-serving Financial Press Agent. Ian Van Ammel was fulsome in his praise. EMI was a valued client of his firm, Streets Financial. Joe was furious, marched up to Van Ammel, and berated him in full view of the dispersing audience. Virtually grabbing his collar, he exploded: "You know perfectly well what you said is not true!"

Some may have noticed mention in the Annual Report of significant changes at the "very top". John Kuipers and Finance Director Richard Watt were appointed Group Managing Directors, to share the title Dr Powell held in 1974. Tillings's wife, Molly, collared me at Ralph Gordon-Smith's retirement party. "Why were they appointed?" She obviously did not approve of Kuipers or Watt. I could not tell her Read had put them in to protect his own position by having *three* managing directors.

As if this was not enough, Powell, Kuipers and Watt were appointed "Vice-Chairmen" on 1st July 1978. By coincidence, Joe had been invited to address a "Seminar on non-executive directors" at the Institute of Directors in Pall Mall on 15th June. Also attending were McKinsey's, who illustrated their talk on management with advice given to a recent client, whose name was not mentioned: "The real problem with this company, Mr X, is you!" It took Joe an effort not to show he knew they were talking about Read. To have done so would have blown open the question of the non-executive directors' role. After all, that was what the seminar was about. Joe, Otto Clarke and Shawcross had done their best to control what eventually transpired. Who ever heard of *three* Executive Vice-Chairmen?!

We saw two films in production during 1977. Rudolf Nureyev failed to start as a recording artist, but he was now to be a film star, portraying the other Rudolf – "Valentino". Sandor Gorlinsky, his manager, boasted that this would be a rich new source of income. We were invited to watch the scene where Valentino dances with Nijinski in a nightclub. Anthony Dowell from the Royal Ballet was to be Nijinski. We found Leslie Edwards on the set, seated well-placed to watch the action. "That young man has been ever so attentive finding me a chair," he said, pointing to a stagehand. "He is madly in love with Rudi and Rudi found him this job, but he is desperately ill." I recognised the pale creature he referred to as the bumptious new boy in bum-freezers I had last seen twenty years ago in my Eton House. I recalled Conway was diabetic and had to inject himself every day. It was pathetic how he came to me and Leslie, desperately grasping at any means to remain close to Nureyev, his obsession. Sadly, he had not long to live. Nureyev's acting fared little better than his singing career. The film was not a success with the critics, although "Nureyev dances agreeably often but his acting is hopelessly under-directed by Ken Russell".

In December, Richard Goodwin and Lord Brabourne invited us to the set of *Death on the Nile*, their second Agatha Christie production for EMI. Arriving at Pinewood Studios, we were shown to Bette Davis's dressing room, where she greeted Joe warmly. Dressed from neck to ankle in crisp white Victorian lace, she said the girl who designed her costume was very talented. Brabourne was impressed how well Joe knew the film star, and Joe later sent him a copy of the double-album *Miss Bette Davis*. We had lunch in the refectory with Peter Ustinov, who made swift pencil sketches of the other artists on his napkin. Children crowded the other tables, making it difficult to know who belonged to Mia Farrow and who to Jane Birkin. Dame Agatha Christie attended the premiere in a wheelchair the following October. I was seated at the supper party at Claridge's at a table with Ian Fraser and the director who had sold EMI a chain of hotels, neither of whom had a clue who I was.

1978

The Chairman's Wife Boasts

The new year began with another film premiere. It was a modest affair, but for Joe it turned out to be a significant occasion. A mysterious American called Earle Mack offered the Royal Ballet School the first screening of a documentary, *The Children of Theatre Street*, about the Kirov Ballet School, narrated by Princess Grace of Monaco. The School would benefit from the premiere, but it had to be attended by a Royal. We gave a private showing of our own, and invited some RB dancers for supper afterwards.

Harriet and I rushed all over London looking for a suitable venue, as the film was unlikely to go on general release. We settled on BAFTA, the film industry's premises in Piccadilly, with a cinema and dining room. We booked the evening for 10th January. A film show followed by dinner made an attractive proposition. Earle Mack was reputed to very rich and to move in the highest circles. This turned out to be true. His friend, the beautiful Lady Leonora Lichfield, the Duke of Westminster's daughter, agreed to be chairman of the event. Her husband, the photographer Patrick Lichfield, was related to the Royal Family, and the couple persuaded Princess Margaret to attend. Lady Leonora came to tea with Joe at the flat. Harriet and I went to Kensington Palace to meet Davina Woodhouse, the Lady-in-Waiting. Everything seemed to fall into place. Accommodation would be limited, tickets would be expensive, and special guests would not be expected to pay. The invitation list would be select. As long as we did not make a loss, and knowing it was unlikely to be very profitable, the arrangement became fun. Caterers came up with an all-Russian dinner menu. The RB School would send four children dressed in "Nutcracker" costumes to greet the important guests.

Joe had retired and been succeeded by Drogheda at the School.

But Harriet firmly ruled that Drogheda and the governors were not to be invited. This was to be Joe's evening. And so the evening of 10th January 1978 turned into a wonderful farewell party for Joe, quite by chance. The School was represented by the ex-director, Michael Wood, who had been offered the film, and the new director James Monahan. Joe was photographed with the children, and beamed indulgently at the charming way they helped him greet the guests and bow to Princess Margaret. Lady Leonora's grand friends, including the Duke and Duchess of Grafton, simply melted at the two boys and two girls in their costumes from Act 1 of *The Nutcracker*.

Junior School Students greet Princess Margaret at premiere

The seating plan for dinner was Leonora's work. She placed her attractive twenty-five-year-old brother, Gerald Grosvenor, beside Princess Margaret, which was a huge success. Joe was on her other side. Freddie Ashton, who sat opposite, had recently received the Order of Merit. He wrote to Joe: "It was so unexpected it gave me a shock, on recovering I was thrilled – a breakthrough for Ballet." Patrick Lichfield lent across to recount his recent experience at Heathrow: occupying a nearby table in the VIP Lounge were some noisy yobs disrupting the place. Asking who they were, he was informed they were EMI Music executives!

Princess Margaret rang Leonora the next day and said she had never seen Joe so relaxed. Later that day, a parcel arrived from Kensington Palace, containing her signed photograph in a silver frame. And a letter came from Aileen, Julian, Vincent and Lisa:

> We found it very interesting meeting all the visitors. It was super presenting the flowers. We had never met Princess Margaret before, and it was exciting for us to talk to her. We thought she looked lovely. Thank you for inviting us to the party.

Earle Mack's partner for the evening was Emma Soames., Winston Churchill's granddaughter. He turned up a few days later at Hatchet Wood with yet another girlfriend, our neighbour Henry Ford II's daughter.

Joe found himself sitting next to Princess Margaret again one morning the following month. They were in the empty Covent Garden stalls for the General Rehearsal of Kenneth MacMillan's new three-act ballet, *Mayerling*. I was a few rows back with her detective, who had been at BAFTA. Like everyone else, he had no idea what was going on on-stage. The scene was set at the Imperial Palace in Vienna. Handsome Principal Dancer David Well, as Crown Prince Rudolf of Austria, was approached by his friends, four Hungarian officers. They knew he sympathised with their schemes to secede from the Empire. The detective commented: "I thought they were trying to pick him up!"

Joe's connection with the Royal Ballet was strong. One afternoon we went scouting the West End for a suitable theatre for the Royal Ballet Choreographic Group's annual performance. Investigating our New London Theatre, we found the auditorium in complete darkness. No one was around. Suddenly the silence was broken by a woman's voice coming from the stage. She was very angry, and she was swearing. "Where is everyone? I'm on time. I'm dressed. I'm here for the lighting check!" Not a sound. "I'm waiting!" she continued. Then, a slight rustling from the back of the stalls was followed by an empty lager can rolling very slowly down the aisle.

"That woman is absolutely right!" Joe stormed. "I'll have someone do something immediately!"

"But, we are not here. You can't," I said. "That woman is Marlene Dietrich!"

"I don't care who she is!" Joe responded, and he meant it. But we slipped away unseen. It was Dietrich's last one-woman show. It was being made for television to be shown later in the year.

The facilities of the Royal Opera House provided several means for entertaining potential donors. There were lunches in the Ante-Room to the Royal Box that featured Queen Victoria's loo. There were dress rehearsals. There was the popular 45-minute backstage tour. And there was the King's Smoking Room (the KSR), decorated with furniture from the Royal Yacht, for entertaining during the intervals. The eighty-six-year-old millionaire Sir Charles Haywood, father of the better-known Bahamas-based "Union Jack" Haywood, brought his wife and secretary to a combined lunch, rehearsal and tour which Joe hosted. The Haywood charity donated £100,000 anonymously. A property tycoon complained at being served a cold meal, and a banker's wife noticed the dessert "was what we had last night!" Felicity Davis, whose husband, Sir John Davis, was the Joe Rank Family Trustee, admitted the draw was to see and meet Placido Domingo rehearsing *Otello*. This produced £60,000. Joe had occasion to boast a singular achievement. A Dr Cohen requested a backstage tour. He came, not in response to one of Joe's 200 individually typed letters, but from the circular addressed to a long list of charitable trusts. Some instinct inspired Joe to arrange to meet Dr Cohen at the stage door. The individual he encountered did not appear particularly distinguished: "He even had a pen sticking out of his breast pocket." He was a GP, but also a hospital inspector. At the end of the tour he concluded the working conditions he had just witnessed were worse than in any hospital he inspected. As a result, Dr David Cohen donated £100,000 from the John S. Cohen Foundation, and went on to be a major patron of the arts and Governor of the Royal Ballet School.

Some donations required no red-carpet treatment. A highlight of the appointment at Eaton Square was to collect a cheque for £100,000 in person from His Excellency Kamal Adham. Joe encountered the Arab Potentate's bodyguards glued to children's television in the entrance hall.

Two films were made to promote the appeal. Julian Pettifer got in first with his documentary for BBC Television. His approach gave a fly-on-the-wall impression, as he knew many of the dancers. More formal was Prince Charles's version, intended for the larger screen. This involved preliminary meetings at Buckingham Palace, where the Private Secretary referred to the Prince of Wales as "One-Take Wales".

Joe was surprised to be invited to represent the Royal Opera House during the Royal Ballet's visit to Houston, Texas in June. He was reluctant to accept. However, the fact that Houston was the headquarters of Shell Oil, who were sponsoring the Royal Ballet on this part of their tour, was too good an opportunity to miss. If he could get Shell Oil to make a major donation to the appeal, it would be easier to make other the major American oil companies, drilling in the North Sea, to follow suit.

Joe went on his own. As usual, he had far more fun without my being there. However, being apart from each other for a whole week made us realise how much we missed each other. He had never been in such proximity to the dancers. Finding himself on one occasion alone in the hotel lift with one of the young males, he admitted to feeling quite excited. And he formed a romantic attachment with a ballet fan, who worked in property and changed his name from Cohen to Cullen later. To have such success at his age must be admired, but

I had a sneaky feeling the young man involved was a little unstable being in such need to change his name. Houston had a large gay community to support its own Houston Ballet Company. Earlier visits by the Royal Ballet caused much excitement, as Donald MacLeary recalled, being wined and dined by many admirers in the late 1950s.

Joe was made a Citizen of the City of Houston by the Mayor, and an Honorary Citizen of Texas by the Governor. To accept these honours, Joe had to go on stage in front of the First Night audience. As he went through the curtain, Principal Ballerina Leslie Collier whispered: "Good luck!" as if he were one of the performers. He breakfasted each morning with Norman Morrice, the director, Tom Macarthur, the technical director, and Peter Brownlee, the General Manager: "We are very lucky to have such excellent people," he reported to John Tooley, who was upset at the high-handed way Joe had treated the President of Shell Oil, who had done so much to sponsor the tour. This is worth elaborating on.

Shell Oil was only 37% British-owned, and considered itself to be an American company. It did not give money to arts institutions outside the United States. Tooley accepted this situation, but Joe was not prepared to, as he had the other major North Sea American oil companies in mind. Shell UK had already donated £60,000, and BP £50,000.

The Shell President had declined to host a fundraising reception for the appeal as he was not contributing, but he "would be most pleased to host a luncheon for Sir Joseph to meet the leaders of Arts Groups in Houston". Joe described what happened: "In the President's Speech to welcome me he said that Shell was a great supporter of the arts, and altogether Shell USA gave $250,000 per year, and it was all given in Houston. In my speech of reply I could not avoid saying that their petrol sales included sales in Montgomery, Alabama, and there were arts in areas other than Houston. I recognised that New York and Los Angeles were perhaps as rich as Houston! (and I know they don't like that part of America), but that was no reason why they should not be rather more broad-minded. I also said the arts were an international thing and they should not be parochial. I mentioned that we, for instance, were struggling to find the money to bring the New York City Ballet to London. I also found out that under the American Government rules Shell would be allowed to give (deductible for tax) 2% of their profits, and this would have meant a figure of about $15 million a year (or $30,000,000 if it is pre-tax profits), as against their $250,000. The President then had to make a second speech to point out that their profits were very badly affected by Mr Carter's (the US President) refusal to allow them more than double the price of oil instead of four times the price as the Arabs had obtained, and their oil magnates told me they wished Texas had remained independent so they could have been members of OPEC."

The National Theatre was at a critical stage when Joe assumed chairmanship of the SBTB. The Press knew things were not going well. "The NT is on course for disaster". Headlines in the *Evening Standard* in March referred to author John Elsom's strong criticism of Max Rayne and Peter Hall's management. Elsom had been commissioned to write the history of the theatre, but discovered costs were running high as equipment failed to work. Once the problems were sorted out, the SBTB could hand the building over to the NT board. Until then, the SBTB was still responsible for the mounting costs. Joe was determined to get the job done and not put up with excuses from Rayne and Hall. In this he was gratified to receive Goodman's support, which he had not counted on, as Goodman was Rayne's lawyer.

Peter Hall describes the SBT Board Meeting on 12th July in his diary, where he was accused of delaying the technicians finishing the job:

I went on to suggest that the clear thing to do was for SBTB to close us down until the work was done. At this Joe Lockwood thumped the table angrily and said "All right we WILL close you down!" The Civil Servant asked how much it would cost. I said in loss of income between £36,000 and £40,000 per week, quite apart from any redundancy payments. We then began a long period of reconciliation which ended in all kissing and making up. Max [Rayne] and Victor [Mischon, an NT Director] arrived late when all the fun was over and we were in a warm glow. Horace

Cutler said we'd had an excellent argument. Joe Lockwood said I'd been very rude to the Board (this of course with an Establishment grin) but all was now well. A good meeting.

The main problem was the drum-revolve in the Olivier Theatre, which was sticking and not revolving. It occupied most of the open-plan circular stage. Plays were being performed without using the revolve. The only time the drum could be tested was after 11.30 p.m. and at 6 a.m. Not to be put off, Joe had me fetch him at 11.15 p.m. on 10th June. We were led under the stage, and found ourselves inside the massive drum "as high as a five-storey building" with a diameter of thirty feet. It was quite dark and frightening, like being in the Wall of Death at a fairground and expected to climb on a motor bike. But in this case the floor revolved in both directions. The floor was in two halves, or lifts, which rise and fall as they revolve. Unfortunately, they were not revolving. The technicians concluded, after considering all alternatives, that the weight of the drum was crushing the ball bearings it rested on.

Joe reported:

The drum cannot be completely ready for handing over unless it is operated regularly for a few hours every day for a period which might extend to a few months. Apparently for some productions the sets for the stage are brought through an opening at the bottom of the revolving drum and then lifted up to the stage through half of the drum-revolve. This requires that when such sets are being installed for the next day's production it is impossible for the drum to be revolved. I arrived at the appointed time and there were 17 stage hands who sat about doing nothing waiting whilst some work was done on the drum. I sat for about 40 minutes but the drum could not be revolved and then after a short period the 17 stage hands got to work to bring the sets by the above-mentioned system. I was not able therefore to see all I wanted to see because the 17 men would probably have been occupied for the next two hours or more.

A few days later we arrived at 6 a.m. in my car. The security guard barred the way, expecting a Roll Royce. Joe shouted: "Let me through! I own this place!" We soon learnt the sets for the two new productions, *Brand* and *Women*, could not be moved at night. Peter Hall sat silently at the back of the stalls as Joe ranted: "The engineers have contractual rights of access. They'll be making heavy claims." He came up with three remedies:

1. Design sets that can be dismantled at night. The NT said this would interfere with artistic policy.

2. Build a temporary stage 6" above the revolve. Cancel *Women* which uses a trap-door. Copy theatres which manage without a stage-revolve.

3. Close the Olivier Theatre for two to four months, allowing work to be done efficiently and on time.

Eventually we were able to witness the drum-revolve moving silently, slowly and rapidly with both lifts raised and lowered to pre-set heights.

On 28th September, Joe chaired a panel of six experts, including William Bundy, the NT Technical Administrator, to interview engineers applying for the all-important job of maintaining this complex organisation. The interviews lasted all day.

Things at EMI were taking a surreal turn. It was all so well-intentioned. In May, Leslie Hill invited Joe to a big concert Freddie Mercury and Queen were giving. On the way to Wembley Stadium, he revealed he was paying Queen a £1 million advance. Joe hesitated, before replying: "How are you going to pay?"

"That won't be our problem", Hill responded. "We won't be around. That'll be for someone else." Joe practically jumped out of the car.

In June, Sir John Read invited Joe to Glyndebourne. He was

obviously using the complimentary seats EMI traditionally received for advertising in the programme. Joe accepted. A few days before the event, Read checked: "I gather you don't really like opera," giving him the chance to change his mind. Joe said he was looking forward to going. So was I. We were to see a new production of *La bohème* by Rayment Leppard's friend John Cox.

It turned out to be an excruciatingly embarrassing and significant evening, although Joe behaved perfectly throughout. As they sat down to dine in the restaurant during the interval, Read lost his voice. Joe conversed with him as though nothing was amiss. This left Dorothy to me. She was brimming with excitement: "I have discovered my own pop star!" she boasted and elaborated throughout the meal on her amazing experience. I froze when she mentioned the name. The more she elaborated, the more certain I was she had been conned. The wife of the Chairman of EMI had been taken for a ride. The horrifying thing was, there was no way of telling her. How could it happen? What does that say for Read? The moment she mentioned Rick Springfield, she had to be talking about the Capitol artist EMI Records were asked to promote in October 1972. Joe attended the party on the *Sloop John D* moored at Chelsea Embankment in his honour. Nothing was heard of him, in the UK at least, and that was all of six years ago.

Dorothy's story was almost predictable, and I grew numb as I listened. The Reads had been on holiday in Bermuda. The hotel receptionist rang to say there was a young American downstairs whose father was a doctor and who was interested in the EMI scanner. Could they meet? Invited up, the young man (Springfield), accompanied by his girlfriend, proceeded to charm John and Dorothy. The couple revealed the "boy's" ambition to make an album. The Reads promised to help. As if by magic, Abbey Road Studios were put at Springfield's disposal, and an album was produced. To promote it Springfield was booked a season at The Talk of the Town. EMI Records were pressured to release the former rock star's LP. Delfont must have offered The Talk of the Town to please Read. Thames TV may even have given him a programme. Did no one dare to tell Dorothy her protégé was second-hand? EMI's catalogue for 1973 listed Springfield's Capitol album. Ironically, it was titled *Beginnings*. I checked on record sales and nightclub show reviews, and wasn't surprised to find Springfield had made little impression during his London visit.

Returning to our seats after the interval, Read was surrounded by his City cronies. His voice was fully restored. In September, the Press were increasingly worried about EMI's to-be-announced results. Was the company cutting its dividend? They were confused by Read's plans for EMI "to get more involved in electronics". Rumours abounded about a takeover. Decca and Racal were mentioned. A bid for Decca or a bid from Racal? In the event, Racal took over Decca, and EMI was spared – for a time.

The year began with Joe celebrating retirement as Chairman of the Royal Ballet School. It ended on another high note. Somehow Joe managed to mingle four of his principal interests, the RB School (still), the RB Company, pop music and industry. On 29th November, he booked EMI's box and the KSR to introduce Kate Bush, whose EMI recording 'Wuthering Heights' topped the charts for four weeks, to the Directors of Smiths Industries and the boys in the Royal Ballet. Kate Bush was unusual for a pop star. She used movement and dance in her stage act, and had studied ballet. Joe arranged a session at the School with the Contemporary Dance teacher. She sat on the floor and rhythmically beat a drum, secretly observed by the Ballet Principal. The Chairman of Smiths, three Air Chief Marshals and wives were in the stalls, and joined Kate, Hilary Walker, her manager, Joe and me for drinks in one interval. By the second interval the airmen were very jolly, and the management asked them to make less noise in the KSR. The programme that evening was a triple bill including Ashton's *Jazz Calendar*, and the boys, who had asked to meet their pop star idol, were able to show off their versatility. They did not let Joe down.

Joe's assistance was sought in the case of a talented South African girl at the Royal Ballet School, who, despite having a British passport, was denied a chance to dance in the UK by Equity. Commonwealth Citizens were treated as foreign since Britain's entry into the EEC in 1973. This applied to Canada and New Zealand as much as South

Africa, where Ninette de Valois found some of the greatest talent. Joe was determined to tackle not just this one case, but the whole problem. Foreign students were given the benefit of training at the RB School, but the RB Company was denied the opportunity to employ them and reap the benefit of the unique teaching, training and tradition. It was time to face up to the situation, and, he went direct to the Union. He requested dispensation for two dancers a year. His request was modest, and he was successful. He received a letter dated 15th December from the General Secretary of British Actors Equity Association incorporating the Variety Artistes Federation Affiliated to the TUC and STUC:

Royal Ballet School, Senior Students

Following our conversations and your submission of the memorandum regarding the possible employment of ex-students of the Royal Ballet School, I am glad to say the Council have approved the scheme subject to annual review, and I have asked our Organiser to make necessary the formal arrangements with the appropriate official of the Opera House.

Yours sincerely
Peter Plouviez, General Secretary.

Apart from receiving deepest gratitude from the student, now able to achieve her ambition to dance with the Sadler's Wells Royal Ballet, congratulations poured in from Moser, Drogheda, de Valois, Markova, Monahan, Tooley, Sainsbury, Bonham-Carter and Lord Hastings. He had achieved the impossible, but there was more to do. It would take another year to persuade the Department of Employment to grant work permits (in addition to Equity cards) to two students "who would be depriving UK Citizens of employment". This awaited the return of a Conservative Government.

Julian Hosking

Junior School, White Lodge, with Dame Ninette de Valois and Headmistress

1979

Whistle-Blower: Curtains for EMI

The new year began and ended again with ballet. In January, we visited Rotherhithe to see Richard Goodwin and Christine Edzard, who made *The Tales of Beatrix Potter*. They had converted their warehouse-home into a film studio, which was barely adequate for what we saw. Boys and girls from the Royal Ballet, dressed as vegetables, were performing *Pas de Légumes*, a ballet created by Ashton to be part of a children's film, *Hans Christian Andersen's Stories from a Flying Trunk*. Fifty years after the still-performed *Facade*, and now in his seventy-fifth year, Freddie was imagining fruit and vegetables from Covent Garden market springing to life. In the confines of the Edzard costumes, the dancers were not enjoying the experience.

In February, Spooner came into his own, when he supervised a major fundraising event for ROHDA. A banquet was held in the Great Hall of the Guildhall in the presence of Prince Charles. Kenneth Cork, the Lord Mayor of London, chose our appeal as the charity he would support during his term of office. All the City Livery Companies were automatically invited and expected to contribute. As five of them contributed £5,000, this was considered a great success. But the evening produced one embarrassing outcome, for which I was responsible, although nobody knew I was to blame. It all revolved around the guest list. As in *Sleeping Beauty*, someone of great importance, who should have been invited, was overlooked. Joint hosts Drogheda and Moser had paid more attention to the seating plan than to the invitation lists. I decided to leave Sir Charles Clore off the list as common sense. He supported the Royal Ballet School performances generously in the past, but for the last three years he had not replied to Joe's letters to his Mayfair home. It seemed sensible to invite his daughter, a Patroness of the Arts, instead. Vivien Duffield was "the charming girl" who gave the School £50. It was her first charitable donation. Now, the future Dame was a tough, short-tempered harridan. She exploded: "Why has the Opera House overlooked my father? He could have paid for the whole development." She was implacable and determined to make everyone suffer. Poor Moser! I saw her make him quake. He had no explanation. Amends were impossible to someone in her emotional state. Her father had cancer, and he died five months later.

I felt insulted at the banquet too. Prince Charles met Grace Bumbry backstage when filming the Opera House conditions. "Absolutely the lowest thing on the totem pole!" She was rehearsing Giacomo Meyerbeer's *L'Africaine*. "The Palace" asked Spooner to get a recording of the little-known opera for the Prince before attending a performance. There was no such thing. However, Patrick Saul at the BIRS found an illegally-recorded live performance. He stressed it was a "bootleg" copy, quite inferior, but the only one in existence. I told Spooner to make sure Prince Charles appreciated this. The Palace sent the Opera House a draft of HRH's speech. Mention was made in it of "warm spoons". What had he in mind? It turned out he associated banquets with low-cut evening dresses and bosoms popping out. To replace the bosom in a décolletage, he recommended a readily warmed spoon. Our future King, immature and still a bachelor, certainly could put his foot in it, with me, as much as with anyone. He continued: "I am looking forward to seeing *L'Africaine*. I hope it is better than the truly atrocious version I have been listening to!"

The Prince Charles film was shown in EMI cinemas. Princess Margaret agreed to introduce it to potential benefactors in five American cities. Her tour was tailored to terminate at her Mustique holiday home. She invited Joe to lunch at Kensington Place on 19th March to discuss it. This was a Spooner venture. Joe took him along. As they set off, Spooner was visibly trembling at the prospect of such an informal lunch invitation. Margaret was surprised to learn that Joe would not be accompanying her on the tour, fixed for October. She would be going to Los Angeles, Houston, San Francisco, Chicago and Cleveland. On 30th May, the film was shown to members of the Royal Family at St James's Palace. Joe escorted Margaret. The Queen Mother and her guest HSH the Princess of Hesse entered from Clarence House, which adjoined the Palace. Freddie Ashton was seen to bow twice, as Peggy Hesse was of equal status to Queen Elizabeth.

Lord Mountbatten and members of his family were murdered by the IRA whilst on holiday in Ireland on 27th August. We were at Hatchet Wood when we heard the news. We were still there when John Barrett rang to say Joe would be attending the funeral at Westminster Abbey on 5th September. The ceremonial and the service had been planned in detail years before. Joe and two others were to be especially invited. In his *The Life and Times of Lord Mountbatten*, published ten years previously, the flyleaf of Joe's copy had a personal message: "Inscribed for Joe Lockwood who has played such a part in the latter years of my life." Entering the Abbey, "By Poet's Corner Door at 10.40 am", Joe found himself seated next to Read's friend Sir James Carreras. The grand Memorial Service at St Paul's Cathedral, later, lacked such a personal touch.

Some said Princess Margaret would be in danger in America, but she insisted on going. Lord Snowdon, her ex-husband, rang Covent Garden to find out what she was up to. To compensate for not going with her, Joe saw her off at Heathrow on 14th October. We were ushered to the Allcock and Brown suite, away from the Terminal 3 Departures building. Lord Napier, her Private Secretary, fussed around, thanking everyone he could find, including me. Sure enough, she ran into trouble. She was barracked by hostile Irish crowds in San Francisco. But Spooner, her knight in shining armour, rushed to her defence. "I would rather be an Irish pig than an English bore": a placard referred to her alleged remarks in Chicago. She was unlikely to get involved, but Spooner had to tell the Press: "She is far too gracious and too much a lady to respond to that! She has been so calm and serene. She deserves a medal."

Drogheda caught up with the Royal Tour and wrote to Joe:

Things went pretty well in Chicago until the grotesque episode which only arose after we had all moved on elsewhere. I must say that I could not help feeling that it is in a way somewhat humiliating that we have to go round begging bowl in hand, and I feel strongly impelled to send a letter to the Prime Minister telling her this: What do you say?

Seeing her off to Mustique, she asked Spooner what his plans were. "To chill out on Barbados," he responded, hoping for an invitation to Mustique. "You must come to lunch," joked Princess Margaret, aware of how inaccessible her island was. Undeterred, Spooner made it, and, on return, regaled his staff with his experience. Discarding formality, his swimsuit-clad hostess invited him to perch on the bed as she made phone calls.

Meetings of the ROHDA Executive Committee, comprising Joe, Spooner and his very efficient Swiss assistant, Valeria Ossola, were held over lunch at Marcus Sieff's Marks & Spencer office. We were told proudly that all the food came from his store. Food was something M&S had only just started, so we showed we were pleasingly surprised. Sieff generously praised the way the appeal was going. Touching on other matters, he was outspoken about the BBC World Service for its biased attacks on the Shah of Persia. This was only a few weeks before the Iranian Revolution took the world by surprise and sent the Shah into exile.

M&S was again at our disposal in December, for a meeting of the Grand Council of Committee Members, when Joe was presented with the Royal Opera House's Medal for twenty-five years' service. Peter Plouviez was a member, and Joe thanked him for Equity's support of our dancers. Also attending was Sir Robert Clark, Chairman of Hill Samuel Co. Ltd. His bank was about to float a record company on the Stock Exchange. With the glamorous title "Solid Gold Discs", it was re-marketing old hits. I recognised its MD as the EMI man a boy told me flogged LPs filched from the stores around Brentford Market ten years previously. Joe must have trusted me. With so much on his mind, I never expected he would bother Robert Clark with the tip-off. But he did, and nothing more was heard of the record company.

EMI's downward spiral was rapid. Not a week went by without mention of another disaster, until the final demise in October. In March, Joe was asked to sign a new service agreement for Read, lasting until 1981. Roger Brooke, from IRC days, was headhunted to become managing director. The *Daily Mail* reported EMI was "in the middle of a nightmare year". Shares once tipped to reach £3 languished at 120p. In April, the *Evening News* reported EMI Records was losing market share. This was anticipated by the *Sunday Express* in February: "entrepreneurial flair vital in the record and film business is somehow not right". It was subjected to "bureaucratic control systems".

Kenneth Fleet was more specific on 6th May: "Sad though I am to say it, the time of decision has arrived for Sir John Read and the EMI Board. I do not believe they can responsibly continue to embrace electronics and leisure activities with their strained financial and management resources". The following Sunday, Joe received a phone call in the country from Read, who had to see him when we got back to London. He would have to wait, as we were breaking our return journey to have tea with the Droghedas in Englefield Green, which would be a leisurely affair. We admired the garden, Joan's Biedermeier furniture, and a painting of Drogheda's castle in Ireland, burnt down in The Troubles. Read was waiting. Afterwards, Joe told me: "That man admitted he does not know what to do". We only read the *Sunday Telegraph* the next day, but Read had seen it:

EMI: time runs out for Read

By far the most intriguing report is that Lord Delfont, who runs EMI's Leisure Division (about the only one that is actually prospering at the moment) could team up with some kind of bid for control. That would not bode well for Sir John. Already Sir Joseph Lockwood, his predecessor as Chairman and the man who built the Company to what it is (or rather was) is said to be deeply unhappy with the way the company's affairs have been managed since he retired five years ago.

On 15th May, Joe received a letter from an ex-EMI employee: "In my opinion the company has failed during the past few years to adhere to the maxim you preached viz: 'Why spend a penny when a halfpenny will do?' Some of us worked very hard in the 50s and 60s and took a lot of knocks in the process … I am passing my thoughts to you with the hope that you can do something to improve matters." Joe replied on 17th May: "I think you will be hearing of some changes to be made in the next day or two." At the EMI Board Meeting the previous day, Dick Watt, the finance director, admitted for the first time that the company was insolvent; i.e. in breach of its bank covenant. Despite frequent requests from Joe over the years, he had never produced or been allowed to produce cash flow figures, a matter of routine in other companies. Delfont was appointed Chief Executive at the meeting.

The name Delfont, the great showman, produced big headlines, which continued for four months. On 20th May, the *Sunday Telegraph* splashed "Delfont's Titanic Task". This was mirrored by the *Melody Maker*: "Question: What is the difference between EMI and the Titanic? Answer: The Titanic had a good band!" Delfont moved to Manchester Square, with his Rolls Corniche parked prominently in the garage, attended by his chauffeur and bodyguard. Electrically-operated gates secured his office. There was reason for this: Edward J. Sieff, the Marks & Spencer scion, had recently almost been murdered in cold blood, and eminent Jews were targets of a terrorist organisation led by Carlos the Jackal. Joe and I saw the set-up when we walked over from Duke Street one day on the spur of the moment. Joe was being mischievous. No one could have been more secretly amused at treading on a few toes. Sure enough, he encountered Dr Badman, Chairman of Blackpool Tower Company, waiting to see Delfont, furious at being starved of non-existent funds by head office.

The company was paralysed. Technically it was being run by Read (still chairman), Delfont and Bhaskar Menon. Brooke had left. In effect, it was under the sole control of a thirty-year-old junior partner in EMI's bankers, Lazards. John Hignett's vintage classic car was parked regularly in the basement garage beside the Corniche. A secret skeleton staff, under a recently-retired assistant company secretary, moved into rented Duke Street offices. Their brief was to produce parallel accounts to show the company in less dire straits than the actual accounts. And how bad they were! Read's PA asked for my assistance. The request was nothing out of the ordinary. The chairman must have four seats for the Opera, but Covent Garden was completely sold out. A word from Joe with the box office manager did the trick. There was one condition, the tickets had to be paid for on collection. This arrangement was made clear to the PA. Nothing was heard for a couple of months, until Joe found he had been charged for the tickets on his personal account at the Opera House. It was not the inefficiency of Read's office, so much as the shocking revelation that head office had imposed a nine-month delay on paying creditors.

In July, Delfont managed to push up EMI's share price. He was the largest individual shareholder, from the sale of the Grade Organisation. Paramount in America was to buy half of EMI's music operations, including Capitol, until the deal fell through. "The Vultures Gather as EMI Deal Goes Pop" announced the *Daily Mail*. In August, EMI announced it would not be occupying its new headquarters in Tottenham Court Road, "The EMI Centre". Delfont's efforts were doomed to fail from the moment Joe blew the whistle on the company. It was pure chance Joe had sat next to Peter Moody at Laird's AGM lunch at the Savoy on 4th June. Moody, a Laird non-executive director and Chief Investment Officer of the Prudential Corporation, was a brilliant acquisition by John Gardiner. The Pru owned the EMI Centre's freehold, and agreed a sale and leaseback policy for £33 million in February, half payable on 30th June, "the remainder being due in stage payments thereafter". The Pru was also EMI's largest institutional shareholder. Obviously Moody had something to talk about. Joe's role as whistle-blower may have been inadvertent, yet it was lethal, as described by Kenneth Fleet in the *Sunday Express* on 23rd September: "Will Men from the Pru help save EMI? Men from the Pru led by Peter Moody, the grand investment vizier, have been along to learn more about EMI's deteriorating fortunes." Bhaskar Menon received one of these visits at Capitol in Hollywood. No advance warning had been given, and Bhaskar was completely taken by surprise. As he was central to negotiations on EMI's future, he expected to have had notification. Just how secret things were soon became clear. One person to be kept in the dark was Joe.

One 27th September, Dorothy Read cut Joe dead at a farewell party for a member of staff. She never spoke to him again. On 12th October, Sir Godfrey Hounsfield was awarded the Nobel Prize. On 10th October, Joe and I were at Covent Garden to see a revival of Ashton's 1937 ballet *A Wedding Bouquet*. We encountered a more florid than usual Thorn Chairman Dick Cave, in the interval. "The Reads are here," Joe informed him, indicating the EMI box. "Oh, is John here?" responded Cave, turning an even darker shade of pink.

On 16th October, Thorn announced it was taking over EMI for £147 million. Jules and Joe had been kept in the dark. They both learnt about it at the same time. Jules invited Joe round, and they watched Thorn shares fall on Jules's Teletext screen. "Sack Cave!" Jules screamed. It transpired Hambros had been negotiating the takeover of EMI Electronics, when Lazards suggested "Why not go for the whole company?" Delfont did a brilliant selling job. Cave was flattered. When he found out the mess he had inherited, he sacked the EMI non-executive directors. Joe had in theory already retired, but Shawcross was incensed. Joe went to see Cave at Thorn House to negotiate some compensation for Shawcross. It was a near miss for Geoffrey Howe's reputation. No longer a director, he was safely in the Cabinet as Chancellor of the Exchequer, since the election on 3rd May. His parting shot to Read, admittedly after dining too well, had been: "My son knows more about the music business than you!" Read was to fade away, described by Cave as "A burnt out case". Delfont took his business away to form First Leisure, in partnership with Max Rayne and Charles Forté. EMI Music became part of Thorn EMI under sole survivor Bhaskar Menon, who managed to keep his department intact.

On 6th November, a press release from Thorn announced the terms of what was called a merger between Thorn Electrical Industries Limited and EMI Limited. On 7th November, the newspapers gave their own interpretation: "EMI accepts new Thorn bid … since the bid Thorn shares have slumped from 410p to 354p, trimming the value of the 7 Thorn for 20 EMI offer from 144p a share to 122p." That afternoon, Joe had tea with Jules Thorn and dinner with Ted Lewis. Both died in 1980.

EMI's published figures for the half-year to 31st December 1979 showed a loss of £7.6 million. Taking into account "below the line extraordinary items" of minus £42 million, actual losses shown in the final accounts to 31st March 1980 were £49 million. Combining these figures with reported profits for the previous five years, EMI had made an overall loss.

Joe and I were not thrown out of our office. No one even suggested it. The music industry was confronted with masses of income being lost from illegal taping of copyright materials. Joe agreed to chair a committee set up by the BPI to tackle the problem. Consideration would be given to methods of preventing copying, with spoiler signals on discs. The possibility of taxing tape- recorder manufacturers was also discussed. The most-favoured solution was to impose a levy on blank tape. Having defeated pirate radio stations, music publishers and composers over the years without losing popularity, Joe now faced upsetting the majority of music-lovers by calling them criminals for something they were doing in their own homes. His aim was to get the Government to introduce a "Home Taping Bill". There would be meetings at the Industrial Property and Copyright Department, and with Government ministers. The BPI gingerly and discreetly engaged political lobbyists in the form of a small "Government Relations Office" consultancy to promote its case.

Things got off to a bad start. Invited to lunch with two QCs, expensively engaged by the international equivalent of BPI to advise on Anti-Piracy, Joe arrived at the Garrick Club on time. He was shown into a room and kept waiting for the arrival of his hosts. The long delay fuelled his hatred for barristers and the IFPI. They were a waste of time and disproportionately funded by EMI. After twenty minutes he was fuming, and, had he not sent his car away, he would have left. With meetings fixed for 2.30 p.m. at Rothschilds and 5 p.m.

at the Opera House, his day was messed up. BC, on the Club's Wine Committee, wished him a happy seventy-fifth birthday for the next day. BC, celebrating his own fortieth, was well-trained to ignore Joe's mood.

The campaign headed "Home Taping is Wiping Out Music" and "Support the Levy" ran for two years. A Green Paper was produced, but the Government decided not to take the matter to the floor of the House of Commons for debate.

We were involved in plans to set up a Music Industry Charitable Foundation called "Solid Rock". Meetings were held at Chrysalis Records. Chrysalis had taken over George Martin's independent production company. I was amused when George, now the businessman, came armed with a pocket calculator. Also at meetings was Jim Beach, Queen's manager. This was before Freddie Mercury had plans of his own for supporting charity. Ballet was on Freddie's mind.

Joe and I admired the rapid progress Wayne Eagling and Julian Hosking made in the Royal Ballet Company. Kenneth MacMillan created principal roles in *La Fin du Jour* to Ravel's 'Piano Concerto' for them. We were at the premiere on 15th March, when Princess Margaret presented MacMillan with the Evening Standard Ballet Award. Dancers' ticket allocations are limited, but we were able to help:

Dear Sir Joseph and William,

Thank you so much for the tickets for Thursday, I had been having trouble trying to get some for my friends and your pair has eased the problem.

I hope you enjoy yourselves on Thursday, it is a light short ballet but very technical and with difficult pas de deux's. I look forward to seeing you at the Party in the Crush Bar afterwards.

With Love and thanks, Julian Hosking.

Wayne Eagling and Principal Dancer Marguerite Porter had booked the Coliseum Theatre for a charity gala performance on a Sunday in October. Their friends had a mentally handicapped child, and they were supporting MENCAP. Wayne and Freddie had become close, and it seemed inevitable Freddie would agree to help. At dinner on 3rd September with Wayne, Freddie and Marguerite (who cooked beautifully) in Chiswick, we learnt of Freddie's plan to dance with the Royal Ballet. He had only a month to become a ballet dancer.

Joe and I were at Little John Reid's thirtieth birthday party on 9th September aboard the *Silver Barracuda* moored at Charing Cross Pier. Joe sat next to Patrick Procktor and spilled all the gossip. Patrick painted the cover picture on Elton John's double-album *Blue Moves* for EMI. "Sir Joseph, you know more about what's going on in the gay world than I do!" he exclaimed, pruriently reprimanding Joe for his indiscretions. Marguerite had not been impressed by Freddie's superstar status, remarking that he was a rather weedy little thing. Come the evening of 7th October, Freddie proved fearless. Thrown into the air, and diving into the arms of six Royal Ballet boys ("Do you know they all call each other by girl's names?"), he danced convincingly to a medley of 'Bohemian Rhapsody', 'Crazy Little Thing Called Love' and 'I Want to Break Free'. "When I had my entrance to do I had to fight my way through Merle Park and Anthony Dowell, and all these people, and say 'Excuse me, I'm going on next', it was outrageous!"

Charles Murland was in the audience at the Coliseum, the home of the English National Ballet, where his interfering was getting under the skin of the Artistic Director, Beryl Grey. He admired Freddie's performance. It was the last time Murland and I spoke.

There was good news at the National Theatre, and the Royal Opera House also ended the year on a high note.

The drum-revolve in the Olivier Theatre was running smoothly on 10th October. At a preview of Peter Shaffer's *Amadeus* on 1st November, Joe saw "the hoists operating" for the first time. I was experiencing a memorable performance. Paul Scofield was Salieri. As he listened to the clarinet merge with the oboe in Mozart's 'Adagio from the Serenade in B Flat Major', he sat transfixed. The music soared from enormous speakers suspended either side of the stage. His eyes were drawn to heaven. Turning to Peter Hall, the play's producer, and his wife Maria Ewing, sitting behind us, Joe was spontaneous with praise. He followed it up with a letter the next day. Peter Hall replied:

> Thank you so much for your generous and perceptive letter. It made today. I am most grateful. I think this theatre is now beginning to work in every sense and we can look forward to an exciting future. It may have all been worth it!

> But seriously – thank you very very much.

On 30th November, the Surveyor's report was approved. On 19th December, the lease of the theatre from SBTB to the NT board was signed in Max Rayne's office. But Joe was not yet free.

Although Equity and the Home Office responded favourably to Royal Ballet School-trained dancers from abroad joining the Royal Ballet Company, the Department of Employment cast an evil spell on the proceedings. It was a Kafkaesque situation. Work permits were not to be granted, as long as there was a possibility that the positions applied for could equally be filled by applicants already in the UK workforce. I visited the local Labour Exchange to pick up leaflets explaining the ROH, as employer, "would have to demonstrate they had carried out a search of the resident UK Labour force for someone capable of doing the task". Joe tried to explain Margot Fonteyns do not grow on trees. A direct approach to Alan Clark MP, Secretary of State for Employment, once married to a ballerina, had no effect. The breakthrough came in November, when Clark's superior, Jim Prior, saw sense. Joe explained the outcome in a letter to Princess Margaret:

> After a few months struggle, and thanks to John Sainsbury, who gave all the papers connected with this to Mr Jim Prior, the Minister for Employment has now agreed to overrule his staff. But he made one condition that this case cannot apply to any other Ballet Companies, and

any students of non-British nationality leaving the School may not be given work permits for other Ballet Companies in the United Kingdom.

You will be interested to know that John Tooley would very much like to apply the principle to 18 year old Opera Singers who show potential, but I do not think he has a hope of success.

May I take the opportunity to thank you very much for all the help you are giving us with the Royal Opera House Development Appeal. I have heard some glowing reports about your meetings in five American Cities.

Princess Margaret replied:

Oh well done you. I bet you put up a tremendously good fight and I do congratulate you on beating a Government Department! What a wonderful thing we will be able to employ our nice old Commonwealth friends again. I am delighted at this news.

I hope I managed to scrape together a few dollars whilst in the U.S. With many thanks, yours very sincerely, Margaret.

The prestige of the Royal Ballet was firmly recognised in the Employment Minister's endorsement for its exceptional standing and reputation, and "its particular link with the School".

1980

Fresh Interests

Not a month went by without Joe and Jules meeting to discuss Thorn EMI. At Jules's suggestion, they met at a restaurant, his flat, or the office he kept at Thorn House. They would read what Patrick Sergeant wrote in the *Daily Mail* on 30th April:

> Thorn EMI is a sad tale of a merger that got the thumbs down from the City as stories went round that Thorn found things far worse in EMI than they expected when they won their bid battle in December. Shares in Thorn EMI have come down from 385p to 256p so far this year and they are 39% lower than May.

On 4th July, Joe's tax adviser was invited to join them at Stone's Chop House. He had put Joe into silver and wine dealing businesses, and was now suggesting they join another client in buying a bank. Joe had already talked to Jeffrey Sterling, "who is a Director of P&O who own the 20th Century Bank", but did not think they would want to sell it. Like so many other projects put up to Jules, it came to nothing.

On 4th August, Joe escorted Jules and Jean Thorn to a gala ballet performance in honour of the Queen Mother's 80th birthday at Covent Garden. On 12th September, Joe and Jules were at the lunch after Thorn EMI's first AGM. Lunch was in a private room at The Ivy, customarily chosen for its proximity to Thorn House. This must have been an ordeal, but less than going down to the City for the meeting.

In November, they would have read the list of *The Times 1000 Companies* for 1979:

Question: What was the biggest takeover last year and what was it worth?

Answer: Thorn acquired EMI to form Thorn EMI for £148,267,000 in cash and shares.

Thorn was not among "The Top 25 Charitable Donations", but EMI came in at No. 22 with £168,638. This compared to £40,000 in 1974, when Joe was last in charge of the EMI Appeals Committee, with me as its secretary.

Joe was at Jules's office for lunch at 12.30 on Friday, 5th December. On 12th December Jules died, aged 81, on the operating table during an emergency prostate operation. Jean told Joe later "there was blood everywhere". Joe was wryly able to see the funny side: Jules regularly sent the College of Surgeons funds and cases of wine. It was his form of insurance. Yet it failed to save him from the surgeon's knife.

Jules and Jean had posted their charity Christmas cards early. Proceeds from the sale provided motor cars for disabled people through Goodman and Sterling's MOTABILITY Charity.

Goodman wrote to *The Times*:

The Obituary did refer to his Charitable benefactions, but in terms which I do not think really did them justice. In 1964 he established and endowed with many millions of pounds an important charitable foundation which bears his name. From then onwards it was one of his principal interests ... His principal concerns were advances in medical science and the care of the sick and disabled and of the elderly but the trust ranged wide in the purposes it supported.

Although Jules's support of ROHDA was limited to £5,000, he did pay for tickets and suppers and drinks in the Crush Bar from his charity.

With Halford Reddish already gone, followed by Ted Lewis in January, aged 79, it only took John Wall's suicide at Christmas for "things to come in threes".

Joe still had Goodman, but Goodman was now Master of University College Oxford, and dinners became fewer. Paul and

Helen Hamlyn filled the gap with hospitality, which was lavish. Staying the night at their country house in Gloucestershire, Joe sat next to Jacob Rothschild. The future Lord Rothschild strongly recommended buying gold. A week or so later, the price of gold dropped through the floor. The Hamlyns devised an original way to help ROHDA. They created a limited edition of Wenceslas Hollar's etchings of pre-fire London, including Inigo Jones's Covent Garden Piazza. The originals are in the British Museum and the Hamlyns made facsimiles with the rare Calotype they discovered still existing in Czechoslovakia. Half the 250 sets were donated to the appeal to sell at £1,500. A set was put on display in Asprey's Bond Street store. City companies framed the prints for their boardroom walls, and Lloyds of London bought two sets. Joe persuaded Max Rayne to buy a set for £5,000, bypassing Goodman's veto on his client supporting the appeal.

Another original way of raising money was provided by a gala evening auction held by Sotheby's on the Opera House stage. It included 115 unusual items, donated by Royals as well as opera and ballet stars, including Prince Charles's cello, to bring in £100,000.

Paul Hamlyn continued his spirited support by bidding £2,600 for Elton John's rhinestone-encrusted bicycle "on behalf of his children". John Reid and Prince Charles, in Grand Tier boxes, bid against each other for a George III bureau bookcase. Princess Margaret sent two cases of Kensington Palace 1976 vintage wine. The Duke of Devonshire's piece of Blue John was valued by Sotheby's at £65, barely worthy

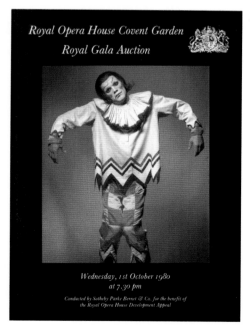

Auction in aid of ROHDA

of a Chatsworth attic sale, but he discreetly added two Blue John jars, to raise £650. Nadia Nerina donated the original Petrouchka costume worn by Nijinsky from her collection of ballet memorabilia.

Joe and Nadia Nerina arrive to promote the auction

At a ROHDA meeting, Moser flippantly wondered: "How had she got hold of it?" hinting at Charles Gordon's shady deals. Drogheda put him down: "One doesn't talk like that. No more of that thank you!" An American museum bid £8,500 for it. ROH Director Sir Isaiah Berlin's wife, Aline de Gunzbourg, donated Natalia Gontcharova's vast backdrop for *Le Coq d' Or*. Knocked down for £1,000 to her BBC

producer friend and Diaghilev expert, it eventually went to the
Theatre Museum, as John Drummond had no possible use for it. Apart
from one piece of silver, this was the only contribution from a ROH
board member. Joe got Dawnay's successor, Sir Ian Fraser, probably
out of a sense of guilt for EMI's collapse, to donate a £60,000 maroon
Corniche convertible. Fraser was Chairman of Rolls Royce and wrote:
"I will talk to my chaps at Crewe and see if they can come up with
what you want." It was bought back by Jack Barclay Ltd, at a pre-
arranged price when it failed to find a bidder. Joe travelled in it with
Nadia, who was wearing one of the costumes donated by designers,
including Hardy Amies, to publicise the event. They were greeted by
Sergeant Martin as they parked outside the Opera House. Not to be
outdone, Ken Thorogood, who owned the BMW concession, donated
a 1977 Batmobile worth £8,000. We entertained Thorogood and his
young wife in the usual way, with backstage tour, Royal Box lunch
and a performance plus Crush Bar party. Mrs Thorogood remarked
with envy on how slim the ballet girls were. This caused amusement,
as her remark was addressed to Briony Brind, who was distinctly
skinny. We left the Thorogoods with Spooner to discuss details of their
gift. I was behind Joe as we departed, and was able to hear Spooner
say: "Now we can get down to business". I was hurt that anyone could
be so dismissive, disrespectful and disloyal, after all Joe's trouble.

Joe was a guest of the McAlpines at Wimbledon in July. He had
never been to the tournament. Moser was there too. He took Joe
aside: "Who are your friends?" he asked, indicating Ken and Fanny
Thorogood, who were expecting him to know who they were.

It was almost unheard of for Moser and Drogheda to join backstage
tours and lunches in the Royal Box for potential donors. An exception
was made for Dr and Mrs Armand Hammer, owners of the Occidental
Petroleum Corporation. Dr Hammer traded medicines for Tsarist
treasures after the First World War, befriended Lenin and continued
to befriend world leaders and royalty. The Royal Box lunch list
included Lord Napier – Dr Hammer had met Princess Margaret in
America. Also at lunch was Denys Sutton, Editor of *Apollo* magazine.
An exhibition of Dr Hammer's collection was planned for the Royal

Academy at Burlington House. Tim Halford, the Hammers' PA and Occidental's Public Relations Director, wrote to thank Spooner:

> Dr and Mrs Hammer thoroughly enjoyed the lunch – I certainly much appreciated both the food and the chance of meeting the remarkable people. I thought Sir Joseph Lockwood was especially fascinating.
>
> I enclose a copy of Dr Hammer's catalogue and book.

The book was entitled *Larger than Life: A Biography of the Remarkable Dr Armand Hammer*.

Joe invited Tim Halford and his wife to a performance of *Sleeping Beauty* when Julian Hosking and Marguerite Porter were dancing. Dr Hammer was soon to list Prince Charles among his acquaintances. Buckingham Palace hinted to the Opera House management that Spooner should cultivate Tim Halford less patronisingly. He was very important to the Hammers, who would be donating £161,000 to the appeal, after the Prince of Wales's visit to Occidental's oil-drilling platform in the North Sea. Mrs Thatcher also visited the platform, later destroyed, in the Claymore Oil Field blowout. Partly as a result of her visit and partly encouraged by Norman St John-Stevas, once again Minister for the Arts, the Prime Minister and Mr Denis Thatcher held a reception, 6.30 p.m. to 8.00 p.m. at Downing Street on 24th June for ROHDA. "The Blessed Margaret", as Norman nicknamed her, kicked off her shoes, stood on a chair, and exhorted the purposely invited oil tycoons to contribute generously. Norman was able to announce from his Privy Council office in Whitehall, as Chancellor of the Duchy of Lancaster as well as Arts Minister, that Mrs Thatcher had agreed to a further £1 million donation to the appeal, with a quarter coming from the Department of the Environment. This was the million from the Government that Joe had been to see Shirley Williams and Lord Donaldson about. Moser and Drogheda reported the appeal had reached £7.8 million, but another £2 million was needed. Joe warned of an imminent cash flow problem. Donations were actually long-term commitments, and not immediately payable.

He wrote to Frank Harris, who was asking for his help at the Institute of Economic Affairs: "I am sorry that you are having cash problems like everybody else." Now was the time to publicise the "Interest Free Loan Scheme" he had worked so hard to introduce in 1977, his own personal way of helping the appeal. At the time, Joe had £60,000 on deposit at his bank, paying 18% interest (15% inflation indexed, plus 3% for privileged clients). With Denis Healey squeezing 83% "from the rich" on unearned income, this deposit income would be considerably more valuable for the Opera House, provided it was tax-free and lent for a short period. The Finance Act of 1976 exempted Capital Transfer Tax on interest free loans. To be safe, Joe wrote to Sir William Pile, Chairman of the Inland Revenue, for confirmation, who replied:

> I should perhaps add that a condition of the exemption is that interest must be for charitable purposes only, but the proposed use by the Opera House raises no doubts on that score. So far as Income Tax is concerned, the bank interest will be for the Royal Opera House and exempt from tax … I hope this will prove to be the helpful reply you wanted.

After three years, Joe retrieved his £60,000 and was listed among donors for his "generous contribution" of £13,500.

He had hoped to tempt other people with surplus funds, but interest rates were dropping. Nevertheless, Kenneth Fleet wrote in the *Sunday Express* on 21st December:

> This particular technique of giving to charity was winkled out by Sir Joseph Lockwood … Now the publicity conscious Abbey National Building Society has latched on to it, with a scheme to benefit Barnardo's, the RSPB, and the Society for the Promotion of Nature Conservancy.

Joe accepted the invitation from Norman St John-Stevas to join "The Chancellor of the Duchy of Lancaster's Committee of Honour on Business Sponsorship of the Arts."

The committee of fifteen, whose purpose was self-explanatory, met infrequently at Norman's Privy Council office. It included Goodman, Charles Forté and Countess Spencer, before she became Prince Charles's step-mother-in-law. Bumping into us one day, Norman was surprised to hear Joe was not joining the visit to the Spencers' seat at Althorp: "You are missing a great treat".

Norman was unable to accept an invitation to a dinner party I arranged for Frederick Ashton, but his friend Adrian Stanford came anyway. Freddie adored being invited out to dinner. He had the reputation of being the last to leave. I booked the private room at The White Tower in Charlotte Street, popular for stag parties, and crispy duckling. Freddie brought Tony Dyson, Ken Fleetwood came with Hardy Amies, and my Cambridge friend Hubert Chesshyre made up the numbers. Hubert was Chester Herald of Arms and responsible for creating the Royal Ballet School's coat of arms, with its "Strength and Grace" motto.

A coats of Arms for the Royal Ballet School: "Strength and Grace"

He found a private client to sponsor the cost, which the governors of the school had declined. Freddie and Joe discussed their early lives in South America. They were born two months apart. Freddie, the senior, was born in Guayaquil and educated in Lima. Joe described the flour mills in Ecuador and Peru. André Levasseur's ballet costumes were recently auctioned at a fundraising event for the School. I knew he was a favourite Ashton designer, who brought a special French chic to Freddie's work. His costumes and décor are represented in *Birthday Offering*, the ballet Freddie created for the Company's 25th anniversary in 1956.

The dinner's crowning success was when Freddie recalled that The White Tower was indeed the same Le Tour Eiffel where he had dined frequently between the wars. Despite the lateness of the night, he insisted on touring the kitchens. The next day, an enormous sheaf of lilies was delivered to my flat. The bouquet had a humorous touch. It was responding to the bouquet I sent him after the *Pas de Légumes* premiere, when he wrote:

Sweet William (almost my favourite flower!) It was a delightful surprise to receive your beautiful bridal bouquet, all I then needed was to be led up the aisle and my bouquet would have been the Talk of the Town. It was a very touching thought on your part and I enjoyed receiving them. Perhaps some carrots would have been more apt but not so nice. I am really grateful for your kind thoughts and I hope we can meet again soon, ring up and come and have a drink. With much affection Freddie glad you liked the legumes.

Choreographers earn less than other creative people, as they only get paid when their work is performed. I thought it unfair he got nothing from EMI's low-price Greensleeve label using pictures from his ballets on their record sleeves. *Birthday Offering* was for Glazunov music, *La Fille Mal Gardee* for Herold, *A Month in the Country* for Chopin, *The Dream* for Mendelssohn, *The Two Pigeons* for Messager, etc. It was particularly galling when Tony Dyson told me Fred was upset that HMV had omitted the coda in *The Two Pigeons*. Of course, I had to do something, and when it was restored I took a copy round to his rented flat near Harrods. "After thirty years in one place, I can't find anything." We discussed Gérard André. Was I Diana Cavendish's son, he asked. Yes. But probably not the Diana Cavendish he was thinking of. Freddie was now eighty. The full ballet, recorded by the Bournemouth Symphony Orchestra, was reissued digitally on HMV, in a double sleeve, depicting no less than ten photographs from a recent production. Freddie wrote: "Thank you so much for the record – right at last with the important pas-de-deux which ends the ballet and is by far the best of Messager in the score. It was kind of you to use your influence to get it right at last."

Two of the appeal's main benefactors were our own gay contacts, and all the more entertaining for that. No one at the Opera House had heard of Fred Kobler, despite his support for the English National Opera and Glyndebourne. Lady Ellerman, widow of the shipping tycoon Sir John Ellerman, reputed to be the richest man in England, was unapproachable. Joe and I became acquainted with both.

Peter Brown, along with Geoffrey Ellis, Brian Epstein's closest friend, was writing his memoirs. *The Love You Make: An Insider's Story of the Beatles* upset the Beatles when it was published in 1983. But in November 1980, Joe was happy to grant Peter an interview. After the meeting Peter rang to thank me, and say he thought he could help the appeal. In a nutshell, Kobler's boyfriend was mad about him, Peter Brown, and would do anything for him. Within a week, Joe was lunching with Fred and the boyfriend, whom he found delightful. There was much criticism of the Opera House, including how much more accessible they found the Coliseum. Nevertheless, the Kobler Trust donated £10,000 and we were invited to Glyndebourne as Kobler's guests.

George Borwick, who spent part of the year in South Africa, borrowed a copy of the film of Prince Charles at Covent Garden to show in Cape Town. Cape Town's ballet company was closely linked to the Royal Ballet, and offered to help the appeal. George invested in theatre productions, and had no particular interest in ballet. A confirmed bachelor, quite out of the blue he married Esther Ellerman. They met on an Ellerman Lines sea voyage to Cape Town. He sang and she painted. She was slightly bohemian, not at all grand, not, obviously, very rich. "I wish I had known you sooner," she told Joe, when she heard he was a friend of Jules Thorn. She occupied the two floors beneath the Thorns' Nash Terrace flat in Regent's Park. When he died, she had tried to buy the whole house. Her trustees donated £25,000 to the appeal, and were instructed to continue their support whenever required.

In August, Peter Andry kindly offered Joe an office with his Classical Artists Division in the Gloucester Place building shared with EMI's International Division. Tony Locantro, who ran the International Classical Repertoire Committee founded by Joe, had made the suggestion in the first place.

Our neighbour the Indian accountant cornered me in the washroom after we moved in: "Sir Joseph tells me he is a silver dealer!" he said in wonder. It was quite true. We were partners in L&Co., a private company trading in silver. To qualify for tax relief, Joe's accountant explained the company had to genuinely trade in silver. Joe took a course with commodity merchants in the City. Trading consisted of buying and selling warrants for silver in units of 10,000 ounces. With silver fluctuating in value between 200 and 1,400 pence per ounce, skill was required. When Nelson Bunker Hunt gambled on cornering the market, the price fell by 50% overnight. Joe was not caught.

My friend in the next office was keen to attend the Thorn EMI AGM on 12th September, and I agreed to go down to the City with her. Jules Thorn's long-time secretary was traditionally presented with a large bouquet at the start of the meeting. The awful EMI Treasurer, still around, hovered over the Thorn finance director. Read, Delfont and Menon were up for re-election. When Read's name was put to the vote, a young man stood up to object. Lady Read, in hat and long-sleeved gloves, and Dr Powell's wife were sitting behind us. Dorothy seemed mildly concerned: "What was that about?" she enquired. I talked to the young man after the meeting, hoping to hear something damning. "My mother lives in Loughton. She sent me. She considers Read morally unqualified to be a director of a company." Read lived in Loughton when he was with the Ford Motor Company.

Joe received a card from EMI's Classical Artists Division on his birthday:

> Over 25 years much admired, highly respected – sometimes feared, but universally liked and trusted – Sir Joseph you never cease to amaze your friends by your enthusiasm and energy. We wish you all happiness on your 76th birthday.

It was signed by Peter Andry, Tony Locantro, Mike Allen, Charles Rodier and Diana Chapman.

George Martin introduced Joe to Chris Wright and Terry Ellis, the owners of Chrysalis Records. They invited Joe to lunch at the Connaught Hotel to discuss their plans to bid for the first commercial "breakfast" television franchise. His knowledge of the early days of ATV, Thames TV and the abortive bid for Yorkshire TV, plus his high standing with the IBA, made him the ideal consultant to their consortium. His City connections were equally valuable, when he took Chris to meet Sir Peter Thornton at Hill Samuel, who agreed to underwrite the bid. Thornton and Joe were both Directors of Laird. Other heavyweights were added to join Thornton on the board of Good Morning Television Limited, which met frequently, appropriately for breakfast, at the Savoy. This became a bit of a joke in the City. An *Evening Standard* cartoon depicted two tycoons at a cocktail party, captioned: "I was just going to ask him to join my TV consortium when he asked me to join his."

The creative side of Good Morning TV included Julian Pettifer, Ned Sherrin and Tim Rice. I wrote to my mother: "It is one of eight companies all hoping to get the franchise, but although an outsider, I wouldn't be at all surprised if they get it, as they very bright and enthusiastic."

Chris Wright wrote to Joe:

I would like to express my sincere thanks for all the help you have given us over the last two or three months on this project without which there is no doubt that the application would not have been presented to the IBA. I look forward very much to our working together for a successful conclusion to the venture when the franchises are granted at the end of the year.

For two weeks Joe attended training sessions to prepare the Good Morning team for their interview at the IBA on 11th December. This was followed by lunch at the Connaught, where it all began.

The IBA awarded the franchise to David Frost's consortium on 28th December. From the start, some people said his "TV AM" bid would win.

Seasonal greetings from the Thorns and the Walls were overtaken by events. But Joe had buckets of cards at Christmas to remind him of good moments in the year. They came from Chrysalis, Queen (signed by all four), Cliff Richard, Hardy Amies, the Rothermere family, Patrick Sergeant, Max Rayne, Arnold Goodman, Dick Cave and Norman St John-Stevas, whose card depicted Queen Victoria, Prince Albert, the Emperor Napoleon III and the Empress Eugenie in the Royal Box at Covent Garden in 1855.

1981

Trouble at the Opera

Norman St. John-Stevas, Arts Minister, with Moser, Tooley and Drogheda

On 7th December 1981, Joe was handed a cheque for £11,500 by the Chairman of the British National Oil Corporation. A year and a half of effort had gone into achieving this donation. Sir Philip Shelbourne was determined to have his pound of flesh from the ROH in return. He would make things very difficult for the staff. His big row erupted in 1983. It was the hardest donation that Joe had come by. To see the goodwill he had achieved shattered by the Opera House Board requires describing in full.

It was essential for BNOC to support the appeal, to make fifty or so North Sea oil companies follow suit. BNOC provided 51% of the output. Shelbourne clearly was not going to be an easy touch. The fact he had been on the Laird Group Board had no effect. He referred to Lawrence Tindale, another Laird man and ex-NRDC colleague Joe had gone to for advice, as "Joe's Spy". Bachelor Shelbourne lived with another Laird director in a grand country house near Aldeburgh. It was close to an even grander house belonging to elderly Harold Drayton, who had been Shelbourne's boss. As one of his "117 Old Broad Street boys", Shelbourne succeeded him as Chairman of the Drayton Group. An ex-barrister specialising in taxation, he was now "a patrician City Establishment figure". A lover of opera, as was Tindale, he was friend and advisor to Sir George Solti, former Musical Director of Covent Garden.

Waiting for Shelbourne, four months in the job, Joe tackled him on 16th October 1980 at the Royal Academy *British Art Now* exhibition, sponsored by ESSO. The confrontation again emptied the room. Joe reminded him in January:

> You have been very kind to tell me that BNOC would look at our Appeal sometime in 1981, and this letter is in no way intended to put pressure on you. I thought however that you would like to know we have been given £40,000 by ESSO Petroleum Co. Ltd, and Getty Oil have given us £22,000.

Shelbourne replied: "As you say, WE have therefore done pretty well out of the Oil Companies."

Invited to tea the following December at BNOC's grand Stornoway House in Cleveland Row, St James's, Joe described the occasion to Spooner:

> Herewith a cheque for £11,500 from BNOC. I had a lovely meeting with Mr Shelbourne, who put me in the category of one of his oldest friends in England. He attached a condition to giving this money before he gave me the cheque, that he acquire four premium seats, one night a week. He provided a beautiful silver tray, Christmas cake and three or four types of cake, in a marvellous atmosphere of (his own) antique furniture etc., so I was really expecting a mammoth cheque. However, I came away with balance sheets and a lot of data about BNOC, and this is the first year they have made a profit. He is very well disposed to the Opera House and we might quite well get something like this on an

annual basis, but I don't know. You will see the cheque is dated two months ago, so we have lost interest on it during all that time.

Joe also came away with a phial of North Sea oil encased in a Perspex block.

Joe's efforts were rewarded with a note in April 1982, that said: "We are very much enjoying our seats in Row T."

Eighteen months later, in his eightieth year, Joe had all his past criticisms of Covent Garden confirmed. Shelbourne wrote:

> On two occasions my booking of the KSR, made well in advance, when I reserved tickets has been cancelled arbitrarily on the grounds that the room was needed for a Director. As Corporate Members we "can book the KSR for dinners and drinks in the intervals in an attractive Edwardian setting which comfortably sits eight for dinner and more for drinks". There is, as you observe no qualifying statement which would permit of cancellation by the Opera House after acceptance of a booking.

This hint that the ROH was breaking the law had all the elements of what Joe always warned it about. For Gala Performance evenings, premium seat holders, with pre-paid tickets for a whole season, were offered their seats at gala prices "if they wished to attend the performance". No mention about confiscation was made in the terms of purchase.

Joe replied:

> As you know in business the customer always comes first. I will be in touch as soon as I can trace the villain. There are so many individuals at the ROH who think that the ROH is something more important than Buckingham Palace and they ought to be put in their place.

And to Moser:

> There are certain people who are perhaps stubborn and can be easily

offended and become enemies for life of the ROH. I could produce a list of friends who refused to help the ROH Appeal because at sometime in the last 20 years they considered they had been treated unreasonably. There may be some good reason why Shelbourne had the KSR taken away after he had booked it, such as a member of the Royal Family suddenly wanting the room but in that case it would be wise to give reasons and no fair person would object. However for the KSR to be suddenly taken away for the use of a Director of the ROH is not in my opinion a good reason. The ROH needs and will probably need even more in the future and relationships it can get. I don't know how to answer Shelbourne's letter. He is a Barrister and can be very stubborn.

Brit Oil, as BNOC became, was returned to the private sector in 1985, making it vulnerable to takeover in 1988. Despite Shelbourne's preference for Atlantic Richfield, BP won, having the support of the Government's "Golden" controlling share. BP reported their findings: Shelbourne as chairman had negotiated a £90 per day lunch allowance, four Centre Court seats for the Wimbledon finals, four free tickets for each ROH booking period, continued use of chauffeur and company car, and £40,000 per annum "in lieu of the withdrawal of office and ancillary services". BP did not honour the agreement. Shelbourne, openly discredited, retired to a beautiful Queen Anne house in the Close of Salisbury

Invitation in aid of the Royal Opera House Development Appeal

In the presence of

His Royal Highness The Prince of Wales, KG, KT

*THEME
AND
VARIATIONS*

Her Serene Highness Princess Grace of Monaco

with distinguished actors, singers and musicians

*Goldsmiths' Hall
Monday 9th March 1981*

Cathedral, with Edward Heath as his neighbour, and died in 1993 aged sixty-nine.

There were growing signs of off-handedness towards Joe by the Royal Opera House from the start of the year. Peter Andry had prophesied he would get no thanks from that quarter.

Spooner initiated talks with Richard Hazell, the Leader of the Royal Opera House chorus, about doing an album for the appeal. He then went off to America to plan Prince Charles's New York visit the following June, having lost interest. Joe was left to tell Hazell the project was of no interest to EMI. We looked in on Spooner's office, to be cut by his secretary: "Pat is on the phone. He is in a New York Police Department helicopter flying above Manhattan. This is much more important!"

Later in January, we were waiting with Terry Ellis to see John Tooley, with a proposal to put on a pop concert at Covent Garden with Chrysalis artists in aid of the appeal. Moser stormed out of Tooley's office, obviously in a tearing hurry. Before Joe had a chance to speak, he brushed past explaining "I'm not here!"

But what really rankled occurred in March. The occasion was a verse recital by Princess Grace of Monaco at the Goldsmith's Hall, in the presence of Prince Charles for ROHDA. It was a black tie, "By Invitation" affair, with £50 tickets offering refreshments at 7 p.m. and buffet supper at 9.15 p.m. As usual, Moser and Drogheda were hosts for the evening. Spooner heard from Major John Winter, the Buckingham Palace Equerry, in December that "HRH would like to entertain Princess Grace, amongst others, to a buffet supper here after the recital, so long as this does not conflict with any plans already made by you or the Goldsmith's Company." Joe pencilled in his diary "Princess Grace concert Prince of Wales Buffet supper Buckingham Palace".

Between December and March, Charles became engaged to Lady Diana Spencer. The evening took on a new significance. This was to be the first public outing of the couple. There was a photo call at 7.50 p.m. for the arrival of Prince Charles, and at 9.45 p.m. for his departure with Princess Grace. Tickets were bought by Charles and Diana's hunting and skiing friends, to give the young couple moral support. They would all "be going on afterwards".

Diana and Charles
with Princess Grace

Joe went to the recital alone. I took my mother. Charles and Diana mingled with the guests after the recital, and departed on schedule. At the same time, the Mosers, Droghedas, Tooleys and Spooners surreptitiously slipped away. Joe found himself on his own, dutifully entertaining appeal supporters.

Spooner could not resist ringing me the next day to say how sorry he was he and his wife had been to the party and Joe had not. He did not quite put it that way. Not only had Joe not been consulted, he was left to conclude, as would anyone in the circumstances, that he had not been wanted. If the matter had been raised, he would have politely declined. He should at least have had the opportunity. In that case, Spooner would have in all decency declined too. But the temptation was too great. I was outraged. Joe had every reason, I thought, to resign at such casual treatment. Instead, he had a spontaneous anger attack, and raged at Spooner's secretary when he could not get hold of the man himself. (She resigned from the appeal.) He next tore a strip off Tooley. He dropped the matter. Tooley reassured him: "It was not really a very good party".

There was a much better do at Buckingham Palace on 29th July, for the Wedding Breakfast after the service at St Paul's Cathedral. Harry Williams told me all about it. As Charles's Pastoral Tutor, he blessed the couple, and "was invited back afterwards". Princes Andrew and Edward livened up proceedings at lunch no end, and charmed Harry in the process.

The future of the appeal was suddenly in jeopardy. Blows came from two opposing directions, the GLC and the Royal Opera House Board itself. In May, the papers reported: "GLC cuts Royal Opera cash. As a first presumably symbolic act on taking office, the GLC's new Marxist leaders have stopped payment of the outstanding part of the Council's £1 million grant."

The sum involved was £575,000. I watched the debate in the Council Chamber, which resembled a schoolroom. "Red" Ken Livingstone, future Mayor of London, Tony Banks, future MP, and Paul Boateng, future High Commissioner in South Africa, feet up on desks, aimed paper darts at the Conservative opposition. No wonder Mrs Thatcher abolished the GLC in 1986.

An outcry arose from ordinary operagoers, and Equity "was greatly disturbed" at the threatened confiscation. The Labour MP Andrew Faulds, spokesman on the arts, wrote to Drogheda:

> I think we may all have to join the fight against the political immaturities of the new GLC. I hope to see Tony Banks shortly with the minute hope that I can talk some sense into his addled pate.

Goodman's advice was sought and had the required effect: "As the donation was a commitment made with certain conditions, the Opera House have grounds to issue a writ as a last resort."

To be on the safe side, Joe brandished Dr Armand Hammer's business card, on which was scrawled:

Sir John Foster c/o Tim Halford

Dear John

Sir Joseph Lockwood has a problem. Please take care of it. I will cover the costs.

Affectionately, Armand.

It was typical of Hammer to keep England's top barrister on a retainer, to ensure Foster would represent him whatever the circumstances.

Although Livingstone's "Socialist Action Group" lost the motion in July, and the GLC's inflation-proof £1 million was safe, the Opera House was still £2 million short of its target. The *Financial Times* reported: "the appeal fund expects to run out of money in October."

There was no room for complacency. If the appeal failed, and the redevelopment failed, contributions made on the condition that the building was completed would have to be returned. It was a blow. The Directors of the ROH were summoned to a board meeting at Commercial Union's head office in the City one evening to consider their position. They were aware they might each be individually liable for any deficiency. ROHDA's Honorary Treasurer, Lord O'Brien of Lothbury, former Governor of the Bank of England, and Joe were summoned. I waited in the car, rather hoping to hear the axe fall. It was no skin off Joe's or my back. When they emerged, Joe was accompanied by Moser, who was cadging a lift: "We have got the go-ahead," he told me. He could not hide his relief. We were on our way to the National Theatre for a first night performance. Moser felt he was missing out on something. This was ridiculous. Joe was getting tickets, he was not. It should have been fairly obvious why we had privileged treatment. Paul Channon, Norman's successor as Minister for the Arts, invited Joe in August to continue as Chairman of the SBTB for a further year, "with the task of settling the outstanding final accounts of the main contractors and pursuing claims against them and consultants where necessary". The drum-revolve continued to give problems. The noise made as it rotated meant it was not being used in productions. We watched tests, as before, at unusual times, such as 9.30 a.m.

Joe and Moser were together in New York in June as guests of the American Friends of Covent Garden to celebrate the Royal Ballet's 50th Anniversary Royal Visit. They were booked into the Park Lane Hotel on Central Park. This was the hotel where Joe and John Gardiner stayed overnight in March on Laird Group business. This visit was for longer. Joe described Moser setting off each morning for a run in Central Park, clad in a tatty old pullover, through the hotel's elegant foyer.

Prince Charles arrived by Concorde on 17th June, attended by two Private Secretaries, a Chief Inspector and a valet. After a flight around Manhattan in a British Airways helicopter, he was driven to the South Street Seaport, where Joe, Dr Hammer and other guests were waiting aboard the *Highlander*. Joe partnered Mrs Vincent Astor, the eighty-year-old doyenne of NY society. Brooke Astor, whispered: "Isn't he just a pixie!?" alluding to fellow host Ed Koch, the diminutive Mayor of New York. Nancy Reagan joined the cruise between the Statue of Liberty and George Washington Bridge. It was a very hot day, and the NY Harbour Police boat divers on the dockside postured and stripped to their barest minimum. Malcolm Forbes Jr., the owner of the *Highlander*, was known to be into that sort of thing.

The Royal Ballet performed *The Sleeping Beauty* at the Met in the Lincoln Centre. Clive Barnes reported: "The company dances better in New York that any other place on Earth." Joe admitted that Anthony Dowell excelled as never before by taking advantage of the full range of the vast Metropolitan Opera stage. When Dowell made guest appearances with the American Ballet Theatre, Joe said he should have been sacked: "In business we never take back anyone who leaves the company." A gala ball and banquet following the performance took place in a marquee, making it difficult for the police to protect Charles from Irish nationalists. Guests were barracked with cries of "British murderers", and placards proclaiming "Royal Creep", "Down with the Monarchy", and "England out of Ireland". The American Friends contributed substantially to the appeal, but this was met with comments in the press as to whether it had been advisable for Prince Charles to go to New York.

The year also saw the Sadler's Wells Royal Ballet celebrating its 50th anniversary, and Princess Margaret her 25th as its President. In June, she decided to attend a meeting of the Royal Ballet Charter Body at the Royal Opera House for the first time. We delivered her copy of the agenda for the board meeting to Kensington Palace by hand. She said she would not bring a lady-in-waiting, provided Joe was waiting to greet her at the Floral Street entrance opposite the stage door.

In November, suntanned and radiant after her holiday in Mustique, Margaret attended a masked ball at the Dorchester Hotel. The hotel was fifty years old and wanted to share its celebration with the ROHDA. Entitled "Un Ballo in Maschera", the invitation read: "A Champagne Reception, a Banquet prepared by Internationally acclaimed maître Chef de Cuisine, Anton Mossiman, served in the Hotel's Ballroom, accompanied by selected wines".

Sir Joseph Lockwood - For Information

In the presence of

Her Royal Highness The Princess Margaret Countess of Snowdon

Un Ballo in Maschera
Banquet and Masked Ball

at The Dorchester, Park Lane, W.1.
Monday 23rd November 1981
in aid of the
Royal Opera House Development Appeal
on the occasion of The Dorchester's 50th Anniversary

Champagne Reception 7.30 pm

R.S.V.P. on
enclosed form

White or Black Tie and Masks

Margaret, wearing a jewelled mask, "a little like a chandelier", was with her current escort Norman Lonsdale. The former owner of EMI's World Record Club was with Margaret on Mustique. He told Joe that her private detective had a magnificent physique. Joe danced with Merle Park, "a charming girl". Merle told him, "we women, Monica Mason and myself, are capable of running the Royal Ballet." It was a fair prediction. They would both become Dames for running the Company and the School.

Guests were encouraged to buy £100 raffle tickets with exclusive prizes on offer. Requested to find a suitable item, I asked Carl Toms, the stage designer, to donate a sketch, as he had promised one at the time of the auction. He came up with a drawing of a prophet, which was not particularly appropriate, and not helped by its heavy frame. Princess Margaret graciously picked the winners from the raffle drum, and Norman was mortified to find his prize was "the hideous picture", which he modestly rejected to much hilarity from Colin Tennant, the Lichfields and Freddie Ashton. Carl Toms asked me later whether it had been Margaret's idea that he should give something. I had no inkling they were friends, through Tony Snowdon, and that he had designed her diamond-scattered mask.

We increased our popularity with the Royal Ballet by bringing Sheena Easton, EMI's newest pop sensation, to a performance of *Cinderella*. Merle Park and Wayne Eagling were dancing, as was Stephen Beagley in a lesser role. Beagley wanted to impress his idol, but Sheena came with her boyfriend. She made up for it by sending tickets for her next concert.

We sat in the otherwise empty stalls for the General Rehearsal of Kenneth MacMillan's new three act ballet, *Isadora*, in April. The big opening number was set in the Gare du Nord. The American girl, Isadora Duncan, was arriving in Paris for the first time. It was like a West End musical, with a whole cast of porters, bellhops, stationmaster and passengers dancing at full throttle. The scene was cut before the first night. During a break, we were surrounded by some of the boys. I recall the occasion distinctly. Three of the most extrovert boys were to die of AIDS. But that was in the future, and something Joe would never know about. Julian Hosking was studiously running through his part, and did not join us. Deep concentration was visibly etched into his handsome face.

Joe lobbied for eighty-four-year-old Dame Ninette de Valois to receive greater recognition. He was gratified when she was created a Companion of Honour at the end of the year. Boasting of his efforts to Freddie Ashton, he was surprised at Freddie's lack of enthusiasm. Already a C.H. and O.M. himself, Sir Frederick did not appreciate competition.

1982

Covent Garden Attracts Strange Benefactors

Joe's older brother Fred died in January, aged seventy-seven. *The Times*, *Daily Mail* and *Evening Standard* carried long articles about "Big John the Donkey King", who:

> left behind him nearly 800 animals – 500 donkeys, 45 horses, goats, sheep, dogs, cats, rabbits, chickens and ducks – all of which he rescued. Big John, who could often be seen carrying young donkeys across his broad shoulders, never turning away an animal in need, even though, in the end, it was costing £85,000 a year to keep them.

Joe and Charles made no comment. He was now more famous than Joe. Charles in Argentina kept quiet, so quiet in fact that when the April-to-June Falklands War blew up, he made no comment. Arriving with Mabel for their regular visit to Europe in July, it was as though there had been no battle to interfere with their plans. Charles maintained there would have been no need for conflict if the Falkland Islands Company was listed on the stock exchange and not treated as a Sovereign Territory. He admitted he had underestimated the volatility of the Argentinian character until the day he attended a football match in Buenos Aires.

When seventy-eight-year-old Vladimir Horowitz expressed a wish to play for a member of the Royal Family, Prince Charles jumped at the opportunity to hear the virtually retired virtuoso pianist. As a result, two concerts took place at the Royal Festival Hall in May. One, attended by Prince Charles, was for the benefit of the appeal. Horowitz's piano was brought over from New York on a chartered plane, and the Horowitzes were installed at the Connaught Hotel. Horowitz chose the Connaught because it did not have air-conditioning. Every smallest request was granted, and all his manager's demands were obeyed. In return, I made a request of my own. Would Maestro sign the Gramophone Company's Golden Book, as a favour to Joe? His manager made sure of it. And one evening I went to the Connaught to collect the album. As I sat waiting in the foyer, I imagined I saw a lonely little old creature in a black cocktail dress standing in the corridor. It was the ghost of Mrs Alfred Clark, the last owner of the album. Here was I, reliving the occasion ten years ago when she joined the EMI Board lunch for dessert, as I waited in the foyer. She probably died in that hotel. Eventually, a secretary came downstairs with the album. But no signature! The page which Arturo Toscanini signed on 2nd June 1939, was scrawled in pencil: "Wanda Horowitz Toscanini Revised name of town where MY father was born". Mrs Horowitz had crossed out Palma and roughly inserted Bussento. What a bossy woman! It was Wanda who insisted on three weeks' hotel reservation at our expense, and said her husband performed at 4.30 p.m., and only at weekends. This was a little too much. Prince Charles did not do weekends, and a concession was necessary.

Following the concerts, Buckingham Palace forwarded a letter to the Royal Opera House for advice. Claudio Arrau, the seventy-nine-year-old Chilean pianist, reputed to be the greatest living interpreter of the classical repertoire, also requested the opportunity to play for Prince Charles. As far as I know, he did not so much as receive a reply from Covent Garden or the Palace.

At the Horowitz recital, Prince Charles was introduced to Mr Herbert Armstrong, the American President of the Ambassador Foundation, Pasadena, California, who offered him £100,000 for the appeal. Later, Joe called on Armstrong at the Dorchester, and must have been convinced of the donor's credentials. Spooner was able to boast in a widely circulated memo:

I am sure you will be glad to know that when I went to the Dorchester Hotel on Friday afternoon, Mr Herbert W. Armstrong decided he would like to see his name on the Commemorative Plaque in the Foyer and thereupon gave ME a cheque for $185,000 instead of the $100,000 he had mentioned the previous day [referring to Joe's visit]. This brings the Appeal total to just over £9.5 million, and helps our cash position considerably.

Armstrong was invited to 10 Downing Street on 23rd July to be personally thanked by Mrs Thatcher. But that was not to be the end of the matter. Front page headlines in the *News of the World* on 1st August carried the shocking story:

Kinky Churchman Fools Maggie and Charles:

A bizarre Church Leader with a sordid past of sexual and financial scandal has bought himself a private meeting with Mrs Thatcher with a £106,000 cheque ... The sleazy activities of 89 year old Herbert Armstrong, head of the Worldwide Church of God, Pasadena, California, should shock security chiefs ... a catalogue of abuse of funds included Armstrong flying to Rumania for sex therapy lessons and taking his Gulfstream jet to London to buy a sex toy.

Consideration was given to returning the cheque, but not pursued.

The appeal attracted other somewhat less blatant approaches, where money and ambition were linked, some conditional, some unconditional. A former Lord Mayor offered support, but wanted paying for his services. Drogheda received a cheque for £10,000 from a patron of the arts as a personal gift, "which was to remain secret at all costs". The patron later received a peerage . Moser was offered £20,000 in return for a seat on the Opera House Board. Claus was outraged and ensured the individual never achieved his ambition. Joe wickedly speculated as to which of our major Appeal donors was the perpetrator who dared to overstep the mark.

The Royal Opera House extension was opened officially on 19th July.

ROYAL OPERA HOUSE DEVELOPMENT APPEAL

Press Release

Prince Charles unveils plaque

ENQUIRIES TO: APPEAL DIRECTOR, ROYAL OPERA HOUSE, COVENT GARDEN, LONDON WC2E 7QA
TELEPHONE: 01-240 1200. CABLES: AMIDST, LONDON WC2

JULY, 1982   No. 24

PRINCE CHARLES OPENS EXTENSION

On Monday, 19 July The Prince of Wales opened the extension to the Royal Opera House at a ceremony attended by the Rt. Hon. Paul Channon, Minister for the Arts, and the Lord Mayor of Westminster, and by many of those whose generous contributions over the past four years have made the building possible.

Prince Charles, accompanied by Paul Channon, unveiled a plaque beside the new stage door entrance. Moser paid tribute to Joe in his address to the guests:

In the House itself, miracles have been performed by our magician/impresario fundraiser Sir Joseph Lockwood, together with Pat Spooner. I don't know how they did it, but they have done it.

I so wanted to tell Moser one does not bracket unpaid patron with paid employee. By failing to differentiate, praise becomes empty. As he continued to include them in the same breath, he was not doing himself a favour. He was anxious for Joe to take on the next, far more ambitious, phase, which would include a second dance space and refurbished Floral Hall. Joe was not interested, and secretly thought it would never be achieved. He suggested a younger man for the job, Henry Keswick, Chairman of Jardine Matheson, who impressed him at United Racecourses Board Meetings. The post was eventually filled by Vivien Duffield, after she buried her vendetta with the Opera House.

In August, Channon asked Joe to stay on the SBTB for a further year. The drum-revolve in the Olivier Theatre was still an issue. However, the Certificate of Practical Completion for the last part of the stage equipment at the National Theatre was issued by the architects on 5th July 1982.

Joe was starting to slow down generally. In July, he became confused whilst demonstrating the scale model of Opera House future plans, and had to be rescued by Robin Dartington, the project director. Admittedly, the concept of the project, to put it mildly, was ambitious. A woman with a strong Lancashire accent came up to Joe at the press conference in the Crush Bar: "I'm Joan, Jack Rowland's lass," she announced. Only after she had gone did Joe realise that Joan Bakewell, the BBC arts correspondent, was the daughter of his senior engineer at Henry Simon.

In September, he cancelled joining Hartley Shawcross's eightieth birthday party, blaming low blood pressure.

In October, it was time to retire his elderly London housekeeper, who was no longer up to looking after him. I moved in to replace her. Every day I would walk across the Park to keep an eye on my flat. We were now, at last, "a couple". One evening, Harry Williams dined with us.

The couple upstairs, Sandor and Edith Gorlinsky, always in full evening dress, he in white tuxedo and smoking a cigar, she brightly jewelled, were now our friends. Forgotten was Sandor's lack of apology for overflowing bathwater through Joe's ceiling. Forgiven was his non-support of the appeal: "I'm listed as Anonymous!" He had an original sense of humour.

They took us backstage at the Coliseum, after Rudolf Nureyev's *Romeo and Juliet* production. Pushing past the fans outside Nureyev's dressing room, including Jessie Norman, Sandor put a copy of the programme in my hands. "Ask for autograph!" he instructed, anxious to have Nureyev in the right mood for signing the contracts he was brandishing. Dining later at Giovanni's restaurant nearby, Nureyev put in a brief appearance. "Your hair is receding," he addressed me. Such formality! Perhaps, seeing me with Joe, he confused me with Ivo Brunner. I noticed he remained fully covered with his trademark woolly knitted "Beanie" cap.

The Gorlinskys regularly saw in the new year at Claridge's Hotel, with their same table in the dining room. We were now their guests, and this was likely to become a fixture. Making up the party were Georges Prêtre and his wife. As usual, I was not properly introduced. Only halfway through dinner was I sure I was sitting next to the great conductor when he hummed 'The Barcarolle' from *The Tales of Hoffman*, which he was conducting at Covent Garden. Joe and he were discussing Maria Callas. I was greatly attracted to the handsome Frenchman's gentle, modest manner, which surely was one reason for Callas choosing to live in Paris. Sandor whispered to Joe: "He is the greatest conductor!" We already knew all Sandor's artists were "the greatest".

Joe encountered Malcolm McDowell on the crowded dancefloor. "How's William?" Malcolm hailed. Mary Steenburgen, his wife, must have wondered who I was. Edith reminded me years later how we three couples walked home across Grosvenor Square in the early hours, still in paper hats, holding presents and coloured balloons. We said goodnight to the Prêtres, "The Greatest", who were staying nearby.

Barney Ales, Tamla Motown boss at Hatchet Wood

Dolly East and Mitzi Ales at Hatchet Wood

George and Judy Martin at Hatchet Wood

1983

AIDS Takes its Toll

The year saw the appointment of a new chairman and a new director at the Royal Ballet School. There was also a new chairman at Thorn EMI. Joe was not concerned about Thorn EMI. For Sir Dick Cave, "the integration of two such large and complex companies had been a major task". He was ill, and died not long after.

Joe still found himself treated as the School's elder statesman. He would attend Governors' Meetings, travelling alone by tube to Barons Court. Before word got to Drogheda, the chairman, to Sterling, the Financial Committee chairman, or even to the Director, Joe got wind the Opera House was imposing Merle Park on the School to replace the director. Despite being Chairman of the Royal Ballet Charter Body, Joe could not resist the odd indiscretion, and let the School have the information. He knew the effect it would have, and was amused to stand aside and watch developments. The director, James Monahan, had once been married to Merle, and refused to believe the news. As an author and former ballet critic, Monahan claimed his ex-wife was incapable of writing a letter. Barbara Fewster, the ballet Principal, was overlooked and convinced it would not work.

Jeffrey Sterling went to congratulate Merle in her dressing room after a performance. Drogheda reprimanded him, he was not yet chairman: "I think I should have been the one to do that," he remarked shirtily.

The Royal Ballet were off on a world tour in June. Joe received postcards from Japan. Wayne Eagling wrote: "Working hard and eating raw fish. Hong Kong here we come."

Leslie Edwards wrote: "NY went very well especially for Fred, and I'm loving being once again in Japan."

Monica Mason wrote from Shanghai: "What a really wonderful

time we're having. NY and Japan were super again, but we were disappointed in Korea, although we had a big success there. They loved Romeo! Of course this has to be the focal point of the whole thing, and what a Country it is. The audiences are noisy and demonstrative and the Co. is dancing wonderfully. We're managing a lot of sightseeing by getting up at dawn like all the Chinese do."

They were all looking forward to seeing us on their return. Merle got stuck in as director, and held the post for fifteen years. She was keen to keep me involved, inviting us both to lunch at the School on 12th October. James Monahan came to the flat the previous evening to have a heart-to-heart with Joe, wishing he was still chairman. His criticism of Merle proved to be quite wrong.

The Sadler's Wells Royal Ballet mounted a stage version of Ashton's *Pas de Légumes*. Taken from the film, it worked well, and we went to see a performance in January. In December, Merle wrote to Joe, proving she was quite capable of writing a letter:

Dear Sir Joe,

The score and parts of the Pas de Légumes ballet are lodged in the Royal Opera House Music Library and Barry Wordsworth has informed me that they cannot be released without the permission of the film company (i.e. EMI). Would you please be so kind as to approach the relevant person to obtain permission for the release of the score and parts (or tell me who to contact)? It is, in fact, a rather pressing matter, since, apart from the planned School performances at Sadler's Wells Theatre for 23-28th July next year, we would also like to perform the work at Eton on two nights in November 1984. The Precentor, Graham Smallbone would like to see the score as soon as possible.

When Princess Margaret visited White Lodge in November, Merle insisted I was included in the party. A boy traditionally presented the Princess with a posy. We all sat at a round table, which Joe explained was the arrangement Margaret preferred, for everyone to join the discussion.

Merle danced at Fred's 80th Birthday Gala the following year, possibly her last stage performance. She wore her original André Levasseur costume from his *Birthday Offering*.

Joe received approaches from the Royal Academy of Dancing, the Dance Teachers Trust and the Institute of Choreology. London Contemporary Dance Trust and Rambert Ballet were the only ones of interest to us. We followed the career of handsome young American dancer Robert North, who progressed from the School to LCD, and then Rambert Ballet, where he became artistic director. At the ninety-four-year-old Dame Marie Rambert's memorial service at St Paul's Church, Covent Garden, Robert was ushering, and put Joe and me in the front row pew to hear Ashton and de Valois address the congregation. John Sainsbury's wife, Anya Linden, the ballerina, implored Joe "on bended knee" to support the Rambert Ballet. He agreed to attend a fundraising cocktail party its thirty-two-year-old chairman was giving around the corner in Mount Street. By not taking me, it was clear that he had no intention of participating with the organisation. So, I never met Adrian Ward-Jackson, a prominent figure in the art world, who set up home with Julian Hosking. When Julian died of AIDS in 1989, another lover told me Ward-Jackson gave him the disease. Ward-Jackson himself died of AIDS in 1991, aged forty-one. By that time he was a Governor of the Royal Ballet, and the Princess of Wales broke her holiday at Balmoral to rush to his bedside at St Mary's Hospital, Paddington. *The Times* mentioned "he was capable of the most profound and quiet friendships, particularly with strong and gifted women". No doubt he impressed Anya Sainsbury at Rambert.

Charles Murland died of AIDS at St Mary's in November 1983. He was one of the very first to be known to die of the disease. He had been moved from another hospital. His friends came to see him. Edith Gorlinsky said they could not understand why they had been made to put on protective overalls and face masks. AIDS was still referred to as herpes. By chance, I developed a minor case of shingles, also known as herpes. For a brief moment, I thought I had AIDS and went for a blood test. One wonders how these things happen. In Murland's case, I have a good idea where he picked up the disease. Our office window in Duke Street (1975 to 1980) faced a newsagent's across the street, above which was a flat. Activity in the flat convinced me it was a male brothel. Dark, Italianate occupants permanently closed the curtains to be sure of privacy. One mid-morning I was passing the newsagent's, when Murland came storming down the front steps practically knocking me over, in a tearing hurry. He was unkempt, and his zip was undone. Apart from the newsagent, the only other door leading from the steps belonged to the flat above. It bore no nameplate. Naughty Charles had evidently overslept.

Even when at his busiest, Joe always tried to get away to the country on Friday mornings. I had hoped to attend Eric Abbott's memorial service at Westminster Abbey. Unfortunately, these ceremonies take place at noon on Fridays. As Joe was unlikely to consider it important enough to vary our routine, I did not pursue the matter.

By the end of the year, the only commitments remaining were the Royal Ballet School and the South Bank Theatre Board. Lord Gowrie, the new Minister for the Arts (I had been to Eton with him), invited Joe to continue for a further year at SBTB "to finish the job: I know you are willing to put in this final stint".

The Smiths Industries Harrods hamper containing a ham and two bottles of champagne, the Christmas gift to pensioners, was delivered to Hatchet Wood. It was a relief not to have a turkey this time.

1984

"Happy 80th"

The first signs arose to indicate something serious was happening to Joe's health. Had there not been a heatwave during July, to coincide with my jury duty, nothing would have given cause for concern.

As a Chelsea resident, I was summoned to spend two weeks at the Crown Court, situated in Hans Crescent near Harrods. I was chair of a jury which reached its verdict on the Friday of the second week. The judge decided not enough time had been taken to deliberate, and called us back the following Monday. I objected, to no avail. The system sucked. The potential jurors' pool mainly comprised old lags, happy to sit around earning £18.50 a week. They advised me never to believe a policeman's witness statement. They looked on pityingly when I did.

I went down to the country on Friday afternoon to join Joe. I found him lying on the thick sitting-room carpet. It wasn't as if he had fainted from his well-known low blood pressure. He was quite conscious, which was puzzling and frightening. Rather than call the couple who were in their cottage, he preferred to wait for my arrival, which could have been at any time. He complained his body ached. This was later attributed to "postural tension in the muscles on the right side of his neck". I suggested we visit the public baths in Ironmonger Lane E.C.I., for stimulation. Here we received some basic massaging after a Turkish bath. Recovering in the changing room, with towels to cover our modesty, we were joined by a young man similarly attired. I was slightly apprehensive, but nothing more arose than a friendly conversation. I bought a teach-yourself massage book, and some baby oil. Joe was my willing dummy to practise on in the Hatchet Wood sauna, and I became proficient.

Charles and Mabel Lockwood were in London throughout July.

Luckily they were not to know anything was amiss, although we were together frequently. They came for drinks at the flat, and lunch in the country. They went up to Southwell by train for the day with Joe. He took them to see the Royal Ballet at Covent Garden, and to see the School perform *Pas de Légumes* at Sadler's Wells Theatre. They went off for one of their Continental tours throughout August and September. Back in London during October, they entertained us to lunch and a matinée. During the interval at Her Majesty's Theatre, I made Mabel's day by pointing out handsome actor James Fox in the audience.

Joe invited Paul McCartney and his family to a ballet rehearsal and vegetarian lunch in the Royal Box on 16th July. We met them at the stage door at 10.45. I memorised the doorman's name, plus those of all the front of house and security staff. We were expecting a party of five, but Paul and Linda brought six-year-old James, Mary, Stella and step-daughter Heather. They were escorted to the empty stalls, when disaster struck. We were expecting to see the General Rehearsal of *Sleeping Beauty*, but the dancers were in practice costume. Joe was in despair. The Company was disputing for equal pay with the Opera Chorus, led by Equity representative Wayne Eagling. Joe was unaware his favourite was the culprit for ruining his day. Linda was quite happy, breaking all the rules by photographing the dancers. The mixed attire added to the occasion she was capturing. Sitting on either side of him at lunch, Paul and Linda asked Joe about his favourite Beatles tracks. Unable to get over his disappointment, and at a loss, he called down to me at the bottom of the table. I was discussing Constantin Brancusi, the sculptor, with Heather, who worked in ceramics. My favourite tracks were from the Lennon/McCartney era, and it would not have improved the situation to choose a Lennon composition. Playing safe, and knowing Joe's preference for ballads, I suggested 'Blackbird'.

Throughout the visit, Spooner was hovering in the background with projects he wished to discuss with Paul. Joe was determined his personal guests should not be propositioned. In this at least he could claim to be successful. An enormous bouquet arrived at Hatchet Wood the following weekend, "With love from Paul and Linda".

Approached by Joe, Roy Sisson, Chairman of Smiths Industries, agreed to become Chairman of the London Contemporary Dance Trust. Robin Howard, Director General, sent Joe some claret from his cellar as a thank you. Howard founded the Company and its School in 1966 to provide training in the Martha Graham modern dance technique. The London City Ballet, a small upstart company existing on a shoestring, announced Diana, Princess of Wales, was to become its Patron. Howard, who had been looking for Royal Patronage, asked Joe if there was anything he could do to rectify this injustice. Joe rang Edward Adeane at Buckingham Palace, who was very sympathetic. His comment, "there is a bit of a problem", was a diplomatic way of saying that Diana did not welcome advice.

Joe had originally created EMI's International Classical Recording Committee to keep Walter Legge under control. He joined Peter Andry, Bhaskar Menon and Ken East at its 25th Anniversary Dinner, which he enjoyed and at which he sparkled. It was such a contrast to the Thorn EMI AGM lunch at the Ivy in September. The new chairman, Peter Laister, did not last long, and not surprisingly failed to merge the company with British Aerospace. He was boasting of buying INMOS, a high technology semiconductor and microcomputer manufacturer of "transputers". The company was "in the forefront, in world terms, in its chosen technologies", Colin Southgate, the new Thorn EMI Director sitting next to Joe, elaborated. Joe diplomatically kept quiet on his own story. Jeffrey Sterling and John Gardiner recently found themselves on the same flight to NY. Jeffrey told John he had just brokered a deal for the Government to sell their "dead loss company INMOS" to Thorn EMI. Joe told me that Southgate "had something to do with information". I concluded this meant public relations, in the old Bryan Samain role. He was in fact an information technology man, founder of Software Sciences, another recently acquired company and somewhat similar to INMOS. Years later, Southgate recalled his meeting with Joe that day as "memorable".

John Read, who had a new job with the Trustee Savings Bank, was also at the lunch. "How could anyone put that man in charge of a Bank!?" had been Hartley Shawcross's comment. Read had a conversation with Joe: "I am now forgiven," was how Joe put it. But the subject matter confirmed that lessons had not been learnt. Read extolled his new great friend, Robert Maxwell, someone Joe had been avoiding for years. Surely Read had not forgotten the lunch at Manchester Square, when Maxwell had made such a poor impression? To be fair, until his downfall, Maxwell fooled many more people than Read.

The year ended on a familiar note. The Harrods hamper was delivered from Smiths Industries. The porters at the flats received their annual tips, with a special fifty Dunhill cigarettes for the night porter.

1985

Final Resignations: "The Bastards!"

A lunch was held at Covent Garden in Joe's honour on 25th February. No doubt it came about on prompting from Lord Sieff, who had written to him: "Phase II requires another Joe Lockwood because without him it will fail. I do hope Claus, in due course, will arrange something to recognise your outstanding contribution to the Appeal for Phase I."

Moser began his little speech: "You are a flour miller." Joe nodded, "Yes, five generations of millers!" He might have responded: "You are a statistician!" I sat opposite Sir Robert Armstrong, Secretary to the ROH Board, the post that traditionally accompanied Cabinet Secretary and Head of the Home Civil Service. He was impressed to hear Joe had read forty Anthony Trollope novels and that there was such similarity between Barchester and Southwell. Next to me was Robin Hambro, Secretary to the ROH Trust, whom Polly Lansdowne claimed the Board preferred to herself. Robin chivvied me to get EMI not to delay any longer in adopting the new digital compact disc system. Ken East was reluctant to switch to a format invented by competitors.

Spooner was on the guest list but not present. Moser spoilt things by being visibly disappointed he could not congratulate him too. He simply did not get it. Yet letters Joe wrote to Spooner and circulated could not have been clearer:

I have received the attached papers from the Opera House asking for my authorisation to pay for certain entertaining. One of these is for £40 for a Christmas lunch for the Development staff. You probably know that in business, although firms have Christmas celebrations, and give them drinks (sic), the Inland Revenue will only allow an expenditure of £1 per person to be free of tax. The Finance Director of the Company is obliged to disclose any excess expenditure which is then charged for tax to the individual concerned.

As regards the Charity, it is completely illogical to spend money on entertaining staff. At the Ballet School recently, a dinner was given for the retiring Director, but has been disallowed by the Solicitors acting for the School, and with the advice of a QC that it was illegal.

As regards the entertaining of Mr Tim Halford for lunch, this again would not be allowed. He is a very nice young man and very helpful, but that is not a good enough reason for entertaining him at our expense. He has already been entertained through our expense account. Any appeal to Occidental Oil has to be made to Dr Hammer. I have collected vast sums for the Opera House over the last four years. I have never spent one penny of my own or the Opera House's money in entertaining any one of these donors except when they have been entertained at the Opera House, when my own personal expense has been tips to the waiters. It is, I think, counter-productive to ask people to give us money, and then entertain them to lunch or dinner with their money.

And again, two months after the Halford lunch:

I have received your list of expenses for your two week tour to Singapore, Brunei, Hong Kong, Tokyo FOR MY APPROVAL. I have NEVER authorised any of these overseas visits since the Development Fund was completed. On your weekly telephone calls you have told me you were going on these visits and I was under the impression you were working under instruction from John Tooley's assistant, Paul Findlay.

The cost of £2,042 plus presumably air fares is a lot of money. If the Opera House thinks money can be raised for it, it is of course for them to settle the bills. As regards the Development Fund we have not raised any money since winding it up a year ago. I have not felt inclined to approach anybody since then, for I lose interest when I see money wasted. You have given me the impression Sir Claus Moser knew of these recent visits and approved.

Joe's no-holds-barred rant over Spooner's extravagance was indicated by the figures: between 1976 and 1982, £9 million was raised at a cost to the appeal of £143,000. Subsequently, a further million came in at a cost of £123,000 by the time of the Singapore, Brunei, Hong Kong jaunt. Despite everything Joe flung at him, Spooner remained at the Opera House until 1990, and Phase II was still on the drawing board.

Much of Joe's contentious mood was caused by ill health. In March there was a major flu epidemic, and he did not escape. Always so careful about his health, this was something he could not cope with, and he lost patience. Hearing that the head porter at the flats had a prescription, he wanted some of the same medicine immediately. He had the same GP (i.e. Dr Hatchick) who looked after EMI House for twenty-five years, and had received classical records from Joe each Christmas. As arranged, I collected the prescription and medicine from the chemists in Edgeware Road. I was surprised to find Dr Hatchick behind the counter when I arrived. It did not occur to ask whether this was something he did regularly or made some special arrangement. It just seemed strange at the time. Joe deteriorated rapidly and a large rash covered his body. I was very concerned and summoned my own family doctor, who diagnosed an allergy. Had Joe never known he was allergic to penicillin? Whether Hatchick was in awe of Joe and obeyed his command, or simply failed to bother to examine him, remains a mystery. Joe recovered, but again, in too much haste, he insisted on returning to the office before he looked fit. People may have remarked on this, or maybe it was a coincidence that, soon after, he took a phone call from the office manager at Gloucester Place, asking him to give up his office.

"The bastards!" Joe exclaimed. Menon, East and Andry, so effusive just a few months ago, were invisible. Bhaskar was "abroad for six weeks". He did make up for it, rather, by expressing his gratitude in a letter from Beverly Hills: "You brought our company dignity, class and success." Meanwhile, Ken was delighted to inherit the Geochron World Time Clock, the gift from Capitol, which Joe had kindly left behind.

We had already decided to sell the flat and leave London. Joe agreed it was ridiculous packing up to go down on Fridays, and, once there, immediately prepare for the return on Sundays. Christie's and Phillips came to value the furniture, Bishops Removals came to estimate, and estate agents brought round Swedes, Saudi Arabians and Greeks. Eventually a Greek cement tycoon made a firm offer, but left the flat unoccupied. I was puzzled to see the curtains I had carefully dry-cleaned remained untouched, as I drove round Grosvenor Square in subsequent months and years. It transpired the Greek purchaser was assassinated by terrorists on motorbikes in broad daylight in Athens.

It was time for final resignations. United Racecourses had already expressed sadness to lose Joe, and John Gardiner mentioned his "Terrific contribution to Laird". SBTB now congratulated him on achieving seventeen years' service. And the most touching farewell from the Royal Ballet came from Merle Park at the School. "It's not the same without you and William visiting us!" she wrote, enclosing a slim volume entitled *The Cycle*, "with admiration, thanks, and love … these poems of Madam's [Ninette de Valois] have just been published. I thought you might like a copy."

I returned the company BMW to Thorn House garage. It was so casually received, I wondered whether such laxity was generally pervasive in all aspects of the company.

During the last week of July, we said goodbye to the Coliseum, the National Theatre and the Royal Opera House. The London Festival Ballet was performing *Romeo and Juliet* at the Coliseum in Ashton's version for the Danish Ballet, and not seen before in London. It was inferior to Kenneth MacMillan's later production for the Royal Ballet. In one of his less discreet moments, Joe said almost as much to Freddie, who was in the audience. At the National we saw an Alan Ayckbourn play, which Joe hated. He did not get the humour, and he expressed a wish never to go to a theatre again. Things were much better at Covent Garden. Wayne Eagling made a one-act ballet, *Frankenstein, the Modern Prometheus*, with music by Vangelis and scenario by Antonia Douro (later Duchess of Wellington), which he dedicated to Joe. We went to the fourth performance, which coincided with Princess Margaret presenting Wayne with the 1984 Evening Standard Award. This was for his outstanding dancing rather than for his choreography, which the critics had not liked. On stage afterwards, Margaret greeted Joe: "How well you are looking Sir Joseph." In fact, Joe did not feel or claim to be well. A friend wrote to Joe:

My wife and I went to see Frankenstein last evening and we thoroughly enjoyed it. It was so different and so exhilarating that the cast got a tremendous ovation. It is only critics who do not understand these things! Warmest congratulations on being a dedicatee. You should feel both pleased and proud!

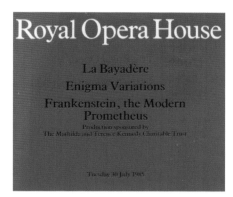

Wayne Eagling's "Frankenstein" ballet programme

The year witnessed a major outbreak of AIDS. Charles Murland was the forerunner. The greatest shock was the news that Rock Hudson had died of the disease. Richard Goodwin's *The Mirror Cracked* was one of his last films. Tony Cloughley, who designed Hatchet Wood, succumbed. And Nick Eden, who Joe caught me in bed with, died. When I knew him, he was head of the Territorial Army. Now, as The Earl of Avon, Prime Minister Anthony Eden's son, and in the Lords as Under Secretary at the Department of Energy, he was one of the most eminent people to die. Fortunately, it was not treated as a Profumo type of scandal.

In August, Joe dined with Pathfinder Bennett, who still lived at Farnham Royal. Before delivering him to the house, we made a detour, searching for East Burnham Well. We couldn't find it! This gave me the idea for another expedition. After the thirty-nine-year lease of the flat had been sold for £425,000, and we were settled at Hatchet Wood, we took a well-deserved break. We spent two nights at the Saracen's Head in Southwell, visiting Joe's retired housekeeper in St Albans on the way. We met his elder brother Frank and his Caudwell cousins. Walking back up Station Road from Caudwell's Mill, which was now flats, we paused to rest on a park bench. Pointing back at the row of Victorian villas we had already passed, Joe indicated, "That is where I was born." Gazing across the fields behind the Minster in Westgate, he imagined he could see his rich uncle's house in Eastgate. By the time we reached Derbyshire, for the next two nights, he was tiring, and remained in the car as I looked at Chatsworth and Hardwick Hall. But at the mill in Rowsley, still run by his cousins, he could not help but be impressed that it was in working order. It still used millstones to grind flour for Chatsworth. The manager produced a copy of *Flour Milling* for his signature, when he discovered Joe's identity.

From Hatchet Wood, Joe visited the Hamlyns in Gloucestershire and Arnold Goodman in Oxford. Paul Hamlyn mistook me for BC, who sold him "excellent cases of claret". Despite his scorn for universities, Joe enjoyed lunching in Hall with Goodman, now Master of University College. The young dons were less interested in having serious conversation than getting away on time to support Oxford United.

Oxford became my regular shopping destination. The Golden Cross Hotel, where I stayed as an articled clerk, was long gone. Replacing it was the enlarged covered market, good for coffee beans and sirloin steaks.

Joe and Max

1986 – 1991

Country Retreat:
"I'm making the bread now"

I was now looking after Joe entirely on my own. The couple preferred to leave, when they no longer had the place to themselves. Housekeepers seemed impossible to find. One applicant boasted how she would join Lord Black for a nightcap. Realising she was referring to the ninety-year-old Bill Black, who he had known at NRDC, Joe recoiled at anything so abhorrent happening to himself. Luckily he got on well with my mother, who stood in for me at Hatchet Wood when I spent a day buying a cottage in Cornwall.

In February, we received a visit from Granada Television about their forthcoming programme on the twentieth anniversary of the Beatles' album *Sgt. Pepper's Lonely Hearts Club Band*: "Twenty years ago today, Sergeant Pepper told the band to play."

We could not leave thirteen-year-old Maximilian on his own, when we went up to London for the filming in June. Having picked up a prescription from Dr Butcher in Devonshire Place, we abandoned the car in Northumberland Avenue, and the three of us walked the remaining distance to the Royal Commonwealth Society's premises. I should add the country was experiencing a heatwave. It seemed rather a grand looking building for a film crew to choose to rent. Sure enough, we were pounced upon by the commissionaire, who had instructions to bar Max from entry. Joe exploded, and, despite concession being made for Max on condition he wore a lead, Joe had difficulty recovering during the interview. Granada said they would of course have come to Hatchet Wood to film, if they had known about the dog. Joe described the upper classes lounging in dinner jackets and long dresses, listening to the *Sgt. Pepper* album. It was only later, and after the programme had gone out, I realised it was the *Revolver* album that had been entertaining the dinner party guests.

I went to London on my own, and travelled by train. The sole purpose of my visit was to find a new investment register to replace one which was full. Stocks and shares were very important to Joe, and he specified the special book required for recording and updating entries.

Don and Ly Bennett came to lunch at the end of August. The Air Vice-Marshal sought advice on raising money for an RAF monument. He wrote to thank us for lunch on 1st September, and died suddenly on the 14th. Joe attended the memorial service at St Clement Danes Royal Air Force Church in the Strand on 21st November. As he entered, an Honour Guard of Air Cadets saluted him. This simple act quite overwhelmed him, and he could not resist a tear. He was what Peter Lendrum called "a softie", a term equally applied to the other rather frightening characters, John Davis of Ranks, and Lord Mountbatten, whose exteriors, Peter said, hid sentimental hearts.

Sir Harry Platt Bt. FRCS, Emeritus Professor of Orthopaedic Surgery at the University of Manchester, died on 20th December at the age of a hundred. He qualified as a Bachelor of Surgery in 1909, aged twenty-three. Seventy-six years ago he had attended Joe's father.

Anna Burdfield, the new housekeeper, came for interview on 21st October. Max inspected her and approved. We learnt she had five cats. She started work on 8th November and stayed for twenty years.

We followed the routine of getting up at 6.30 a.m. and going to bed at the regular hour of 9.30 p.m. Joe's nephew Michael Lockwood and Janet came for the weekend in June 1987. They recognised the strict discipline as something he inherited from his mother. The way he said, "Have you put the water beside my bed William?" it could have been his mother speaking. One evening I asked to stay up late to watch a TV programme. Joe told Michael: "William spent all night up in London at nightclubs!" Quite untrue. My infrequent visits to Cornwall were also dramatised: "William treats this place like a hotel!"

We took the Lockwoods to see West Wycombe Park, the nearest National Trust property. In the car park, a sign indicated that no dogs were permitted in the grounds. Max remained in the car. As we approached the house, a man slipped out of a side door with his dog, and set off across the park. It was Sir Francis Dashwood, who lived there. Joe was outraged. "If that man can do that, so can I!" The visit was not a success.

Joe treated me generously to show his appreciation. He passed on the rental income from the fields and the sale of timber from the woods. The Hatchet Woods were dedicated under a covenant with the Forestry Commissioners. This meant maintenance costs could be set against income, and timber sales profits were not taxed. Best of all, they supplied free logs for our two log-burning stoves, which remained lit throughout autumn, winter and spring. The woodlands rose steeply behind the house and provided both a positive and negative effect. They sheltered us from the Great Storm in October, when hundreds and thousands of trees were blown down in Southern England from 90mph winds, with whole woods decimated. Our neighbours suffered but we were untouched. On the negative side, they blocked TV reception. Joe overcame this by renting a small spot further up the hill for the aerial, but permission lapsed after twenty-one years. People are so difficult! Engineers from EMI Electronics located a signal above the tree canopy, and we installed a sixty-foot mast. From a distance it resembled a mini Eiffel Tower.

One Sunday, a large package was handed to Anna with no explanation. It weighed three pounds, and was correctly addressed to Joe. We lived fairly remotely and its delivery was a mystery. We treated it as a suspicious item and left it in the drive and rang the police. Joe entertained the Thames Valley constabulary as we waited for the Bomb Disposal Unit to arrive with sniffer dogs and remote control equipment. Joe explained he was a former director and pensioner of Hawker Siddeley, who had supplied the Hawker P1177 Jump Jets for the RAF in war zones. He might be a target for terrorists. The item was dismantled and revealed a glossy coffee-table book. *Goldfields, A Century Portrait 1887-1987* was a complimentary gift to shareholders from the Chairman of Consolidated Goldfields. Possibly some other shareholder in the area had received Joe's copy inadvertently, and kindly brought it round. Joe promptly sold the shares he had bought in 1972 for a £12,700 gain. The book was an omen of doom for the company.

Charles and Mabel Lockwood came to lunch on 2nd August, bringing daughter, son-in-law and grandchildren. The next day, Joe fell heavily in his bedroom and broke his hip. Michael Elliott, our GP and friend, gave instructions not to do anything until he arrived. He trained as an osteopath and knew what he was talking about. An ambulance arrived in the evening to convey Joe to the Chiltern Hospital in Great Missenden. They must have operated immediately, because the phone went early the next morning. It was Joe with instructions to fetch him, followed by detailed directions of the route to take. This was extraordinary, as he could have no idea where he was, and had travelled the twenty-odd miles in the back of the windowless ambulance. They kept him in for thirteen days. I was surprised not to get a call from the hospital that first morning. Apparently they had not felt it was necessary. They had spoken to Charles, his next of kin.

It was most unfortunate that Charles happened to be in this country at the time of the mishap. He journeyed to the hospital by train purposefully. Joe had already refused to share the cost of a memorial for their mother in Southwell Minster. This was a double-life-size bronze rood, entitled *Reclining Christ*, commissioned anonymously by Charles to hang high above the nave. The family came over for the installation. Joe's vulnerable state left him open to a plea to provide for his four nieces, "who might be poor one day". Not mentioned was the new thirty-four storey head office the Roberts family were erecting, that became the tallest building in Buenos Aires. Again, he found his brother unforthcoming. If Joe intended to support anyone, it would be his brother Frank's family. One benefit from Joe's accident was that he was now taking me into his confidence.

Determined to get out of hospital, a walking stick soon replaced crutches. His reason for refusing to use the hydrotherapy pool proved he could be very ungracious at times, as well as stubborn. He was not prepared to share the water with a poor Iraqi boy, recovering from wounds inflicted in the Iran–Iraq war. As a condition to leaving hospital, he agreed reluctantly to have a carer for two weeks. His rapid recovery was mainly due to proving this had not been necessary. Impatience was nearly his undoing: in the welcome home, Anna and Max, together, caused him to trip on the front door step.

On the recommendation of his physiotherapist, he ordered a special armchair. We visited Parker Knoll's head office in High Wycombe. The furniture manufacturer was founded in the Chilterns, where it obtained raw material from the extensive beech trees in the surrounding woodlands, such as at Hatchet Wood. Joe was measured and tested for posture. The end product was manufactured to his specifications, unique and for his exclusive use.

LG, now retired, a widower, but still living in Gerrards Cross, welcomed an invitation to lunch. It was good for both of them. Despite being the Grand Old Man of the UK record industry, LG was still considered a subordinate by Joe. On the subject of the Company Pension Scheme, Joe was cagey, in case LG was on a lower tier. Afterwards, LG wrote:

> It was marvellous to have a good chat with you again. It really took me back to the "old days" when you used to chase us around but always knew exactly what was happening and would always help us out of difficulties once you were satisfied we had done our best. Sadly, I don't see the old spirit around much these days.

As if on cue, the press exposed Read again. Memories of his previous mismanagement had been all but buried. As Chairman of TSB, he was bidding to take over Hill Samuel, which was in trouble. A price was agreed, but a massive slump in the equity market made Hill Samuel shares fall dramatically. The City could not believe it when Read did not withdraw or lower his offer. The stock market crash was reason enough. Headlines in *The Times* said it all: "Anger as TSB deal is approved", and, "Read denies Board battle". The *FT* reported: "TSB shareholders' fury fails to stop £777 million bid for bank". It turned nasty: "Sir John Read the Chairman of the Trustee Savings Bank and

Sir Ian Fraser, a Director, have begun libel proceedings against the *Observer* newspaper. The action concerns an article published in December about the fees paid to Lazards the Merchant Bank for handling the bid for Hill Samuel in October." As usual, Read was caught paying too much.

In December, we received a visit from Capitol Records' lawyers from America, who were staying at the Savoy Hotel. The request came from the Thorn EMI Company Secretary. On the surface, it was purely a social call. But I learnt later that Thorn EMI was threatened with confiscation of Capitol Records. The Anti-Trust authorities were on the trail. They had picked on an article in an American music industry magazine some years ago, when an EMI executive boasted EMI owned Capitol. We heard no more. I believe the lawyers went away happy to report Joe was not fit to face subpoena from an American court of law.

Two of the finest people in music and ballet died in 1988. David Bicknell, as head of EMI's Classical Department, had treated me as an ally. And Freddie Ashton bestowed a touch of his aura. It was also the year that Joe began to fail. I never saw him look at his presentation set of encyclopaedias; his general knowledge appeared self-sufficient. But now he was frequently consulting *Collins Home Doctor* and other medical books.

In October, pernicious anaemia was diagnosed, and a district nurse came to give him a jab for iron deficiency. This was the only time we saw the district nurse at Hatchet Wood. It did no good, and Michael Elliott consulted Dr Peter Butcher, who gave EMI executives annual check-ups. This was something Joe introduced, and Sir Ernest Simon innovated at Henry Simon. Joe had gone to Butcher for years, and, if anything was amiss, he should know about it. Other than prescriptions for sleeping pills and the purple hearts Joe used as a stimulant when he needed to sparkle, Butcher invariably provided a clean bill of health. He now confirmed Joe showed no atypical symptoms.

A blood sample was taken at the Hamleden surgery. Tests were made at Wycombe General Hospital. Things took off. Michael Elliot told him, "a young lady was taking an interest in him". This was Dr

Susan Kelly, consultant haematologist at the John Radcliffe Infirmary in Oxford. His condition was extremely rare, so rare that it was conditioned by a single gene of the 100,000 genes dispersed between the chromosomes spread around the body. She knew of only one other person with a similar defect, and she was a girl in her teens. It might take two years to locate and repair the gene. With Joe's permission, she would treat him as her guinea pig, monitoring and providing transfusions of blood from the best donors in the country, Oxford undergraduates. Joe had myelodysplasia, where the bone marrow manufactures too many white blood cells. Transfusions would restore the balance. The white cell imbalance indicates cancer, but this did not apply to Joe, for a simple reason: it was the condition diagnosed as uninsurable by Ernest Simon's doctor in the 1930s. A second opinion from Lord Evans, the Queen's doctor, gave Joe a clean bill of health. And there the matter rested for fifty years.

Subsequent research reduced genes from 100,000 to 20,000, lessening Dr Kelly's monumental task. But each gene mutates millions of different ways in the human genome, so she was on a hiding to nothing. Nevertheless, never one to turn down a deal, Joe agreed to trade his cure in two years for free blood and free treatment. Transfusions would take place at five-weekly intervals as an outpatient in High Wycombe NHS General Hospital.

Week one coincided with the visit of two cameramen, an interviewer and Brian Southall, EMI's PR man, to Hatchet Wood. A fresh attempt at a book on the history of EMI met with Joe's co-operation. A visual record of Joe seated with Max at his feet was unexpected. The questionnaire, submitted to refresh his memory before the meeting, was dismissed after a cursory glance as unnecessary. LG had made such a questionnaire a condition of participating. He told Joe: "I hope the 'invasion' on Tuesday goes off well – don't be too hard on them! I will certainly get advance notice of the questions I shall be expected to answer." Joe gave a virtuoso performance, talking without a break for an hour and thirty-five minutes about NRDC, Shoenberg, Hounsfield, Sinatra, Capitol and the Beatles. Southall received a case of cigars which he treated as a souvenir of the occasion. In his book *Abbey Road*, Southall gave Joe credit for blocking the sale of the studios.

Thorn EMI now had a non-executive chairman, and, surprisingly, it was Joe's old colleague Sir Graham Wilkins, Chairman of Beechams. Chief Executive was ambitious Southgate. LG told Joe, in mock horror, that the Chief Executive signed letters to staff using his Christian name. Southgate might well have recalled that lunchtime conversation with Joe. The truth about INMOS was revealed in *The Times'* leading article on 13th December:

End of a Thorny Problem

A few people in the semiconductor industry will have a sneaking feeling that the transputer will go the way of the hovercraft and other Great British inventions: Sold to an overseas buyer to develop rather than exploited in the United Kingdom … INMOS, the Semiconductor manufacturer set up by the Labour Government in 1978 was purchased in a rash moment in 1984 by Thorn EMI … For most of the time Thorn has owned INMOS, it has wanted to sell it.

It seems incredible so much could go wrong in a single year at Hatchet Wood. Electricity, telephone and water were all off at different times in 1989 for varying periods, even as long as a week. Cables were replaced, substations were moved, and water pipes were dug up. All this with an invalid in the house, and an intolerant one at that. It was important to remain in contact with the outside world. We managed, sometimes kept warm by log stoves, and sometimes, in the dark, staring enviously at neighbours' lights fed by a different source.

Max died on 1st February. It was sad to see him pass away after sixteen years.

My parents' house in London was burgled when they were away in June. Furniture was left piled up, as though the intruders planned a second visit. That night, after Joe had gone to bed, I slipped back to London, and kept vigil in the empty house. Back at Hatchet Wood by dawn, no one was to know he was left alone all night.

Continuing from that initial dose in November, transfusions were administered at five-weekly intervals throughout the year. To begin with, a sample was taken at the surgery and sent with "the blood collection" to High Wycombe. Here, Dr Kelly would check the haemoglobin level, before booking Joe into hospital. Soon Michael Elliott was coming to Hatchet Wood himself to take the sample. I would be dispatched direct to High Wycombe, avoiding double-handling. When Joe heard I was taking it to the Pathology Department, he was horrified. He associated pathology with death. Better to have called it the Haematology Department.

Spending all day attached to an intravenous drip was tiring, and Joe was encouraged to remain overnight. Once was enough. In future, he insisted on going home to bed. One late evening we were going down in the lift, when an administrator got in. At first she ignored us, then something struck her. Looking at Joe in his wheelchair, she remarked: "So you don't fancy staying with us tonight?"

Susan Kelly was solicitous: "If for some reason during this period you felt you needed the blood transfusion earlier, of course we would be able to accommodate that, but I do know that you do not like to come more often than you have to."

We grew to like Dr Kelly, especially when she admitted to an indiscretion. Bruce Chatwin, the gay travel writer, was a patient in the Radcliffe Infirmary. Since 1986 he was known to have AIDS, but he denied it to the end, claiming he had picked up a rare virus in Africa. He was not one of Dr Kelly's patients, but she was intrigued and persuaded a colleague to let her take a surreptitious look at him. He died in the Radcliffe. In the same year, Julian Hosking died. This drove me to obtain a copy of *Living and Working with HIV*, the booklet intended to train Frontliners. When people of a similar age to myself, such as Sheridan Dufferin, were dying, it seemed sensible to have a copy at hand.

Joe planned my future. He started in a small way, by buying our internal telephone system from BT, so that I would not incur future subscriber rental charges. This was not as simple as it sounds, because by law BT retained ownership. Joe had to persist even when the law was changed to permit ownership purchase. He gave me £40,000. I was now in charge of his stocks and shares, monitoring his capital gains position, and writing his letters. Apparently my handwriting became so like his, even his brother never found out. Joe was relieved to learn his considerable capital gains were not taxed on death. Inheritance tax would take care of itself in his absence. He personally knew the manager of the EMI Group Pension Fund, who came from Smiths Industries, when Joe was on the SI Pensions Committee. Hoping for a sympathetic response, he asked for consideration be given to me, but received this reply:

> As I understand the situation, you are particularly concerned to make provision for a gentleman who has been in your employment for some considerable time … a person may be considered to be dependent for the ordinary necessities of life upon someone else who is, in effect, taking care of them. I am sorry that it is not possible to do anything through the Thorn EMI retirement and death benefit arrangement.

This was disappointing. Joe had previously been told EMI had absolute discretion to provide for spouses, parents, grandparents, children, grandchildren *and* dependants. He hated the thought of his pensions being written off.

In August, Joe wrote to congratulate Joe Loss, the band-leader, on his eightieth birthday. Joe Loss claimed to be the longest serving artist on HMV:

> It made me feel so happy to remember the exciting years when you were Chairman of E.M.I. I first remember recording for them in 1935 on Regal Zonophone and the other artists I remember on the same label were The Salvation Army Band and Gracie Fields. The price was 1s. 3p. per record and I did not receive any Royalties either!

During the year, apart from Charles and Mabel, Janet and Michael and their two sons, and LG, we were visited by Ken and Dolly East, and Wayne Sleep, the dancer and his friend George Lawson, the rare book dealer. We went to lunch with George and Judy Martin. Little John Reid and his current boyfriend entertained us at their large country house. We paid another visit to see Joe's old housekeeper. In December, Joe brought his Christmas card from the Royal College of Physicians to show off to Dr Kelly that he was a friend of the President of the College.

We listened to John Major, the new Prime Minister, interviewed on *The World at One* on New Year's Day 1990. Joe had been a strong supporter of Mrs Thatcher, especially when her views were not meant to be popular. He agreed that the Commonwealth was wrong to impose sanctions on South Africa. He agreed the breaking down of the Berlin Wall would be bad for West Germany: unification with the East could only lead to dilution of the economy.

On 25th January, we experienced a storm even greater than that in 1987. Electricity was off for four days, and we were making hot water from saucepans balanced on the Norwegian log stoves, which we huddled round for warmth.

In March, Joe had further news from LG on Southgate, who was now chairman. Joe had written to Graham Wilkins to remind him of EMI's great pioneers, Berliner, Blumlein, Shoenberg, and Hounsfield, suggesting it was time to restore the EMI scanner from oblivion. It was an unpopular suggestion, and it is doubtful Wilkins was shown the letter, as the acknowledgement came from Southgate.

According to LG, Southgate proudly announced to the Thorn EMI Board that he, Southgate, had built up a personal arrangement with David Geffen to buy Geffen Records for about $750,000,000. The deal was to be signed in London, so he said, and then he and Geffen would immediately fly to Hollywood for a press conference. Unfortunately, on the day of the signing, news came through that Geffen had signed with MCA for much less than Southgate had offered. Geffen had not been in touch with Southgate to tell him what he had done. "So much for the personal arrangement!" Chairman of MCA was Lew Wasserman, who Joe met with Mike Nidorf. The story had been fed to LG by Bhaskar Menon, after a Thorn EMI Board Meeting. Bhaskar came to lunch, along with LG in April. Very full of himself in his role as Chairman of the International Federation of the Phonographic Industry, based in Beverly Hills, he boasted of employing a British ex-diplomat as consultant. He said Sir John Morgan was also employed by Mirror Group owner Robert Maxwell, "who bullied him". This was the John Morgan, on duty at the Foreign Office when Charles Lockwood was first kidnapped. Bhaskar wrote to Joe:

> It was so wonderful seeing you yesterday and I am most grateful for your warm and generous hospitality. At the present point in my EMI career there could have been no tonic more reassuring for me than the hours I was privileged to spend with you. As you know, to three generations of EMI people you will always represent the leader who personally built the glory of the Company and inspired each of us to bring the highest standards of effort and values to our service with EMI. I, as you know, have always felt a special and deep pride as having been employed by you as well. I return herewith the Philip Andrew's letter, which William so kindly lent me yesterday. I am moved beyond words that you should have kept it for these last 34 years. I am looking forward to seeing you again soon.

They never met again, and the following press release explains why:

Bhaskar Menon held Captive

In June Mr Bhaskar Menon was detained for 34 days in Kuwait. His plane, which was destined for Madras, landed in Kuwait at the beginning of the Iraqi invasion. The passengers were forced to alight and Mr Menon was taken to a hotel where they remained for over a month. Mr Menon escaped on 3rd July and has now returned to Los Angeles.

Michael and Janet came to lunch in May. Michael mentioned visiting his cousin Betty Lockwood in Yorkshire. Joe realised he was talking about the daughter of one of his farmer uncles, where he spent school holidays. She was his age and a spinster. "Get rid of Anna!" Joe told me, fantasising on having cousin Betty keep home for him. They spoke on the phone but he never mentioned what he had in mind. She was amused and a little flattered when I told her later.

Dick and Peggy Adderley came to lunch in July. Peggy was Joseph Rank's granddaughter. She asked me whether I had kept a note of Joe's anecdotes, as she had Dick's. I presume she was referring to Joe and Dick's gay bachelor days in the 1930s. She meant the war. Dick's memory served him better, recalling events with Charles in Brazil, rather than with Joe in Belgium and Ireland. Peggy bought Dick a farm in Yorkshire, to ride around on horseback. He still had the physique of a jockey.

Charles and Mabel came to lunch in September. They were worried about a law in Argentina requiring their grandchildren to register by a certain date to retain British nationality. The children's parents were not reliable. Our local High Wycombe MP once held a senior post in the British Embassy in Buenos Aires. Would I or Joe write to him? We were not really up to it. Back in London, Charles wrote to me, sending his letters recorded delivery. At first I thought that was a sign he did not trust me enough, but he probably considered our postal system was as unreliable as in Argentina. A granddaughter studying at Bath had instructions to come and see Joe. It was all quite innocent, but it was Joe's turn to feel he was being checked up on.

Life was by no means at a standstill. We had visits from a young clock repair expert who restored the Swedish Hyungens grandfather clock. It now required rewinding less often. He persuaded Joe to buy another antique long-case clock. The two grandfather clocks rang on the quarter hour.

Most of the outings, apart from hospital visits, were to the optician and the dentist. Joe had a new plate fitted on the NHS rather than privately. It was a ridiculous way of saving money, and was to cause problems. He had to go private in the end.

My family decided to sell the Victoria Cross awarded to my great-uncle. It was extremely valuable, as it was the first VC awarded to an airman. The RAF Museum at Hendon, where it was on loan, claimed ownership. The matter was sorted out, and the medal went at auction to Lord Ashcroft for a record price. When the museum director was being difficult, Joe incredibly generously agreed to intercede with the chairman of its trustees. This was Marshal of the Royal Air Force, Sir Denis Spotswood, one of the Smiths Industries directors Joe had entertained at Covent Garden. He lived locally, and Joe offered to lobby him, which probably meant sitting in the car outside his house until we were asked to leave. This proved unnecessary, but the offer was appreciated by my family.

In October, our nearest neighbour started a Sunday clay pigeon shooting school. The noise was horrific. I told him the valley we were in was shaped like an amphitheatre, which amplified the gunshot noise spectacularly. Today, he would be convicted for anti-social behaviour, but at the time he remained uncompromising.

A less offensive noise emanated during the otherwise silent autumn nights. Joe Brown, the blond mop-top 1960s cockney pop star, lived in a cottage at the bottom of the field. He was having a skiffle session. Joined by George Harrison over from Henley, and Joe's "Bruvvers" group, songs from the Swinging Sixties would ricochet up the valley. They were unintentionally serenading Sir Joe, the former "King of Pop".

I was brought up with a start on 1st October, when Joe exclaimed: "Has he done it yet?" As far as money matters were concerned, Joe was still on top form. Without telling me, he had instructed his bank manager in Southwell to transfer money on deposit to a higher-yielding "three month Crown Reserve Account". He would need to live for three months to qualify, and he succeeded! I rang the manager of NatWest, who sounded confused at being caught out. Perhaps he hadn't carried out Joe's instructions. Rather than confess, he rapidly credited the £13,500 interest. Joe's plan had been clear cut: close the account on 1st October. To continue the Crown Reserve by one day into a further three-month period was a commitment he had no confidence of honouring. It was essential to act on 1st October or risk being penalised. "Has he done it yet?" I can still hear the urgency in his voice. It was imperative. The sum on deposit was very large, about £480,000. We decided to put it into equities of our own choice. Joe had lost confidence in stockbrokers. The point of contention was a company called Cookson. "I've never heard of it! It's not even a Blue Chip! What's it doing in my portfolio? Get rid of it!" The stockbrokers bought Cookson on his behalf in 1989 at 316p. We got out at 90p. We now invested in five reputable companies. All prospered over the next three months. For example, £79,000 invested in Glaxo rose to £103,000.

The November hospital visit coincided with Joe's birthday. He was presented with a card signed by his ten nurses. Susan Kelly wrote: "What a way to spend the day!"

When we got home in the evening, Anna said "A strange woman rang up! She sang!" We worked out that Edith Gorlinsky saw his name in *The Times'* list of birthdays, and wanted to sing "Happy Birthday"! Sandor had died suddenly of throat cancer in May, and his Thanksgiving service was on 6th November. She must have been feeling rather low. We felt we should have supported her.

I went up to London for my fiftieth birthday on 6th December. My father did not join us at lunch. He told me Joe rang, asking when I would be back! I had also hoped to spend Christmas Day with my family. "If you do, I will find someone else!" Joe threatened. No more was said. I was not keen to be thrown out on my neck.

The 19th December visit to High Wycombe General Hospital was much like any other. I did not know at the time that Joe had decided to make it his last. The two years of the contract were up.

Jeffrey Sterling received the peerage he was after. "As the £540,000 Chairman of P&O Company that operated the doomed ferry Herald of Free Enterprise in which 193 died," he was shown by the *Daily Mirror* under the banner "IT'S LORD ZEEBRUGGE". The paper continued: "Families blast Thatcher's honour for ferry boss." Resignation Honours Lists are always controversial.

Wayne Eagling announced he would be leaving the Royal Ballet in September, to run the Dutch National Ballet.

As usual, a Christmas hamper was delivered by Smiths Industries.

On 15th January 1991, John Major announced that the American-led Operation Desert Storm had driven Iraqi forces out of Kuwait.

Joe saw this as a sign that the Prime Minister was blessed with "a lucky streak".

Despite the January blood test indicating further transfusions were essential, Joe had decided not to continue. Another three years were required to cure the "defective gene". In a moment of bravado, Joe asked me whether to hang on. His pension income was growing consistently from indexing and bonuses. The longer he lived, the richer he and I were. He was playing devil's advocate. This reminded me of the way he once teased the EMI Board. "Shall we sell Capitol?" he asked, half seriously, at the time its share price momentarily reached $60 on Wall Street.

He was visibly weakening and scarcely eating. Michael Elliott, a good shot, brought us duck, woodcock and a pheasant from his game locker in an attempt to improve his appetite.

On 27th January, I took a phone call from John Repsch. He asked to be remembered to Joe. This was very strange. His regular calls had stopped once his book *The Legendary Joe Meek: The Telstar Man* was published in 1989. Why was he calling now, two years later? Did he think Joe could still tell him something significant? The man obviously had Joe Meek in mind as he circled round us like a vulture. Today, the "Joe Meek Room" in the National Sound Archive at the British Library in Euston Road commemorates the first independent recording manager.

On 30th January, Joe woke up declaring he was to have three teeth out. The private dentist he now went to in Marlow gave him an appointment for the same afternoon. It was a struggle to get there. The receptionist obviously thought we should not have come. She should have been told it was her job to make patients welcome, rather than treat them as something the dog brought in. No teeth were removed, and Joe was none the worse from the outing.

Michael Elliott came on 11th February for another test. He knew there was no point in persuading Joe to restart transfusions. He said Susan Kelly was in tears, and that they were booking him into the private Chiltern Hospital to rest for two days. I asked the doctor in charge about his treatment. "There is nothing I can do," he told me.

No transfusion was given between when he went in on the 13th, and when he came out on the 15th. There was no charge for the stay. I concluded that Elliott and Kelly were taking this cautionary step to preclude any accusation that they were allowing him to die when it was still preventable.

On 24th February, Joe fell out of bed in the night and broke some bones. He wanted to get to his special Parker Knoll chair, where he could smoke his pipe. Of course, this was impossible unassisted. To sit up all night smoking a pipe is rather an original concept. The young locum, summoned to attend, was torn off a strip for prescribing a single paracetamol pill: "What do you mean by not giving me two, you idiot!"

The lack of red blood cells and solid food was making Joe light-headed. "What shall we do with the other William?" he asked. "Shouldn't we give him something?" I told him I was the only William. He was quite certain there was an additional younger version of me around to look after him.

One morning, he woke up exclaiming: "I'm making the bread now! And it's going to be wonderful! Far better than that plastic rubbish!"

We were left alone for ten days. Michael Elliott came on 5th March. He took me aside. Gently he warned it could not be much longer. He was amazed I had kept Joe going these last days. Fame and fortune meant nothing. What remained was our all-embracing physical companionship during those final hours. Suppressed for years, it was now Joe's driving force.

That night, he pointed to his bedside desk. "Get rid of the rubbish!" he instructed. In the drawer I found two nude photographs. One was of Julian Hosking, the Royal Ballet Principal dancer. The other was of myself. It was a compliment to be matched with such beauty. He asked me to lie beside him. He said I was as perfect as when we first met. He died in his sleep in the early hours of the morning.

PART 4

Me Again

Me with Max and Min

Life After Joe

The days that elapsed between Joe's death on 6th March and cremation on 11th produced conflict emotions of unimaginable intensity.

Elation sprang from a sense of freedom and release from twenty-seven years, a fossilised fly in amber. Anguish and despair fed from the prospect of an empty future. Free of responsibility, yet drier than a squeezed lemon, I was totally exhausted.

Critics disapproved of the delay in reporting Joe's death until after the cremation. Only Michael and Janet Lockwood and LG were informed. I needed to recover and cope on my own. But it did produce an episode that might have been less hurtful, had I not been so secretive.

Michael Elliott came as soon as called, despite the early hour. He explained a second doctor was required to see a body intended for cremation. I was kept waiting until late afternoon. The day passed so slowly. The doctor chose to give precedence to the living over the dead. I needed to note the closing prices of Joe's Channel Islands investments. I asked her to bring a copy of the *Financial Times*. She said she had never received such a request. Her comment on observing Joe – "How tall he is!" – served no particular purpose. The undertakers were kept waiting too, down the hill, the hearse's engine running all afternoon. They were surprised at the unnecessary delay.

I was joint executor with two of Joe's solicitors at Herbert Smith. One rang in a panic a couple of days later, having studied the will. Had I followed Joe's instruction to cut open an artery? Apart from modest bequests to his nephew and great nephew, I was sole beneficiary. This was expected. That the will was drawn up in 1974 did come as a big surprise. He never told me. Anyway, he had no cause to change it.

On 6th March, I let brother Charles, Max Rayne, Paul Hamlyn, Jean Thorn and Jeanie Lewis among others know that "the end is near". This would spare surprise at reading the obituaries on 12th March.

The newspapers carried long tributes. *The Times* and *Telegraph* were first, having received notice immediately on my return from the cremation and lunch with the Lockwoods and LG.

Alongside Margot Fonteyn, Robert Maxwell and Freddie Mercury, Joe appeared in *Lives Remembered: The Times's Obituaries of 1991*, a hardback published the following year. This confirmed the interest in his passing that I anticipated, and deflected, in the wording of the notice I composed:

> On March 6th peacefully at home aged 86. Funeral has taken place. No memorial service at own request.

Freddie died of AIDS in November. When their wills were published, it was revealed they had both left £5 million. Yet Joe's working life had been twice as long as Freddie's. The comparison symbolised how values had changed dramatically over the last twenty years. Pop song writers and recording artists had no greater supporter than Joe, and they knew it. At the same time, they were aware he considered them obscenely overpaid. Freddie's continuing royalties made him richer in death than in life.

Hugh Massingberd, Obituaries Editor of the *Daily Telegraph*, was instantly on the phone. His CV for Joe "stopped short in the early eighties". What had he been doing since? "Please send a fax". Massingberd took trouble to make his obituaries a little bit more entertaining than his competitors. I was unable to help. What appeared was fairly innocuous, but, unintentionally, caused me considerable distress, from one anecdote he managed to find to flavour his piece: "At his home in the Chilterns Lockwood had a remarkable collection of original cartoons, mostly featuring the faithful Nipper of His Master's Voice."

The morning, 12th March, a message was left, whilst I was out, to ring the secretary of the Company Secretary of Thorn EMI. I could not believe what I was hearing: "The Chairman has read about Sir Joseph's cartoons and would like to have them. We will of course make a donation to his chosen charity."

The cartoons were Joe's personal property, and now mine. Over the years, cartoonists were flattered to be asked for originals of their work, and rarely asked for payment. And the chairman making the request was Southgate, who had snubbed Joe so recently. Now, the great Music Industry Mogul, Southgate, was photographed beside a Berliner gramophone, and no doubt had visions of bedecking his office with framed dog and trumpet cartoons. Bryan Samain, who had negotiated with some of the cartoonists, was luckily available to confirm my ownership. When Southgate visited me to make amends, I could not resist showing him Alfred Clark's Gramophone Company "Golden Book" of autographs, which I also owned. He promised to honour a promise to donate £2,500 to the Royal Ballet School, Joe's chosen charity. Despite boasting about cancelling EMI's Box at Covent Garden (and Wimbledon debenture seats), he asked what he could do to help the Royal Opera House. He later became Chairman of the ROH Board, where he learnt the Opera House depended on pre-selling boxes and premium seats at the start of the season to supplement its income.

The Times gave Joe a generous amount of space, ending conventionally: "He never married". An unsolicited tribute came later, in what is now called its "Lives Remembered" column, from the Director of the Cancer Research Campaign:

> Sir Joseph helped boost CRC's income by about 70% in just five years. CRC reluctantly saw Sir Joseph retire in 1967, due to growing pressure from his business commitments.

It was left to Max Rayne to refer to his work for the National Theatre and the Opera House: "To all his activities he brought a wisdom based on his huge experience as well as great good humour albeit coupled with an intolerance of inefficiency and procrastination."

This was endorsed by Peter Brinson in *The Independent*. As former director of the Royal Ballet's "Ballet For All" company, Peter wrote as someone who knew Joe personally:

> He turned up suddenly, I remember, at a Ballet For All performance I was directing, gave useful opinions and remained a friendly adviser to us afterwards. Such visits gave him a knowledge at performance level that he would use to place his expertise where it mattered … He fulfilled the major requirement of a chairman as defined by David Webster, then General Manager of the House: 'What's that?' I asked, 'He must be able to pick up the telephone', said Webster, 'and say Get me the Foreign Secretary'. And the Foreign Secretary responded with help. Lockwood could do that and more. He was kind and gave good council to the Arts. May the Business World do more!

I was attracted to Peter, who had the figure of a danseur noble, which he aspired to being, but, which he was not. He addressed some of us keen ballet fans at Cambridge in 1960. To add interest to the lecture, he brought one of his young male dancers, not, as it happened, a ballerina. He stood the boy on a desk to illustrate the poses, attitudes, and physical properties he was describing. Werdon Anglin, Peter's partner, told me he was diagnosed with cancer and not long to live. This was why he wrote such good obituaries. He died soon after.

John Sainsbury, Chairman of the Opera House, arranged to dedicate the final performance of the Royal Ballet season on 25th June to Joe's memory. It was Peter who provided the programme note. This was the moment to remind everyone about the £6 million Joe had raised personally for the redevelopment project. Imagine my shock when the programme came back from the printers with half docked from Joe's contribution. This was the work of the current General Director, Jeremy Isaacs, in thrall to Vivien Duffield, the Opera House's new fundraiser in chief. A pity, as Joe had once been the former MD of Thames TV's boss.

Meeting Janet Lockwood at Kings Cross on the day of the performance, who should rush up to me on the busy concourse but the delightful Donald MacLeary. Such a coincidence. Back in 1959, Donald was the boy in the company Joe had a thing about. He had no idea the evening's performance was in Joe's honour. John Sainsbury resigned suddenly as chairman, and little was done to foster his instructions.

I ordered a cold supper for the intervals in the Crush Bar. My guests consisted of Janet, Edith, George and Judy Martin, Dolly East, John Reid and boyfriend, Robyn Pratt (Charles's granddaughter) and fiancé, and Valeria Ossola. Wayne Eagling and his girlfriend Jane Wellesley joined us for a moment. All efforts to pay were brushed aside by House Manager Trevor Jones. Sainsbury had personally taken care of it himself.

The *Evening Standard* review next day was headed "Strength and Sensuality". It called *Raymonda Act III*, *A Month in the Country*, and *Elite Syncopations*, choreographed respectively by Nureyev, Ashton, and MacMillan, "An excellent triple bill programme."

Under Sainsbury's auspices, again, the Royal Ballet School's annual performance on 20th July at the Opera House was dedicated to Joe. Charles and Mabel, who were in London, came, as did Julian Gibbs and Nicholas Ferguson. Charles could not make out Joe's connection with Julian and Nicholas. Dame Merle Park wrote in the programme: "Sir Joe's advice was much valued by me. His favourite composer was Mozart, and in this connection, it is fitting that David Bintley has choreographed a new ballet to Mozart's 'Les Petits Riens' for this performance". Lower School pupils performed Scottish, Irish and Romanian dances. In *Valse Fantasie* by George Balanchine, the principal role was taken by Christopher Wheeldon, who is now the internationally famous choreographer. *Elite Syncopations* was performed as a tribute to Joe exclusively. The programme in its entirety was dedicated to Margot Fonteyn, Prima Ballerina Assoluta of the Royal Ballet, who died two weeks before Joe.

A final word on obituaries: I continued adding to the press cuttings book with the sixty people Joe came across, one way or another, during his long life.

As sole beneficiary, rich overnight, I should have been happy. But

I was really miserable. For months I dreaded what the next day's post would bring. At liberty to change the terms of Joe's will, I doubled Michael's settlement to include his two sons. As expected, Charles was along to claim for his four daughters. By coincidence, the amount he requested matched what Michael's family was receiving from me, and I was able to satisfy him. He showed no interest in what I was doing for his poorer relations. Had he asked for more, he would not have got it. He was inclined to be patronising, but in this instance he was reasonable. Joe had made the situation easier, by letting him know I had money of my own and my father did not need to work.

Joe had bank accounts in Jersey and Guernsey to hold his foreign investments. To obtain probate, which had been no problem in the UK, a separate firm of solicitors based in the Channel Islands had to be engaged. In addition to the two firms of solicitors, I had EMI to deal with. Joe's estate owned the company's subsidiaries in Ireland and Turkey. Unique to these two countries was a law requiring ownership of a company to be registered in the name of a responsible individual. It makes one wonder what corruption was afoot in these territories. Fortunately for EMI, Joe's reputation was acceptable, and equally fortunate for EMI, a codicil in his will returned the subsidiaries to the parent company.

Joe had nine pension policies supplying half of his income. Contacting the individual fund managers to cancel payments, I discovered how unique the pension arrangements for non-executive directors that Joe had invented were. At Beechams, I was referred to the Consumer Products Division, which presumably covered Macleans toothpaste, Brylcreem, Horlicks, Lucozade and Ribena. At Hawker Siddeley, I felt I was being treated like an old friend of Sir Tommy Sopwith.

About a month after Joe died, the solicitors received a letter from BC enquiring about his inheritance. His arrogant tone did not find favour, especially as there was no provision for him in the will. Even less favour resulted from another letter that followed, worded in an extremely persistent tone. Joe had created a Discretionary Trust from half his share portfolio in 1974. I received the Trust's income in lieu of salary. In the event of my death, the Trustees had discretion to dispose it among a list provided by Joe, which included his godchildren, the Royal Ballet School, and BC. Herbert Smiths were the Trustees, with clear separation between the Estate and the Trust. I decided to close the Trust in 2010, to create the Sir Joseph Lockwood Scholarship at the Royal Ballet School. The 1974 portfolio had grown considerably in the interim, the underlying assets remaining practically untouched. By transferring it intact to a charitable body, there was no vast Capital Gains Tax to pay. I incurred no taxable penalty from the transaction. Each year one boy or girl receives tuition and lodgings the School would not otherwise be able to afford.

Joe's bank in Church Street, Southwell, where he kept an account for seventy years, paid him a final courtesy. There was a locked black tin box inscribed "J. F. Lockwood" in the vaults. The manager invited me and Michael to watch him unlock it. We were not surprised to find it empty.

Executing Joe's will was a way of keeping in touch. Another was to trace his existence, starting with his ancestors in Huddersfield, and following the trail to Doncaster, York, Southwell, Chile, Paris and, eventually, Manchester. Another was to fill the Golden Book with signatures of people he valued.

I started with Arnold Goodman, who said he would be happy to listen to me. The way he put it, I took it as a warning not to be a bore. When Angus Wilson died, Tony Garrett "was inclined to go on rather, and test the patience of even the most sympathetic friends". "But I live in Oxford!" Goodman parried, not knowing I had his new address after he retired as Master of University College. His home turned out to be a modest house on the outskirts. He received me reclining in a converted dentist's chair which minimised the need to move. Throughout the interview I could hear his two cooks busily preparing the aptly-named "Two Dinners" Arnold's lunch. I asked about the episode when Villiers confronted him with rumours Joe was being blackmailed. "The man's a fool!" Goodman brushed the matter aside. He surprised me by saying he hardly knew Joe. Yet he had invited him to dinner or supper no less than thirty times in one year. His most recent Christmas card was signed "With Warm Regards". He even asked Joe who trimmed his ear hair (me actually!), indicating his own bristles. I was reminded how Joe dismissed friendship with Brian Epstein using the same words: "I hardly knew him". As I was leaving, the great lawyer could not resist asking: "Has Sir Joseph written his autobiography?" Hearing he had not, Goodman responded with much self-satisfaction: "I have!" *Tell Them I'm On My Way* did not appear until 1993. Rumour had it Goodman delayed publication until he had seen Barbara Castle's. Mutual dislike, jealousy and competitiveness endured, even at the highest level.

I went to see Godfrey Hounsfield at the office he was still provided with in CRL. Later, he agreed to be the subject of an interview filmed at Hatchet Wood, paid for by me, and uniquely, made possible with the encouragement of Bill Ingham, former Director of the Labs. They both were able to put their side of the EMI scanner story on record. It was fascinating to hear Godfrey describe his "Eureka" moment, an inspired guess, to cut corners and solve the formula for computerised tomography. Lord Hinton, the atomic scientist, admitted that the equation exceeded his own comprehension.

Godfrey Hounsfield and Bill Ingham with Video Arts producer

Two memories remain from that day of filming. First, I requested the local airfield to refrain from sending up glider-releasing craft for a few hours. The thermals and air pockets directly above Hatchet Wood provided the perfect place for this manoeuvre. Secondly, the expressions on Godfrey and Bills' faces when they saw the life-size portrait of "Gervase" Joe commissioned from Patrick Procktor were unmissable. Almost as disapproving was the look they cast in the direction of bookshelves lined with low-brow paperback novels. I gave copyright of the interview to the British Institute of Radiology.

Wayne Sleep invited me to his dance studio in South Kensington, where he taught Princess Diana the *pas de deux* that surprised her husband at a ROH gala. She had practised getting from the Royal Box to the stage undetected. In 1962, as a thirteen-year-old, Wayne was awarded the Royal Ballet School's Leverhulme Scholarship by Ninette de Valois with Joe's encouragement. He signed the Golden Book with kisses, and I took him to lunch at a restaurant in Brompton Road, that had once turned him out for misbehaving.

Four Prima Ballerinas were the last to sign. Merle Park and Dame Ninette signed on "Madam's" ninety-third birthday; Alicia Markova and Nadia Nerina, over lunch at an Italian restaurant. Alicia supported Joe regularly at Royal Ballet Governors' Meetings. Nadia was hard-up and asked me for help. Charles Lockwood was furious when he heard a Prima Ballerina was after his late brother's money.

The Golden Book, signed by King George V and Queen Mary in 1916 and by my ballerinas in 1991, is now the property of EMI Archive Trust.

Joe would have been distinctly unimpressed to know that I visited his black sheep brother's Lockwood Donkey Sanctuary at Godalming. Fred's widow was still in residence, tending 800 abandoned animals. I had not expected "the private rescue home" to be so extensive. Paddocks and sheds were jumbled together haphazardly around Kay Lockwood's house. A plaque read "This Recovery Block erected in Memory of Mr John Lockwood was opened by Leonard Rossiter". Another read "This Plaque was unveiled by Lord Baden-Powell in Memory of Mr John Lockwood". The whole place was a memorial to

Fred and paid for by animal lovers, including one woman who gave £40,000 "for the donkeys". Any minute I expected to repeat nephew Michael Lockwood's experience of being challenged "by a large man in a dirty old donkey jacket and frayed trousers kept up with string in his filthy yard". The voice would be rough and gruff, as described by the manager of a donkey sanctuary in Lincolnshire (Fred's was unregistered), who got phone calls from him. I slipped away as Mrs Lockwood opened the door to let out her cosseted fluffy manicured pets, near a sign that read "No Dogs Please".

Living alone at Hatchet Wood for four years, I maintained a routine of lifting weights, swimming in the unheated pool, followed by a sauna and run around the woods in all seasons. This had given stamina to support Joe, in his declining years.

I made a sentimental journey to Mullaghmore, near Sligo, where Lord Mountbatten and his family were murdered by the IRA. This was my only visit to Ireland. I had been beside Joe in 1979 when the phone call came telling him of Mountbatten's funeral instructions. On a skiing holiday with the Mountbattens in 1936, Lord Louis's sister-in-law once told my father: "You're a riot with the Commander!" On the gates of Classiebawn Castle overlooking the harbour was displayed the Mountbatten coat of arms.

Raef came to stay soon after Joe died. He provided warm and genuine sympathy. I was grateful and surprised by how fond of me he still was. We rarely met during his seventeen years as a Housemaster. Resisting pressure to stay on, he had escaped in retirement to his family home in Shropshire. The remoteness and tranquillity of Pentre Uchaf made the release from Eton's grip all the easier. We went up to London to inspect progress on Shakespeare's Globe Theatre on Bankside. Raef was sponsoring a brick to support its construction.

I learnt that Harry Williams was a regular visitor to Pentre Uchaf from his retreat at Mirfield. Elizabeth Cavendish was no longer able to provide a bed for him in London, and Raef made him welcome. I believe I may have brought about their friendship. True, they had known one another at Trinity, and Harry stayed with Raef when preaching in College Chapel. Raef would send him "round the house" after Boys' Dinner and Evening Prayers.

I was invited to stay with Raef on Harry's next visit, but I declined. It was time to start afresh, to move on from old company, but I did not know where to. Realising it was foolish to turn down this well-intentioned request, I changed my mind. Raef instructed me to come by the scenic route he described, and not by "the ghastly motorways". Harry, Raef and I visited a local garden centre to choose a tree to plant over Joe's ashes, which were scattered at Hatchet Wood.

School and university memories were revived at reunion dinners held during the year, both of which I attended that one time. My Tutor's Old Boys preceded Trinity's, and was held at Boodle's. I was disappointed, almost as much as My Tutor, and surprised that Robin was not at the reunion. But I had a strange experience to make up for it the next morning. I discovered that My Tutor and I were both staying at my club. As we sat together at breakfast, My Tutor, without any prompting, started talking about JC. That name still struck my heart at every mention. JC had married three times, first time with a cousin, "they were too young" I was told. JC was without a job. He was having a bad patch. Why was My Tutor telling me all this? There was no way he could know my feelings. There were plenty of people from the previous night he might have mentioned. Yet he chose JC.

My Tutor invited me to stay with him in Scotland. He lived in Perth, where he had some involvement with the university. His son, John, at the Trinity reunion dinner, gave me driving instructions. I strained my back lugging a heavy suitcase in Cambridge, and arrived in agony in Perth. My host was unrecognisable. No longer My Tutor, or "Grags", or "Spot", "David" now greeted me like a new man. Before I could stop him, he was grabbing my suitcase. What had caused the change? David explained he had suffered from a terrible hernia, so bad he had been invalided home in the war. In addition, guilty feelings at the loss of friends in battle turned the witty and brilliant sportsman into a dour Scotsman. For years he had to wear a truss. Recently he had given up smoking a pipe. Simultaneously the pain had disappeared. To prove it, he presented me with the truss, to relieve my suffering, and to retain as a memento of him. Joan Graham-Campbell took me aside for a discreet word: "Please, take care not to get David overexcited whilst you are here!"

From Perth, I went on to stay with in Argyllshire with Tommy Russell, now aged eighty and recently widowed. Joe never visited the house he built at Colintraive, overlooking the Kyle of Bute. They kept up a correspondence, although unknown to Tommy, the letters were written by me latterly. Arriving in mid-afternoon, I was greeted with a familiar voice: "Don't come upstairs, I've got nothing on!" Had the caution been a summons, rather than a warning, no doubt I would have obeyed without hesitation. We were both in a low and vulnerable state. Out came the cine-film of his wedding reception. Joe was best man, and against all convention, carried the bridegroom to the "going-away" car.

We sailed across the Kyle to Tighnabruaich, inevitably in a storm. Tommy manned his yacht single-handed; I do not count as crew. We had to take shelter. I had visions of our drowning together.

Every day he would look across the waters to Bute. Not long afterwards he sold up, and passed his last years on the island.

In 1992, at last, I set about doing things that were not possible before. I spent a couple of nights in Paris to see the new Bastille Opera House. There had been missed opportunities to experience Concorde. I now made up for them by flying to New York and back. Wherever I went there were reminders of Joe. Sitting in front row seats on Concorde were two chairmen he helped get promoted. I thought better of introducing myself. "Are you going on business?" they would have asked. "No, I am looking for your old colleague, who did so much for your careers!"

Raef and I went to Stratford-on-Avon for a couple of seasons, staying at a bed-and-breakfast. In the interval at a production of *The Oresteia*, the Headmaster of Eton came up and embraced Raef warmly as "an old friend". Eric Anderson told me his uncle, EMI producer Kinloch Anderson, had left his son his vast collection of HMV records. As Kinloch was in charge of all the sessions at Glyndebourne, they were something to treasure. It was impossible to get away from EMI!

The Head Man's wife, Poppy, taught English Literature, and wanted to know what Raef thought of the play's Greek translation.

I drove to the Lincolnshire coast. Joe was rarely photographed with his mother, but some pictures were taken on the millworkers' outings at the seaside. I went to Mablethorpe, where Joe swam with Bombardier Billy Wells. Then on to Kingston-Upon-Hull, where I was told I could find old Joe Rank's father's windmill. Mr Rank's birthplace adjoined the mill, which is preserved in his memory. York was my next destination. At the museum, where uncle Frederick Lockwood's prize "Pat the Giant Bull's" head once hung, the specimen was no longer in evidence. Cousin Betty Lockwood's roast beef and Yorkshire pudding made up for any disappointment. I was advised against visiting Betty's Famous Tearooms in York and Harrogate: "The prices they charge tourists is something terrible!"

I admired how Edith coped with her loss. She and Sandor would go to Barbados for a couple of weeks in January and February. Now, she was bravely going alone. Bernard Delfont took Edith under his wing and made her stay enjoyable. In March, I took her to Covent Garden. We looked forward to Kenneth MacMillan's new ballet, *The Judas Tree*. We should have waited for the reviews. We hated it. It shared the bill with Balanchine's *Stravinsky Violin Concerto*, performed on a bare stage with dancers dressed alike. It was difficult to tell the girls apart with their hair scraped back in identical fashion. We were sitting in front stalls. As the curtain went up, Edith exclaimed loudly: "Is that Sylv?" She had picked out Sylvie Guillem. "Naughty girl!" she muttered.

I learnt Sandor had negotiated for her an unheard-of twelve-year freelance contact with the Royal Ballet. Apparently, she asked Rudolf Nureyev: "Do we have to pay Sandor?" Nureyev made her an Etoile of the Paris Opera Ballet in 1984, aged nineteen, and introduced her to the Royal Ballet in 1988. Paris refused to grant her freelance terms, and Nureyev asked Sandor for help. She partnered Rudolf on his fiftieth birthday in 1989.

Margot Fonteyn was more forthcoming. She presented Edith with a fur coat.

"Naughty girl!" was an expression I was to hear one more time. Edith girded herself to close Sandor's agency. She claimed not to be involved in his business affairs. Joe saw differently, telling her: "You are very much a part of the business". Clearing Sandor's desk, she came across letters from Maria Callas, which shocked her. A prima donna's prerogative is to be unreasonable, but these were quite something. She had, among other things, perjured herself in court over a shipping dispute between Onassis and her former lover. I was not shown the letters. Edith decided to destroy them. Like Joe, I appreciated Edith's strength of character. She always behaved like a normal, ordinary, calm and unassuming person to help artists unwind. Never without a bottle of smelling salts in her evening bag, they were intended as much for herself as for artists. She was North Country and forthright. No snob, she preferred the Lyric Opera in Chicago to the Met, and La Scala. I was determined to visit Chicago.

She decided to revive the parties she and Sandor gave at Claridge's to see in the new year. Sitting on my right at dinner was Elizabeth Connell, the large Australian opera singer. As the waiters lifted in unison the silver lids for the first course dish, she whispered: "Edith is making sure everything is exactly as before." Edith confided later: "Elizabeth is lost without Sandor," indicating the singer's career had depended on Sandor. On my left was Alicia Markova, sharp and chic, belying her eighty-two years. We were given funny paper hats, which I hate. Alicia made hers look as if it was designed with her in mind. She told me she was still made to feel a little girl in Madam's presence. Ninette de Valois acted as her guardian when she joined the Diaghilev Company aged fourteen as a "baby ballerina".

One day Madam came to class, late, tetchy and ruffled. Her Irish housekeeper had mislaid her stays. Alicia giggled like any schoolgirl at the memory of her teacher's discomfort. Soon after midnight, Elizabeth Connell announced her car was waiting. In genuine awe, a fellow guest exclaimed after she had taken her leave: "Ah! To witness the departure of a Diva!"

Rudolf Nureyev died in January 1993. Earlier rumours arose that he had AIDS, which Edith loyally dismissed: "He is tired and works too hard".

She and Maude Lloyd, Nigel Gosling's widow (Maude and Nigel were the ballet critics known as Alexander Bland) flew to Paris for the funeral. Edith said: "I have lost a son." Edith always stayed at the George V Hotel. Nureyev's coffin was borne up the steps of the Paris Opera, and set down to rest in the foyer. The whole company lined the Grand Staircase and balconies in silence. He was carried away to a secret destination to applause. So dramatic was his departure that I determined to visit his resting place.

In February, I set off for Chile, after re-reading letters Joe sent his cousins in the 1920s. I planned to cover his five-week sea journey from Southampton to Concepción in twenty-four hours, flying via Washington and Miami. Approaching Santiago airport on schedule, the plane was diverted to Mendoza in the Argentinian Andes. It seemed fate was preventing me from exploring Joe's past. Twenty years ago, it was Allende's Marxist government that caused a last-minute change of plan. This time smog was to blame. Chile is a long, thin country, leaving little space between ocean and mountains. Smog arises from the rapidly expanding city and is blown inland by the Pacific winds. Trapped against the mountain, a pall forms which deflects the morning sun-rays into the pilot's eyes. The blinded United Airlines pilot has no recourse but to land elsewhere and wait for the air to clear.

I found my hotel, the San Cristobal Sheraton, occupied the site of Joe's old flour mill, Molina San Cristobal de M. M. Williamson & Cie ("Capacite: 60,000 Kilos par 24 heures").

Arriving after the long flight, I was determined not to waste a minute. The landmark I was looking for, the Cerro San Cristobal, towered above the city like Rio de Janeiro's sugar loaf mountain. The view from my hotel room matched the photograph Joe took from his bedroom at the mill. I took the teleferico, which rises in two stages to the peak. The build-up of anticipation, the bright sunshine, the rarefied air, combined to produce an indescribable moment of epiphany. The shimmering city spread out beyond, but my eyes were elsewhere. Below, I observed the Rio Mapucho, which once brought supplies to the mill. On the far bank the Apoquindo plains, where Joe rode mill horses, stretched to the hills, where he fished for salmon and explored local gold mines. A smart residential area filled the space between the mountain and river. Among the neat avenues of two-storey villas I looked for Joe's "casa". The mill and stable yard were long gone, but the mill manager's house survived.

Down from the Cerro, I wandered along "Calle el Carro" lined with crape myrtle and crimson bougainvillea. Many casas had copied the balcony, shutters and roof tiles pictured in the photographs. But without silos, power house and bullock carts, it was difficult to envisage the bustling, noisy mill in what is now an exclusive suburb.

Santiago, rather than Southwell, provided Joe's happiest moments. But the flour mill that brought him to Chile lay further down the country. Concepción is off the beaten track, occupying a major fault line, subject to earthquakes, where there is little sign of development since the 1920s. Arriving on the *Beagle* in 1835, Charles Darwin witnessed the aftermath of a massive quake. I had planned to spend the night, but was recommended to take a day-return flight. This was partly due to Concepción being so much less important than Santiago. I did notice passengers on the morning flight who were the same on the return journey.

The offices of Messrs Williamson & Co., where Joe reported on arrival, were still as imposing as in any minor city. Across Independencia Piazza, where he sat smoking his pipe and looking twice his nineteen years, stood the old cathedral. Reduced to rubble from an earthquake that struck the city in 1972, its replacement was noticeably inferior. Recently there have been further disturbances.

Molinos de Concepción, the Santa Rosa Milling Co. Ltd's mill, to my amazement remained exactly as Joe would have seen it in 1924. Five silos, so shiny in the photographs, were now a dull rusty brown. It was still pressing 50% more grain a day than the smaller Santiago mill. In Joe's time, it produced "La Rosa Blanca Harina Flour" and "Gavilla Rolled White Oats". Now, a notice board stated "Cie Molinera el Globo S.A." were "Fabricantes de Avena Quaker". Undoubtedly the area was run down, with marshalling yards on one side and shanty town on the other. Horse and cart were still in use for local transport.

The wide Bio Bio river now flowed aimlessly to the ocean. Silted up and blocked by a new dam upstream, it remains sacred to the Mapuche indians, the most southerly indigenous race in South America. Concepción is the home of the country's main university, with a well-tended campus. Parks and avenues are noted for their rare araucaria trees. It has its own Cerra Caracol, a smaller version of Cerro San Cristobal. A short distance along the coast are the summer resorts, where Joe swam. Talcahuano Bay nearby provides the Chilean fleet's securely guarded base, where photography is forbidden.

The Hotel de France, where Joe lived, and the British Club, are gone, but I could share the excitement he must have experienced on his first trip abroad to this remote area.

My journey home took me via Buenos Aires and New York. Charles Lockwood said I had "come to check up on us!" One of the four sons-in-law sent to meet me at the airport was not around. By the time he appeared, I had called the family residence in Hurlingham. This created a bit of an atmosphere, as the whole clan had assembled specially to greet me. Charles appeared to dislike Chile. He described it as backward, and Santiago "a very run-down city". He imagined the streets were dust tracks. Nothing could be further from the truth. American investment meant it had some of the most spectacular hotels in the world. Of course, he was getting at his brother. Chile's vineyards were superior, and, until Allende messed things up, Industrias Electronicas y Musicales Odeon S.A. sent Joe a case each Christmas.

Charles maintained this attitude back home, when I drove him to Nottinghamshire on his annual visit. The mills he managed in North, South and Central America were all so much bigger than those two in Chile. Once in Southwell, I would slip away for a quiet moment on my own.

With Charles and Mabel Lockwood

Down at Caudwell's mill, gazing into the slow-running mill stream, I had another epiphany moment. My watch stopped at 12 o'clock. Never had this happened before. With no idea how long I had been standing there, I rushed back to join the lunch at the Saracen's Head.

Everything was done to make my visit to Buenos Aires enjoyable. A piece of sheet music with a hymn written for Southwell Minster by Joe's mother was presented to me graciously. I was given a tour of the Teatro Colon, the largest Opera House in the world. On its stage Nijinski danced in 1913. The marble-clad structure had taken twenty years to build, compared to our own Opera House's nine months following the 1858 fire. I inspected the dressing rooms with en suite baths, but noted no sign of any opera in production. Then on to Banco Roberts, the Lockwoods' thirty-four-storey skyscraper. One of the daughters' friends whispered "They are very proud of this!" as we took the lift to the penthouse. Spread out below was the whole

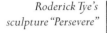

Roderick Tye's sculpture "Persevere"

city, with the brown Rio de la Plata, so wide its far banks were out of sight. In the docks, I could make out the giant 150,000-ton grain elevators built by Simon Engineering before the war.

Back home, I supervised the installation of a memorial statue at Hatchet Wood. This was the larger-than-life bronze torso I had commissioned from Roderick Tye, a young sculptor who exhibited at Royal

Academy summer exhibitions. It represented Joe's motto, "Persevere", and depicts the unbearable strain put on male dancers' backs. We had witnessed this, with the boys rehearsing Glen Tetley's demanding new ballet *Voluntaries*.

In August, Edith Gorlinsky introduced me to a secret part of her life. I knew of the rose-covered cottage in Sussex where she spent weekends with Sandor. No mention had been made of the stone cottage tucked away in the Yorkshire moors of her childhood. It fitted Anthony Trollope's stricture in *Is he Popenjoy?*: "the married woman who has not some pet Lares (lair) of her own is but a poor woman". We shared an interest in the Yorkshire Summer School founded by David Gayle, ex-Royal Ballet dancer. Joe paid David this tribute: "Anyone starting a ballet school in Yorkshire has my admiration!" Edith was waiting for me at the cottage to take her to a performance in Ilkley. Imagine my surprise to find her cottage a scene of permanent chaos and disorder. She and Sandor preferred to keep their Grosvenor Square flat private, entertaining elsewhere. They were such perfectionists. I imagined their London home so immaculate and full of fragile treasures, visitors would only spoil it.

Whilst in Yorkshire I explored the surroundings familiar to Joe's Victorian relation, Sir Frank Lockwood. I was struck by the similarity in their character. Both were larger than life and driven by the uncompromising ambition, yet affable and accessible. They both were called to protect their Prime Minister's reputation. The Liberal-leaning Solicitor-General ruthlessly prosecuted Oscar Wilde to quash the gay rumours involving Lord Rosebery. Joe was able to stop the scandalous picture of Harold Wilson, naked in bed with Marcia Williams, going any further. By taking immediate action to clamp down on and fine The Move group, the Profumo-like scandal was avoided and soon forgotten. He had to be ruthless to disassociate EMI from any blame for distributing the 'Flowers in the Rain' disc.

On the easternmost fringe of the North York Moors National Park, and overlooking the sea, I came upon the modest red-tiled brick Victorian villa that Sir Frank had built in 1890 as a shooting box.

Stained glass window and lynch gate in the nearby Church of Cloughton were donated in his memory, by "Sir Henry Irving, Mr Kendal, the Earl of Rosebery, Lord Feversham and others". Sir Frank was the Liberal MP for York and an amateur actor in his youth.

In October, Raef and I spent a week in Crete. Twenty years ago, Joe and I had docked at Heraklion, and not set foot on the island. I was now keen to see Knossos and Phaestos. Raef had seen Knossos already, and was not anxious to repeat the experience. I understood what put him off, when he agreed to come. Tourist buses were parked nose-to-tail, engines running, exhausting thick diesel fumes. It was like Park Lane in summer. We drove across the island to Phaestos, and the atmosphere could not have been more different. We were alone, on a beach where we swam, with nothing between us and the North African coast.

Raef in Crete

Raef, so calm and mild, was a better companion than I deserved. It took a great deal to ruffle him. So when he said my driving terrified him (the hire car was left-hand drive), and insisted on taking over, I realised I was still in a nervous state. I was not used to criticism. We rented a modern villa in a run-down village above Chania. Raef was interested to meet the architect who built and owned it. The surrounding houses were mostly empty, in need of repair or half-built.

An Arcadian encounter

Local boys playing football on a piece of waste ground were the only sign of life. Raef befriended the one with an American accent, and he was invited to meet the parents. Greece was in election fever. Every conceivable space was plastered with PASOK posters, and the incumbent Papandreou government was making impossible promises. We met a young student working part-time in a shoe shop on the harbour front. He was intelligent and planning to further his studies in England. To our disappointment, he supported PASOK.

Byzantine chapels dotted the island. Some we came upon were abandoned, some were pocked with wartime bullet holes. Domes, resting on classic cruciform vaulting, absorbed Raef with their simplicity. Looking back on his photographs of crumbling pediments and faded wall paintings, I see again their fascination.

The novelty of visiting places of my own choice was wearing off. In November, I went to Washington DC, simply because I had never been there before. This inspired me to return the following April for the Royal Ballet's 1994 American Tour, which was to open at the John F. Kennedy Center for the Performing Arts. The occasion was the premiere of a new production of *Sleeping Beauty*. This was the ballet that caused a sensation on the company's debut in America after the war. This time, American audiences would be seeing a new production before London. The novelty of the situation was rather lost when the production turned out to be a disappointment. Nevertheless, my second visit to Washington was enjoyable. It was good to see familiar ballets in an unfamiliar theatre. Dining one evening with the dancers, Donald MacLeary came over and embraced me. So many times had Donald been the Prince Florimund awakening his Sleeping Beauty, Princess Aurora, from a hundred-year spell. With this simple gesture, Donald was now releasing me from dreams that lasted thirty years.

Having displayed "the virtue of constancy" in my relationship with Joe, I was now at a loss. Two years of daily tears were followed by one further year mourning. Joe had speculated who I would be living with at Hatchet Wood when he was gone. "No one!" I interjected. But loneliness can be a disease. The *Book of Genesis* states: "It is not good for man to be alone." I had saved Joe loneliness in old age, and at the same time given him something more. In William Blake's words: "The basis of true love is mutual need."

Another pet dachshund like Max would be a partial solution. He must be standard-sized, long-haired, and have a coat of that special red tone. Crufts annual dog show was now held at the Birmingham Exhibition Centre, just a short trip up the M40. I chose the day devoted to the hound category. In one particular stall, I came upon a dachshund bearing a remarkable similarity to Max. An elderly lady dressed smartly in tweed coat and skirt was its owner. I told her my story: "Twenty years ago I bought a puppy just like yours. The owner was a Mrs Martin. She lived in the New Forest." "My name is Martin, and I live in the New Forest," she replied. Forgiven for recognising the pedigree, but not the owner, I was promised to be informed of her next litter. Jean Martin was still in business.

Driving back from Birmingham, almost home, I had a strange experience. There, all by itself, in the middle of the road, was a small dog. It had escaped under the security fencing and CCTV surrounding my neighbour, Sol Kerzner, the South African tycoon's, property. It was his wife's pet Highland Terrier. I stopped the car at the gates and rang the intercom. Meeting two interesting dogs, both on the same day, had to be a good omen.

With the possibility of companionship from a dachshund, I had something to look forward to. But out of nowhere came a new craving. There was just one thing that would restore happiness: to find Charles Selby, who had disappeared to America, out of my life, in 1966. This thought was so private and ridiculous that I did not contemplate sharing it with anyone. Research into the Lockwoods' family history had taken me to the Public Records Office in Chancery Lane, to Somerset House, and even to the Mormon Church in Exhibition Road. I now followed the same route in a search for Charles. Concentrating on the Home Counties, I came across a "C. Selby" of about the right age in Godalming. It was a ridiculous wild goose chase, and I was becoming obsessed and miserable at the same time.

Edith died on 24th October. I received a phone call. She had left a list of people to be informed in the eventuality. Vernon White, the vicar at her local church in Sussex, but now Chancellor of Lincoln Cathedral, was "summoned back" to take her funeral service. He told us her enduring wish was to join Sandor. Her friend Donald Sinden read the lesson. Alicia Markova, Ram Gopal, the Indian dancer, and David Gayle attended the burial. The occasion added to my misery.

As a founder shareholder in Eurotunnel PLC, I had the opportunity to be one of the first cars through the Channel Tunnel in November. It was an unusual experience, driving off a train into France. I spent a week in Rheims, Rouen and Paris. I saw *La Bayadere*, Rudolf Nureyev's last production for the Opera, premiered three months before he died. It was impossible to get a ticket, but I queued on the off-chance. Someone sold me a seat in their box, which was an arrangement one does not come across at Covent Garden.

It seemed appropriate to visit Nureyev's grave on my way to Rouen. I followed the route taken by his coffin from the Opera to the Paris suburbs. The Russian Orthodox church at Sainte Genevieve-des-Bois was designed with a familiar onion-shaped dome by Alexandre Benois, fifty years ago, as a resting place for exiles. Buried in the cemetery were Grand Duke Andrey Romanoff, Tsar Nicholas II's nephew and his morganatic wife, Prima Ballerina Mathilde Kshessinska. It was not difficult to find "Noureev's" grave, festooned with fresh flowers. Just two plots away rested Diaghilev's lover, Serge

Lifar. Although he died six years before Rudolf, he was receiving many more floral tributes. He would consider this his due after a life devoted to the Paris Opera. It had been his intention to be buried beside Auguste Vestris and Vaslav Nijinski in Montmartre Cemetery. He had even re-interred Nijinski there, previously buried in St Marylebone in 1950, where Ram Gopal stood silently at the graveside as he did for Edith. Come 1986, there was no space for Lifar nor for Rudolf in Montmartre. One day someone may suggest placing the four "Dieux de la Dance" alongside each other.

Driving from Rouen to Calais, I made a detour to Caen. Southwell Minster was reputed to be modelled on its Norman Abbey aux Hommes where King William I is buried. Sure enough, the twin spires dominating the narrow Caen streets were recognisable as duplicates of the towers casting shadows over Joseph and Mabel Lockwood's shared gravestone.

On 8th December, I took a deep breath and wrote to Charles Selby at the address where Stowe School still had him listed. This was Fisher Scientific Worldwide in Pittsburgh, where he worked in 1966:

Dear Charles,

You were an assiduous letter writer between 1960 and 1964! Your letters were good, apt and typewritten, and I have kept them. I do not know why you bothered, as I was an insufferable person at the time, but less so now, I hope. They are a fascinating compendium of the pre-swinging sixties, and I am glad I kept them.

I should very much like to hear from you again, how things are with you – just one letter would be more than sufficient!

Joseph Lockwood died in 1991, and I never regretted the 27 years with him and EMI. Starting as one of his 60,000 employees and ending as his one remaining employee (plus housekeeper and dog) – it all passed so rapidly and is now a closed episode. I would do the whole thing again.

So if you get this letter, Charles, please do make contact, as it would be absolutely tremendous.

Yours, Bin.

On the 13th January 1995, Fisher Scientific Worldwide returned my letter. They kept no record of their former employees.

I went to Germany in January, and signed on for a three-week French language course in London during February. The plan was to join my cousin Eddie, who had a photographic appointment in Munich. The job fell through, but I decided to go on my own anyway. On my last visit in 1959 I bought a postcard at the Neue Pinakothek Gallery, which had its intended effect. It was of Marc Chagall's *Daphnis and Chloe*, and I had sent it to Raef. So far, no such luck with my letter to Charles.

I commuted daily from Hatchet Wood to the French course organised by Alliance Francaise in a building off Tottenham Court Road. Each morning I looked across at the ugly EMI Centre, now the headquarters of an oil company. Its oppressive tower blighted the skyline above Bloomsbury's Georgian squares and terraces.

On 19th February, I heard from Mrs Martin: "The puppies have arrived!" I asked her to reserve the two males in the litter of four. Things were starting to go my way. The rest of the litter were girls, and they were already accounted for.

My search for Charles so far had been a total failure. Something like fifty lines of enquiry went nowhere. I was contemplating hiring a private detective. Charles played the church organ, but the Royal College of Organists had not heard of him. Dr Barry Rose "could not recall Charles Selby playing the organ at Guildford" when he had been choirmaster. But he had "fond memories of EMI, since it was they, through Brian Culverhouse who first 'discovered' the choir at Guildford Cathedral, and they made their first recording with us in 1965 – just four years after the Consecration. I think I am right in saying that Sir Joseph Lockwood presented us with Gold Discs in 1976." This must have been for Stainer's *Crucifixion* conducted by Barry Rose, issued on Classics for Pleasure in 1969.

So much for the classical world. I next turned to pop. Charles's boy-band "Footprints" played gigs in the Camberley and Richmond areas, occasionally fronting Long John Baldry, Rod Stewart and others at Eel Pie Island. I asked Elton John if he had heard of him, but got no reaction.

Charles's National Service colleagues, friends and families also proved fruitless. In the end, I swallowed my pride and asked Eddie for help. I felt he owed me a favour after backing out of the trip to Bavaria, which he had initiated. Slightly reluctantly, he rang the 1st The Queen's Dragoon Guards headquarters at Cardiff Castle, reluctantly because he had not kept up with his regiment. Sure enough, the adjutant parried: "Where have you been all this time?" Nevertheless, he was helpful and suggested Eddie contact their ex-Commanding Officer, who was Charles's uncle. Lt Colonel Harold Selby was eighty-three and in poor health, the adjutant warned. In fact, he died later that year. Eddie said he was an outstanding horseman and Olympic showjumper in his day.

It was so simple. Col. Selby told Eddie that Charles's sister Anne lived in Camberley, a few streets from his former family home. It had never occurred to me! Charles was living in Southern California, and Anne even had an address for him: "But we've lost touch since he moved to the mountain." I re-addressed the returned letter to an unpromising box number, which turned out to be a Fire Department. Enclosed with it I placed a note dated 8th February 1995:

The sentiment in my letter still applies. Stronger if anything. And I do hope I can 'locate' you.

'We only part to meet again
The mighty boundless waves may sever
Remembrance oft shall bring thee near
And I will with thee go forever'

Edgar Allen Poe (recently discovered poem).

On 24th February, the phone rang late at night. It was Charles, professing his undying love. It must have been a dream. But no. An envelope franked 24th February "Running Springs, San Bernardino, California", embossed with a "Snow Valley" Snowflake (a ski resort now! What about the Fire Department?), arrived on 27th February:

> Dear Bin,
>
> Overseas mail is invariably bad news so I turned the envelope over to identify the sender, and WHAM, it was just like when I first met you – the weak knees, dizzy etc. We were trying to get away from the party and were on the floor, leaning against a refrigerator, shoulders and knees touching, wanting to hold hands, but someone was there. Maybe we should have held hands anyway, and then never let go!

He went on to recount the intervening years. Nothing mattered. I prayed they were already behind him, and we were going to start where we left off.

Nothing could be so completely romantic. There was no denying the pressure and demands I had once put upon him. These I referred to in my reply:

> Written at 3.30 to 4.00 am Monday Feb 27/95 … It is not the physical attributes that one loves, although they do help. It does not matter when they inevitably mellow. They remain in the memory and cannot be removed. They are always there … What about the future? Who knows? I feel it is sufficient that I will be appearing at your doorstep – in the past (those whole four years!) it was always you appearing on mine.
>
> Yours – yes it's true! Bin.

But his letter of the 26th was already on its way:

> Bin, I seem to be saying that I think I could spend the rest of my life with you. There it's finally said! My travel agent just called. I could fly

over, take you out to dinner, fly home, stay over one day … Everyone I have been attracted to over the years was held up to my memory of you for comparison. You were the model that they were to be judged by.

By the time I received a letter dated 4th March on the 10th, it was already fixed. He was coming to stay forever. There were practicalities to be faced: "I would like to do the big race weekend at Monterey in April. Laguna Seca is one of the most beautiful and challenging race tracks in the world, and I'm already committed to be there." As explanation, a photograph was enclosed showing "My Alfa Romeo Balocca on my transporter – That is me!" An arrow pointed to the tall, unmistakable figure striding manfully, pipe in mouth, alongside the desert track … "After that I think I should get on a 'plane and never come back!"

Charles at Willow Springs International Raceway in California

Apparently I had a rival: that Balocco! Inserted with the photograph was a monologue:

The Alfa Romeo Logo – The True and Previously Untold Story

The Alfa Logo is an adaptation of the Coat of Arms of the aged Italian City of Milano, which is named after a quite delicious Pepperidge Farm cookie. The Logo is divided into two fields. One depicts a serpent chewing into a small red person. The other is a red cross on a white field. Both these images have origins in ancient and colourful European …

On 5th March, I received a phone call at dawn from an unfamiliar voice. No introduction was necessary. It was Charles's friend, Mike Smith. So sensible to have conscripted an independent party. Eddie had voiced misgivings, but here was Mike firmly, respectfully and sincerely endorsing Charles's decision. Such a reassuring voice, telling me Charles was "a gentleman, the loyalest friend in the world: he would do anything for one", and confirming he had already bought his air tickets. Everything was going to be all right.

The flight was booked on Virgin Atlantic, arriving at Heathrow at 11.45 a.m. on Friday, 17th March, and returning on Monday 20th at 3.00 p.m. The enormity of the whole situation was tearing the poor fellow apart, when he wrote on 8th March:

Bin, we will be better, and stronger, and happier together than we could ever be apart. I believe this implicitly, and so must you. If we doubt, then we will fail.

Doubt was creeping as he wrote these words. He continued:

I don't think we should ever consider my staying after the initial visit. It will be wonderful seeing you, and we can rationally discuss the future, and be open to any and all ideas, allowing a much broader scope to our thoughts. What do you think?

As he came through the Arrivals gate at Heathrow, it was joy unbound! All was decided. The figure approaching seemed to glow, embodying all the hype of that golden, sun-kissed, Sunshine State of Southern California. Beforehand, I had recalled dank, unpressed suits, dank hair, dank skin, all imbued by the dull matt sheen of sticky, drizzly London evenings. Now, all was lightness and vigour.

That evening Raef telephoned, his voice full of concern that the dream was over, and I was facing reality and my dream smashed. But the moment of rapture was not destined to end. All obstacles to Charles staying had mysteriously disappeared.

I had one moment of panic. It was overwhelming, and struck like a physical blow. Did I have the necessary resolve? Could I assume responsibility for someone else's future? Once before, I had rejected my schoolboy admirer, only to regret my decision later. But Joe had given me the opportunity to accept or reject an offer, and I had made the right but equally difficult decision. I must make the right decision again.

Charles's sister, Anne, was adamant: "He will not be staying – a sister knows!" Eddie's view I already knew: "When will he be going back?" My father, who admired Charles and gave him the introduction to a career in electronics, shared Eddie's view. But my father had not favoured my joining Joe.

Charles has not returned to America. He decided we should keep the dachshunds, both of them. We went down to the New Forest to see Max and Min for the first time. Inevitably, the smaller one, Min, bonded with 6'4" Charles. We were to become a happy foursome.

Charles with Max and Min

There remained one obstacle to perfect happiness. I was still jealous, painfully so! Yet I had years to learn how destructive that emotion can be. Who was I to disapprove of Charles admiring attractive boys? After all, I had once benefited. One evening, he returned from a motor racing event at Castle Coombe, purring with pleasure at "a wonderful

*Alfa Romeo
"Balocco", now at
Hatchet Wood*

*Sailing in the
Greek Islands*

experience", the afternoon spent lounging on a grassy bank alongside
a young motor racing enthusiast. They planned to meet up. He
returned the next day, but his new friend failed to appear. Missing his
Balocco, and contemplating returning to racing, he went up to
London to look at an Alfa Romeo in a South Kensington showroom.
Inevitably, the salesman was young, attractive, public school educated,
and, on top of that, heir to a baronetcy. Another Sir John Bradford! It

was no more than a professional relationship, but it took an effort to suppress my jealousy. The fact is, Joe and Charles flourished in the company of the young. Someone prepared to abandon his life in America did not deserve to be met with sulks and silliness.

Anthony Trollope described jealousy as: "This corrosive emotion's paramount place in daily life. Only a few, rare, people have the courage to admit such an infection."

My great-aunt Linda Rhodes-Moorhouse, on her honeymoon in France, admitted to pangs of jealousy. With her husband, Will, and a journalist, she was about to enter the history books, the first three to fly across the English Channel by plane, in 1912. She went to bed the night before the venture, as Will stayed up late with an attractive female aviator: "They discussed aviation technicalities, which were of course absorbing to both of them … these were a closed book that I could not share."

Max and Min inspect Ringo Starr's 1974 present to Sir Joe

Charles was a complete stranger to jealousy. One day, soon after his arrival, I had an unexpected phone call from Robin, who taught me to tie my tie that first morning at Eton. It was quite out of the blue. I had not spoken to Robin for some years, and he had never called me at Hatchet Wood. He was at home in France. On sudden impulse, he wanted to tell me he was still aroused at the memory of our most intimate moments: "Billy, you were wonderful!" Charles was in the room, paying scant attention to my blushes.

That autumn we stayed with Raef in Shropshire. Charles was motor racing again with the Alfa Romeo Club. Raef and I drove to Oulton Park to support him. Loyally we stood on the exposed hillside overlooking the circuit. It started to pour. We were miles from shelter, without a mac or umbrella between us. We were drenched. Quite enough excuse to return to the car. That was out of the question! Loyalty was tested to the limit, and proved not to be wanting.

I once quoted a poem by Edgar Allen Poe. the first verse expressed my sentiments exactly. This was the final verse:

> And oft at midnight's silent hour
> When brilliant planets shall guide the ocean
> Thy name shall rise at heaven's highest star
> And mingle with my soul's devotion.

THE END

Index